THE **SECRET LIFE OF**
Lady Liberty

D0427960

"The words on the Statue of Liberty base: 'Give me your tired, your poor, your huddled masses yearning to breathe free . . .' reflect indigenous and feminine values of nurturing, caretaking, welcoming; 'I lift my torch . . .' a symbol of bringing light and consciousness. I marvel at the weave, depth, coverage, and yet readability of this very well-researched book. How wonderful it would be to have a couple of its chapters excerpted into a text for American history, a high school required course."

JEAN SHINODA BOLEN, M.D., AUTHOR OF
GODDESSES IN EVERYWOMAN

"I could not agree more with the premise of this well-written book. I truly believe that more women in positions of power would do much to alter the political landscape for the good. We men seemed to have messed things up. . . . let's give the ladies a chance."

GRAHAM NASH, OF CROSBY, STILLS, AND NASH

"*The Secret Life of Lady Liberty* is a rich, thoughtful, and fascinating excursion into many of the concepts, ideas, and ideologies that have influenced thoughts of freedom throughout humanity. It examines how we have struggled with various kinds of freedom and have been forced to weigh them against other values. This work of Hieronimus and Cortner is truly a cultural tour de force."

BARRY MORENO, HISTORIAN AT
THE STATUE OF LIBERTY NATIONAL MONUMENT

"No other figure today exemplifies patriotic esotericism more than Robert Hieronimus—and in this historical feast of a book he and his longtime collaborator Laura Cortner lay out a vision of the meaning, myth, and purpose behind America's most iconic symbol. The authors sweep away conspiracism and in its place leave us with a resplendent vision of the centrality of Lady Liberty in our inner life and ideals as one people united."

MITCH HOROWITZ, PEN AWARD–WINNING AUTHOR
OF *OCCULT AMERICA*

"A feminist and multi-ethnic history of the Statue of Liberty is way overdue. This account, which sparkles with insights, evokes the work of Katya Miller on the statue atop the U.S. Capitol dome. Both histories help complete the record. This work, which provides a new lens on our history, is a unique history of rediscovery that I hope will reconfirm our nation's responsibility to foster freedom for all peoples (resisting patriarchy, assisting peace), in the tradition of the Statue of Liberty as a symbol for empowerment."

BRUCE E. JOHANSEN, PH.D., PROFESSOR OF
COMMUNICATION AND NATIVE AMERICAN STUDIES AT
THE UNIVERSITY OF NEBRASKA AT OMAHA AND
AUTHOR OF *FORGOTTEN FOUNDERS*

"As the daughter of a Clan Mother, a true matriarch and descendant of those intrepid women leaders of the famed Iroquois Confederacy, I deeply appreciate the work of Hieronimus and Cortner in bringing to light the central role of those we call 'lifegivers.' For those around the world seeking the source of feminism, life, liberty, and justice for all, I highly recommend *The Secret Life of Lady Liberty*."

JOANNE SHENANDOAH, PH.D., HAUDENOSAUNEE
(IROQUOIS CONFEDERACY) AND
GRAMMY AWARD–WINNING SINGER

"There are many books on women's struggle for equality but most of them ignore the actual roots of this worldwide movement. Hieronimus and Cortner set the record straight. This is a remarkable story told with style, humor, and keen insights based upon exceptional scholarship. A new pillar in the study of the struggle for women's rights."

DOUGLAS GEORGE-KANENTIIO,
AKWESASNE MOHAWK AND VICE PRESIDENT OF
THE HIAWATHA INSTITUTE FOR INDIGENOUS KNOWLEDGE

"This powerful and timely portrayal of Lady Liberty includes an exploration of the artistic, cultural, and historical contexts that have informed this cultural icon. The book packs a great deal of political punch and history while explaining the symbolism of women's role in our political life—past and present—missing from even our higher education today."

EDITH P. MAYO, CURATOR EMERITA IN
POLITICAL AND WOMEN'S HISTORY AT THE
SMITHSONIAN'S NATIONAL MUSEUM OF AMERICAN HISTORY

"The Statue of Liberty isn't just a statue. It represents many things from the past, and over time it has evolved to represent much more. Among the female elements of this enigmatic statue, as expressed in *The Secret Life of Lady Liberty: Goddess in the New World,* are the earth-bound respect, fondness, and acknowledgment for Iakonkwe (womankind) that dwells within traditional Haudenosaunee (Iroquois) culture."

JOHN KAHIONHES FADDEN, COFOUNDER OF
THE SIX NATIONS INDIAN MUSEUM

"An eye-opening treasure of the history of America's greatest icon. This must-read provides an enlightening understanding and a new appreciation of the concept of liberty."

STEVEN SORA, AUTHOR OF
THE LOST TREASURE OF THE KNIGHTS TEMPLAR

"This book takes an important step by pointing out that goddess traditions need to be examined and revised for what they can teach us in this age of male domination and the exploitation of nature. Filled with fascinating historical facts and mythological sagas, this work points the way toward an extension of the American Revolution to social and spiritual changes that are crucially needed in the 21st century. This book is rooted in the past but, like the torch of Lady Liberty itself, is a beacon meant to illuminate the future."

STANLEY KRIPPNER, PH.D., COAUTHOR OF
PERSONAL MYTHOLOGY

"This sweeping encyclopedic study of the Statue of Liberty includes a rich collection of rare historical and modern images. Hymning the male/female polarity on which creation is based, this book issues a clarion call for balance. May the power of this iconographic symbol of the sacred and optimistic principles underlying the American experiment continue to triumph over cynicism and authoritarianism."

JAMES WASSERMAN, AUTHOR OF
THE SECRETS OF MASONIC WASHINGTON AND
THE TEMPLE OF SOLOMON

"A brilliant and extraordinary look into an important part of America's history that's surprising, inspiring, and offers tremendous hope."

THOM HARTMANN, PROGRESSIVE NATIONAL AND
INTERNATIONALLY SYNDICATED TALK SHOW HOST

"Who would have imagined that you could draw our country's entire history through the iconic image of Liberty gracing the New York Harbor? That's precisely what the authors do in this engaging and well-documented journey through the long-neglected outtakes of our past. The exploration of Native American and feminist history and values, combined with contemporary scientific research, lead us to envision a sustainable future where liberty indeed prevails."

SALLY ROESCH WAGNER, PH.D., EXECUTIVE DIRECTOR OF
THE MATILDA JOSLYN GAGE FOUNDATION

"A brave and wonderful retelling of the hidden history of America. This fascinating, well-researched, thought-provoking book gives us great insight into the true history of the Statue of Liberty, our debt to Native Americans, the imbalance created by the suppression of the Sacred Feminine, and a true vision for a more enlightened future."

TRICIA MCCANNON, AUTHOR OF *RETURN OF THE DIVINE SOPHIA*

"The authors have created an exceptional work . . . an extraordinarily free piece of writing on multiple levels, written in an engaging and readable style. In a world hidebound by convention, why not read this book and let this most talented public artist and his far-seeing coauthor take you on a remarkable journey?"

JOY PORTER, PH.D., PROFESSOR OF INDIGENOUS HISTORY AT
THE UNIVERSITY OF HULL IN THE U.K. AND
AUTHOR OF *NATIVE AMERICAN ENVIRONMENTALISM*

"*The Secret Life of Lady Liberty* is an in-depth, intriguing, and insightful examination of mythic, spiritual, social justice, and political dimensions of Lady Liberty as Goddess of Freedom and Her connections with other iconic Divine Feminine forms in the USA and beyond."

SELENA FOX, SENIOR MINISTER AND
HIGH PRIESTESS OF CIRCLE SANCTUARY AND
FOUNDER OF THE LADY LIBERTY LEAGUE

"This amazing book shines a fresh light on the history of not just Lady Liberty but the whole American experience. The authors have generated an interesting hypothesis that resonates with my worldview of why women and their biology are both impactful but also at times misunderstood."

C. SUE CARTER, PH.D., DIRECTOR OF
THE KINSEY INSTITUTE AND RUDY PROFESSOR OF BIOLOGY
AT INDIANA UNIVERSITY AT BLOOMINGTON

THE
SECRET LIFE
OF
Lady
Liberty

GODDESS IN THE NEW WORLD

Robert R. Hieronimus, Ph.D., and Laura E. Cortner

Destiny Books
Rochester, Vermont • Toronto, Canada

Destiny Books
One Park Street
Rochester, Vermont 05767
www.DestinyBooks.com

Text stock is SFI certified

Destiny Books is a division of Inner Traditions International

Library of Congress Cataloging-in-Publication Data
Names: Hieronimus, Robert, author. | Cortner, Laura, author.
Title: The secret life of Lady Liberty : goddess in the New World / Robert R.
  Hieronimus, Ph.D., and Laura E. Cortner.
Description: Rochester, Vermont : Destiny Books, [2016] | Includes
  bibliographical references and index.
Identifiers: LCCN 2016004085 | ISBN 9781594774935 (pbk.) —
  ISBN 9781620551592 (e-book)
Subjects: LCSH: Statue of Liberty (New York, N.Y.) | Liberty in art. |
  National characteristics, American, in art. | Women—United States—Social
  conditions. | Goddesses in art. | United States—Civilization—Indian
  influences. | United States—Civilization—French influences. | Signs and
  symbols—United States.
Classification: LCC F128.64.L6 H54 2016 | DDC 974.7/1—dc23
LC record available at http://lccn.loc.gov/2016004085

Printed and bound in the United States by Lake Book Manufacturing, Inc.
The text stock is SFI certified. The Sustainable Forestry Initiative® program
promotes sustainable forest management.

10   9   8   7   6   5   4   3   2   1

Text design and layout by Virginia Scott Bowman
This book was typeset in Garamond Premier Pro with Alexa, Futura, and Gill
Sans used as display typefaces

Figures 5.6, 7.3, 7.6, 8.6, and 9.4 appear courtesy of Creative Commons; license
available at https://creativecommons.org/licenses/by/2.0/legalcode.

To send correspondence to the authors of this book, mail a first-class letter to the
authors c/o Inner Traditions • Bear & Company, One Park Street, Rochester, VT
05767, and we will forward the communication, or contact the authors directly at
www.secretlifeofladyliberty.com.

Contents

Foreword

J. Zohara Meyerhoff Hieronimus, D.H.L.

The topic of liberty is one that appeals to all human beings, because it is our nature to desire freedom. As sovereign men, women, and children, all human beings thrive when given broad and egalitarian boundaries within which to unfold their particular character and talents.

So often throughout humankind's history, freedom comes at the expense of great loss of life. For example, the drive for liberty in order to remove a tyrannical government or individual is a necessity that millions of people will give up their lives to have and leads to a chance for both the soul and personality to evolve. This natural instinct for individuality is nurtured in certain societies, but often it is restricted only for certain people, while it is completely withheld from others. Worldwide today, women and children are generally omitted from this natural right of having autonomy and protection based on equality.

Matrifocal cultures of the goddess traditions, which are profiled in this coauthored work, were not cultures in which power was the exclusive domain of the women. Rather than being subjected to exploitation, if not outright enslavement as is the case for millions of women and children today, women in matrifocal cultures were emancipated from the global construct of male domination and the exploitation of human, animal, and natural resources. In matrifocal cultures, some of which exist even today primarily among Indigenous peoples, women are held in the highest esteem; they are deemed to be more intuitive, kinder, and inclusive than their male counterparts. For these reasons, they are considered the ones best able to judge right from wrong, as exemplified by the Jewish prophetess Devorah (2654–2694 BCE), who, even though a woman, was so highly regarded for her insight that during her lifetime she was the only judge allowed to pass sentences.

Matrifocal societies are organized primarily around protecting the women and children and assuring their sacred value, as well as fostering their creativity, independence, and leadership. Historically, in these progressive and ancient communities, women owned the land, selected the leaders, and discharged those failing in their moral and ethical duties. Bound together with valuing the Earth, the goddess tradition honors all that is protective and nurturing for the world.

In the 1980s I named my communications business Liberty Works and featured the Statue of Liberty on my business card. It was under this banner that I spent more than a decade writing, speaking, conducting radio broadcasts, and engaging in other communication efforts. As a registered Libertarian and as a human being who believes that peace is humanity's destiny, I chose the name Liberty Works because of my love for action as well as truth. To have peace, one requires freedom. The name Liberty Works emphasized my own belief that serving liberty is sacred service, and from liberty, autonomy and balanced collaboration with all people are possible.

These are some of the reasons I'm pleased to write the foreword to this book. As collaborators, Robert R. Hieronimus, Ph.D., and Laura E. Cortner represent an interesting mixture of talents, generational perspectives, and history. Bob Hieronimus, my husband since 1980, is a world-recognized muralist, "artcar" creator, symbologist, author, historian, and broadcaster. His reporting on American history has always featured the vital role that the League of the Iroquois played in America's founding, based on the form of representative lawmaking they gifted to the Western world. Bob has championed numerous people who, because of race, nationality, or religion, were diminished and marginalized— so taking up the cause for women's equality is a continuation of this impulse. Bob's appreciation for the intuitive excellence of women and their capacity for working well in a collaborative way explains why he has chosen to work almost exclusively with female assistants all his life.

Laura E. Cortner, the coauthor of this book, has been the executive producer and research assistant for Hieronimus & Co. for many years, producing *21st Century Radio* and several of our other media ventures. As a trained editor and writer, she has acted as our in-house editor, tidying up or even ghostwriting magazine articles and online postings, and helping both of us edit many of our previous books. Although Laura has helped research and write several of Bob's other books, this is her first experience as a primary coauthor. Knowing her excellent skills as an editor and researcher, and from a writer who has benefited by our shared publisher, Inner Traditions, I say, "Welcome to the club!"

This book springs in part from a radio series on *21st Century Radio,* during which Bob interviewed leading pioneers in the field of women's spiritual histories and quest for equality. Bob wrote and hosted the interviews and, together with Laura, drew content from these transcripts and added more research. Together they have created a book on the goddess tradition hidden within the story of our beautiful Statue of Liberty. They have done this in a manner that no other authors have done. All of Bob's life work—from his numerous murals, other artworks, books, and appearances on international television programs— consistently features the themes of America's sacred origins, hidden history, and destiny. This book follows that same theme, through an examination of the history and symbolism of the Statue of Liberty in the ancient and near past.

The Hindu tradition would say we are coming to the end of Kali Yuga, the Dark Age. The Maya people call it "the sixth sun," a time of cross-fertilization between all peoples and all traditions. From my own decades of studying the Kabbalistic tradition, which has resulted in two books on the female and male prophets of ancient Israel published by Inner Traditions, we would call it "the age of Yesod." Yesod is the last of the ages before we are stationed as a civilization at the bottom of the Tree of Life and begin an ascent to higher awareness and worldwide peace. According to Kabbalistic prophecy, in about 220 years we will enter the blessed time of global equality and freedom, the age of Malchut, the age of the woman, a time of global awakening to the female divine, to our natural intuitive talents. In Judaism this is called an awakening to the Shechinah, the indwelling presence or feminine aspect of God that fills each life-form.

The prophesied age of Malchut will bring with it a more elevated awareness of all life systems. It will be a global movement of female leadership and restoration of the Earth, and it will be a time when women's heart-centered intelligence and leadership will be the crown upon the world's head. Lady Liberty also wears a radiant crown, suggesting that this reality is America's special calling as well. Liberty for the world's people will come with women's liberation in education, occupation, and in the home. In a vision I had in 1985, this was called "the New Order of the World Mother."

The Secret Life of Lady Liberty reveals the various threads that weave together the fabric of our nation's commitment to freedom, a desire for individual liberty, representative lawmaking and keeping, and humanity's eventual emancipation from suffering and oppression. Lady Liberty reminds us all of this sacred duty and holy call to freedom and how it leads to justice and equality for everyone. Learn how this lady, this great emancipator as a world mother, warrior, protector, and healer, is found worldwide in various forms and how she eventually came to be cherished as an American symbol of personal commitment, liberty, and national identity.

J. ZOHARA MEYERHOFF HIERONIMUS, D.H.L., is an award-winning radio broadcaster and author, as well as an activist for social justice, environmental causes, and animal rights. A pioneer in the field of holistic health care and founder of the Ruscombe Mansion Community Health Center in 1984, she has been called both a visionary and futurist. From 1992 until 2001, she hosted the popular daily "whistle-blowers" radio program, *The Zoh Show*. Together with her husband, Dr. Bob Hieronimus, she continues to host *21st Century Radio,* broadcasting since 1988, making it the longest-running alternative-themed radio show in the country. Her book titles include *The Future of Human Experience* (Destiny Books, 2013), *Kabbalistic Teachings of the Female Prophets: The Seven Holy Women of Ancient Israel* (Inner Traditions, 2008), and *Sanctuary of the Divine Presence: Hebraic Teachings on Initiation and Illumination* (Inner Traditions, 2012).

Acknowledgments

By Robert R. Hieronimus, Ph.D.

The most important soul of this incarnation is my beloved wife of thirty-five years, Dr. Queen Zohara. She is a wise soul who knew we were to join forces when we first met. She was aware of my purpose in this life and from the very beginning gave me the glorious freedom to focus on what we needed to accomplish together as a team. From this bonding a great deal of good and sacred work has been accomplished and continues to be accomplished. We still have much to do! Since 1978 Zohara has stood behind every important accomplishment I have made, from the founding of Ruscombe, which she transformed into a holistic health care center, to the founding of the AUM Center and *21st Century Radio,* which draws near to its thirtieth year on the air. More importantly, Zohara has taught me what families are all about, and by that I mean not just our children but also all four-legged, winged, and crawling members of our environment. It's no wonder that all my important writings and paintings are dedicated to her. She is truly the center of my life and work.

The coauthor of most of my books, Laura E. Cortner, has worked with Zohara and me since the inception of *21st Century Radio* and has helped to make that show the success it has become. Her ability to multitask never ceases to amaze me, and all of our guests on *21st Century Radio* have praised her extraordinary abilities. I am the most difficult person to work for, and I'm certain that her upbringing in a military family prepared her for tolerating my militant personality when it comes to getting the job done at all costs. Whenever I bite off more than I can chew, she alerts me to the dangers. We have worked together as co-creators of many projects, including other books, and I am proud to say that this book is our best co-creation to date! The reason for that is Laura's magic with words and her extreme desire for accuracy. She is a brilliant researcher who goes to great lengths to uncover truths that others are not able to find. While we worked together on this book for more than five years, I was also called away to restore several murals, which took most of my energy. Knowing this, she led the way and carried the work to its conclusion.

We would also like to thank our publisher, Inner Traditions International, especially Jon Graham and Ehud Sperling. They were instrumental in shaping the ideas behind this book and then showed extreme patience in allowing us to consider and reflect upon what we had discovered and to perfect the documentation of those discoveries. One look at our bibliography proves how long that took!

Others I want to mention include my sisters, Dolly, Nancy, and Barbara, who were essential to my upbringing, often protecting me from our violent household. They introduced me to the joys of movies, and music, and singing in harmony, and gave me some sense of security. Today, I receive some of the same comfort from my astrologer, the Rev. Linda Newman, whose precision with her craft has opened many closed doors for me. About two years into this project I received an unfinished manuscript by the late Herbert Bangs titled *The Feminine Face of God*. His widow, Chris Bangs, also gifted me a part of her husband's library, which included a great number of books on gnosticism. I am grateful to these contributions for influencing our understanding of those areas dealing with the Nag Hammadi library and the works of Marvin Meyer and Elaine Pagels.

Most importantly, I want to thank my mentors, starting with U Maung Maung Ji, who was introduced to me by his student, the former secretary general of the United Nations U Thant. Maung was a retired statesman, diplomat, and lifelong occultist and mystic. He was a disciple of Master Koot Hoomi, a highly evolved spiritual being, an Arahat in Buddhist terminology. Maung visited us in 1972 at the *Apocalypse* mural at Johns Hopkins University to tell me who had really channeled that work, which I was fully restoring even as this book went to press. Ever since the original completion of the *Apocalypse* mural in 1969, my mentor has been the Thrice-Greatest Hermes Trismegistus, who also had a hand in this manuscript. So mote it be!

By Laura E. Cortner

I am filled with gratitude for the many people and beings who gifted me with the honor of working on this book. Thanks to Bob and Zoh Hieronimus for giving me a career wherein I could exercise my independent mind and stretch it to explore new subjects and frontiers further than I ever dreamed possible. I thank them for their support over the years, but particularly in the past five years as this book came into being. Thank you especially to Zoh for the demonstrations of courage and sustenance you've given me, including the supply of matzah ball soup you provided as the deadline loomed. And special thanks to Bob for the encouragement and faith you showed in my abilities by giving me so much responsibility for this book.

To my sisters, Jennifer and Cathy, thank you for supporting me through this project and throughout my life. Jennifer was particularly brave to wade through some early drafts and to give feedback on what little coherence there was at that stage. To my mother, thank you for giving me the chance to switch roles of caregiving with you in your elder years. Hopefully I can demonstrate some of the unconditional love you gave me all your life. To both of my fathers now in the spirit world, thank you for the years of hardship in defense of a nation and the national values you held dear. To all my grandmothers and aunts, nieces and relations, I thank you for being part of my family tree and part of the clan with whom I share social bonding. Thank you for nurturing me.

To the ancestor spirits and goddesses who guided the writing of this book, showing up with inspiration at the oddest of hours and making connections where none seemed possible, thank you for keeping me healthy while the hours of reading and editing grew wearisome.

Thank you very much to Amy Ford for serving as an early outside reader and contributing essential editing help and suggestions. Amy also contributed valuably to the illustration-gathering and research. Her brother Joe Ford attentively transcribed hours of interviews with almost no errors. Mike Donahue also contributed several hours of transcribing, as did Laura Finney and Meg Bowen, whose many hours of transcribing included a lot of cheerleading on the side. Thanks guys. Thanks also to all my friends at Ruscombe for their continuing support and healing.

Thank you to Jon Graham at Inner Traditions International, who was always available to answer our many questions on the themes we wanted to cover and for lending his considerable intellect to our ideas. The entire staff at Inner Traditions is always a delight and consistently professional to work with, and in this case, special thanks to Jennie Marx, our excellent project editor. Thank you also to John Kahionhes Fadden of the Six Nations Museum for remaining patient with our numerous inquiries and for bolstering the Native American sections by sending us dozens of ideas and referrals to experts. John also gave us permission to use several of his artworks as illustrations in this book.

And finally, to all the women whose histories inspired us through this book, and their daughters and descendants to follow, thank you. May the light of Liberty be free to shine through *all* of our hearts and minds in the years to come.

Image Contributors

We also wish to thank all the people and organizations for uploading the public domain artworks that so enrich this book.

1

What Do We Mean by "The Secret Life of Lady Liberty"?

This is not your typical Statue of Liberty book. As a matter of fact, it's not even the kind of Statue of Liberty book we originally set out to write. What we first proposed to our publisher was to write a simple book about the evolution of the symbolism behind this famous statue. We thought we would review how her image had evolved from the Indian Queen of the earliest days of European contact in this land, through the Revolutionary patriot artwork of Minerva and the Indian Princess, and then trace how these figures eventually became the green colossus we all know so well in New York Harbor. Our publisher liked the idea but wanted us to expand the theme. They suggested examining the Statue of Liberty from a new perspective as a "Goddess in the New World."

These two loaded concepts, Goddess and New World, broadened our examination quite a bit, and we quickly realized we needed to do more research—a lot more research, in fact. To fit all of this new reading into our schedule, we reorganized our radio program for more than two years to create a Lady Liberty interview series. We asked a lot of questions and read through one bibliography after another. We interviewed a number of feminists and art historians about the peculiar contrast between the way women are treated in art and how they are treated in society, and gradually we formed a perspective on how *Liberty Enlightening the*

World, the Statue of Liberty's given title, could be considered a goddess in the New World. She turned out to be one of many figures who could claim that title, and we looked at several of them.

We found ourselves way back in the Neolithic era, learning about the goddess-worshipping cultures that predominated on this planet for millennia before so-called civilized history began. It turns out that a long time ago on this planet, most of humanity envisioned their creator God in the form of a woman. We realized that what we had learned to call the "dawning of civilization" was actually the transition point between these goddess-worshipping cultures and the patriarchal cultures that have dominated ever since.

Reflecting on the Statue of Liberty as a goddess led us to question just what is the nature of a goddess and what it means that the people of the United States of America have chosen to identify themselves and their nation as a goddess. Considering the Statue of Liberty is used around the world as a symbol to represent the United States of America, we wondered how we might use these insights about the female divine to shift the American paradigm. We believe seeing the Statue of Liberty as America's goddess could facilitate the transition to the partnership lessons of the goddess and away from the domination patterns of the current patriarchy.

A Goddess Is Better than **No** Goddess at All

Some of what we learned in this study of the Statue of Liberty is critical of allegorical female art, and we don't shy away from that. In his book *The Statue of Liberty,* architectural historian Marvin Trachtenberg said monuments are "a way men transmit communal emotions, a medium of continuity and interaction between generations . . . for to be monumental is to be permanent."[1] Some critics say all allegorical statuary of virtuous females contribute to the perpetuation of an unobtainably idealistic role for women. Others complain that they mask the imperialistic intentions of American exceptionalism in a deceptively maternal guise, especially the depictions of armed females. Public monuments are, after all, generally the propaganda of the dominant class, designed to establish

Figure 1.1. Detail from the 1750-square-foot mural *We the People* by Dr. Bob Hieronimus, Baltimore, Maryland, 2013. Notice that the Statue of Liberty is placed next to the Iroquois Tree of Peace and below is the George Washington Covenant Wampum Belt. Photo: Stuart Zolotorow.

their preferred renditions of history, ideals, and virtues. Because of their cost, monuments are almost always the product of the elite, designed "to engineer memory and create a particular vision of the past . . . and to manufacture consent," as art historian Albert Boime put it.[2]

The Statue of Liberty may not be the perfect symbol, but at least it's a permanent monument in the form of a giant female, which is a start. *A* goddess is better than *no* goddess, because over time the archetype will impact consciousness toward female empowerment regardless of the intentions of her creators. No other American symbol has the international appeal that the Statue of Liberty has. In fact, the majority of the four million people who make the pilgrimage to this particular Lady Liberty every year are not Americans. After they visit, they take back home with them her inspirations for personal independence, and assuredly these many private ideas about freedom that the Statue of Liberty inspires around the globe are not all related to her American identity.

Meanings of public monuments tend to change along with the tides of public interest, and in America, the melting pot of change, our national ideals have also continued to change over the years. In the United States, where we pay homage to our national myths, our monuments to them fill the role of religious pilgrimage sites. With all the changing identities of America, the Statue of Liberty has managed to represent us effectively for more than 130 years no matter what we seem to stand for. She has been changing from the start, even during the dedication ceremony wherein she was presented to America by her French creators. As the last firework dimmed in the sky, the interpretations and dreams that the French people associated with her were quickly forgotten, replaced by new American interpretations and dreams.

Some of the not-so-secret symbolism behind the Statue of Liberty is her ancestry in the Greco-Roman pantheon, as she is based mainly on a Roman goddess named Libertas. The secret part of that particular symbolism is revealed in the earlier deities of the goddess-centered cultures such as those of Minoan Crete and Mycenae on which many of these Greek and Roman gods and goddesses are based. The Greek myths that we all learn in elementary school come to us from stories recorded by Homer and Hesiod in the eighth century BCE, but many of them can clearly be recognized in the traditions of these much earlier cultures. When the prepatriarchal originals are compared to the way the myths are told today, one can begin to see accounts of one culture being overlaid on top of another. Suddenly there are stories of heroes slaying serpents or dragons, when in the more ancient goddess-centric myths, serpents were a symbol of the Great Mother Goddess herself, or of the regeneration and renewal sponsored by the goddess. Rape appears in the goddess myths for the first time after they were recast by the Greeks, where sexual domination was used as another metaphor for a warrior culture subduing a goddess-worshipping culture.[3]

Who We Are

To simplify, we use the pronoun "we" throughout this book because, even though our discoveries were different, we collaborated on all the research and on the *Lady Liberty Radio Interview Series,* the content of which serves as the basis for this book. Robert R. Hieronimus, Ph.D., is the interview cohost on *21st Century Radio,* and Laura E. Cortner is the long-serving executive producer and research assistant. Since 1988, along with Dr. Zohara Hieronimus, we have interviewed thousands of groundbreaking researchers who are advancing the fields of consciousness, the interconnectedness of all life, and unexplained phenomena. We also enjoy interviewing other researchers who take maverick approaches to history like the one we've taken here with the Statue of Liberty. All the quotes in this book not otherwise attributed are from the interview series we did focusing on Liberty and the goddess, and biographies of the participants in this series are listed in appendix 1. On the Lady Liberty radio series we interviewed Native American wisdomkeepers about their creation myths, theologians on the Virgin Mary, and Jungian analysts on the psychology of the Goddess. For an understanding of the African traditions that blended with those of slaves and Caribbean Natives, we interviewed a Yoruban priestess and discovered how syncretized traditions resulted in a veneration of the divine in female form that is uniquely American. And because coauthor Bob Hieronimus has been dogged by conspiracy theorists his whole career, we made a special point of learning the paranoid fantasies about the Statue of Liberty and what they tell us about the psychological tendencies of Americans.

We are two coauthors who come from very different backgrounds, each with our own set of prejudices to overcome. Robert R. Hieronimus, Ph.D., was born into an abusive, coal-mining family and was raised in the post–World War II world of Baltimore. Indoctrinated by old-time radio, television, and his surroundings to believe that women are capable of making decisions pertaining only to home and family, he is ashamed to read in his journals how at one time he believed women were simply not the mental equals of men. He pulled himself out of these prejudices as part of his greater spiritual growth beginning in the 1960s when he participated in the women's movement as a natural extension of the greater spiritual movement. An artist and a student of the ageless mystery traditions, he was especially drawn to ritual practices that were based on equality and balance between the genders. When he joined the Freemasons, he selected the branch called co-Masons because they admitted both men and women. He composed "The Earth People Prayer" (see the last chapter) in the early 1970s in which he points out that despite all the perceived differences between humans, we are all Earth People. He became a feminist by way of his spiritual path, seeing all people as Earth People.

Today he is privileged to work with his wife, Zohara, on many philanthropic endeavors pertaining to the underprivileged, the environment, social justice, the arts, and supporting the middle class.

Laura E. Cortner was born into a middle-class military family and came of age in the post-feminist era of the 1970s and 1980s. Despite the fact that she attended a women's college in the 1980s, she did not proudly embrace the label of feminist until she began researching this book. To many girls who followed the second wave of the women's movement, "feminist" was considered almost a dirty word, associated with unshaven armpits and rage. The media reinforced the idea that the women's movement was successfully concluded by showing women excelling in any profession. As that old perfume ad encouraged, you could work all day to bring home the bacon, and then come home and neatly fry it up in a pan.

What persuaded her to declare as a feminist was learning about early advocates for women's rights. As far back as the early 1400s, people like Christine de Pizan were writing about the need for gender balance for overall peace, but most exciting to learn about are the audacious women of the suffrage movement such as Matilda Joslyn Gage, Lillie Devereaux Blake, Belva Lockwood, and Alice Paul, whose histories reveal how much more the women's movement has yet to accomplish. As has been the experience of other men and women learning to identify as feminists, the clincher is the data. Countless statistical studies show that gender balance in the workplace and the funding of social programs for the family improve a corporation's profits and/or a nation's health.[4] Advocating for women's rights, it turns out, really means advocating for human rights, because gender balance leads to greater social harmony and growth for everyone across the board.

Lessons from Community Art and Public Art

We learned a lot while writing this book about how public art is used to manipulate our opinions regarding domination and compromise. As a community and public artist himself, coauthor Bob Hieronimus has a unique perspective on the creation of the Statue of Liberty. His firsthand experience with designing and executing large works of art meant to survive in the public eye for a long time has taught him that when working in the genre of community and public art, the artist is always faced with opposition from some members of the community in one form or another. He has seen his murals vandalized, his sculptures denounced from the pulpit, and some pieces completely painted over without his knowledge. He tells of one community meeting where, to his astonishment, both Jimi Hendrix and Thomas Jefferson were "voted out" of his proposed *A Little Help from Our Friends* mural.

Like all public art projects, the Statue of Liberty is a story of compromise and perseverance. Its history is one long scramble to assemble the right moneymakers over almost two decades to complete the project

LET THE ADVERTISING AGENTS TAKE CHARGE OF THE BARTHOLDI BUSINESS,
AND THE MONEY WILL BE RAISED WITHOUT DELAY.

Figure 1.2. The meanings of the Statue of Liberty have been changing since the very beginning, driven largely by editorial cartoons like this one. "Let the Advertising Agents Take Charge of the Bartholdi Business, and the Money Will Be Raised without Delay," *Puck*, April 18, 1885. Reproduction on display at the Liberty Island Museum. Author photo.

on two continents. Big pieces are expensive and require the cooperation of the authorities, and artists working in the community require special diplomatic and salesmanship skills in addition to being artists. Even so, Auguste Bartholdi, the sculptor of the Statue of Liberty, was also a true believer in the transformative power of public art. His biographers stress what a savvy marketer he was, but his inherent talents for promotion should in no way overshadow his success at tapping into a cultural insight that allows his colossal creation to speak to the hearts of people worldwide more than a hundred years later.

Hieronimus is also fond of repeating the advice that every one of us is an artist in some form. Everyone is born to create and should find the manner of creation that makes them happy. It doesn't matter whether it's visual, verbal, musical, sewing buttons, gluing things together, or creating positive relations or a comfortable home, it is the act of creating that sends fire up the spine. Sadly, art classes are being cut from school curricula, and when included they are so short as to allow no time for true inner reflection. Give artists a long enough period of time to create, says Hieronimus, and you're going to have a revolution—at least a revolution of consciousness.

Using the Statue of Liberty as a New Lens on History

As we attempted to define the secret life of Lady Liberty, we discovered along the way an entirely new way of appreciating not just the Statue of Liberty but also a new way of appreciating the United States, and even what qualifies as history itself. Following the threads of what was happening in the United States around the time of the Statue of Liberty's creation uncovered for us the contributions to the building of this nation of those not generally acknowledged in history books: women, Indigenous people, the slaves, and the working poor. One of the conclusions we reached is that liberty for the female—meaning real women—is a key to humanity's survival on this planet, and we'll spend a lot of time elaborating on that.

Even with the public relations gloss removed, however, we found that the Statue of Liberty, especially when viewed as the descendant of a long line of goddesses, still represents an America we can admire, and in fact, admire even more. Using the Statue of Liberty as a new lens on American history opens up our American story to one that values all its peoples, reminding us that this country, with all its mixed-people glory, is truly alight with potential. Though it took a surprising amount of arm-twisting to get Americans to accept this gift from France and to pay for her pedestal, once she was up it took almost no time for Americans to embrace her as their own. The Statue of Liberty has come to stand for all the ideals that each of us thinks is special about American liberty, which is why she is so effective as a symbol of protest. Because most of us identify with her, it is especially jarring to see images of her in parody or under attack by vandals.

Seeing the Statue of Liberty taken over by protestors immediately exposes the discrepancy between our ideals of "liberty for all" and the less than equal distribution of liberty in reality. Rousing speeches about Lady Liberty can inspire us to live up to her virtuous image, but at the same time they can make us critical of the manipulation of her symbolism by the privileged class. Attempting to explain her effective adoption by various, and even opposing, causes over the years, Albert Boime called her a "hollow icon," and Marvin Trachtenberg called her a "polymorphic iconographic blank."[5]

Our journey took us up the helixlike stairway inside the body of the Statue of Liberty to peer at the world through her crown and see what it looked like through the lens of ideal liberty. The real world comes up sorely lacking through this lens, and that inspired us to seek out new partnership-oriented methods that apply her ideals of liberty to more long-term solutions. As we take this fresh look at American history based on the standards of our nation's divine female, we will be accused by some of writing revisionist history and judging the past by today's standards. Of this we are probably guilty, but not ashamed. If history is the lie commonly agreed upon, as Voltaire said, then a little revision is necessary from time to time, when today's standards cause us to judge past actions differently. Suffragist Matilda Joslyn Gage believed that when you see how the world needs to change, it allows you to see his-

Figure 1.3. Lady Liberty makes the perfect symbol for just about any kind of political or satirical statement. Here Dr. Bob Hieronimus enjoys his vintage 1975 *MAD Magazine* featuring the mini-poster titled "Ms. Liberty," which replaced letters on the tablet to read "Women's Lib 1975," and a 2013 *National Geographic* that used the Statue of Liberty as a measuring stick to show how far the tides will rise around the world if all the ice melted. Author photo.

tory differently. Gage's biographer Sally Roesch Wagner stressed during our interview with her that embarrassing and controversial issues must not be avoided when teaching history, because it "deprives citizens the tools needed to make wise decisions."

Traditional history is told as if it were an endless series of wars and conflict, numbing us into accepting murder and genocide as necessary evils. Until recently, the atrocities committed by Columbus and his fellow explorers, when mentioned in history books at all, were glossed over in favor of pumping up the glorious accomplishments of the navigators. Historian Howard Zinn described this "learned sense of moral proportion coming from the apparent objectivity of the scholar" as deadly, but also warned against getting angry at the past. It is not always possible to clearly define who was wrong, and sometimes the dominators had the best of intentions, while victims of oppression will often turn on others even less fortunate and continue the cycle of domination. However, it was not inevitable for the Native Americans to be decimated so that the westward march of "progress" could reach its end. We should not accept murder for progress; genocide should not be taken for granted in any era. Zinn's *People's History of the United States* documents many cases of "fugitive moments of compassion" as a counterweight version of history, and we highly recommend it. These moments of resistance hold the hope for our future and remind us that when looking at history from a new perspective, it is important to keep our attention focused on correcting the ramifications of the past that continue to plague us today.[6]

Another big discovery we made while examining U.S. history from the perspective of Lady Liberty is that the Christian Church is the main source behind the social conditions that repress women in this country. The early suffragists also saw these heavily engrained religious beliefs as the cause of female suppression and pointed out how religious symbols and rituals reinforcing the authority of a male God have encoded the norms of gender relations. Actually, all the organized religions of the Abrahamic traditions suppress women, but it's organized Christianity that teaches most Americans that the female portion of the divine should be a source of suspicion and fear. "There's a reason why religion has been a pivotal battleground in establishing systems of domination," says historian Max Dashú. Religious symbolism, like mass advertising, has the power to manipulate and motivate human feeling.[7] We learned a lot on this subject from religion professor Elaine Pagels, particularly about the early Christian Church heretics and their adherence to Jesus Christ's radical acceptance of women as leaders in the church.

There Is Power in a Name

One of the first things we discovered when starting this research was how much of the terminology that we grew up believing was historically accurate is considered offensive to those on the receiving end of subjugation. Without getting tangled up in politically correct absurdities, we present here a brief primer explaining our choice of some of the terms used frequently in this book. Our definitions will also give an overview of some of the material we intend to cover and why we chose to capitalize certain words and phrases.

Goddess: Let's start with why we use this word in our subtitle, and why it makes so many people uncomfortable. As we noted, in the countries where Abrahamic religions predominate, the term "goddess" can provoke superstitious fear, but this is generally based on cultural ignorance. The monotheistic belief system that posits there can be only one male God teaches that representations of the divine in female form are suspect at best, and hell-spawn at worst. Today, most people in the United States associate the term "goddess" with an oversexualized movie star or a singer with an inflated ego. "It's hardly a reverent term," says Dashú, noting how desacralized and trivialized it has become in popular culture.[8]

Nor does it translate well to describe what most Indigenous traditions refer to as their creator or ancestral spirits. Oneida Joanne Shenandoah told us that Native Americans use words that are mostly ungendered and refer to "celestial beings" or "spirits" rather than deities. In chapter 6 we review the essential concept of relationship in which Indigenous people dwell with their creator spirits and with life on Earth, guiding all their actions. Feminists take a diverse approach to goddess research and veneration, and some prefer to say "Goddess" instead of "the goddess" because the latter implies a *thing* as opposed to a presence or an essence. We use the terms "Goddess" or "the goddess" somewhat interchangeably to mean a female expression of the divine.

Matrifocal: This is the word we have chosen to use to describe cultures that are gender balanced and that acknowledge women as equal partners in life instead of as dependents or slaves. We decided not to use the word "matriarchal," which might seem the logical choice when contrasting with a "patriarchal" culture where lineage is traced through the father, and culture is dominated by the man. Unfortunately, "matriarchal" has become a controversial word, because it has had mistaken assumptions attached to it causing some to see it as a threat. The mistake is that woman-focused cultures do not become dominated by the women at the expense of the men. No one has ever found a mirror-opposite to patriarchy, in the sense of a culture where women are in complete control of the society and culture. No one has ever found a female monotheistic deity either, because in mother-ruled or matrifocal cultures each gender is valued for its strengths, cooperation is encouraged, and the deities reflect this pattern as well and manifest as gender partners.

Archaeologist Marija Gimbutas revolutionized this study of history when she brought an interdisciplinary approach combining archaeology with linguistics, ethnology, and religious studies to reexamine the nearly omnipresent female figurines found in archaeological digs around the world. Uncovered by the thousands across Europe, Russia, and Mesopotamia, in fact worldwide, in the past few decades, these goddess figurines and rock art date as far back as thirty thousand years ago. These figurines and patterns emulating the female form and sexual regeneration were previously dismissed as fertility fetishes or pornographic toys before Gimbutas began to interpret them as symbols of reverence for the life-giving powers of woman. Cultural historian Riane Eisler and others who have continued Gimbutas's research describe the goddess-worshipping cultures as partnership oriented, as opposed to domination oriented. Art historian Merlin Stone described this time period as "when God was a woman." The veneration for the fecund female form reflects the spiritual concerns of the people who created them and basically shows that "the original direction of our cultural evolution was more in a partnership direction," as Eisler puts it. "It was not an ideal, but a less violent, less unjust, a more humane, if you will, and sensible way of living."

New World: This is a term we will avoid using except in the context of those who used it in the past. Instead we use the term "the Americas" to refer to the region of the North and South American continents during the time of European discovery and exploration. Calling it a *New* World implies that the *Old* World was following a natural progression to overtake and dominate the new. It implies the old ways were civilized and the new ways were primitive. Those pushing the agenda that "civilization" had the God-ordained manifest destiny to move westward were blind to the advancements of the so-called primitive peoples they were rolling over. This blindness is why it was not until the latter half of the twentieth century that we began to learn about the Native American cultural norms that, by today's standards, were more civil than those of the European conquerors. The European explorers and colonists came from a society where the top tenth of 1 percent controlled all the wealth and land while the majority lived in impoverished squalor. Slavery was popular and cruel, and women were literally the legal property of their husbands and fathers. In the Americas, the Europeans encountered cultures where slavery was abhorred, women led the clan systems, and people practiced earth-friendly land management, advanced agricultural science, and effected natural healing techniques. Everyone was equally fed and healthy. The Indigenous people rubbing elbows with the early English colonists along the East Coast of North America enjoyed egalitarian government structures, rights for women, and no squalid poverty. Together with the silver the Europeans stripped from South America, the Europeans assimilated these Native American advances in medicine, food science, and social structure into their own cultures and then spread them around the globe—literally creating a "New World." The discovery of the Americas and the self-governing people who flourished there truly had a global impact, as we detail in chapter 6.

Native Americans/American Indians/Native People: We use these terms interchangeably on the advice of the many Native scholars we have questioned on this matter. It is inaccurate to refer to all the people on these continents as one culture, however, and the most respectful way of talking about any of the Native people is by using the names they use to refer to themselves. When we use the three above-referenced terms it is usually in broad generalities to distinguish between the cultural approaches of the Indigenous people when compared to the European people. "Native American" is a new term invented to try to correct Columbus's error of calling these people "Indian," but "American Indian" is the term still used by the U.S. government that carries the legal weight of counting people for the census and in treaty negotiations for land sovereignty. It is also what many Native people, especially the elder generations, are accustomed to calling themselves. In this book, we focus mainly on the League of the Iroquois, a confederation of six Native nations that joined together under a nonaggression pact in upstate New York more than five hundred years ago. They include the Mohawk, Seneca, Onondaga, Cayuga, Oneida, and later the Tuscarora. Iroquois is a French term, and Haudenosaunee, or People of the Longhouse, is how they refer to themselves.

Euro-American/American/Colonist: In a book where we make a lot of comparisons between Native ways and those that followed, it would be confusing to use the term "American" by itself. Therefore, when we talk about English settlers before the American Revolution we refer to them as colonists. After the ratification of the U.S. Constitution, and to distinguish these settlers from the Native Americans, we have adopted the term "Euro-American," in preference to describing them as "white," as is customary for many historians.

Black People/African American: "African American" is meant to be a more respectful term, but it has the obvious problem that many Black Americans do not have ancestors from Africa. Some are the proud descendants of slaves, but not all. We acknowledge that many activists object to being identified by a skin tone, and in fact, the color black is not a good description for most Black Americans' skin tone. But most of the researchers we polled did not find it offensive, and out of respect for the fact that we are distinguishing them at all as a group of people, we will often capitalize it as Black Americans just as we do for Native Americans. We use both of these terms to contrast the suppression of certain peoples in the domination culture.

Founding Fathers/Revolutionary Generation: Throughout our previous books, *Founding Fathers, Secret Societies* and *The United Symbolism of America,* we purposely capitalized the term "Founding Fathers" out of respect for what this generation of individuals did in separating state from church and monarchical control and founding a self-governing nation. With our new perspective on women and the suppressed histories of so many people, a capitalized "Founding Fathers" no longer feels appropriate. We have begun to use the term "Revolutionary generation" as a more inclusive description of the astonishing collection of minds that was born at the right time to usher in these changes. This gender-neutral term also includes all strata of society that each contributed to this revolution to the extent of their abilities.

When we refer to those who designed our nation's images and symbols, we sometimes call them our "founding artists." Otherwise we will use the lowercase "founders" when referring to the group of public servants who shaped the new United States government. Even John Adams objected to the term "Founding Fathers," warning against over mythologizing the Revolution as a golden time. In an 1812 letter to Benjamin Rush he said, "It was patched together and piebald policy then, as it is now, ever was, and ever will be world without end."[9]

Republic/Republican: Just briefly for those who don't remember from civics class, a constitutional republic is what was formed by our founders. The democratic republic or representative democracy we refer to is not to be confused with today's names for the political parties of Republican and Democrat.

Feminism/Woman Suffrage/Women's Suffrage: The so-called third wave of feminism starting around the 1980s challenged the power of words and labels and criticized the earlier waves of feminism for being too focused on the concerns of white and middle-class women at the expense of disenfranchised women. Some have suggested new terms like "womanist" or "humanist" to describe the continuing struggle for women's rights, but we are going to stick with "feminist" and embrace it as it could be: a label for both men and women of all class structures and colors. Recognizing the label of feminist as one to be supported by everyone will help us reach gender parity in politics and business, which won't happen without quotas and exemptions. As we learned from historians Sally Roesch Wagner and Edith Mayo, the women of the suffrage movement who worked hard for more than seventy years were not *given* the right to vote, they *earned* it. Just like the activists who launched the American Revolution, women's rights activists discovered that guided anger, channeled appropriately, can create necessary and lasting change. At the beginning of the movement they used "woman" suffrage, but today it's more common to use "women's" suffrage, which is why you'll see both in this book.

Climate Change/Environmental Upheaval: "Climate change" is a term we've been using for years as being more accurate than "global warming," but by now "climate change" has also become politically charged and inaccurately used. When we talk about the environmental problem or crisis, we are really talking about the human problem, because the environment and the Earth will still be here in a hundred years—the question is, will it be a livable place for humans? Throughout this book you will see we are assuming the near future will bring some kind of global adjustment or environmental upheaval, because, more than likely, we have already passed the tipping point. The changes are accelerating, and it won't be long before no one will deny that humans have impacted the climate. With the inevitability of temperature increases assured, the best we can do at this point is to concentrate on how to survive the changes and learn how to take care of one another. It's time now to value who we are over what we have and practice treating all life-forms with compassion. If we adopt the Native American practice of weighing every one of our decisions with regard to how it will affect the seventh generation to come, we will inevitably affect the way we treat the Earth as well.

The Power of Symbol

Hieronimus's doctoral dissertation is a humanistic psychological analysis of symbols, particularly the symbol of the reverse of the Great Seal

Figure 1.4. Being a metaphorically hollow icon makes the Statue of Liberty an even more powerful symbol. This image shows the statue under construction in New York and reveals that her hollowness is literal as well as metaphorical. Reproduced from an 1886 engraving on display at the Liberty Island Museum. Author photo.

of the United States. In our previous book *Founding Fathers, Secret Societies* we included a long section on symbols as the formative agents of communities. In sum, myths, symbols, and archetypes are more than just sources of historical knowledge of the objective world, they are also significant forces in the psyche. Symbols are a bridge between the conscious and unconscious mind, cultivating wholeness and resulting in self-realization. When a symbol contains both conscious and unconscious elements, it can relate to the entire psychic system and be assimilated in consciousness relatively quickly. From the standpoint of humanistic psychology, the development of a symbolic mythological system is deemed necessary to a culture's health and stability. Our society's contemporary disintegrative state is partially explained by our failure to create meaningful myths and symbols.

Our founding artists had a much better grasp of the language of symbols than we have today, which is why they were all comfortable embracing non-Christian images to embody American liberty. Even the most extreme Christians among them did not raise an eyebrow at the many goddesses adorning the state seals, coins, and capitol buildings, because they lived in the era of the Enlightenment when it was understood that female imagery represented the virtues to which everyone should aspire. Today the conspiracy-minded grasp only a black/white level of interpretation, and because they have been taught to fear any image that associates the female with divine power, they have lashed out at the Statue of Liberty, as well as the statues of Justice and Peace and Freedom, calling them false idols and messengers of Satan.

Images and myths are far more effective at motivating people's emotions than words and facts are. Television and movies are such powerful drivers of social movements because they reach us through imagery. Neurosurgeon Leonard Shlain saw the redeeming qualities of television and the Internet in rewiring our brains to once again be image-readers, an action that regularly exercises our right brains. This return to the more image-driven side of our brain is in contrast to the past centuries, pre-television, when humans were immersed almost exclusively in the left brain of words and linear thinking, leading inexorably to an over-emphasis on the Word as law.[10]

The Statue of Liberty as Energizing Symbol

Accepting the goddess as part of the American tradition is a path that could lead many to the monumental paradigm shift we are advocating in this book. Using the power of concentration to study the symbolism of ancient female iconography can transform consciousness and create change within. Recognizing the goddess can help us recognize life as sacred, and our responsibilities to each other to keep it that way. That humanity thirsts for the unifying symbol of the goddess is evidenced by the substitutes that manifest in everything from the spiritual, as in veneration of the Virgin Mary or the Catholic saints, to the banal, as in veneration of the icons of pop culture, who are called "divas"—literally "goddesses" in Italian.

The new awareness we are talking about has nothing to do with religion, but instead it is a conceptual shift from a pattern of domination and separateness to one of inclusion and wholeness. The shift requires that we act on the understanding that life is sacred. "If we move from the heart in how we relate to each other," said Dashú, "then that is manifesting Goddess as far as I'm concerned. That is the ultimate." How we relate to one another and to the Earth around us would be affected if we honor the Statue of Liberty as our American goddess. Throughout this book we have chosen to consistently refer to the Statue of Liberty as a "her" rather than an "it" because we want you to embrace her as the goddess she is. She is the conscience of our nation and has the ability to strengthen the qualities of female power in all of us.

Our contemporary society is enchanted by the spell of consumerism. In this materialistic age, we are offered female role models who disguise selfishness as power and encourage us to find happiness through shopping. Reclaiming the goddess and allowing room for the female divine in our culture would lead to a more inclusive view of American history. Valuing the contributions of suppressed peoples will open the door for us to shift our behaviors in the present.

And shifting our behaviors in the present—and on a very large scale—is exactly what needs to happen if humanity is to survive the next one hundred years of environmental upheaval. Why do we bring up the environment in a book about the Statue of Liberty, you may ask? Because studying American liberty embodied in the female form led us to a very pro-environmental conclusion. One of the main messages of goddess veneration is a reminder to honor our relationship with the Earth and all living creatures, something that has to change radically right now if humanity is to survive on this planet. Despite a natural abhorrence for change, especially when it comes to habitual comforts, change we must—and, as we'll see in this book, Americans have a duty to lead the way.

Throughout this book we also advocate strongly for electing more women to positions of power, but that's only because the imbalance in female leadership in the United States is still so severe that action is required to achieve parity. As Sheryl Sandberg says, "In the future there will be no female leaders. There will just be leaders."[11] And we add that these future leaders will be people who no longer see the world around them as merely a source of potentially profitable resources for extraction but as a source of life and power that must be treated with respect. In the end, what we need is both male and female leaders who operate from the human drive for caring and compassion. These qualities may be seen as female characteristics in today's mind-set, but that is mainly a result of social conditioning. Men can be just as caring as women when social norms accept it, and women can be just as warlike as men when social norms encourage it. We advocate any changes that support gender balance in business, politics, and the home, including legislation to support childcare, elder parent care, flextime, and infant nutrition for the developing years. Families are the nexus of shared power, and parents are the role models for how the next generation will advance, so supporting equal responsibility in the home is crucial to creating a more balanced next generation.

We want you to start noticing the American goddesses all around you in seals and statuary, but also the goddesses in your personal life as seen in the nurturing qualities of the people you meet, especially your mothers, sisters, and daughters. And men, too, a new generation of whom are beginning to embrace caregiving as a symbol of strength. The goddess is all around us in nature as well, as she makes her presence known in the changing seasons and cycles of birth and death.

Once you start looking, you will literally see American goddesses everywhere! There's Lady Freedom on the Capitol dome, the old Liberty-head nickel, the blind Lady Justices at the Supreme Court, and even vestiges of the Indian Queen, the former personification

Figure 1.5. It's easy to notice American goddesses all around you when you visit Washington, D.C. Here are two named America and History from the first panel of the *Frieze of American History*, designed by Constantino Brumidi in the Capitol Rotunda. The standing figure is named "America" and wears the Phrygian cap. Seated at her right is the Indian Princess and to her left is a figure labeled History, recording events. Both are balanced by eagles. Architect of the Capitol.

of America, in cigar-store Indians. The more we learn of their backgrounds, the more we talk about them and form opinions about them, the more we will energize their ideals of freedom, liberty, and justice in our national consciousness.

No, this is not your typical Statue of Liberty book. If you are looking for a definitive history book about the Statue of Liberty we recommend you start with any of the fine books Barry Moreno has written on the subject, or the many other greats listed in our bibliography. This book is about recognizing the goddesses in the real women around you and noticing the goddesses in our official insignia in order to help you tap your own full potential to create and change the world in the special way that your talents were designed for. American women, especially women whose children are grown and who have more time to serve their country now, must begin to see themselves as leaders. These are the women the Dalai Lama spoke of when he said, "The world will be saved by Western women."[12] Even though they may not yet think of themselves as leaders, in the West more women have the means, education, and motivation to see what kind of future is in store for our grandchildren if we allow corporations to dictate policy within the same domination paradigm built on a cycle of eternal war. The Statue of Liberty, with her torch of enlightenment/wisdom held high, reminds us that through education and reaching for the infinite goodness of divinity we can secure true liberty. This is why we love America so. This is the American Liberty, based on enlightenment and embodied by a goddess.

How did this symbol become so powerful? Her original French creators described her future as energizing hope for liberty in all countries of the world, not just in America and France, and they gave her a name that speaks to this international destiny: *Liberty Enlightening the World*. But we doubt even they would have predicted the enormity of her success. This book is an attempt to consider how she might also be called a Goddess of the New World. Studying her this way has led us to rejoice in her idiosyncrasies as we realized that she has become a symbol of both the myths that unite us and the diversity that strengthens us.

2

Where Are Your Women?

Where are your women?" That's what our Native American leaders asked the European settlers as they gathered around the council fires trying to negotiate peace terms. "How can we possibly talk to you about peace if your women aren't here?" This profound question sums up the enormity of the cultural clash between the hierarchical patriarchy of the Europeans and the cooperative and matrifocal practices predominating on the northeastern coast of the Americas before the Europeans arrived.

The Europeans were just as shocked at the question. "How can we possibly trust the counsel of a woman if women are cursed by the temptation of Eve?" they wondered. Europeans did not trust the intellectual capacity of women, especially in deciding anything as important as war and peace. The Natives' trust in their women was even used as further justification by the Europeans for their periodic policies of genocide against the Natives. Europeans were brought up to believe that anyone who allowed themselves to be ruled by a woman, especially in spiritual matters, must be allied with the devil.

In this chapter, we look at some of the mothering aspects of the Statue of Liberty. The title of "Mother" is the highest honorific Indigenous people can assign to anyone. First Nations people all over this continent honored the strength and wisdom of their women and valued their life-giving powers with respect. Among the Iroquois—or Haudenosaunee, the Native culture with which we are most familiar—women were assumed as absolutely necessary for balance in all tribal relations. Contrast these beliefs of inclusiveness and respect for their elder women, or Clan Mothers, as the wisest of counselors to the status of mothers in the United States today, wherein mothers are one of the groups discriminated against the most, especially single mothers and elderly widows.

Although the colonists borrowed extensively from the Native culture and governing practices, they ignored this key element of gender balance when constructing their new government, leaving Euro-American women struggling for centuries to gain a seat at the liberty table. The United States government today lags way behind when compared to the rest of the world in terms of the percentage of women in power. Only 19 to 20 percent of the U.S. Congress is led by women, ranking the United States at number 71 on a list of 190 countries comparing the percentage of women in government around the world today. That puts us far below all of Europe and even much of Africa and Asia and Central America, where they have elected considerably more women into power than we have in the United States.[1] We argue that creative solutions are required to more rapidly achieve gender parity in the United States government, because we believe that it is our best hope in achieving lasting peace with other Earth People and with the environment.

The Love Hormone

When we heard that chemical differences between male and female brains were being used in the argument to include more women in positions of power, we were determined to learn more. The more we learned, unfortunately, the more disappointed we became about finding a simple neurochemical argument for gender parity. The popular press is dangerously oversimplifying the data on the actions of the hormone system oxytocin,*

---

*When referring to oxytocin, one is talking about a system of many hormones working together with other chemicals, including oxytocin, vasopressin, cortisol, estrogen, and opiates all working in combination. Interestingly, research has indicated the effects do not pertain to just the sending of the hormone—it turns out the receptor sites are just as important, if not more so, than the production of the chemicals themselves. Estrogen and testosterone have an effect on the receptor sites, and when lab animals have their receptors blocked, it is shown that they exhibit antisocial behavior no matter how much oxytocin they are producing.

which is naturally produced in both men and women, and reporting on the new field of scientific inquiry around this hormone has the tendency to stray into hyperbole. This is especially true when translating the data into conclusions about oxytocin's role in learning to trust and bond and feel safe.

It was formerly believed that only women used the hormone oxytocin because it had been identified as being responsible for the physical and chemical changes related to pregnancy, childbirth, and breastfeeding. When we sought out the leading researcher on oxytocin and social bonding, we learned how far the research has come in the past few decades. It is now clear that oxytocin is produced equally in both genders during times of stress to assist humans in reaching states of calmness and connection. The curious point is that the hormone estrogen increases a woman's ability to receive more oxytocin in times of stress than can men, and this is being extrapolated into social science studies including those showing how men and women excel at different types of problem solving.

Twentieth-century neurochemistry is beginning to validate what Native Americans practiced instinctively: men and women approach solutions differently, and the best results for all are gained when both genders are included in the decision-making process. When the sexes are balanced in the boardroom and in government, solutions that are more creative and productive and long lasting are reached.[2] As we learned from cultural historian Riane Eisler, we need to expand the discussion beyond simply increasing the number of women on boards of directors and in political office. It's not so much about adding nurturing policies into the workplace to enable women to work and tend their families at the same time. It's more about adding nurturing policies into the workplace so that all humans can work more productively together and care for their families at the same time.

Companies in the United States are losing out by not having the input of women. No matter that more college graduates are women, the numbers reaching the top leadership positions remain in the single digits. Capable women drop out of the workforce all the time, even when they are on track for prestigious and influential executive

Figure 2.1. *Clan Mother's Warning via War Chief* by John Kahionhes Fadden. Seated Seneca chief, with standing Clan Mother and war chief before him. The wampum is the Women's Nomination Belt, which gives authority to the women to nominate a person to the position of chief as well as the power to remove him from office for negative behavior. Two colonials in the background are learning about the operations of the League of the Iroquois government. Photo: John Kahionhes Fadden.

posts, because they are making the decision to take care of their families instead. Companies that realize this and have implemented policy changes to allow flexibility in schedules and expectations have discovered the results are that both men and women feel encouraged to value their nurturing side, and everyone benefits. Health improves, creativity increases, and the corporation's profit margin goes up.

The Female Governesses Beg Leave to Speak

The cultural norm of honoring the female was not exclusive to the Iroquois. From the Cherokee people, or Aniyunwiya, we have the accounts of an individual known as Attakullakulla and his niece Beloved Woman, or Nanyehi, both leaders from the mid-1700s. Cherokee women were fierce warriors as well as key participants in negotiations, and any nation that presented itself without women was immediately suspected as being violent and out of balance. Attakullakulla is the one recorded as saying to the Europeans, "Where are your women?" at a peace negotiation in 1759 in the South Carolina region.[3] When his niece took over the leadership of the Clan Mothers of the nation there are several accounts of her following the same tack.

"Beloved Woman" is actually a title of leadership, not a name, and Nanyehi is more often identified by her European name, Nancy Ward. In 1781 and 1785, as white settlers began streaming into her people's territory, she is on record as reprimanding the representatives of the new United States for not including their women in negotiations. She implored them to let their women hear her voice. She advised those listening to remember that they were all sons of mothers and stressed the traditional roles of kinship among her people as her basis for authority. The proper approach to diplomacy was kinship, as opposed to the "white father" and "elder brother" patronizing terminology used by the Europeans.[4]

The Haudenosaunee are also on record expressing their concern to the Europeans about lack of female representation during peace talks, believing as they did that the presence of women would ensure the peaceful intentions of the other. Oneida chief Good Peter is quoted in a 1788 speech as saying, "Brothers, our ancestors considered it great offense to reject the counsels of their women, particularly of the female governesses. They were esteemed the mistresses of the soil. Who, said our forefathers, bring us into being? . . . The female governesses beg leave to speak with the freedom allowed to women, and agreeably to the spirit of our ancestors. . . . They are the life of the nation."[5]

Before 1800, many treaties were signed by both male and female sachems, but still Europeans probably didn't realize the power that women wielded behind the scenes. The Native Americans tended to assign the role of public speaker to men, and wise counselor to women, so more often Europeans were speaking only with the men.[6] Iroquois men acted as the elected public leaders, but women controlled the election process. One way of looking at it would be to say that the men spoke in public what the women told them to say in private. The founders of the United States of America incorporated much of what they learned from the Iroquois Confederacy into their own republican experiment, as we review in chapter 3, but they had blinders on when it came to understanding that the key to the Iroquois success was balance between the genders.

Respect for the Mother Starts with the Creation Stories

The wide expanse between the different notions of women in political power starts at the very beginning with two very different notions of the creation of humankind. We talked to two Iroquois, Mohawk Douglas George-Kanentiio and Oneida Joanne Shenandoah, about their ancestral being known as Skywoman from whose daughter the Mother Earth and the Grandmother Moon are formed. We hesitate venturing any further into retelling Native American mythology at the risk of disrespecting them by misinterpretation. Their sacred teachings are meant to be handed down orally in the appropriately ritualized settings, and rather than presume, we instead recommend you to Kanentiio and Shenandoah's books *Skywoman* and *Iroquois Culture and Commentary*. What seems logical to assume, however, is that growing up with a tradition that the world was created by a female guiding spirit and that male and female humanity were created in balance would result in a self-governing system based on balance between the genders.

The Europeans' opinions of women were likewise the result of generations of conditioning. English colonists grew up with a tradition that the world was created by a male guiding spirit and that male humanity was created first, with female humanity created to serve him. Centuries of this training explain why they were so surprised by the Natives suggesting that they honor their women. It also explains why Native American spiritual practices were so poorly translated, filtered as they were through the Europeans' own very different beliefs.

For example, the concepts of balance in Native American teachings were often mistranslated into the Christian concept of duality between good and evil. Common among many Native American myths is the tale of a divine woman or ancestral spirit who is the mother of twins. According to Seneca Barbara Alice Mann, these twins described balance. "Male and female were but one of a series of bonded pairs evident everywhere in the culture," she said in her book, *Iroquoian Women: The Gantowisas*.[7] Skywoman's daughter, Gusts of Wind, is one example of an ancestral spirit who bore two male twins. The tale of these Iroquois twins was translated by the Christian missionaries as a reference to good and evil, but Kanentiio said the "evil" twin was really more of a mischievous spirit and the countering balance of dark to the "good" twin's light. "He introduces even greater tension on this planet," said Kanentiio. "The conflict, the tension, the ignition that produces other

Figure 2.2. *Skywoman Falling* by John Kahionhes Fadden shows the Iroquois creation story with the ancestral spirit Skywoman leaving the Skyworld for the watery planet below. The animals and birds below cooperated to provide her enough shelter, and thus Turtle Island, the Earth, was formed. Growing up with a tradition that the Earth was created by female guiding spirits and that male and female humanity were created in balance would shape a culture's approach to gender balance. Photo: John Kahionhes Fadden.

forms of life . . . It is from him that the Earth, the mother, is given the specific form."

Native American traditions often honor a female ancestral spirit together with a male counterpart as balance. For example, the Sky, the West Wind, and Thunderstorm are often portrayed as male in balance to the Earth as female. The Sun as male and Moon as female are often paired, and throughout most of the Americas, the stem of the peace pipe is paired with the bowl of the sacred pipe as male and female. "You find these male and female counterparts all over the world," said history and comparative religion professor Jordan Paper, "not just in the Americas." Archaeologist Marija Gimbutas showed the prevalence of this same partnership in the goddess-worshipping cultures of Old Europe, where evidence points to an Earth Mother paired with a male consort or son.

Indigenous people assign the title "Mother" to the spirits that guard their most sustaining food source. In her essay "Meanings of Goddess," historian Max Dashú lists page after page of mother essences from South America, as in mothers of waters, mothers of animals, and mothers of sacred places. Mother spirits range up to the Far North where "the Inuit speak of the Sea Mother, who created the great ocean mammals, and the Caribou Mother," Dashú writes. "These Mothers are old women, like the primary female spirit of the Cheyenne, Old Woman."[8] The Sioux creation myth tells of White Buffalo Calf Woman bearing a pipe representing the covenant between the Sioux and the buffalo, with instructions on how to live. Indigenous people in Africa are also full of mother veneration. "The Yoruba speak of *awon iya wa,* 'our mothers,'" reports Dashú, "or a collective term for female ancestors, female deities, and for older living women, whose power over the reproductive capacities of all women is held in awe by Yoruba men. . . . They are called the owners of the world."[9]

All along the East Coast of North America, the Indigenous people traced their family through the women. This was discovered with surprise in the mid-1800s by suffragist historian Matilda Joslyn Gage as she prepared her multivolume *History of Woman Suffrage* and was searching for examples of nations where women were not oppressed. She recorded observing how many of the Native American nations living around her in upstate New York assigned to women "almost the whole legislative authority, and in others a prominent share."[10] No sale of lands was valid without consent of what she called "the Council of Matrons," which elected the chiefs and settled all the disputes. She reported that Mohawk Clan Mothers forbade young braves to go on the warpath, and she found treaties "among the State Archives at Albany, New York, signed by the 'Sachems and Principal Women of the Six Nations.'"[11]

The Statue of Liberty as America's Mom

In our consideration of the Statue of Liberty, we realized that the value our nation places on nurturing has contributed to how we tend our liberty. If you can consider the Statue of Liberty as a symbol of strength in nurturing, we'll show you a few ways she's turned into America's Mom. Symbolically, the Statue of Liberty is unlike a traditional European mother goddess figure, because there is no emphasis on the life-giving parts and she is fully clothed. The Statue of Liberty did pick up the name the Mother of Exiles, but this was not a designation given to her by her creators, nor is it a comprehensive description of her many layers of meaning and intention. She is not cradling a child, and her facial expression is rather fierce.

It was not until we talked to Sue Carter, Ph.D., in fact, in our search to learn more about the hormone oxytocin, that we suddenly had our *aha!* moment. Carter likes to describe her research in the study of the oxytocin system by using a metaphor of safety, and she immediately saw how the Statue of Liberty fit into that discussion. "Obviously, she's a woman, she's welcoming, she's offering safety—all the same stuff, isn't that a metaphor?"

The reason the Revolutionary generation surrounded themselves with a multitude of images of the female divine in the form of Lady Liberty, Minerva, and the Indian Princess was, in part, to fill an unconscious need for a mother figure. By the time French sculptor Auguste Bartholdi unveiled his version of Lady Liberty in 1886, Americans were well primed to accept a matronly goddess figure as American Liberty and were very quick to adopt her as a substitute mother goddess.

Outwardly, the Statue of Liberty is not intended to be symbolic of motherhood, but Americans soon overlaid the mother image onto this statue and assigned to her symbolic renderings never intended by her creators. In addition to becoming the Mother of Exiles thanks to poet Emma Lazarus, she also became the female domestic partner, we might say wife, of Uncle Sam, thanks to political cartoonists like Thomas Nast.

We want to resurrect the name of Georgina Schuyler here, a friend of Emma Lazarus and the one actually responsible for attaching to the Statue of Liberty her new identity as the mother offering "worldwide welcome" to anyone "yearning to breathe free." Lazarus had died only a year after the statue was dedicated, at the young age of thirty-eight, and if it weren't for Schuyler, Lazarus's poem may have been forgotten forever. Schuyler herself had forgotten about it until she rediscovered it years later in an old bookshop. Becoming inspired by the words of her late friend, she enlisted the aid of several wealthy patrons who created a plaque that was later accepted in a formal presentation at the statue in 1903.[12] Until this more public association with Lazarus's "The New Colossus" the tendency had been to interpret the statue's actions more along the lines of *enlightening,* as the creators had intended, rather than with the idea of a motherly *welcoming all peoples* that she is identified with so strongly today.

Bartholdi, His Mother, and the Statue

There is a popular story retold in most Statue of Liberty history books that claims the face for the Statue of Liberty was based on that of the sculptor's mother, Charlotte Bartholdi. By all accounts, Auguste Bartholdi was somewhat of a momma's boy, though deferential respect for one's mother would certainly have been conforming to the social standards of his class and time. For reasons we explain in chapter 5, however, this mother and son were especially close, and Bartholdi's life-long devotion and care for his mother are noteworthy.

In some ways, Bartholdi used his Liberty project to get out from under his mother's shadow, according to Barry Moreno, the librarian and historian of the Museum Services Division at the Ellis Island National Museum of Immigration in New York. She had controlled her son's career well into his thirties, and it was not until he left for several extended research trips to the United States that he was able to find a wife. At the age of forty-two, he worked up the courage to write home to France and ask his mother's permission to get married. After he and his new bride nervously obtained Charlotte's blessing and returned to France, they moved in with her and she remained the matriarch of the house until her death. Bartholdi's love and respect for his mother are enough to speculate that he poured some of that maternal devotion into his statue by seeing her face when he thought of the highest ideals and virtues that he was trying to capture in his colossus.

However, there is a problem with the popular story that the face is modeled on his mother. It is based on only one comment made to only one person at only one time, and it was made somewhat in passing at that. Of course, the lack of corroborative evidence doesn't mean the story is not true, but upon closer examination, it does sound more like one of the numerous clever marketing ploys finessed by the sculptor Bartholdi and his fundraising committees in their various attempts to get this expensive public monument off the ground.

The story originated at the Paris Opéra in 1876. Joining Bartholdi in his box seat was his friend Senator Jean Bozérian, an early supporter of the Liberty statue project and fundraising committee. Bozérian had just visited the foundry where the face of the statue was on rush for completion so that the head and crown could be displayed at the Paris World Expo of 1878 (figure 2.6, p. 47). As Bartholdi ushered the senator into his box, they were greeted by Bartholdi's mother, Charlotte, and according to Bozérian's numerous retellings of the incident at dinner parties and fundraising events for years afterward, Bozérian immediately gasped in astonishment at the resemblance of this woman to the face of Liberty.

He turned to Bartholdi and said, "This must be the model for your statue!" To this Bartholdi is supposed to have said simply, "Yes," before proudly introducing Bozérian to his mother. To the best of our knowledge, Bartholdi never claimed in public that his mother was the model for the face, and no writing of his has been uncovered to corroborate

Figure 2.3. Portrait of Charlotte Bartholdi, the mother of the sculptor of the Statue of Liberty, rumored to be the model for the face of the statue. Reproduction on display at the Liberty Island Museum. Author photo.

the story. There is nothing in the extensive surviving correspondence between mother and son mentioning a sitting or a modeling or even a comparison of her likeness to his Liberty. Bartholdi was present at some of these fundraising dinners when Bozérian retold his story, however, so it's important to note that he never denied it either. As the consummate salesperson he was, Bartholdi surely would have recognized how this humanizing element would help manipulate public opinion across two countries.

Bartholdi had a keen understanding of the elements of classic colossal statuary, making it unlikely that he would have erred on the side of sentimentality. Inserting the face of any actual human model would risk making the statue appear to be of the present moment. To give a work

Figure 2.4. The face of the Statue of Liberty circa 1885, nearly unrecognizable without the hair and crown, was designed to have an androgynous and timeless expression. Reproduction on display at the Liberty Island Museum. Author photo.

of art a timeless quality required creating an androgynously featured face with a somewhat vacant stare, meant to imply the distant unknown future. Bartholdi's goals were for the facial features to be pleasing and discernable from great distances, while generic enough to be infinite. We might conjecture that when Bartholdi answered in the affirmative, he was thinking in metaphors himself. Both he and his mentor on this project, Édouard de Laboulaye, took several opportunities to characterize their version of American Liberty in maternal terms. "Liberty is the mother of a family who watches over the cradle of her children," said Laboulaye, who was intent on ensuring that their statue of Liberty would be matronly and conservative in design.[13] Yes, when you compare the portraits, the face of the Statue of Liberty does look like Charlotte Bartholdi. But as a generic face, it also looks like a lot of other people, including Laboulaye himself, a curiosity we review in chapter 10.

Women Are Different from Men

Even though it was not originally conceived as a Mother of Exiles nor a deliberate tribute to his mother, the Statue of Liberty has filled the role of a mother figure for this nation, providing a symbol of strength that is also nurturing. It is our perception of her as being both strong and a caretaker at the same time that we'd like to see adopted in diplomatic and domestic policies, and why we advocate that more women be cultivated as leaders in order to achieve that state of balance as practiced by our Native American ancestors. It may set some feminists' teeth on edge to hear this, but women *are* different from men. Sue Carter told us that, genetically, women and men have adapted different biological systems for survival, and, perhaps because historically women have had less participation in war and defense than men, their brains have evolved differently.

Humans as a species use more than one strategy to address challenges. In general, social science studies show women are less likely to take high risks, are less likely to cause conflict, and tend to value personal relationships differently from men. Both genders surpass the other at solving various kinds of problems. For example, women have better recall when hearing a story and display better fine motor coordination, while men are better at mentally manipulating three-dimensional shapes and at target-directed motor skills.[14] The different skills adapted by men and women seem almost chemically designed to facilitate advanced problem solving when the two are brought together. The Iroquois figured this out centuries ago and never made any political decisions that weren't guided by the council of the Clan Mothers.

Feminist critics of the overblown reports on oxytocin research charge these scientists with "neurosexism" as well as improper science.

After battling their way out of centuries of belief that women's brains were inferior to men's, naturally some feminists are very sensitive to any claims of distinction between men and women. They warn against becoming distracted by supposed brain differences leading to a search for a chemical fix for inequality. Focusing on equal parenting and placing value on nurturing in the workplace, they suggest, would be more effective than time spent researching any neurochemical gender differences.[15] Still, learning more about the potential of oxytocin could actually open a new door in humanity's evolution, especially when it comes to tapping hormones that are activated in both genders by feelings of peace and safety or war and aggression.

Involving women more deliberately as peace diplomats has been proposed many times before in this country. Suffragist and peace activist Julia Ward Howe, for example, conceived of an International Mother's Day after witnessing the carnage of the Civil War, followed immediately by the border dispute that blew up into the Franco-Prussian War in France. She called for women around the world to rally together to keep their sons from being sent to kill other mothers' sons in needless wars. Women of all nations should come together and promote "the great and general interests of peace," she said. Many have noted how the pain of the birthing experience makes women more careful about taking life. "An Occasional Letter on the Female Sex" published by Thomas Paine in 1775 argued that "in giving [the State] our sons and our husbands we give more than ourselves. You can only die on the field of battle, but we have the misfortune to survive those whom we love most."

Oxytocin and the Human Potential

As we noted earlier, oxytocin was considered a woman's hormone, because about a hundred years ago it was first identified as playing a role in triggering contractions of the uterus during childbirth and in letting down milk during breastfeeding. It was from the work of psychiatrist Jean Shinoda Bolen that we first picked up on the excitement over the new oxytocin research, and in particular, those studies implying that women make better diplomats due to their estrogen-enhanced advantage of absorbing oxytocin in times of stress. Incidentally, Bolen's current mission is advocating for a United Nations' sponsored version of Julia Ward Howe's idea of an international women's gathering for peace.

The material on oxytocin is complex, and we are grateful to Sue Carter for walking us through the technical papers that report on her primary research as well as the research of her colleagues. Carter believes that oxytocin and its related hormones had been ignored in the research lab for so long because they were mistakenly identified as being relevant only to women's health. When her work showed that oxytocin also played a role in monogamy and social bonding (i.e., "love"), oxytocin suddenly became a hot topic. Social science trials have shown that when humans are given nasal sprays of oxytocin before playing games of risk, both men and women exhibit more trust and empathy for their fellow players. This led to implications for the financial world given that those administered oxytocin are also more likely to trust a stranger with their money.[16]

In short, oxytocin is not just about uterine contractions and breast-feeding anymore. Swedish researcher Kerstin Uvnäs-Moberg did some of the first studies on oxytocin to show that it is released in the brain simply from skin-to-skin contact, meaning massages or hugs. She then coined the term "calm and connect" to explain what a flood of oxytocin impels us to do. Perhaps not surprising to dog lovers, Uvnäs-Moberg and her colleagues have shown that petting a dog can produce the same state of dreamy, bonding euphoria described by mothers who breast-feed their children, because both actions trigger the release of oxytocin. Meg Daley Olmert, the director of research for the Warrior Canine Connection, believes the oxytocin release that occurs in both dogs and humans upon contact was likely instrumental in the domestication of the wolf thirty thousand years ago. The calm and connected response from oxytocin led to what she calls "a triumph of trust over paranoia."

New research is showing that oxytocin is released in times of stress, and the better you are at using oxytocin, the better you will be at dealing with stress. What Carter uncovered was that the systems developed by mammalian evolution that regulate social bonding are the same ones that regulate reaction to stress.[17] Men and women appear to produce oxytocin equally. It's how they use it that differs—but even there we are in danger of oversimplifying, because the effects of estrogens and androgens on oxytocin and vasopressin, its mirror hormone, are not well understood. Oxytocin binds to and stimulates receptors in a way that may be regulated by estrogen, in part. Estrogen's effects on oxytocin are due to complex effects on the estrogen receptor, but its function appears to be to stimulate quiet time, like bonding with the baby or breastfeeding. There is also some evidence that testosterone can enhance the synthesis of vasopressin in brain areas that are involved in defensiveness or that facilitate activities like defense of the home or one's mate. The two appear adapted to function together for species' survival.

Oxytocin evolved because human infants, like most mammalian infants, need many years' worth of attention in order to develop the sophisticated cranial capacity of the brain. Biological parents are not necessary to provide the proper nurturing to trigger this chemical wiring, of course, just someone to love the baby and to make it feel safe. Neglect is worse than abuse for brain development, and solitary confinement is the worst abuse of all. Children can somehow adapt to abuse, but neglect will stunt the brain beyond repair. Very simply, if your brain never gets past survival mode, it can't expand to the higher-learning functions. Again using metaphor, Carter says we are wired for love, with an ancient biology that evolved before our brains developed the ability to communicate in words. What we can potentially learn from oxytocin about the non-gender-specific human potential is that the giving and receiving of love are essential components of human existence.

To grasp the enormous implications of how the oxytocin system makes us human, Carter and her team studied the brains of a tiny mouselike rodent, the prairie vole. Finding a socially monogamous mammal suitable for laboratory study has allowed for great strides in oxytocin research, but considering that Carter is studying what is called the love hormone, it's not surprising that she jumps to assure us that the prairie voles in her lab have far more pleasant lives than those in the wild. Unlike all other rodents, and even all other voles, prairie voles live in large extended families that work together to raise the pups. Sometimes, even before the mother can interact with the newborn pups, the father will be with them already, licking and tending his children. What sets the prairie vole apart from other rodents is the amount of oxytocin in their brains, and by studying their behavior as the oxytocin supply is manipulated, scientists have extrapolated on the motivations behind the social bonding of humans.

Tend-and-Befriend as Opposed to Fight-or-Flight

Almost everyone will experience a wash of oxytocin that is stimulated by the sight and smells of a baby. Regardless of whether you had anything to do with birthing that child, the hormonal release of oxytocin you feel is designed to generate tending behavior. Adoptive parents, grandparents, women who deliver by C-section and do not breastfeed— all of them will produce oxytocin merely by being in the presence of a baby. Carter conjectures that this very old and complicated system of hormones evolved as a security measure for the survival of the species. "These ancient molecules allow individuals to manage apparently contradictory tasks," she says, "such as reproduction, forming social bonds, and at the same time self-defense in the face of a threat."[18] It's what turns off the fight-or-flight (antisocial, animalistic) reflex and makes you run back into a burning building to save a child, overriding the self-preservation instinct to flee. It's what makes humans bond with their children and trust each other.

Yet so much remains unknown about how the oxytocin system works, especially the long-term effects. Exciting but incomplete research is indicating oxytocin can improve social interactions for people with autism and post-traumatic stress syndrome,[19] but Carter warns about unknown long-term side effects. Researchers are manipulating a primordial system, and some people are now self-medicating with over-the-counter "likeability" sprays. The common use of a synthetic version of oxytocin to induce labor, together with the popularity of C-sections that bypass altogether the production of oxytocin during labor, have

Figure 2.5. *L'Amerique Independante*, 1778. This painting featuring Benjamin Franklin shows him in Roman attire with his arm around the Indian Queen and surrounded by goddesses, including Liberty with her pole and cap, Minerva behind her with her shield and spear, and Mercury and Ceres in the left corner with the plow. Antoine Borel engraving after Jean Charles Le Vasseur. National Portrait Gallery, Smithsonian Institution.

begun rewiring generations of children. Any time you substitute for a natural function, you suppress the body's ability to do that function by itself. Oxytocin research is clearly still at the threshold, and anyone claiming that it can explain the differences between men and women is not considering all the implications.

Democracy Starts in the Family

The discovery that estrogen facilitates the absorption of oxytocin, helping women remain calm during stressful situations, brings us back to the model of the Clan Mothers as the necessary diplomatic counselors. Fostering dialogue from all participants, comparing the opposing points, truly listening to the other rather than projecting one's own solution, these are the keys to successful peaceful negotiation. This is why we say women should be present at every stage of conflict resolution.

In the past two generations, public opinion has shifted enormously in the West about the father's role as the nurturer and partner in domestic duties. Riane Eisler takes great encouragement from these shifts, saying, "It has to start with a more democratic family, because that's the model people grow up with." With a new generation of men becoming more hands-on parents, work/life balance will naturally improve, given that men raised by strong, liberated mothers, when starting families of their own, become a new kind of father role model for their children.

A similar crack in the patriarchal model occurred just before the American Revolution. Eisler shows that new concepts in child-rearing and dealing with servants started in England, where in the 1700s "the rising power of women in the families of the British ruling classes brought important changes in the men who governed England." These changes in the home and child-rearing were accelerated in the colonies,[20] where by the middle of that century urges to republicanize the state were starting to be felt in the family. Patriarchy has always been modeled on the family, with the father operating as a little king with complete power over his wife and children, and social order in the community being maintained by conformity to the family rules. Democratizing the family helped some men to accept larger social reforms.

Eisler developed a new system she calls "caring economics," in which she demonstrates how a country's economic health can best be evaluated by looking at how much money is spent on programs for women and early childhood education. Across the board, when one compares one country to another in terms of the regulations and policies they have instituted to benefit women and children, one finds that the better the women are treated, the better the country is doing economically.

Studying this model of caring economics provides a more accurate picture of a nation's wealth than calculating the gross domestic product.[21] Eisler's Center for Partnership Studies has sponsored and reported on numerous studies indicating that not only do corporations that add more women to their boards increase profits, but so do nation-states.[22] Nordic countries like Norway, Sweden, and Denmark, all of which were suffering from postwar poverty and starvation after World War II, made a choice to rebuild along new lines of partnership. Today these thriving market economies have women in more than 40 percent of their legislature, and an equality has been ensured in the society and in the home. With policies like universal health care, paid parental and eldercare leave for both men and women, early childhood education, and generous support for senior citizens, the status of women, and all people, has risen. Surprisingly, in surveys on quality of life, men, as a rule, do not report feeling threatened by this change. Nordic people rate very high on the happiness indices, given that both men and women of these countries are encouraged to feel safe about expressing their own nurturing tendencies without feeling emasculated. Of course, these are not perfect societies, but they do enjoy lower crime and poverty rates and better health overall.

Study after study shows that the more women leaders a company has, the more profitable the company is, but as of this writing only 5 percent of Fortune 500 CEOs are women.[23] Once again, however, leaders don't need to be women, they just need to care about, and display compassion for, their people. The domination model in place today encourages leaders to act like authoritarian fathers, laying down the law and expecting to be obeyed. When companies make the commitment to hire and promote more women, the result is the implementation of policies that allow for more nurturing.[24] Different perspectives on the career arc are needed to allow men and women to stop and start a career to raise a family or care for a loved one as needed. But beyond all policy change suggestions, what is really needed is an overall perspective shift. We as a people need to value caregiving as a positive force, and one that is necessary to human happiness and success.

Summoning the Mother Bear

Earlier we mentioned psychiatrist Jean Shinoda Bolen and her campaign for a United Nations Fifth World Conference on Women. Bolen's vision is for women around the world to summon their "mother bear" energy and unite to correct the Earth's imbalances. She talks about giving women real power at the peace negotiation table, pointing out that women, as a rule, tend to see the goal as finding a resolution, whereas men, as a rule, tend to see their goal as winning the debate. Women are more inclined to give and take and form relationships, she says, compared to men, who are more inclined to have their opinions heard.[25] Since 2002, when she realized that there was no plan to have another UN-sponsored international conference on women—after they had been happening semiregularly every five years or so since 1975—she began to publicize the need to continue holding them. She talked to us about how much has changed since the last UN women's conference in 1995, most notably the rise of the Internet and the interconnectivity of the world, as well as the many goals as yet unmet from the last conference. An international conference with more than 190 countries and thousands of NGOs dedicated to "women's issues" has the potential to launch what Bolen calls the mother's agenda into global politics. "In sufficient numbers, women have a common sense about taking care of people, the Earth . . . and are especially needed to make sustainability and peace possible," says Bolen.

Bolen's plan includes the creation of sisterships (as opposed to fellowships) wherein wealthier women and wealthier nations would create funds for poor women from around the world to attend the conference and contribute their ideas and problems and solutions. Women with

Figure 2.6. Liberty's head was ready in time for visitors to climb inside it at the Paris Universal Exposition in 1878. Reproduction on display at the Liberty Island Museum. Author photo.

the least resources cannot be left behind while women from affluent societies attend conferences around the globe. The women's movement is challenged to avoid the shackles of power that come with the dominator system and is working to address issues of ethnic and class division as well as gender division. Based on what we know from historical precedent of the Indigenous women leaders, it is indeed essential to include the marginalized women in these discussions in order to find sustainable solutions for the planet.

The other group that is essential in making the change to a partnership-oriented society is men. Woman suffragists had no political power and relied on the cooperation of men in power to change their minds and attitudes before women won the vote. In much the same way, activists in the women's movement today are realizing that men must experience their own consciousness-raising in order for society to achieve any lasting changes for gender parity.

An anecdote from history demonstrates how one woman raising the consciousness of one man had the impact of changing the lives of everyone in the United States. The woman's name was Febb Ensminger Burn. She was a college-educated Southern woman and follower of the suffrage cause. Her twenty-four-year-old son, Harry Burn, a newly elected senator from Tennessee, was on record as being anti-suffrage, as were most of his constituents, though he had indicated he was personally favorable to the cause. Harry Burn wrote later that his mother was a good example of the validity for suffrage, given that she was a well-educated woman prohibited from voting, while their illiterate farmhands were allowed to vote just because they were men. On a hot August day in 1920 when Tennessee was deadlocked over ratification of the Nineteenth Amendment, Harry received a letter from his mother wherein, interspersed between scrawling news about an upcoming family wedding and issues on the farm, she urged him to "vote for Suffrage."[26] He decided to listen to the counsel of his mother, changed his vote, and Tennessee ratified the amendment as the thirty-sixth state, creating the majority nationwide. As the result of one woman writing to advise one man on one vote, women in the entire United States were raised to the level of citizen for the first time in the history of the republic.

In our search for the secret life of Lady Liberty, we encountered dozens of stories of contemporary women in power around the world who are making lasting change. In 2003 women on both sides of the fourteen-year civil war in Liberia banded together and locked their men in the negotiating room until they agreed to stop fighting, leading to

Nobel Peace Prizes for some and the election of the first female president in Africa. The 2013 "Senate Sisterhood" in the United States consisted of Democrat and Republican women bonding over pizza dinners and compromising together during the government shutdown to author almost every major bill passed in that session.[27]

The Goal Is Balance

Women in positions of power are changing the world for the better, but gender equality in humanity overall is the goal. Action needs to be tempered by wisdom. Men and women need to learn to use both hearts and minds to achieve the transformative balance of male-femaleness that elevates us to humanness. Both right action and contemplative meditation are required for wholeness.

On the archetypal level, women are different from men, says esoteric historian and symbologist David Ovason. He calls the female archetype "a symbol of perfection" and the only promise we really have of saving the world. Women tend to be less mired in the material world than men, he says, and have more instinctive contact with the spiritual world, which is often labeled as women's intuition. It is this idealism, in part, that led to virtues being portrayed in art as women, a situation that we will discuss later that both empowered and suppressed women through the ages.

Many women need to learn more about the warrior archetype and mastering the physical world, and many men need to learn more about being quiet enough to hear the still, small voice within, which is accessible when one lets one's guard down. Today's modernizing trends, of course, include many stressed-out and overworked women who could also benefit from slowing down and tapping into their vulnerable sides after having performed as a warrior and provider for far too long. And many men are, in fact, embracing and feeling pride in living the life of a caregiver.

The research currently being done on the hormone system oxytocin is disproving the assumption that it is human nature to be selfish and suffer the survival of the fittest. Rather, we are hardwired for social bonding. The deeper yearnings for justice and caring that we all share, in fact, have been the most powerful motivators of cultural advancement through the ages. We urge all Americans to seize the opportunity of political freedom we have in America. Humanity's next step to enlightenment is to create a nation where everyone can feel safe enough to flourish in healthy prosperity. Enlightened laws are needed to balance individual liberty, and enlightened and informed citizens are needed to maintain and uphold these laws. Each one of us must find our assignment and activate it; your seemingly insignificant actions might be the ones that tip the scales and change history. We can start by honoring the nurturing qualities within us all and acknowledging our female ancestors and the female half of the divine creator.

"Where are your women?" One of the best things we can learn from the Native Americans is to ask this question. Continue to ask yourselves this whenever you have a chance to influence any political or corporate structure or board. Don't take the chance of being presented with a ballot of names with which you are unfamiliar. Research the contenders ahead of time, seek out the best women for public office, and then support them. Volunteer to help women get elected—from the PTA, to the corporate board of directors, to the United States Congress and presidency. Mentor young girls to become leaders. Support policies and legislation that implement caring and nurturing in the workplace and allow women to advance in leadership positions. Ask everyone: "Where are your women?"

The Statue of Liberty feels like a mother to many Americans because it is through her that we see ourselves connected to the whole, to the nation as a whole, and to our national soul. We could look to the Statue of Liberty as a steadfast reminder that in order to maintain the kind of enlightened liberty she is designed to stand for, we, her children, must nurture her. We must tend the laws that ensure these liberties and be on constant vigil to keep them safe. We must guard our liberty as we would guard our cherished mother. To value liberty, therefore, is to value caregiving.

3

What the Statue of Liberty
Learned from the Indian Princess

For five months in 1871, Auguste Bartholdi took an extended tourist trek across the United States. This trip was his effort to "Americanize myself a little"[1] and part of his agreement with his mentor on the Statue of Liberty project, Édouard de Laboulaye. These two French men were endeavoring to create a statue that would embody the essence of *American* Liberty, and artist Bartholdi enthusiastically dove into the research part of his assignment. Laboulaye, on the other hand, a professor of American studies in France and author of several volumes of history and commentary on America, never visited the United States in person. Bartholdi documented his travels on the newly constructed cross-continental railroads through extensive notes, watercolors, and sketches, while also perfecting his skill at the new invention of photography. Although he was not successful at drumming up much practical support for his and Laboulaye's expensive project during this first trip to the United States, he did return to France with a more realistic appreciation of the American people and their understanding of liberty—even if that did not include any insight into the mutually exclusive goals of liberty in terms of European settlers versus Native Americans, or Black Americans, or women, for that matter.

During this trip, Bartholdi would have studied the many depictions of Lady Liberty seen on all the coins in circulation and the statuaries in New York, Philadelphia, and Washington, D.C. Among these many examples of the American Liberty goddess adorning everything from the aristocratic-looking insignia, seals, and flags, to the pedestrian items used in everyday kitchens, Bartholdi would surely have seen vestiges of the Indian Princess, an earlier version of an American Lady Liberty popular during the Revolution. Traces of the Indian Princess are not easy to spot in the outer form of the Statue of Liberty, but they are obvious in her sister statue on top of the U.S. Capitol dome, the *Statue of Freedom,* who wears an enormous feathered headdress. Because Laboulaye and Bartholdi were both intent on creating an *American* Lady Liberty, however, even though there are no feathers on the Statue of Liberty, we will now examine this earlier Native American version of Lady Liberty that art historians have termed the Indian Princess. It's important to point out, however, that this endearing nickname is completely disingenuous, because not only is she not Indian, but the concept of a royal princess was completely unknown to the Native Americans of this part of the world.

For purposes of this discussion we are classifying the proliferation of goddesses and female allegory used to symbolize America before the Statue of Liberty under the term "the American Liberty goddess." The Statue of Liberty is decidedly French in design, but the American Liberty goddess has an extensive pedigree of her own through her British and American ancestors. For a few decades following the American Revolution, the newly minted American people identified themselves and their goals with an allegorical female who looked a bit like a mixed race European/Native American. Studying how and why the founding artists changed the costume of the Indian Princess demonstrates how the Native American influences on the founding of this nation were concealed in our mythmaking.

In this chapter we will review why the Roman goddess Libertas was adopted from British insignia by the patriot propagandists, how she transformed under their pens into the Indian Princess, and how the Indian Princess helped lead the Revolution. We will show how the Iroquois influence theory explains why this free-spirited, feathered figure was so admired by the Revolutionary generation, and then why the Indian Removal policies of the following generations explain why she shed her feathers and donned a Roman stola. We'll also look at how the myth of the Indian Princess enjoyed a renewed popularity after the bloody fighting of the Indian Wars had diminished at the end of the 1800s, when most of the surviving Native Americans had been pushed onto reservations and were being perceived as less of a threat. Convinced by this time that the Indians were a dying race, Euro-Americans resurrected stories of Pocahontas and Sacagawea and molded them into the genre of "the good Indian" where they were cast as characters in the growing myth of American exceptionalism.

More English than the English

Before the American Revolution, female allegories of liberty were already popular in England and, to a lesser extent, in France as well, but the mania for Ladies Liberty achieved truly unprecedented heights in the new United States. Greek and Latin were part of the required education for the educated upper class of the English colonies, and it's important to remember that the colonists did not yet think of themselves as Americans, but rather as Europeans living abroad. Many of the Revolutionary generation had gone on the grand tour through Europe when they were younger and had become intimately familiar with the neoclassical school that dominated the arts and philosophy.[2] The educated elite on both sides of the Atlantic read the same political treatises advocating liberty and prided themselves on England's reputation in Europe as the most liberty-loving of countries. Ever since the Magna Carta, but even more so after England's Glorious Revolution and subsequent Bill of Rights in 1689, Englishmen distinguished themselves from other Europeans in their attempts to circumscribe the monarch's power.

By the mid-1700s British artists had begun dressing their own national female allegory, a figure named Britannia, in elements borrowed from the Roman goddess Libertas. Doing so was an expression of their national pride in the Englishman's rights to liberty and harkened back to an ancient time as a symbolic way of declaring those rights eternal.[3] The Englishmen living in the colonies notched up this pride in an Englishman's right to liberty, and as they got feistier about liberty in response to being taxed without a say-so, colonial artists adopted this Libertas-infused Britannia, added feathers, and made her their own.

In Britain, the figure of Britannia derived from Roman images on coins that had been struck by Hadrian during the Roman occupation. For centuries Britannia acted as a symbol of *place,* usually seen depicted sitting on a rock or a globe, near the sea, with a trident or shield by her side. As English artists caught liberty fever in the 1700s, they began replacing that trident with the liberty pole and cap and depicting Britannia as a sisterly guardian of Libertas. The human allegories and symbolism of the Roman gods and virtues were copied by European and colonial artists after the system codified by Italian artist Cesare Ripa in his influential 1593 book, *Iconologia.* Ripa's and other emblem books like his were enormously popular in both Europe and the colonies, where they were used as guides for artists and students of allegory to follow the accepted meanings inherent in the symbols and the connections between them. The libraries of many of the founders included the 1766 edition of *Iconologia,* and even more of them contained George Richardson's 1779 translation, which was the first version published in English.[4]

In Ripa's illustrations, we see Libertas with her most enduring symbols: the pole, or staff, and the cap. In ancient Roman depictions, she was also commonly accompanied by a liberty-loving cat or a fractured jug or disjointed chain, all symbolic of restraints being broken. The founder of the Lady Liberty League, Selena Fox, told us that in Rome, Libertas was also sometimes seen with a torch or with rays of light around her head, though the floppy cap is far more common. The pole and cap are relics of the ceremony performed in the Roman Republic to free slaves. A magistrate would tap the slave on the shoulders with a staff known as the vindicta, and after the slave's head had been ritually shaved, they were given a felt cap known as the pileus. The pileus is also called the Phrygian cap, because the style was popular among the natives of the region of Phrygia (present-day Turkey). You can see what looks like Liberty's floppy cap in artwork depicting characters from Phrygia, such as King Midas, the figure Paris, instigator of the Trojan War, the followers of Mithras, and the legendary warrior women of Greek mythology, the Amazons.[5]

The ceremony of freeing a slave was common enough in a soci-

Figure 3.1. The Roman goddess Libertas on Roman denarii issued in 42 BCE. Gaius Cassius Longinus, the prime mover in the assassination plot against Julius Caesar, issued these Libertas coins to commemorate liberty from the tyranny of Caesar. Classical Numismatic Group, Inc., www.cngcoins.com.

ety where slavery was elemental; indeed, more than 40 percent of the Roman population was enslaved at any given time. Freedmen of Rome composed a significant sector of the society, as these manumission ceremonies endowed a slave not only with personal freedom but with libertas, or political freedom, as well, which meant they had the right to vote. Libertas became the patron goddess of these freed slaves, and the earliest known temple dedicated to her, on Rome's Aventine Hill, dates to 238 BCE. At first a minor deity associated with just the liberation of slaves, Libertas later came to represent the political liberty of the entire Roman Republic. After leading the assassination of Julius Caesar, Brutus and other conspirators had the image of the goddess Libertas struck onto coins to commemorate how they had liberated the republic from tyranny. Commencing with the reign of Augustus, Libertas came to represent the constitutional government.[6]

The Revolutionary Revolution

Before we look at what attracted the colonists to identify themselves with a Roman goddess of freed slaves, we must first pause to examine what made the American Revolution so radical. Our tendency today is to criticize the founders of the United States for not being radical enough with their Revolution. As a movement of and for the elite white male, what seems obvious to the modern eye are the many glaring social injustices they failed to address. With the help of historian Gordon Wood and his many fine books, however, we have been able to appreciate just how truly revolutionary those beginning steps were. The American Revolution upset so many patterns across so many strata of society, but the biggest change it made was in the way ordinary people thought about themselves.

When the definitive challenge to kingship and authority was declared, ordinary people outside of the aristocracy assumed rights and power for the first time. Thomas Paine and Benjamin Franklin were both born of ordinary means and missed out on the classical education afforded many of the other patriots, and it is from these two that we get the strongest appeals for the participation of the common man in the independence movement. Most of the other founders had very little estimation of the general public, which they considered to be rabble, just as their Greco-Roman role models had. They feared that giving too much power to the people would result in the tyranny of the uneducated poor over the rich, which they believed was the reason democracy had failed in ancient Greece. The common man in the American colonies wasn't really interested in these politics; he just wanted the liberty to be left alone to strike out and move to better land whenever he wanted to.

Englishmen in Britain grew amused at how the provincial rustics in the colonies pushed their penchant for liberty to new extremes. Traditional boundaries everywhere—from homelife to the law—were challenged by the colonists, earning them a reputation for being even more English than the English.[7] British visitors reported in disgust at how unruly the children in the colonies were, and how much more authority the women and common people had when compared to aristocratic England.[8] The customs of doffing caps to one's betters, modes of dress to identify class, and the protocols of addressing a gentleman were all being leveled in the colonies. The American Revolution completely revolutionized army life, as impressment, or forced recruitment, and the severe punishments normal in the British Army no longer worked with these precocious colonial soldiers. Reforms in prisons and a reversal of opinion on corporal punishment in the home also followed the

Figure 3.2. Soon after the Stamp Act in 1765, the Indian Princess was merged with Britannia and Libertas to stand for America. The masthead of the *Massachusetts Spy* newspaper, featuring the Indian Princess holding the liberty pole and cap, was engraved by Paul Revere. Library of Congress.

Revolution. Bridges to the civil rights movements for women and Blacks were laid at this time, demonstrated by the Northern states abolishing slavery soon after the war. At the outset of the fighting the British press lampooned the baseness of the Americans by exclaiming they even gave women rifles! The growing acceptance that women had independent minds was so strong in the colonies that it allowed for a woman, Mercy Otis Warren, to be acknowledged as one of the leading advocates for independence, corresponding with the fledgling nation's leaders and writing effective editorials and histories under her own name.

Separation of Church and State

By far, however, the most radical impact of the American Revolution was the one most relevant to the design of the Statue of Liberty—the unprecedented separation of church and state. Today's adherents to the myth that America was "founded as a Christian nation" are dreaming of a time that never existed. Christian nation adherents cherry-pick quotes and point to the founders' regular church attendance or donations made to build new churches to reinterpret the founders' insistence on freedom of religion. They conclude that by freedom of religion the founders actually meant the freedom to choose which *denomination of Christianity* one could follow. The vision of an American past as a Christian nation actually better describes the repressive Puritan era when religious pluralism and diversity were outlawed. The Constitution was expressly aimed at separating the new nation from this old approach. Concerned more with morality and ethics than dogma, the founders were determined not to encode Christian doctrine into federal laws. The U.S. Constitution was the first of its kind to ban the religious test oaths requiring those taking public office to declare their Christian identity.

The founders claimed a "New Order of the Ages," the motto they struck on the U.S. Great Seal. The old order they turned away from was the church's complete control over society and the law, a system that could be called church-state. They noted how the intolerance of church-state control was responsible for centuries of violence, torture, and suppression and decided the time had come to break the link between the ever-arguing factions of Christianity and the military might of the monarchy. Rather than Christian symbolism, the founders chose images from the republic of Rome to identify their experiment. Part of the explanation for why this shift away from church-state occurred in the Americas was the popularity of the theological doctrine here called deism, a belief that allowed for a Creator God, but left the rest of moral decision making up to the rational mind of the individual. Deists were convinced that religious toleration was essential because no one could ever be absolutely sure their dogma was correct.[9]

A Deistic Enlightenment

While the majority of the population continued to follow the original-sin Calvinistic practices of their Puritan ancestors, the elite who crafted the

Constitution had a new, rational approach to religion. Most of the founders who were influenced by deism—Washington, Franklin, Jefferson, and Monroe among them—continued to attend orthodox churches with their families and outwardly conform. Wives and children of the founders tended to be the more devout churchgoers, illustrated by the example that Martha Washington would remain behind after church services for the Communion, while her husband, George, would go home early.

The religious beliefs of Thomas Jefferson and Benjamin Franklin were unorthodox enough that their enemies accused them of being atheists, and yet both contributed financially to several building projects for churches of different denominations, including Jewish synagogues. The founders all perceived the valuable role of the church in providing social order and encouraging public virtue. They also recognized the power of religion to move the people. Franklin's designs for their currency exemplify how they used religious rhetoric and symbolism to sway popular opinion to build a virtuous nation.

The Enlightenment was a time of great curiosity about science and the natural world, and adherents of deism delighted in examining the driving forces in nature. They determined that virtue and reason were the keys to social justice and harmony. The observation of nature was enough to testify to the existence of God, and deists rejected the superstitious rituals of the church and organized religion. Followers tended to rabidly oppose tyranny in any form.[10] The deists' rejection of the church's ceremonial trappings and rituals partially explains why Freemasonry, with its emphasis on ceremonies but also on reason and independence, flourished side by side with the growth of deism. Both Masonry and deism were antagonistic to organized religion, considering it the main obstacle to the independence of the common man,[11] and Masonry provided a welcome outlet for those rational minds who still enjoyed the social bonding that ceremonial conventions could provide.

British Cartoons

All these radical challenges to the religious hierarchy, social class structure, and subjugation by authority percolated in the colonies to create a

Figure 3.3. British cartoons like this one, *The Reconciliation between Britannia and Her Daughter America*, published by Thomas Colley in 1782, exemplify the cultural tendency to represent the English colonists as the Indian Princess. Library of Congress.

growing sense of separateness. Key to the shift in identifying themselves as something other than British was the development of a new allegory to symbolize a distinct populace. The symbol that the founding artists eventually adopted to stand for their opposition to the tyranny of British authority was the Indian Princess. Her cheeky attitude in political cartoons, showing her thumbing her nose at the British ministers and the king, was a rousing and unifying force for the colonial rebellion.

We used to think these early pro-American cartoons were the ingenious work of our colonial artists, but interestingly, these satires turn out to have been originally designed by British artists and later copied by the colonials. Art had been slow to develop in the colonies, in part because they were behind on the latest technological advances in everything, not just in printing, but also because the old Calvinist prohibition against imagery had discouraged art training or patronage of the arts.[12] The Indian Princess as a symbol for rebellion in the colonies was originally created by British editorial cartoonists. The growing appetite for news, satire, and scuttlebutt in England in the 1700s was fueled by advances in mass-printing techniques, supplying a large new audience for editorial political cartoons.

The Indian Princess could best be described as the rebellious teenage daughter of Britannia. Unlike the muscular Indian Queen whom we describe in chapter 6, the Indian Princess is playful and vigorously engaged in the pursuit of liberty. Gone are the South American parrots and alligators, the club and the ax depicted with the Indian Queen on the maps of the earliest explorers. The Indian Princess does not languidly display her nakedness as her earlier counterpart had done, and indeed, by the end of the century, her skimpy topless, tobacco-leaf skirt costume was covered demurely by Roman robes. Feathers are what distinguish the Indian Princess from Britannia or Libertas, for in terms of their facial features, they often look like the same person. The lines between these goddesses really began to blur when the Indian Princess started wearing Liberty's clothes and carrying her implements.

Almost all of the best cartoons showing the Indian Princess in distress were created for the merchant class in England, who were suffering alongside the colonists as a result of unfair taxes and retaliation boycotts. They enjoyed lampooning their own British ministers for restricting trade with the colonies and for making a mess of diplomacy. Trade was symbolized by the Roman god Mercury usually seen together with stacks of the merchandise being exported from the colonies, such as bales of cotton, tobacco, wheat, rice, and furs. The players in the cartoon contentions were portrayed as a family: Britannia and the Indian Princess as mother and daughter, with Liberty urging them both on. The Indian Princess is often depicted as a helpless, dependent child or as a vulnerable maiden being molested by British ministers, while Britannia looks away in shame. One of our favorites is the 1776 anonymous engraving *The Female Combatants* (figure 3.4, p. 62). In this illustration, Britannia and America are at odds, but more commonly the two were posed together as covictims of farcical British politicians.[13] The elegance of Britannia next to the crudeness of the Indian Princess also summarized how the two cultures were

Figure 3.4. An overdressed Britannia says, "I'll force you to obedience you rebellious slut," to the Indian Princess, who represents America in this anonymous 1776 engraving. Notice the feathers worn in the English lady's hair, a fashion trend inspired by Native Americans. The Lewis Walpole Library, Yale University.

perceived: the citizens of the mother country were sophisticated; the colonists were uncultured.

Paul Revere Was Busy before That Midnight Ride

Before the crisis brought on by the Stamp Act of 1765, the colonists would have found it offensive to be identified as Native American allegory. They spent a lot of time and energy trying to appear as cultivated as their cousins across the sea and were proud of being Englishmen. It was not until people started talking about separating from the mother country—disassociating from their identity with Britannia—that the colonists finally embraced the image of the Indian Princess and began using it as their own national identifying symbol. "American" was a word they had previously used only to describe Native Americans. Now the colonists decided to become Americans, too. The earliest known colonial illustration of an Indian representing the colonists is from a 1766 engraving done by Paul Revere for an obelisk structure erected in celebration of the repeal of the Stamp Act (figure 3.5, p. 64). In the final panel King George is seen introducing America, as an Indian, to the goddess of Liberty.

Paul Revere and Benjamin Franklin were among the colonies' best propagandists. Both early on recognized the need to adopt the name "Americans" and to change their allegorical image. They were also the first to borrow Libertas and other neoclassical images to emulate the Roman Republic as a role model for the growing protest movement leaning toward independence. In the hands of the copyist Revere, the Indian Princess merged with Libertas and took on the cause of American liberty. Whereas in Rome the liberty granted by the goddess Libertas was considered something given and received, in the colonies the Indian Princess version of the Liberty Goddess came to stand for the inherent right of all men to be free.

The symbols of Libertas started showing up in the colonies in the decade leading up to the Revolutionary War. In those crucial years before any fighting began, when the Revolution was taking place in the realm of the imagination, the Native American form of Lady Liberty

Figure 3.5. Paul Revere's design for an enormous obelisk made out of oiled paper and filled with three hundred lanterns and erected in celebration of the repeal of the Stamp Act in 1766. This is the earliest known representation, by an American artist, depicting the English colonists as an allegorical Native American. In the detail magnified from panel one, the Indian Princess is dejected as the goddess of Liberty hovers nearby trying to stop British ministers, one in the form of a flying devil carrying the Stamp Act. In the final panel, King George is introducing America as an Indian to the Liberty goddess. Library of Congress.

took center stage in the war of political cartoons. After the colonial artists put their hands to it, the Indian Princess was soon seen everywhere, supported by the Liberty goddess and surrounded by many other supplemental goddesses representing wisdom, abundance, and victory. Paul Revere designed the masthead for the *Massachusetts Spy* as a figure that looks like Britannia seated on a globe holding Liberty's pole and cap, except that she's wearing a tobacco-leaf skirt (figure 3.2, p. 57). Revere surrounded his portraits of the leaders of the Massachusetts rebellion, John Hancock and Samuel Adams, with Liberty, her pole and cap, and Minerva with her shield. Another masthead design by

Revere for the *Royal American Magazine* features the Indian Princess offering the peace pipe to the Genius of Knowledge (figure 4.1, p. 88). The *Royal American Magazine* also printed numerous illustrations that Revere copied exactly from British prints, such as *Britannia in Distress,* which he changed to *America in Distress* just by adding a few feathers and replacing the shield with a bow.

Once the nation was born, the Indian Princess/Liberty really exploded in popularity. Thomas Paine wrote about the goddess of Liberty in his 1775 poem "The Liberty Tree" in which he describes her coming down from the sky to plant the tree of liberty—a Native American concept. The brand-new U.S. government used a refined version of the Indian Princess as the symbol for themselves on all but one of the earliest congressional medals. She appears in the Daniel Morgan medal of 1790 (figure 3.6, p. 66) wherein the United States is depicted as an elegant Native American woman crowning one of the tactical heroes of the Revolutionary War with laurels. In the 1791 Augustin Dupré diplomatic medal she sits among bales of merchandise and a cornucopia, welcoming Mercury, the god of commerce, to her shores (figure 3.7, p. 67).

Curious Crosscurrents

In order to talk about the influence of the Native American philosophy on the founders, we must start further back in time to just after contact between the two cultures. The American Revolution may be described as a product of the European Enlightenment, the philosophical movement in Europe beginning in the mid-1600s, but without the discovery of the "noble savages" in the late 1500s in the first place, the Enlightenment itself might never have been sparked. The observation that men really could live in a "natural state" opened the minds of the European philosophers to imagine a better life and allowed them to consider the possibility of change.

It is a myth that the *Mayflower* Pilgrims came to the Americas in search of religious freedom. They had already found a haven of religious freedom in Holland, but as foreign immigrants, they were having a hard

Figure 3.6. The earliest congressional medals used the Indian Princess to represent the new United States, as in this medal awarded to Daniel Morgan in 1790 for his exemplary service during the Revolutionary War. Yale University Art Gallery.

time finding work there. Nor, unlike future settlers in North America, were the Pilgrims interested in missionary work to convert the Natives to Christianity. The Mayflower Compact is "all about obedience to the king, obedience to the rulers, there is no concept of personal freedom," said anthropologist Jack Weatherford. "That's the American Indian concept."

In the precontact European mind, the concept of freedom was related exclusively to the concepts of nation and aristocracy. If one nation overtook another, there was a loss of freedom. The people of Europe did not even consider the concept of *individual* or *personal* liberty or freedom. "Personal liberty is when an individual person gets to

Figure 3.7. Engraved in Paris by Augustin Dupré under the direction of Thomas Jefferson, this 1792 U.S. diplomatic medal shows America as the Indian Princess holding a cornucopia and gesturing to her abundance of merchandise, welcoming Mercury, the god of commerce.

decide things for themselves, how to lead a life, what they want to do, the pursuit of happiness," said Weatherford. "These are ideas that really came from the American Indians, and were very shocking to the people who arrived here from Europe."

Right from first contact, the curious modes of deportment practiced by the Native Americans enchanted the Europeans, as they first began learning of the healthful hunter-gatherer life of the Native Americans. In the 1500s and 1600s, many tall and vigorous Indians were brought to Europe and traveled around, on display, and seeing these healthy and athletic specimens in person was stunning for the Europeans. Most Europeans were stunted and sickly and living in comparatively filthy and oppressive conditions. "They had never encountered this before," said Akwesasne Mohawk Douglas George-Kanentiio, "seeing Native people existing without the encumbrance of a centralized state, or a set of privileged class royalty, or not qualified by the teachings of the institutionalized religion. . . . They were not only shocked, they were captivated."

The word "savage" derives from the old French word *sauvage* and literally means "of the woods." When it first came into popular usage to describe the Indigenous people of the Americas, it was this woodland connotation that was implied, not the bloodthirsty one later attached to the word.[14] The term "noble savage" derived from the comparison of the freedom of the Native Americans to the freedom of the nobility in Europe. Both hunted in beautiful game preserves, traveled seasonally, and were not tied to the drudgery of subsistence farming.

The Indian Princess Dances a Ballet

It's true that some travel accounts, especially those backed by the Catholic Church, fabricated and exaggerated claims of cannibalism (a definition that gave them sanction to capture the Natives as slaves), but many other explorers emphasized the nobleness of the *sauvage*. They were described as dwelling in an Edenic or utopian state, with no shame of nakedness, no poverty, and a trusting innocence. Philosophers and political satirists started pointing to the differences between liberty as experienced by the noble savage and the squalid conditions of most Europeans cities, and these comparisons began to subtly change the way Europeans thought about their own place in the world.

Court masques and ballets in England and France from the early 1600s, including Shakespeare's *The Tempest* of 1611, introduced the noble savage to the common people. There was almost no attempt at accuracy in these productions, the main inspiration seeming to be their skimpy costumes of bright feathers worn by dancers cavorting through exotic locations,[15] but these dramas and artworks did spread the news about this different way of life.

This discovery of a living community of self-governing men in an uncorrupted natural environment was the spark needed to set the Age of Enlightenment in motion. Philosophers like Locke, Rousseau, and Voltaire started writing about "man in his natural state," referring to the Native Americans and their realization of individual liberty. As Locke put it: "In the Beginning all the World was *America*." Rousseau said, "The state reached by most of the savage nations known to us . . . [is] the state least subject to revolutions, the best state for man."[16] Europeans feared the Native Americans, but grew to admire them as well, and it was learning about their existence that led the great European philosophers to finally challenge the age-old hierarchical control of the church and state, a challenge that eventually culminated in the American Revolution.

How to Prove Influence

Once the Enlightenment ideas did spark, they disseminated around the world, but nowhere else did they take root into real radical social change except among the English colonists living in the land of the Iroquois. Gordon Wood observed that "Classical Republican values existed everywhere among educated people in the English-speaking world, but nowhere did they have deeper resonance than in the North American colonies."[17] In none of the other colonies settled by the British, Dutch, Spanish, or French did representational democracy spring up. It materialized only in the northeast of America, because it first required the germination from the seeds planted there by the Iroquois. Europe only "imagined the Enlightenment," said historian Henry Steel Commager, but America "realized it."[18]

It's difficult to pinpoint the origin of a philosophical idea, and proponents of the influence theory are the first to say there were many other influences on the Revolutionary generation in addition to the Native Americans. These influences include individuals more commonly named in the Euro-American history books such as the writings by Locke, Montesquieu, and Rousseau. The founders also took great inspiration from Greek tales of overcoming insurmountable odds and learned from them about community and honor. They carefully studied the republican ideal of Rome, even though they knew that both the Greek and Roman systems were designed for the benefit of just a small elite class in relatively small geographic areas. They puzzled over how to put these limited systems and Enlightenment theories into practice across a large landmass with competing sovereign states. Gradually it dawned on them that this very conundrum had already been solved by their Native neighbors. The Iroquois had the most direct influence on the founders, and indeed on the framers of the Constitution, but similar federated unions of Native Americans were observed up and down the East Coast, from the Huron, to the Cherokee, the Wampanoag, and the Abenaki.[19] Living among the Natives since the 1500s, the colonists had absorbed this new concept of individual liberty and then echoed it back to Europe, where it in turn influenced the ideas of the Enlightenment.

For a short while in the United States, the brightest minds of the Revolutionary generation identified themselves as the symbolic Indian Princess. For an even shorter while they were not ashamed to emulate the real Native Americans and acknowledge how much they owed them. Remember, they dressed as Indians when they dumped tea into the Boston Harbor! From our modern perspective, it's hard to appreciate the powerful influence the Indians had over the colonists during this era. For example, in the generations before the Revolution, the Indians completely controlled the balance of power between the French, in present-day Canada, and the British along the East Coast, and they also controlled all the key routes of commerce and negotiation between them.

Ben Franklin was the most forthcoming of the founders in giving credit to the Native Americans for many of his ideas about founding a new nation. When taken as a whole, however, the number of times all the founders wrote about how they considered the Native Americans their role models is astounding. This wealth of data, called the influence theory, has been collated by a handful of academics who all discovered it independently from one another after being challenged to do so by Native American friends. In a nutshell this theory says that our founding fathers deliberately and consciously followed some of the patterns established by the League of the Iroquois when designing the new U.S. government.

Thank You Very, Very Much

If the noble savages can govern themselves peacefully and maintain union with competing sovereign nations over a wide expanse of land, our founders asked, then why can't a community of educated Englishmen? Here are some of the points of practice noted by the founders as practiced by the Iroquois.

- The people had the right to impeach their leaders.
- They united several sovereign nations to act as a unit.
- They added new territories as equal members instead of as colonized dependents.
- They created a set of electors who voted for the leader.
- They gave respect to one speaker at a time in political meetings (something the British still don't do).
- They formed caucuses or special councils for informal decisions.
- They used the title of the political office to refer to a particular leader rather than their own name.
- They prohibited military leaders from becoming political leaders, a critical change from European tradition.[20]

"Democracy was a gift by the aboriginal people, specifically by the Iroquois, to the world," Kanentiio told us. Like many Native Americans, he knew this to be true because his Mohawk ancestors had passed down this knowledge to him through their oral teachings. Bruce Johansen's *Debating Democracy* outlines the evolution of the influence theory in the world of academia and tells how he and his colleagues Don Grinde and Sally Roesch Wagner each stumbled upon these Native American oral teachings and then set about to locate the historical documentation to prove it. Growing numbers of Native Americans in the academic community, such as Roy Fadden, John Kahionhes Fadden, Vine Deloria Jr.,

Oren Lyons, and John Mohawk added their own work to the debate.

The Native oral teachings on the influence theory are quite clear. Kanentiio summarized it well in his book *Iroquois Culture and Commentary.*

> It is apparent to us that the concepts of a true democracy did not come from Europe, since at no time in its history prior to the twentieth century did any nation on that continent grant universal suffrage to its citizens. True, political theorists such as John Locke and Karl Marx were advocates of popular representation, but a truly functioning democratic government free from class, ethnic, gender, or age restrictions simply did not exist. The widely praised Greeks held two thirds of their people in a state of slavery and denied women the right to participate in the governmental process. Romans were simply barbarians with a higher command of technology. The Roman Senate was a debating club for the male elite that sustained its legislative excesses by legions of serfs. Everywhere in Europe or Asia people were oppressed, exploited, and denied what we have come to regard as our basic human rights. It's a wonder that part of the world did not sink into the sea, so great was the human suffering. When the doors of America were opened to immigration, millions elected to venture into the unknown in hopes of a better life. The uncertainties before them had to be better than the despair they were leaving behind. In our Iroquois territory, they found the freedom they longed for. The Iroquois were one of the very few nations on Earth to abide by a constitution that protects free speech, religious tolerance, the right of popular assembly, and the right of its citizens not only to participate in government but also to dissent from its policies.[21]

The influence of the Iroquois on the U.S. Constitution can be traced back to 1754 when Benjamin Franklin outlined the Albany Plan, which was clearly modeled on what he had learned from observing Native American governing techniques, specifically the Iroquois Great Law of Peace. Taking the advice of his Native friends, Franklin urged his fellow colonists at that time to unify in order to better defend themselves against attacks during the French and Indian War and establish harmonious relations with the Indians. Though it was not ratified, the Albany Plan was followed closely as inspiration for the later Articles of Confederation in 1776, the document known today as our first constitution.[22]

The most convincing evidence of the influence theory is to see these opinions in the words of the founders themselves as collected from their writings by the dozens by scholars like Bruce Johansen and Donald Grinde. John Adams wrote in his *Defence of the Constitutions* in 1787 that the U.S. Constitution was the Americans' attempt to "set up a government of . . . modern Indians."[23] Thomas Paine wrote, "To understand what the state of society ought to be, it is necessary to have some idea of the natural state of man, such as it is at this day among the Indians of North America. . . . [Poverty was a creation] of what is called civilized life. It exists not in the natural state. . . . The life of an Indian is a continual holiday compared to the poor of Europe."[24] The Second Continental Congress invited twenty-one Iroquois sachems to observe the debates over independence in May and June of 1776. The Indians camped out in the room above Congress on the second floor, and Secretary of the Congress Charles Thomson, himself an adopted member of the Delaware Indians and whose Indian name translated to "Man Who Tells the Truth," recorded their visit in detail in the official minutes for the Congress. At the end of this observation period, they gave John Hancock, the president of the Congress, an Indian name, Karanduan, or the Great Tree,[25] likening him to their own Great Law of Peace, the central hub around which all their laws radiated.

One of the measures used to push the colonists to action was the clever use of Native American imagery and metaphor, such as Paine's "Liberty Tree" poem or Franklin's Join or Die Indian symbols. Through their efforts, the common man in the colonies was convinced to join the Revolution, even though in the end what the common man gained from the fight was far less immediate than what was gained by the propertied class.

The Great Law of Peace and
the Council of the Clan Mothers

The Iroquois tell of a peacemaker prophet who walked the lands many years ago trying to convince the warring nations to give up their blood feuds and bury the hatchet under the Tree of Peace. Deganawidah is said to have spoken through Aionwatha, and with the help of the first Clan Mother, Jikonsahseh, who convinced her people to listen to the prophetic words, they established the Great Law of Peace. The oral traditions recount that this happened on a date in late summer on which an eclipse occurred, and Seneca Barbara Alice Mann collaborated with astronomer Jerry Fields at the University of Toledo to pinpoint the very year. Combining astronomical data with oral traditions, Mann and Fields have confirmed that the Iroquois Great Law of Peace was enacted in 1142 CE. This means that a representational form of government was keeping the peace over a wide expanse of the Americas for hundreds of years before Columbus was even born.

Notice in figure 3.8 that the role of the Clan Mothers is compared to that of the Supreme Court in the U.S. establishment. That's because the Clan Mothers made all the most important and final decisions in their society. The reason the Great Law of Peace worked so well and so long for the League of the Iroquois but the U.S. Constitution has worked only partially well for the Euro-Americans and only for some two hundred years, is because the Euro-Americans left out the women, the family, and the concept of living in relationship with the Earth. The Iroquois system had a second tier under their confederation, which was ignored or not perceived as important to the framers of the Constitution. That second tier was the clan system of families, and the clan system was ruled by the women. Attention to spirituality and relationship were left out of government decision making when the women of the American Revolution were not invited to inherit the powerful role that the Iroquois reserved for their Clan Mothers. Perhaps the men of the Revolutionary generation believed they could handle only one revolution at a time.

The elevated status of women among the Iroquois was not unknown to the Revolutionary generation, however. Barbara Alice Mann points

U.S. Constitution

Grand Council Under the Iroquois Great Law of Peace

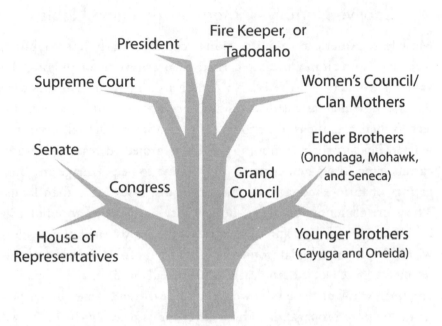

Figure 3.8. Illustration of the Iroquois influence theory and how closely the self-governing structure of the United States mirrors that established by the League of the Iroquois more than five hundred years earlier. Chart rendered by Amy Ford based on the concept in "The Great Law" at Injunuity.org.

to the earliest Jesuit reports on contact with the Iroquois in the early 1700s, where they observed the women's power: "Nothing is more real than the women's superiority. It is they who really maintain the tribe, the nobility of blood, the genealogical tree, the order of generations and conservation of the families. In them resides all the real authority. . . . They are the soul of the councils, the arbiters of peace and war; they hold the taxes and the public treasure; it is to them that the slaves [i.e., captives]* are entrusted; they arrange the marriages; the children are

---

*"Slaves" is a misnomer resulting from the Jesuits' misinterpretation of captives. In Native American tradition captives were not turned into slaves, but rather were usually adopted into the clans as family.

under their authority; and the order of succession is founded on their blood."[26]

Captive Narratives, More Savage than Noble

Most Euro-American colonists didn't read these early Jesuit reports, of course, and simply projected their own criterion for judging the value of women onto the Native Americans. They described Native American women as the drudges and servants of their men and subject to their brutal passions, completely blind to the actual power the women held in their communities. Their projected fears were soon extrapolated into a new form of propaganda to help assuage any misgivings of Euro-American colonists over dispossessing Indian lands. The genre of fiction known as the captivity narrative grew popular in both Europe and the colonies starting in the 1600s, titillating readers with the tales of colonial women being carried off by Natives and suffering the "fate worse than death." Purportedly written as first-person accounts, many of these tales were actually written by men under pen names as pure propaganda. These adventure stories, with their lewd undertones, remained in demand throughout the conquering of the frontier, contributing to the acceptance of the Manifest Destiny way of thinking.

Yet, despite the number of Hollywood westerns that have relied on it as a plotline, rape was entirely unheard of among the Native Americans.[27] They esteemed their women too much to consider such a crime. The truth is that most European women captured by Native Americans grew to respect, if not appreciate, their life among the Natives. When given the chance to return to the European settlements, most refused, saying they preferred to stay where they had discovered more freedom and respect, not to mention cleanliness and health, than they had ever known among "civilization."[28] There was such a steady flow of settlers running away to join the Indians in the early days of colonization that guards were posted to prevent runaways. By comparison, the number of Native Americans "turning European" by choice was almost nonexistent.

"Good Indians" Meet the Indian Princess

No examination of the Indian Princess would be complete without Pocahontas, the name that probably comes to mind when most Americans hear the words "Indian Princess." Like Squanto, Massasoit, and Tammany, Pocahontas was a real live Indian, whose myth recast her in the role of the good Indian. "Good Indian" stories were used to embroider the romance about the superior European culture inevitably conquering the continent. By the end of this version of the story, all bad Indians were dead, and all good Indians were converted to Christianity and had become civilized.

Good Indians either helped the Europeans, married white, or accepted Christianity. In what she deems the "Pocahontas Perplex," Rayna Green says this choice developed two accepted roles for Indian women in our mythology: the virgin-saint or the whore-demon. The eroticized yet pure Indian Princess who saves the Europeans, converts, and defies her heritage, remains pure and removed from reality, peering out at us evocatively from cigar-box labels and bottles of cure-all medicine elixirs. Green compares this Indian Princess to the obscene campfire songs of the cowboys, about their lusty squaws who do whatever the men want for money, showing that actual sexuality converted real Indian women into whores. In fact, many believe the word "squaw" derives from the slur meaning "cunt," so be mindful when you use it.[29]

As it turns out, almost everything we remember about Pocahontas's story is wrong. Considering that most of what we know about Pocahontas comes from elementary school Thanksgiving Day pageants and construction paper cutouts, that's not surprising. Starting with that story John Smith told about her saving his life by laying her head upon his so her father the chief wouldn't bash his brains out—probably not true. First of all, Smith told versions of that same story happening in other foreign countries he visited on his extensive explorations. Second, he didn't tell this story until after Pocahontas toured England and became famous, and beneficial for him to be allied with. And third, his story very nearly parallels a popular Scottish ballad with which he was almost certainly familiar.[30] Whether or not John Smith was telling the

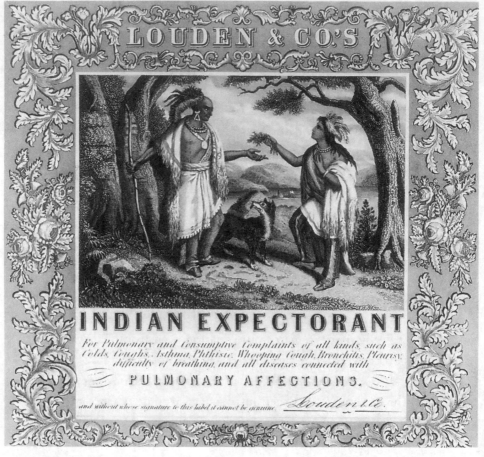

Figure 3.9. The Indian Princess disappeared as the emblem of the United States soon after the Revolutionary War, but she remained a presence in advertising, especially on labels of patent medicines and tonics like this one, circa 1848. Library of Congress.

truth, the image of the young Indian maiden willing to sacrifice her life to save the brave pioneer is embedded in our national mythology. The Pocahontas myth not only established the model for U.S.-Indian relations, it also established the acceptable role that Native American women could play in those relations.

"In a more intimate sense than any peace treaty could accomplish," said John Higham of Pocahontas in his essay "The Indian Princess," "she had given [the European newcomers] an indigenous heritage. She was, in effect, the primal American woman, uniting the land and its conquerors through the mediation of her body and spirit."[31] Many of the Virginia elite today are proud to claim Pocahontas as a direct ancestor through the lineage of the son she had with an English pioneer. The Pocahontas myth allowed us to believe this land was a gift from the Indians to the Europeans. In the "good Indian" version of the Pocahontas myth, the encounter with John Smith would have happened when she was around twelve years old. We are taught that later she grew up, married a Jamestown settlement tobacco planter named John Rolfe, traveled to England to meet the king and queen, and then caught smallpox and died. She is buried in England.

Soon after she passed away, the truce known as the Peace of Pocahontas, which the Virginia colonists had enjoyed for the last five years, dissolved. Far more lasting than the actual Peace of Pocahontas was the false peace of mind her myth gave to the Euro-Americans: that good Indians would see the correctness of the ascendancy of the European culture and gracefully remove themselves so the Europeans could move in and improve the area with *their* culture.

Historian Paula Gunn Allen masterfully extracted a biography about Pocahontas from the Native point of view as preserved in oral traditions as well as traditional documentation. She revealed a complex woman behind the mask, a woman known among her people as Matoaka. Matoaka was sent by her people, the Powhatan, to the Jamestown settlers to play many roles, including diplomat, medicine woman, and spy. Gunn Allen concludes that "young Matoaka, nicknamed Pocahontas, must have been a shamanic prodigy," based on her medicine name Amonute, which identified her as Beloved Woman, or shaman of high degree.[32] She certainly didn't join the Europeans or convert to Christianity of her own free will.

Often left out of the elementary school version of her story is how she was kidnapped by the English, who hoped to hold her for ransom and leverage her in their conflict with the Powhatan. It appears likely that she was probably already married to an Indian at the time of her abduction and may have already had a son. There are Native Powhatan today who trace their lineage to her. After being held captive for many

Figure 3.10. *The Baptism of Pocahontas,* an 1839 oil painting by John Chapman that hangs in the U.S. Capitol, shows the quintessential Indian Princess as the good Indian, converting to Christianity and marrying a Euro-American, reinforcing the myth that European culture was superior and destined to overtake the Native Americans. Architect of the Capitol.

months and forced to adopt English ways, Pocahontas was baptized as a Christian, took the name Rebecca, and entered into the first interracial marriage in the country. This union established the short-lived Peace of Pocahontas, which was the strategic goal of kidnapping her in the first place.

The Indian Princess myth of Sacagawea served the same purpose. Both Sacagawea's myth and that of Pocahontas were popularized in that rose-colored-glasses time of American history after the Civil War and around the nation's centennial. Many of our most treasured patriotic chestnuts were created in this era by enthusiastic writers riding the wave of renewed interest in the Revolutionary generation. This is the time we first hear about George Washington and the cherry tree and Betsy Ross giving flag-designing instructions to a committee in her living room.

It was not until the late 1800s that the story of Sacagawea was extracted from the journals of the Lewis and Clark expedition where it had been overlooked for almost a hundred years. It was rediscovered and publicized by, among others, activists in the woman suffrage movement who were looking for role models of strong, capable women. For the role of a strong woman operating competently in traditionally male roles while retaining her maternal strength, they found a perfect match in Sacagawea. They took a misstep when they labeled her a princess, however, and her roles as guide and interpreter were probably played up, but in terms of diplomacy, her most important role on that expedition was simply that of being a woman. As we reviewed in chapter 2, it was expected that a traveling party with peaceful intentions would include women. Sacagawea's presence would reassure any suspicious Indian who might have challenged, "Where are your women?"

The myths of Sacagawea and Pocahontas were disseminated at the end of the 1800s, not coincidentally, as the Indian Wars were coming to a close. Each time these stories were retold, they enforced the idea that perceptive Indians were the ones who gave their blessing to the "preferred" culture conquering the West. By celebrating her conversion, marriage, and seemingly complete acceptance of the European newcomers, "Pocahontas has symbolically conferred her pedigree upon them," said Higham.[33] Good Indians who helped the Euro-Americans, so the stories went, were also helping their own people rise up—even if they didn't know it yet.

The Indian Princess Worked for the American Revolution, but Afterward, Not So Much

The "good Indian" myths helped Euro-Americans feel legitimized about overpowering the Indians. Rather than hearing about planned exterminations, or smallpox-infected blankets, most Euro-Americans chose to believe the complex myth they told themselves about what they were doing and why. During the course of U.S. history on this continent, the relationship between the Natives and the Euro-Americans has run on a parallel track with these myths, and learning the history of the Indian

Princess—why she was at one time so appealing and then turned into a symbol of derision later on—can help us distinguish between the two.

The Indian Princess was adopted by the founders because she stood for the radicalism of the Revolution. It was radical to separate themselves from centuries of monarchical church rule and attempt to copy the Indians in a system of self-rule. By the time of the Constitutional Convention, it was so commonly understood that the new U.S. system of government was based in part on the Indian manner of governance that everyone referred to it in shorthand. In the early years of rebuffing the British, the new Americans experimented and playacted at being more like the Indians. They started societies and associations of Tammany and of the Red Men, and Indian lodges within Freemasonry, none of which would have permitted a real Indian to join. They loved the symbolism, but the real Indians and the unresolved questions about how to expand into their territory—while remaining true to their ideals of the inherent liberty of mankind—were a constant bother.

Even as the colonists and new Americans adopted Indian ways of dress, military tactics, and governmental policies, they continued to be uncomfortable with the notion of appearing Indian. Their preference to identify themselves with Greek and Roman goddesses demonstrates that many of them preferred to pretend to be what they were not: sophisticated in the eyes of the world. It didn't take long before the symbolism of the Indian Princess disappeared into America's neoclassical age, which started a few years before the Revolution and lasted only a few years after the war was over. The imagery and architecture the founding artists left behind are reminders of their utopian visions of social harmony based on virtuous and enlightened leaders and the republican values of Roman political philosophers and statesmen. The Indian Princess would live on only in the advertisements for tobacco products and in hints of feathers in the hairdos of Ladies Liberty on American currency.

As Auguste Bartholdi traveled across the plains on his 1871 exploratory tour of the United States, he was awestruck at the enormity of the contrasting Rocky Mountains. He described them in letters home to his mother as something out of the "fairy tales," calling them "red

Figure 3.11. This rendering of a cigar-store Indian Princess from circa 1935 includes the word "Liberty" on her headdress. Index of American Design, National Gallery of Art.

masses of rock extravagantly shaped, burnt terrains, grey grass, . . . dried up torrents." After spending three days crossing the plains, with their "immensity which is like the sea," interrupted only by occasional flocks of antelopes or towns of prairie dogs, and a "very few" human towns, he added, "There are sights of extraordinary savageness," he continued. "Only the savages are missing."[34]

Bartholdi's disparaging use of the term "savages" is in keeping with the contemporary Euro-American mind-set about Native Americans, when "bloodthirsty" and "backward" had become the main adjectives touted to justify the forced removal of these noble people. Bartholdi's trip crossing the continent was only eighty-some years after the original colonies on the East Coast declared themselves a new nation and then immediately began expanding westward despite all their promises not to. The ink was not yet dry on the Constitution when the founders were faced with their own hypocrisy of proclaiming liberty for all, yet unable to hold back the tide of settlers breaking every treaty they entered into with the Native Americans. Already by 1871, the wide expanse from the Mississippi to the Pacific had been so decimated by the Indian Wars, and the forced removal to reservations, that Bartholdi crossed the entire country and noted only the absence of people.

Édouard de Laboulaye similarly wrote about the American Indians in terms that displayed his ignorance of their cultural ingenuity. For law-and-order Laboulaye, the written record seemed essential to qualify as civilized, and without it he claimed the Indians "had no past," just "vague memories preserved by their old men." This coupled with his observation that they had "no distinction of property ownership and, in consequence, no State," prevented them in his estimation from advancing beyond "savagery."[35]

It's tough not to judge the opinions of the past by the standards of the present. Laboulaye's blindness to the sophisticated social structure and oral history preserved in prodigious memories is like unto the founders' blindness at recognizing the Native American appreciation of women's worth. Being so focused on establishing a republic unlike anything tried before, and worrying constantly about retaliation from England, the founders were probably too preoccupied to even consider phasing in the role of the Clan Mothers to their government. If they considered it at all, they must have rejected it as too radical a change to upend their culture's long suppression of women. We cannot know why they rejected the Clan Mothers' role when they copied so much else of value, but by so doing, they effectively declared that life, liberty, and the pursuit of happiness were unalienable rights for men only.

We *can* guess, however, that in a world where the founders had been able to introduce women to an equal base of power in their new government, the image of the Indian Princess might have survived as a symbol for America. Perhaps the image would have evolved to look more like a real Native American woman than a European princess imitating an Indian, but any kind of Native-looking allegorical woman standing as the symbol for the United States would certainly have driven the social and moral choices of the United States in different directions. It is clear that the balance built into the Iroquois system for long-term peace was the voice of the Clan Mothers. By studying the family tree of the Statue of Liberty, and becoming acquainted with the Indian Princess, we can recognize the essential ingredient for balance missing from the U.S. government, still, to this day is the voice of our own Clan Mothers.

4

Goddesses Were Everywhere

W hen we began our examination of the Statue of Liberty and the many Ladies Liberty among her ancestry, we wondered early on about the contradiction between depicting liberty as a woman while denying liberty to real women. The Revolutionary generation went mad with virtuous female imagery picturing the ideals of their new republic at every opportunity, and we conjectured that perhaps this abundance of goddesses indicated their psychological need or a race memory inherited from our ancestors of a more partnership-oriented world. The years leading up to the Revolution had been full of arguments from both sides that described the conflict in terms of a parent-child relationship. The king was the father, and Great Britain was the mother country, with the colonies as their children.[1] We wondered if the post-Revolution severance from their mother country was compensated for subconsciously by the founding artists in their urge to design and embed hundreds of matronly Ladies Liberty in their artwork.

This chapter is a collection of some of the peculiar explanations we turned up when trying to answer these unanswerable contradictions. We discovered that folk art explains much of the explosion of popularity of the American Liberty goddess, especially after the eagle and Uncle Sam were added to Liberty as a masculine counterbalance. We also discovered why the truly American-made Liberty goddess named Columbia eventually had to concede her place in national affection to Bartholdi's French-made Statue of Liberty. We confirmed our belief that whether or not the founders were aware of it, the images of female power they surrounded themselves with were essential for building national unity.

Just as the Indian Princess was not intended to resemble a real Indian woman, neither were the many European-looking Liberty goddesses meant to be any statement on the reality of Euro-American women. The long-standing artistic tradition of allegorizing virtues as women is ultimately explained by Latin grammar, which assigns feminine gender to these nouns. In addition to Liberty, the following virtues are others that have traditionally been depicted in female form: faith, hope, charity, prudence, justice, fortitude, and temperance. Romanticizing virtuous ideals as feminine also worked to enforce the codes of conduct for the perceived ideal woman, who was encouraged to faithfully uphold moral principles for the benefit of her sons and husband. The proliferation of Ladies Liberty in the artwork of the new republic is partially explained by the avowal of the Republican Mother concept, the role assigned to proper ladies in the new republic that we discuss in chapter 12. In addition, the American Liberty goddess was popularly depicted as a mother figure urging the public to unite as a family to ensure the future of the Union.

The personal writings of the Revolutionary generation are full of acknowledgments for what they learned from the Native American system of self-government. But when the histories of their era were written, the influence of the Roman model was amplified, and the influence of the Iroquois virtually disappeared. Soon after independence was won, the Indian Princess, who had worked so well to inspire the Revolution, no longer felt right as the symbol for the new United States.[2] She remained in folk traditions, showing up in an increasingly subservient role, but by the first decade of the 1800s, the Indian Princess had been almost entirely cloaked in a new set of Roman robes.

The Vanishing Indian Princess

Symbols and inspirations from Indians are one thing; real Indians and their human needs and wants are another. Fear of Indian retaliation

Figure 4.1. Masthead design by Paul Revere for the *Royal American Magazine* in 1774 features the Indian Princess, symbolizing America, offering the peace pipe to the Genius of Knowledge. Beinecke Rare Book and Manuscript Library, Yale University.

is one compelling reason the Indian Princess symbol faded from use as the official image of the United States. During the Revolutionary War, the Iroquois sided with the British, believing that Indian territories would be protected longer by the promises coming from the foreign crown than those of the local colonists. When the Indians allied with the British and laid waste to the frontier, the stereotype of the "noble" savage was effectively eliminated. Many colonists, especially those squatting on Indian treaty lands, lived in constant fear of reprisal.

Often forgotten in the odes to the mostly honorable George Washington are his orders for a guerilla campaign against the Iroquois in western Pennsylvania during the Revolutionary War to burn them out of their villages, women and children included. Indian reprisal attacks on the patriots, coupled with the daily fears of having to live literally surrounded by people with whom they had broken treaties and from whom they had confiscated land, made the new Americans even less likely to want to identify themselves, on their official insignia, as an Indian Princess.[3]

By the end of the War of 1812, the new motif of the "Vanishing Indian" had fully integrated into national consciousness.[4] Whether or not you advocated assimilation like Jefferson or removal like Jackson, everyone agreed that the Native Americans, their language, and their culture, were soon to be extinct, and the Euro-American civilization would expand across the continent. It was seen as "inevitable because of the superiority of white, Euro-American culture," said art historian Vivien Green Fryd, "as well as the superiority of the religion of Christianity."

We have to remember that one of the main reasons the American Revolution was fought was because land speculators wanted the Indian land on the other side of the Allegheny Mountains, which Great Britain had protected for the Indians against the settlers since the French and Indian War.[5] The framers of the Constitution immediately found themselves challenged with the paradox between their soaring sense of virtue and liberty and how to apply that to their Indian policies, which were in direct conflict with the unstoppable flow of white settlers. George Washington and Henry Knox distinguished themselves after the war in their struggle to keep settlers from disobeying their Indian policies and in trying to retain the ideals of the Enlightenment and Revolution.

After the Revolutionary War, the exploding population of the Euro-Americans by birthrate and immigration forced the founders to make compromises that they had not intended. The "social forces unleashed by the Revolution transformed the society and culture in ways no one in 1776 could have predicted," said historian Gordon Wood.[6] Larger state legislatures open to a wider class of people meant that merchants and farmers were now politicians, too. The specific needs of individual localities were soon at odds with the concepts of unity and public virtue. The Constitution itself was created in part as a response to local uprisings of democratic urges. Many of the aging Revolutionary generation despaired at the havoc that "we the people" waged on their carefully envisioned ideals for a virtuous society of rationalism.

Gradually, however, with the help of the Vanishing Indian notion, public opinion about official Indian policy swayed to the point that during the Jackson administration (1829–1837) Congress approved the harsh removal policies that led to the Trail of Tears and other poorly administered forced migrations wherein thousands of Indians died.

Both the Feathers and the Pileus Had to Go

The decision of the founders to include the sanctioning of slavery in the Constitution is another reason the Indian Princess no longer fit. Slavery was an abomination among the Native Americans from whom the founders borrowed the principle of personal liberty. By comparison, however, slavery was an integral part of both the Greek and Roman systems. Openly emulating the slavery-hating Indians in their national symbolism would have forced the new Americans to acknowledge these disparities. With slavery determined to be integral to the new American nation, subsequent retellings of the Revolution's inspirations downplayed the influence of the Iroquois in favor of the Greco-Romans.[7]

As can be seen in the different architectural preferences, residents in the Southern states emulated the cultures of Greece and Rome more than people in the North did. Below the Mason Dixon Line the architectural style is full of Greco-Roman columns and triangular pediments over porticos with grand entranceways. In the Northern states the plain Federalist and Colonial Georgian styles of architecture were preferred. When defending their liberties to hold other men in bondage, Southern aristocrats merely had to look around them to be reminded that slavery was indispensable to their new republic, because, as they selectively remembered, their new republic was based on the Greco-Roman model of government.

For the same reason that the feathers had to vanish, Liberty's cap, or pileus, attracted controversy. The pileus directly linked the Liberty goddess to the manumission of slaves, and artists in America began avoiding it, especially on currency designs, so as not to embarrass the

Figure 4.2. Goddesses were everywhere as seen on this popular printed cotton toile, the "Apotheosis of Benjamin Franklin and George Washington," circa 1785. Washington drives a chariot carrying a personified America, who is wearing ostrich plumes in her hair and holding a caduceus. Below, Franklin is surrounded by Liberty, with her pole and cap, and gesturing to Minerva, with her helmet and shield, next to Winged Victory and her trumpet. Yale University Art Gallery.

Southern states. Patriots of the South had convinced themselves that American liberty meant they had the freedom to own slaves, and they were very vocal about defending that freedom.

Another reason that the allegorical American Liberty transitioned from the Indian Princess to the Greco-Roman style goddess was timing. The fascination with Greek and Roman culture, art, and style, collectively known as the neoclassical movement, was reaching its peak right when the founding artists were grappling for symbols to depict this new nation. Since the discovery of Pompeii in 1748, everything about the ancient world—from togas to architecture to governmental style—had become the craze in both England and the colonies. The plainness of the neoclassical line particularly appealed to the new Americans looking to replace the overly elaborate rococo style of the aristocracy, which they viewed as ostentatious. Homespun, simple, and practical became the new beautiful, especially after boycotts and the war brought imports of luxuries to a halt.[8] In art, the new Americans were drawn to simple lines and planes, too.

Ladies' fashions were affected by the neoclassical, together with all other art forms. Empire-waist dresses influenced by the Roman look were worn by upper-class ladies, and soon after the signing of the Constitution, this style was donned by the newly designed American Liberty goddess. This nonaffiliated European-looking lady, named in portraits simply as America, sometimes put an ostrich plume in her hair. In a curious throwback to the Indian Princess, the trend for aristocratic ladies to wear a single large feather in their hair started after the Native Americans visited Europe and created a sensation, inspiring fashions. This trend is also behind the lyric in *Yankee Doodle* where the country bumpkin sticks a feather in his cap so he could call himself a "macaroni," or a dandified aristocrat.

How the Indian Princess Went Greek

As stated earlier, at the beginning of the intellectual and political antagonism between Britain and the colonies in 1765, the colonies were depicted in British cartoons as the Indian Princess. Polemicists

Figure 4.3. Paul Revere's commentary on the Boston Tea Party appeared in the *Royal American Magazine* in 1774, faithfully copied exactly from a British print that had appeared in London a few months earlier. America is depicted as a Native American woman in Roman robes being manhandled by several British ministers forcing her to drink tea. America spits the tea back into the minister's face. Britannia covers her eyes in shame, and an allegorical military man stands to the right doing nothing, while France and Spain look on from the left. Library of Congress.

first characterized her as a dependent daughter of Britannia, but by the end of the Revolution, in both British and American art, the Indian Princess had grown up and was more frequently being interpreted as a younger sister of Britannia.[9] In American political cartoons, the Indian Princess became restless and is seen more actively engaged than in British cartoons. The Roman goddess of Liberty appears to assist her, and together the two of them, or sometimes a composite figure made up of symbols from both, are seen reaching for the pole and the cap of Liberty, or stomping on the symbols of monarchy, such as crowns, garters, and scepters.

This swapping of clothing and accessories continued until eventually the Indian Princess lost all her feathers and replaced her arrows with a sword and shield. A clear demonstration of the preference for the Euro-American mode of the American Liberty goddess can be seen in a map used for the peace negotiations to end the Revolutionary War. In 1782, the cartouche of this map included the familiar Indian Princess. By the 1784 reprinting of this same map, the princess had been replaced by a traditional Lady Liberty with her cap on a pole.[10]

America's founders continually interrupted their work on writing the Constitution and otherwise organizing the governmental infrastructure to spend time designing and debating emblems, mottoes, and medals. An apparently natural predilection for what today is known as branding, combined with an attempt to communicate with a largely illiterate populace, meant the founders took symbols very seriously. The consensus was that the symbols that they chose to represent their experiment were just as important to their long-term success as their policies.

The passion for imagery of the goddess in American art began just before 1776 and reached its crescendo during the Madison administration (1809–1817).[11] Goddesses were everywhere. Liberty and Minerva were especially popular, but also making frequent appearances were Justice, Ceres, Victory, Virtue, and Fame. The new composite versions of the American Liberty goddess appeared on newspaper mastheads, seals for states and educational associations, flags, currency, statuary, paintings, songs, poetry, and household goods like needlepoint and weathervanes. The founders had what appears to be a near obsession with female allegory when designing the insignia for their experimental break with society.

Liberty, Britannia, and the Indian Princess were blended to create something new and distinctly American. Sometimes she wears Minerva's helmet to demonstrate she can defend herself wisely in war, and sometimes she carries Demeter's cornucopia to demonstrate that her harvests and exports are bountiful. In the 1800s, this melting-pot American Liberty goddess was the most popular female allegory of America. She was the new icon for civic virtue, and as she donned the

Figure 4.4. Lady Liberty was the face of all U.S. currency until the twentieth century, when presidents' heads were featured for the first time. Top image: 1803, capped bust designed by Robert Scot; middle image: 1808, draped bust designed by John Reich; bottom image: Liberty with Indian headdress, 1857, three-dollar proof. United States Mint, Philadelphia, National Museum of American History, Kenneth E. Behring Center, Smithsonian Institution.

fashions of the day she no longer served as an anchor to the past, but more as a reflection of America's ability to master the future.[12]

When the new national Mint created the first coins in 1792, Lady Liberty's visage was the one chosen to replace the customary monarch's face on the coins. Liberty-head coins stayed in circulation all the way up to the twentieth century, when they were replaced by portraits of presidents. The founders looked for any means to create among the people a sensation of national union, a federated state to hold the former independent colonies together. Ben Franklin jumped at the chance to disseminate emblems of morality on the new paper currency issued by the Continental Congress at the outset of the war. Knowing the novelty of paper money would be closely examined by all who handled it, he designed mottoes and symbols, complete with interpretation key, which sounded straight out of *Poor Richard's Almanac,* instructing readers to spend frugally and moderate their conduct. Franklin's numismatic emblems of morality were popularized further when several regiments adopted them for their battle flags.

Why the Founders Were Drawn to the Goddess

The elite of the Enlightenment saw themselves as cosmopolitan citizens of the world, members of the international Republic of Letters, where men of learning in all countries shared information despite boundaries. The rapid advances in science and philosophy inspired belief that all were connected with a new sense of benevolent purpose. The classic Roman interpretation of virtue had been something martial, linked with manliness and courage. "The new virtue was soft and feminized," said Gordon Wood, "and capable of being expressed by women as well as men. Some in fact thought it was even better expressed by women."[13] Declaration signer Benjamin Rush called natural affections, benevolence, politeness, and love "appropriate to a modern enlightened society."[14] This "domestication of virtue for American culture" was one of the most radical things about the Revolution according to Wood, who described it as a utopian vision written about excitedly in the years

Figure 4.5. Six state seals show the prevalence of goddesses in our official insignia. North Carolina: Liberty with pole and cap and Plenty (really Ceres with the cornucopia); New Jersey: Liberty with pole and cap and Ceres with cornucopia, plus three plows in the shield; New York: Liberty with pole and cap and Justice with scales; Virginia: Virtus (Virtue as an Amazonian warrior); Pennsylvania seal's reverse: Liberty with pole and cap and sword; Wyoming: Liberty with a pole carrying a banner with the state motto, Equal Rights, because the Territory of Wyoming was the first to grant women suffrage in 1869.

leading up to and for a few years after the Revolution. Writers as different as Thomas Paine, James Wilson, and John Quincy Adams were optimistic that a new era of virtue had dawned.

While filling their landscape with images of the female divine, the founders were convinced they had ushered in a new age of benevolence, which Wood says was not "nostalgic or backward-looking," but progressive. "It not only helped reconcile classical Republicanism with modernity and commerce, it laid the basis for all reform movements of the nineteenth century, and indeed, for all subsequent modern, liberal thinking."[15] The Revolutionary generation instilled their symbols with a mixture of idealism and utilitarianism. Virtue among the elected rulers was seen as absolutely necessary to maintain the republic of liberty they had designed. And they were convinced that public virtue was just as essential, knowing as they did that previous republics had failed mainly due to factionalized self-interests.

The founding artists used neoclassical goddesses to assure themselves that their risky experiment was blessed by and aligned with ancient principles. The American Liberty goddess was used in national architecture and adornment to show strength and endurance. She was used on the frontispieces of magazines and journals to show support for the arts and sciences. She showed up in public displays and parades to represent national unity and on international diplomatic seals and treaties to show independence. Lady Liberty was also used to emphasize prosperity in order to capture the imagination of the average American. Jefferson routinely talked about liberty needing to be protected, and he justified his Louisiana Purchase by calling it an "Empire of Liberty."

Lady Liberty encouraged a familial sense of unity. As the Republican Mother ideal, she linked everyone as one united family. Whereas before the Revolution, political discussion was framed in terms of the monarch as father and the subjects as his children, people now started talking about the United States of America as a family where everyone had to agree to work together. Symbols of union were provided for all economic classes, from the familiar thirteen links in a chain to a more refined thirteen candles in a chandelier.[16] According to some accounts, the models for many of the earliest Liberty coins were well-known socialites such as the daughter of the president of the First National Bank of the United States, Ann Willing Bingham, said to be the model for the so-called Draped Bust Liberty-head coin of 1795.[17] Liberty's hair and head coverings were causes for much debate and consternation, with bareheadedness implying a virginal and thus virtuous state, but unbound and flowing hair indicating unbound freedom, and suggesting looseness of character.[18] Hair carefully coifed, as in Bartholdi's Liberty, indicated a liberty controlled by the law.

Liberty Is Balanced by the Eagle

As versatile as she was, to become a successful archetype Lady Liberty needed to be balanced by the masculine principle. The archetypal female in art is usually accompanied by at least a hint of the archetypal male, according to esoteric symbologist David Ovason. "This marks the recognition of the cosmic and biological fact that nothing is entirely feminine, no more than anything is entirely masculine," he told us. Through history, female allegory has been used to assert permanence and stability, while male allegory asserted action and change.[19] Until the invention of Uncle Sam, the masculine symbolism that was paired with Lady Liberty was usually in the form of the bald eagle or a portrait of George Washington. Liberty and the eagle were particularly effective as a balanced pair and reinforced this dualism by appearing on the opposite sides of millions of coins. Associated with Jupiter, the eagle is an active symbol that dives and swoops and hunts its prey, symbolically a good partner of masculine principle to balance the female Liberty. When George Washington is pictured together with Lady Liberty, the subconscious message is urging the public to relate as a family, espousing both liberty and union in one image.

One of the most influential pairings of Liberty with the eagle was the 1796 *Liberty in the Form of the Goddess of Youth Giving Support to the Bald Eagle* by Edward Savage. Savage's engraving was based on a famous image of the Roman goddess of youth interacting with Jupiter in the form of an eagle. Other than the title, there is little to indicate

Figure 4.6. An influential piece from 1796 inspiring many copycats, this image depicts the United States as an allegorical female called Liberty providing nourishment to the eagle. Engraving by Edward Savage titled *Liberty in the Form of the Goddess of Youth Giving Support to the Bald Eagle*. Library of Congress.

that this is Lady Liberty, depicted here as a modern woman in contemporary dress and hairstyle (figure 4.6). There is a liberty cap on top of a flagpole in the background, but the focus is on this elegant lady lifting up a chalice to nurture the gigantic eagle hovering over her. The balance between the masculine and feminine is particularly easy to see. This engraving was reproduced and copied by many other artists and amateurs in many other mediums, like painted glass and needlepoint, and achieved widespread popularity. Thomas Jefferson had this one hanging in his parlor at Monticello.

Earlier "Statues of Liberty"

The statue of "Liberty and the Eagle" is the popular name for a sculpture originally placed above the Speaker's desk in the House of Representatives between 1817 and 1819. This thirteen-foot-tall statue of Liberty was officially named the *Genius of the Constitution* by her sculptor, Enrico Causici, and she can still be seen today on display in the Hall of Congress, faithfully guarded by the enormous eagle by her side. This statue was a replacement for another giant sculpture actually called the *Statue of Liberty* that was sadly destroyed when the whole building was burned to the ground in the War of 1812. Also situated directly behind the chair of the Speaker of the House, this first statue of Liberty made an imposing sight from what we can tell from the one surviving artist rendering and the incomplete descriptions in the correspondence between designer and architect. A seated matronly Liberty, she was between nine and twelve feet high and framed by twenty-six-foot-high columns that were draped in crimson. She held the liberty cap in her hand, and the American eagle stood loyally by her side.

Architect of the Capitol Benjamin Latrobe proposed a giant statue of Minerva for the Capitol's west front that never materialized, but it survives in the form of a watercolor sketch. An even earlier giant statue of Liberty was proposed by Italian artist Giuseppe Ceracchi in 1791 that would have been between sixty and one hundred feet high if he had been able to convince Congress to fund it. What survives today is a five-foot-tall bust called *Minerva as the Patroness of American Liberty* on display at the Library Company of Philadelphia and believed to be a character study for the larger monument.

As with any allegorical female, the symbols surrounding her are essential to identify who she is, especially when she starts donning contemporary dress. In addition to the bald eagle and the portraits of George Washington, the American Liberty goddess by definition was accompanied by at least one of these associated symbols: the pole, the cap, the liberty tree, the motto *E pluribus unum,* the flag, Benjamin Franklin, a rattlesnake, a chain, or a shield.[20] Likewise, there was almost always another classical symbol nearby, something like a pyramid, an altar, a temple, or an obelisk, intended to link the new America with the idealized republics of Greece and Rome.

Other Roman gods and goddesses make regular appearances to prop up the American Liberty or to carry messages about the new republic. Mercury appears as protector of commerce, usually demonstrated by the bales of goods ready to ship from American ports. Minerva, the Roman goddess of wisdom and war, is the most popular of the supplementary goddesses depicted. Generally, she is seen supporting the American Liberty, though sometimes she herself appears as the personification of wisdom, guiding the American experiment in liberty. Other times Liberty borrows Minerva's helmet or carries her shield, complete with the identifying Medusa aegis. The founders were drawn to Minerva in her persona as the goddess of wisdom more than her persona as the goddess of war, and they included her to show that the new American concept of liberty was guided by wisdom or reason.

During the first few years of the republic, it was sometimes difficult to identify which goddess was Liberty and which was the Indian Princess, which one was Minerva, and which one was America. After the successful completion of the War of 1812, however, after beating the British Army twice in one generation, there was a growing conviction in the new republic that the American version of Liberty was what really set them apart. For it is at this time that the image of American Liberty starts to predominate over the other Roman goddesses, the Indian Princess, and neoclassical ostrich-plumed ladies.

Figure 4.7. This is a good example of common folk art of the time wherein everyday objects were fashioned into Liberties and Columbias, like this weathervane dated circa 1865–1875, now in the collection of the American Folk Art Museum in New York City. Artist unidentified; possibly Cushing and White, possibly Waltham, Massachusetts. Paint on copper and zinc, 18¾" x 15" x 2", Gift of Jerry and Susan Lauren, 2006.12.2. Photo: Gavin Ashworth.

Folk Artists Loved Lady Liberty

As the common people gained increased leisure time, they began to experiment with art and play with color and design to decorate their domestic items. The popularity of the American Liberty goddess as a theme in folk art is evidence that this emblem of the female divine had permeated the consciousness of the people.

Lady Liberty summarized in an instant the ineffable "yearning to breathe free," as designer Nancy Jo Fox put it. After surprising herself one day during class with a sudden burst of inspiration to insist that the Statue of Liberty was an example of monumental folk art, Fox was designated as curator of a mammoth exhibit called "Liberties with Liberty" at the American Folk Art Museum in New York City in honor of the 1986 centennial of the Statue of Liberty. The poster series from Fox's "Liberties with Liberty" show ended up traveling internationally, and her work was turned into a successful book, often quoted by researchers tracing the evolution of the Statue of Liberty. She defines folk art as made "by the people, for the people" by nonprofessionals who were inspired by the universal stream of consciousness that directed the hand of the craftsperson and eye of the artist to create unique works that were rarely signed. Distinguishing features of folk art are its free use of color, found and recycled two- and three-dimensional materials, and its restraint of academic tradition. Often these artworks are also practical objects like andirons, cake pans, window shades, or weathervanes. Fox likes to call folk art "a side-door to history," because it can be a record of people's lives and their attempts to make their everyday items beautiful.

Reeling off some of the Lady Liberty objects she collected from historical societies, museums, and private individuals all over the country Fox said: "oil paintings, watercolors, shop-signs, shop-figures, ship figureheads for ocean and interior waterways, reverse paintings on glass, printed and woven textiles, needlepoint, furniture, prints, *scherenschnitte* [German for "scissor cut" designs], cookie and ice cream molds, portraits, architectural elements, circus wagons, carousels, wood blocks, cakeboards, moneyboxes, gate finials, toys, dolls, and even firefighting paraphernalia." All of these were adorned in some way with a loving

Figure 4.8. The popularity of Lady Liberty as a theme for folk art shows how much this goddess permeated national consciousness. The Citizen Fire Company no. 3 used Lady Liberty with her pole and cap as their symbol, beginning in 1836. National Museum of American History, Kenneth E. Behring Center, Smithsonian Institution.

tribute to Lady Liberty created by an obviously amateur artist. There are some exquisite renderings, too, like the scrimshaw carved by homesick sailors into whale or walrus tooth, or bone, while away from home for several years. The Columbia or Liberty figureheads on their ships would have signaled to other ships that these sailors were Americans in defiance of the British Navy's continued insistence on impressing any English-speaking sailors they could overpower. Some of the largest objects featured in the "Liberties with Liberty" show came from firehouses and circuses where the goddess Liberty was a recurring character. Circuses routinely included a United States wagon featuring "a Greek goddess of Liberty flanked by two Indian maidens in feathered skirt and headdress, holding tomahawks and feathered liberty poles and liberty caps."

A large portion of folk art is created by "anonymous," and as Virginia Woolf's famous quote goes, in many cases, "anonymous was a woman," especially in the needlework and quilting arts. Whoever was fashioning

Figure 4.9. *Columbia Teaching John Bull His New Lesson,* watercolor etching, 1813, shows America as an allegorical female wearing the fashionable empire-waist dress and carrying Liberty's pole and cap while she lectures both France and England to treat her with respect. Library of Congress.

these objects, the image of the American Liberty goddess was a source of creative inspiration for millions of people. The folk art depictions have the added dimension of taking on a totemic veneration. When you make a fireplace andiron into the shape of Lady Liberty, it *becomes* Lady Liberty. When you press a cakeboard with a Lady Liberty design into your dough, you partake of the spirit of American Liberty by eating it.

The Trouble with Naming
American Liberty "Columbia"

Although some will give the goddess in these designs the name "Columbia," we found that Columbia as a name appeared more in written works than as an image distinct from the American Liberty goddess. The only distinguishing characteristic about images named Columbia seems to be her penchant for wearing the American flag, and almost never wearing Indian feathers. The name Columbia derives from Christopher Columbus, of course, which adds a whole new dimension of the domination script to her interpretation. Linking the American Liberty goddess with the idea that civilization was on an unstoppable westward flow meant that Columbia became a player in the game of national politics, especially in editorial cartoons.

English writer Samuel Johnson is usually credited as the first to coin the term "Columbia" as a nickname for the American colonies, but an earlier colonial reference has been found in the 1697 writings of a Massachusetts Bay Colony magistrate named Samuel Sewall. Sewall wondered why this continent had not been named *Columbina* instead of America, a question we ask ourselves in chapter 6.

In 1775, Phillis Wheatley, the first Black woman to publish in America, wrote an enormously popular ode to "His Excellency, General Washington" in which she called on the goddess Columbia to protect her hero on the battlefield against Britannia. Wheatley's owners had bought her fresh off the slave boat from Africa at the age of seven and, recognizing her intelligence, provided her with an education that turned her into one of the most celebrated writers of the day. Many other poets copied her, including one of George Washington's favorites, Joel Barlow, who published an epic in 1807 titled the *Columbiad,* intended as a historical concept piece on the spirit of America.

At the commencement ceremonies of the newly renamed Columbia College in 1795, the goddess Columbia was invoked to assist the women of the new republic in their roles as Republican Mothers, nurturing their patriot sons and husbands to be virtuous. "The Genius of Liberty hovers triumphant over the glorious scene . . . may we see the lovely daughters of Columbia . . . thus keep our country virtuous."[21] The song "Hail Columbia," written in 1798, was considered our national anthem until the twentieth century. The U.S. president was traditionally announced with "Hail Columbia," and it was sung at the dedication ceremony in Paris when the Statue of Liberty was officially gifted to the United States on July 4, 1884.[22]

Figure 4.10. Columbia Phonograph Company was founded in 1888 in Washington, D.C., and used this allegorical lady in their logo on their phonograph cylinder packages. Scanned by Infrogmation from his own collection.

Though ostensibly named in honor of Christopher Columbus, hundreds of lakes, rivers, and schools around the country bear the name of the goddess Columbia. In 1786, South Carolina named its new capital city Columbia. There are also cities named Columbia in eighteen other states, and counties named Columbia in eight others. The goddess Columbia—holding a torch and looking a lot like the Statue of Liberty—is seen in the opening credits of some of our favorite movies produced by Columbia Pictures. Columbia Records, a different company, was founded in 1888 in the District of Columbia, and later branched into the television business with the Columbia Broadcasting System, or CBS.

Most significantly, in 1791 the founders chose the name Columbia for their new federal city, built as the nation's capital. Washington, D.C., is the District of Columbia which could be interpreted as the "District of the Goddess." While the thought of a goddess overshadowing our nation's political power base causes conniptions among extremist Christians today, who see demons behind any expression of female divinity, we think it's actually the best hope our leaders have. If they can learn to recognize the American Liberty goddesses surrounding them in D.C. as representing the untapped wisdom of the female divine, then perhaps this recognition could begin to influence their decisions to promote cooperation instead of domination.

Uncle Sam: ISO Powerful Female Companion

As the nation searched for symbolism to provide a sense of national identity, Uncle Sam emerged in popular culture as the masculine balance necessary for a male-female partnership. As we mentioned earlier, if an archetypal female image is to work its way deeply into our soul, it must have a male counterpart. Calling the United States Uncle Sam started around the War of 1812 at a time when the nation was feeling more masculine and aggressive. At first he was depicted very similarly to the potbellied characters John Bull in Britain and Brother Jonathan in New England, who wore striped trousers and a top hat. As homage to President Lincoln, Uncle Sam added a beard and grew tall and thin under the pen of cartoonist Thomas Nast. Nast supported the Union, and his cartoons featuring Uncle Sam and Columbia together as a couple had tremendous influence on public opinion.

In the cartoon couple, Uncle Sam is usually portrayed as America considering the more militant and greedy impulses of the nation, while Columbia/Liberty is portrayed as the soul or conscience of the nation, advising discretion. Nast's cartoons from the Civil War era show Columbia wearing the stylish corsets and hoopskirts of the time, usually scolding Uncle Sam for his dubious policies.

The tradition of portraying Liberty and Sam as a couple for satiric effect continues today. Pulitzer Prize–winner Joel Pett of the *Lexington*

Figure 4.11. A 1918 poster issued during World War I featured Columbia wearing the Phrygian cap and urging Americans to grow a Victory Garden. National Archives.

Herald-Leader in Lexington, Kentucky, who gave us permission to reprint some of his cartoons in this book, often employs this device of relating the two halves of a political debate to the dynamics between a male-female couple. Usually these couples show Liberty doing the right thing, and Uncle Sam being tempted by political connections and selfish desires. "To me the Statue of Liberty means freedom," said Pett, "and freedom to me is about the Constitution and the Bill of Rights. I use Lady Liberty almost exclusively as a symbol, usually a worried symbol, of something gone wrong with liberty."[23] Thanks to Pett and many other cartoonists, Lady Liberty continues to whisper in the ear of Uncle Sam, urging him to straighten up . . . at least in the cartoon world!

Lady Liberty the Propagandist

Columbia as a Lady Liberty image made some of her final popular appearances in propaganda posters for World War I. There she is, sporting the latest art nouveau fashions, standing alongside Uncle Sam, selling war bonds and planting Victory Gardens. After 1920 and the emancipation of women, the classically robed allegorical females declined in popularity in favor of the "New Woman." As real women became participatory citizens, the romantic images of allegorical females extolling virtue felt outdated. The one version of Lady Liberty that has supplanted them all is Bartholdi's Statue of Liberty. Today Bartholdi's Statue of Liberty is even more popular than symbols that had a direct connection with the American Revolution, such as the Liberty Bell or the flag. But just like the other versions of the American Liberty goddesses, the Statue of Liberty is a construction of propaganda designed to elicit national pride.

After the Revolution, it didn't take long for critics to point out that the liberty and prosperity promised to all was being appreciated fully only by the few. Historian and social critic Howard Zinn gave us a new perspective on this abundance of attention to Lady Liberty during our nation's founding years. By combining liberty with other concepts like order and property, Zinn says the elites among the founders were able to attract the middling and lower classes and to unify them in support of independence. The elite made speeches about "our" country and "our" liberty, and even "our" property, with blatant disregard for women, Native Americans, Black slaves, and white servants. "The language of liberty . . . could unite just enough whites to fight a Revolution against England," said Zinn, "without ending either slavery or inequality."[24]

While that hypocrisy may be true in regard to the rhetoric about liberty, symbols of liberty, with their ever-changing and multivalent layers of interpretation, cannot be dismissed so readily. Symbols reach us on an unconscious level and speak to us in a voice beyond conscious understanding. Though deliberately designed with the intention of instilling national pride among Frenchmen in the nineteenth century, the Statue of Liberty escaped those confines long ago to become a symbol of hope and renewal and a million individual things to a million individual people all over the world. Columbia, Minerva, and the Indian Princess all faded from memory as the Statue of Liberty gradually became the image that all Americans refer to when thinking of an American Liberty goddess. The role of virtuous female power—the role that the founders considered essential for a sense of national union—has been completely assumed by the Statue of Liberty.

5

Colossal Statuary Consists of More than Size

A Statue of Liberty Time Line

One of the reasons the Statue of Liberty forms an emotional connection with people around the world is that the concept of personal liberty resonates in something truly large. As sculptor Auguste Bartholdi put it in his 1885 book, his colossus would produce an emotion in the breast of the spectator, "not because of its volume, but because its size is in keeping with the idea that it interprets."[1] The idea of liberty is so enormous, in other words, that it is suitable for interpretation by a colossus. Trying to describe the indescribable emotions that result when viewing effective colossal statuary, Bartholdi continued, "Colossal statuary does not consist simply in making an enormous statue. It ought to produce an emotion in the breast of the spectator." Without a doubt, what makes the Statue of Liberty memorable is its colossal size. There are literally dozens of female allegorical artworks in France that resemble the Statue of Liberty, some with nearly identical postures and accoutrement, but none of them has resonated so memorably for so long, and so completely, as this particular Lady Liberty.

Bartholdi's artistic skill is rated by many art historians as standard and unexceptional. Be that as it may, all seem to agree that his two greatest contributions to the Statue of Liberty were his insistence that the statue be colossal and his ability to convince thousands of people to go along with the idea. His mentor on the project, Édouard de Laboulaye, had in mind a more traditional statue such as the many he and Bartholdi were surrounded by in Paris in the mid-1800s.[2] Laboulaye indeed directed the elements of the statue's design and posture and symbolism, but it was Bartholdi's grandiose vision that made it extraordinary. The success of enlarging an ordinary-looking statue relies on many elements, and we'll review a number of them here.

This chapter was reserved for all the little bits about Bartholdi's biography that didn't correlate to one of the other topics we covered in our quest to find the secret life of Lady Liberty. Most other books about the Statue of Liberty feature a time line, but rather than repeat the standard events one can find anywhere, we created a so-called secret time line. We will review some of the main events of creating the statue in this chapter, but we will also focus on lesser-noticed anecdotes that we believe coalesced to help push this idea out of Bartholdi's and Laboulaye's minds and into reality. Although most people today credit Bartholdi, it was actually Laboulaye who created the Statue of Liberty, and he did so *"with the assistance of Bartholdi,"* as Barry Moreno puts it [emphasis added] in his *Statue of Liberty Encyclopedia*.[3] Not only was it Bartholdi's drive that enlarged it to colossal proportions, but it was his training and skill that situated the statue in the busiest harbor of the United States, with nothing nearby to compete with it—thereby allowing that profound emotion to well forth in the hearts of the viewers.

What was behind this drive?

1834: The Second Baby, Frèdèric-Auguste Bartholdi, Is Born

In the year 1834 the sculptor of *La Liberté Eclairant le Monde* was born. He was named Frèdèric-Auguste Bartholdi and called Auguste. He had an elder brother with the same name who was born earlier in 1831 and died in 1832. There was also an infant sister named Auguste-Charlotte who was born and died in 1833.[4] Giving your surviving children the same names as earlier deceased ones was not uncommon in that day and age, but we point this out in connection to the markedly close relationship Bartholdi shared with his mother, Charlotte. She had borne two children in quick succession who had died as infants, and when the son who was to become our sculptor was born in 1834, there must have been some psychological impact in the sense of his being a replacement child. There was one other elder brother who survived to grow to adulthood, Jean-Charles, born in 1830.

The Bartholdis were from Colmar in the Alsace region near the eastern border of France. This made them culturally French, but they spoke a dialect more akin to German. Unlike most of the rest of France, this region was mainly Protestant, and the Bartholdis were practicing Lutherans. Bartholdi's father was a prosperous lawyer, and the family lived comfortably, owning several properties and vineyards in the region. When Auguste was just two years old his father died unexpectedly, leaving Charlotte a widow at a young age with two small sons to raise. She decided to move them to Paris, where she could devote herself to their education and careers. She maintained all the properties and vineyards in Colmar from a distance, and her management of the businesses continued to bring in a substantial income throughout their lives.[5]

Auguste's Imposing Mother

By all accounts Charlotte Bartholdi was a very controlling woman. She nurtured the interests expressed by both of her sons and hired the best tutors and paid for them to go to the best schools. Bartholdi's brother Charles started out studying art, inspiring his adoring younger brother to follow him, but then Charles switched his interest to the law and became a successful lawyer like his father. Later in life, Charles grew eccentric and eventually mentally unstable. After his mother broke up his twelve-year illicit love affair with a woman whom she considered unsuitable, he suffered a complete nervous breakdown and was confined. His breakdown came just as the the Statue of Liberty was being constructed in Paris, and as Auguste's statue was slowly growing to surpass the city's rooftops, he faithfully made time to visit his brother in confinement. He felt a great loss when Charles died in 1885, just after the statue was officially presented to the U.S. ambassador to France.[6]

When Auguste chose to make art his profession, Charlotte was there every step of the way, manipulating, cajoling, and prodding. She arranged his public appearances and launched his name in the art world. When he was eighteen, she paid for him to open his own studio, and from the age of nineteen onward, he would exhibit in every one of the yearly art salon exhibitions in Paris.[7] From the outset he seemed particularly talented at acquiring the best locations for his work to be noticed. Whenever they were apart, Auguste and Charlotte wrote to each other almost every day. Many of his letters include drawings, especially when he was touring the United States.[8] It is from this loving mother, who saved most of these letters to be preserved today in the Musée Bartholdi in Colmar, that we know as much as we do about the planning and purpose of the Statue of Liberty.

The Statue of Liberty's French Cousins

In 1848, Auguste Bartholdi was fourteen years old, and over the next four years, as he came of age as a budding artistic talent, his country went through a short-lived return to the idealism of Revolutionary days. They established what became known as the Second Republic, and all around him, Bartholdi saw his teachers and the most respected artists of the time creating statues of La Liberté, La Republique, and La France in honor of the renewed optimism that buoyed France when Napoleon Bonaparte's nephew was elected as president to replace the king. For a few years Napoleon III improved the country with modernization projects and republican reforms. During this period, Bartholdi's mentor, Laboulaye, established himself as France's leading authority on the United States of America and taught the first university courses on the U.S. Constitution. Students flocked to his lectures, and he began to influence a generation of moderate republican and abolitionist thinkers.[9]

In a way that was very similar to what had happened at the time of the American Revolution and the first French Revolution, the leaders of the Second Republic in France eagerly created works of art to establish their identity as a new nation. Public statues were designed to show stability and to represent a link to the past. Allegorical females carried the mythic keys to the idealism of the age and showed up in the statuary, seals, and paintings of the salons. Barry Moreno says the Great Seal of France, designed by Jean-Jacques Barre in 1848 (figure 5.1), was almost certainly the original inspiration for Laboulaye's Statue of Liberty and that Laboulaye probably showed it to Bartholdi with that suggestion in mind.[10] Barre's design includes a seated robed woman holding aloft in her right hand a fasces, representing civic authority, and wearing a crown of light that even has the same number of seven rays coming from it.

Figure 5.1. The Great Seal of France, designed in 1848, was almost certainly the model for the Statue of Liberty. She was one of dozens of Ladies Liberty surrounding Bartholdi and Laboulaye when they conceptualized and designed their colossus.

Another contemporary sculpture was *La Republique* by Jean-François Soitoux, one of Bartholdi's sculpting teachers. Soitoux's *La Republique* is a statue of a standing, robed woman with a sword pointing down, and it is still on view today in the middle of downtown Paris. Painter Ary Scheffer, an early family friend who encouraged Bartholdi to take up sculpting instead of painting, created a sketch of his own version of *La Republique,* possibly as an entry in the design competition for the Great Seal in 1848.[11] An entry in the 1848 salon was *La France Eclairant le Monde* by A. L. Janet-Lange with whom Bartholdi would later collaborate (figure 5.2). Honore Daumier produced a scandalous breastfeeding *La Republique* in 1848, and, in 1855, Robert Elias's *France Crowning Art and Industry,* also with seven rays in her crown, was captured in a photograph by Bartholdi and is retained in his collection in Colmar.

Today, the rays of light coming from the Statue of Liberty's crown are the source of some of the wildest speculation by paranoid conspiracy theorists on the Internet. Searching through history to find the inspiration for the rays of light and the torch, the question they never seem to ask is, What did robed and illuminated females mean symbolically to Frenchmen during Bartholdi's formative years in France? The answer is: Robed and illuminated females were created as calming symbols of the conservatism of a secure republic. France was in search of stability in its symbols, having experienced a bloody governmental upheaval approximately every twenty years since the French Revolution, and the artists working for the Second Republic defined this stability in terms of virtuous robed females.

The Second Republic came to a halt in 1852 when Napoleon III decided he would rather be emperor than president, and his coup d'etat squashed most of the republicanizing reforms Laboulaye's crowd had begun to implement. However, this was not before they had had a lasting impact on the imagination and created an abundance of compelling artwork. These robed and illuminated allegorical females of the propaganda of the Second Republic in France (1848–1852) metaphorically stand as a whole trunk of the Statue of Liberty's French family tree.

Figure 5.2. She's wearing robes and holding a torch, and her name is nearly identical to the Statue of Liberty's. This is *La France Éclairant le Monde* by A. L. Janet-Lange, produced in 1848. Reproduction on display at the Liberty Island Museum. Author photo.

Bartholdi Wonders like an Egyptian

At the age of twenty-one, Bartholdi took off on his version of a grand tour with four other young French artists to travel across Egypt for nine months. They also stopped in Nubia, Arabia, and Ethiopia,[12] and in some of his photos he looks like a Native wearing traditional Egyptian galabia and kaftan. This trip was to make a lasting impression on young Bartholdi, as it was in Egypt that he felt that emotion stirring in his breast as he beheld the enormity of the Sphinx, the Pyramids, and the Colossi of Memnon. "We are filled with profound emotion in the presence of these colossal witnesses," he said, "centuries old, of a past that to us is almost infinite, at whose feet so many generations, so many million existences, so many human glories have rolled in the dust."

He could very well have been describing his own future statue of Liberty here. "Their kindly and impassable glance seems to ignore the present and to be fixed upon an unlimited future."[13] Bartholdi's Sphinx-like *Lion of Belfort,* completed in 1880 in Belfort, France, is Bartholdi's only other truly huge work of art. It is seventy-two feet long by thirty-six feet high. Created to honor the citizens of the town of Belfort who had resisted the Prussian Army for 103 days in a siege during the Franco-Prussian War, the lion appears carved out of the side of the mountain, bristling with outrage. With the *Lion of Belfort* and *Liberty Enlightening the World,* he showed a mastery of what he had learned about the Egyptian monuments.

Dinner Parties and Flattery

Usually the first official date for the birth of the Statue of Liberty is listed as 1865, because that is the year Bartholdi named in his book as the first time it was discussed. He describes a dinner party at the Laboulaye house for a group of abolitionists and Union supporters, celebrating the end of the Civil War in the United States. During the party there was apparently a brief discussion about creating a memorial gift to the United States commemorating the liberation of the Union. Whether or not they talked about an actual *statue* of Liberty that evening, nothing more happened with the idea for several years. Bartholdi continued advancing his sculpting career, making traditional busts and statues of prominent men, and dreaming of someday making something that would touch the infinite.

Attending the Paris World Expo in 1867 was the exotic new ruler of Egypt, the khedive, or viceroy, Isma'il Pasha, who was creating a sensation with his modernizing efforts for Egypt, such as building new schools, railroads, and telegraph lines. He had also begun construction on the Suez Canal with French assistance. While in Paris he attended the international congress of abolitionists organized by Laboulaye, and Bartholdi took the opportunity to try to win a commission from the khedive to create a colossal lighthouse at the entrance of the new canal. He called it "Egypt (or Progress) Bringing the Light to Asia," a very common theme for the day. At the highly competitive international world expos every year, each country would show off its latest technical marvel, and the concepts of "Bringing" and "Progress" appeared in the artwork in one form or another every year with examples like *Industry Bringing Peace and Light to the World*.[14]

Not Reconciled to Marriage, and a Return to Egypt

The collection of Charlotte Bartholdi's letters from 1868 reveals that at some point, without her son's knowledge, she planned a wedding for Auguste and even sent out some invitations. When he learned of this he cryptically noted, "I would prefer if you want to reconcile me with marriage that you made it possible for me to see and meet the person you have in mind instead of talking about marriage or making compromising overtures." The matter was soon dropped, and the mystery woman's name has not been preserved.[15]

Bartholdi returned to Egypt in 1869 for the opening of the Suez Canal, and this time he brought with him to show the khedive a sketch and a small model statuette of his proposed lighthouse (figure 7.5, p. 194). He described it as an 86½-foot-tall peasant woman, or fellahin, wearing traditional Egyptian robes. Her arm is raised, as is the Statue of Liberty's, but Progress raises her left arm and is holding a lantern rather than a torch. Bartholdi proposed that the main source of light was to come from her crown, but the khedive would eventually reject the entire proposal as too expensive.

Bartholdi Goes to War

The Franco-Prussian War of 1870–1871 was a short war with far-reaching consequences for both the balance of power in Europe and for the eventual creation of the Statue of Liberty. Bartholdi immediately volunteered and marched out with the French armed forces. He wrote home to his mother, now living in Colmar again, that "I am helping when I can those who are suffering."[16] His mother wrote back that his childhood home was now occupied by Prussian soldiers. The war ended disastrously for France, when Emperor Napoleon III and his army of one hundred thousand men was captured and forced to surrender.

The emperor's capture created a power vacuum in Paris that led to several months of bloody revolution in the streets and a temporary rule of the radicals, called the Paris Commune of 1871. Even more devastating for Bartholdi was the ceding of the Alsace and Lorraine regions, including Bartholdi's family home, back to Germany as part of the conditions ending the war. The region was forced to adopt German culture and give up their dialect to speak High German, the official language of the Second Reich, creating much resentment. Unlike many Alsatians, after the war Charlotte Bartholdi retained her properties there and still made regular visits between them and her home in Paris, now having to travel to a foreign country to go home.

The loss of the regions of Alsace and Lorraine, affectionately called the Two Sisters, was psychically devastating for France. Many commentators have observed how this sort of exile from his birthplace contributed to Bartholdi's personal yearning for freedom. According to some counts, at least ten of his major artworks are related to the losses suffered during the Franco-Prussian War. His commemoration of French heroes made him such a favored son of Colmar that the Nazis sought out his works for destruction when they retook these areas in World War II.[17]

Statuemania!

With the emperor gone and the violence of the Paris Commune sub-dued, Laboulaye and his circle of moderate friends who were in favor of a constitutional republic seized their opportunity for more reforms. The Third Republic began formulating as early as 1871 (formally established in 1875) with an accompanying "statuemania." Statuemania is a nickname created by historian Maurice Agulhon for the huge outpouring of public monuments of political persuasion and moral instruction to which the Statue of Liberty belongs. While gigantism was an exception, statuemania gripped all of Europe, especially France at this time. In France, the monarchy was now abolished, and the people needed to replace all the coins and public artwork that had depicted the sovereign as their ruler.

Feelings of revenge also spurred on French artists as they competed with Germany to make bigger and better artwork. Bartholdi's Liberty would eventually be compared to the allegorical giant *Bavaria,* which was around sixty feet high, and *Germania,* which was thirty-four feet high on top of an enormous pedestal, erected in 1871 right on the border between the two countries where it seemed designed to gloat over the seizure of the Alsace region. Everywhere one turned in France there was a new statue going up to honor past events, men of history, and dozens of female allegorical Mariannes and La Republiques.

Bartholdi Investigates America

On June 8, 1871, in the midst of all of this transition in France, Bartholdi left for the United States. He and Laboulaye had decided to find out if America was receptive to the idea they had been kicking around for years, which by this time they were describing as a gift in honor of the upcoming centennial of the Declaration of Independence. Bartholdi wrote a telling line to Laboulaye as he left, poetically describing the purpose of the trip: "I will try to glorify the Republic and Liberty over there, in the hope that someday I will find it again here."[18] Many years later he would say he knew instantly when he sailed into New York Harbor that he'd found the perfect location for their statue on Bedloe's Island, but in fact, he continued looking and considered several locations in New York and Philadelphia. It would not be until he got to California that Bartholdi wrote to Laboulaye about Bedloe's Island, and it would take years of political manipulation before they could get approval to build the statue there.

Bartholdi Americanized himself for five months, traveling from coast to coast. He was not impressed with how fast Americans moved, lamenting that speed did not allow room for great imaginative works. Using the letters of introduction provided by Laboulaye and his political friends, he gained entree to prominent abolitionists and liberal thinkers in the United States, prevailing upon them to join the team that was making the statue. He met with Brigham Young and marveled at his sixteen wives and forty-nine children,[19] found Henry Wadsworth Longfellow "very enthusiastic" about their project, and sat on the porch with President Ulysses S. Grant smoking cigars.[20] He spent most of his time in New York, Philadelphia, and Washington, but then took off across the country on the new railroads to California via Chicago and Salt Lake City, and then came back East again via Denver, St. Louis, and Pittsburgh. "Everything is big here," he wrote his mother, "even the *petit pois!* [peas]." If anywhere would appreciate a colossal statue to Liberty, it would be here, he decided.

Finding the Perfect Frame

Bartholdi was obsessed with finding the perfect location to suit his colossus, knowing its surrounding frame was as integral as its form to its long-term success. For colossal statuary to work, he explained, it not only needed to consist of large planes, simple lines, and shallow contours to avoid deep shadows, but it also needed to be situated in a place where no other buildings or natural features would distract the eye. It wasn't unusual to have a statue viewed from the water, but for one to look *better* from the water than from on land was unusual. When looking at the Statue of Liberty from what is today called Liberty Island, her back is turned toward you and she appears static, a symbol for stability.

When looking at her from a boat, however, she appears to come alive and begins to move as the view unfolds while you move around her in the boat passing by. Lodging her on an island was a brilliant move in maintaining her surrounding frame, given that she is separated from the city by a fairly large expanse of water. Any tall buildings that may yet rise against the New York skyline will not obstruct or detract from her visibility.

Other foreign visitors to the United States in the 1870s noted its growing social inequalities—from corruption in the Grant administration, to swarms of immigrants packed into tenements, to the westward expansion crushing the Native Americans and the brutal crackdown on the newly freed slaves in the Reconstruction South. None of these conditions of inequality were noted in Bartholdi's many reports home to his mother and to Laboulaye.[21] Instead, Bartholdi saw the embodiment of the optimism they had hoped to find in the American understanding of liberty. In his biography of the statue, he wrote how the Americans inspired him. "If, then, the form of the accomplished work is mine, to the Americans I owe the thought and the inspiration which gave it birth. I was conscious when I landed at New York that I had found the idea which my friends had hoped for."[22]

First the Maquettes, Then the Masons

After returning to his studio in Paris, Bartholdi got to work creating a series of statuettes, or maquettes, revising them until Laboulaye settled on the final design in 1875. Once decided, they launched the official fundraising campaign with a great banquet at the Grand Hôtel du Louvre. During these few years after returning from his American tour, Bartholdi filled several other commissions and began his other colossus, the *Lion of Belfort*.

Bartholdi joined the Lodge Alsace-Lorraine to become a Freemason in 1875, a fact that today causes much consternation among the right-wing paranoids who see any mention of Freemasons as a sure indication of ulterior motives. Fear of the Freemasons is based on an old threadbare conspiracy claiming that the top echelon of Masonry in the

United States was infiltrated by a fictional cabal run by the Bavarian Illuminati, who are now intent on world domination.* Some commentators link the symbolism of enlightening in the Statue of Liberty's official title, *Liberty Enlightening the World,* to the name of the Illuminati, or to the Masons' stated goals of educating men in moral standards to reach higher states of enlightened consciousness and community service. Holes in this theory that the Masons influenced the symbolism of the Statue of Liberty lie in the timing of Bartholdi's constructions. Bartholdi proposed a lighthouse-woman for the Suez Canal in 1867, long before he became a Freemason. He and Laboulaye had settled on the name *Liberty Enlightening the World,* as well as the form of the lighthouse-woman for the Liberty statue, well before 1875.

What *does* correspond to the year he joined the Masons is the launching of the statue's fundraising campaign. It's more logical to assume Bartholdi joined the Freemasons in 1875 because he saw it as one more way he could meet influential and wealthy patrons whose dollars he needed to raise the funds necessary for the statue's construction. This is not to say Bartholdi was not sincere in his attraction to the principles of Masonry. He was, by all accounts, a bona fide believer in the power of virtue, acts of service, and the goodness of humankind, all of which were embodied by Freemasonry.

Laboulaye and Bartholdi launched their fundraising campaign almost exclusively on the strength of Bartholdi's salesmanship, having to downplay the lack of actual commitment they had received from the

---

*This conspiracy originated during the multitude of rumors of plots and counterplots circulating through France during the accelerating violence of the French Revolution. People were reeling to understand who or what to blame for the carnage and thorough eradication of the established order. The by-then defunct group from Bavaria known as the Illuminati was just one of many suggested as the true revolutionaries behind the French Revolution. The conspiracy claimed that these anarchists had infiltrated French aristocracy and were controlling the bread shortages in order to lead to a peasant revolt. In 1797 and 1798 two conspiracy theorists (Barruel and Robison) claimed this same group of plotters had survived in secret, and when their books were published in the United States, several preachers here started a panic by claiming the Bavarian Illuminati had also infiltrated Freemasonry in the United States. These conspiracies were politically motivated and were usually leveled against the leaders with whom they did not agree, Jefferson being their main target at the time.

Figure 5.3. Editorial cartoons in the United States lampooned the Statue of Liberty project, especially the delay in fundraising for the pedestal, as in this 1884 example from *LIFE* magazine describing how the statue would appear by the time the funding was complete. Reproduction on display at the Liberty Island Museum. Author photo.

Americans. They were so fired up by the idea of spreading republican-ism through the light of Lady Liberty, however, that in the end they were able to convince two nations very skeptical of the project to not only fund it, but in the case of the United States, to also authorize the use of prime Manhattan real estate and agree to pay for its upkeep and care in perpetuity.

Merchandising Liberty

The fundraising also coincided with the dawn of the age of advertis-ing, and almost immediately Bartholdi began licensing the rights to the image based on his sketches to raise money to pay for the construction. Indeed, some of the first to see the value in a colossal statue of Liberty were the merchants. The first label to plaster Bartholdi's Liberty on a product was Champagne Delauney of Reims in France,[23] and soon in both France and the United States Lady Liberty was hawking every-thing from sewing needles to Dr. Haas' Hog and Poultry Remedy.[24] Many of the ads emphasize the theme of liberty, such as the liberty to wash with whatever soap you chose. From the outset, both sides of the Franco-American Union fundraising committee were comprised mainly of businessmen and politicians interested in strengthening the ties of trade between the two countries. *Liberty Enlightening the World* was commodified by her very creators, and the commercialization of this ideal has inspired much cynicism.

In France, most of the money for the statue was donated from the wealthy establishment. The fundraising committees were seeded by asso-ciates of Laboulaye, who were naturally a lot like him in temperament: educated, powerful, upper-class people. Many of them believed as pas-sionately as he did that it was their duty to lead the people of France to a more liberal and stable system of government. "His idea of liberty had to fit in with the need for stability," said Barry Moreno, and that included economic progress.

In the United States, the advocacy of the elite was also crucial, espe-cially for securing government approval. Liberty benefited by patrons like the iron magnates Cooper and Hewitt on the New York fundraising committee, with Hewitt later becoming Liberty's lead sponsor in Congress.[25]

Thanks largely to the famous advocacy of Joseph Pulitzer, however, we can safely say the money for the pedestal was indeed raised "by the people," saving the Statue of Liberty from the ignoble distinction of becoming a gift from the millionaires of France to the millionaires of the United States. Pulitzer was frustrated when, in 1885, the statue arrived in America but could not be erected because the pedestal hadn't been finished due to a lack of funds. He decided to restart the American side of the fundraising campaign to inspire the pedestal committee to finish the work. The promotion Pulitzer organized through his newspaper, the *World,* brought in contributions from thousands of people across the country, averaging less than one dollar each.

Bartholdi, Lafayette, and the Torch Arm

As the United States prepared to celebrate its one hundredth birthday in 1876, the new republican French government commissioned Bartholdi to create a statue of the Marquis de Lafayette as a gift from France to the United States. This normal-size statue showing a nineteen-year-old Lafayette eager to distinguish himself in Washington's army still stands today in Union Square Park in New York. It was officially dedicated with great fanfare, including Bartholdi in attendance during his second trip to the United States. Bartholdi was creating his Lafayette statue at the same time as he also began the foundry work on the Statue of Liberty at Gaget, Gauthier, and Company in Paris. Amazingly, this work on Liberty began despite missing two key ingredients: there was still nowhere near enough money to pay for it, and even more surprisingly, there was still no final engineering plan for how to safely construct it.

On his second trip to the United States, Bartholdi traveled officially as a member of the French jury for the world expo in Philadelphia. He was much better known this time around, and he was honored, as a distinguished visitor, with several awards and feted by the New York chapter of the Franco-American Union. He would also oversee the unveiling of his statue *Lafayette Arriving in America,* and, before returning to

Figure 5.4. The torch and arm almost didn't make it in time for the centennial celebration in the United States, arriving just before the closing of the Philadelphia World Expo in 1876, where it was an immediate success.

Paris, he would meet the woman to whom he would later get married. We talk more about his future wife, Jeanne-Emilie, in chapter 9, when we speculate further about who might have been the model for the Statue of Liberty (figure 9.7, p. 259).

The goal had been for the statue's completed right arm holding the torch to be shipped to join Bartholdi at the Philadelphia World Expo in time for the Fourth of July celebration, and several letters Bartholdi wrote home show his frustration over the delays. He was growing faint from the July heat and weary of the endless parades, and he wrote his mother that he would "receive my wretched arm only on August 1st."[26]

The thirty-foot arm and torch would actually not arrive in Philadelphia until September, just in time, prior to the closing of the expo. As a novelty, it was to be illuminated by electricity,[27] and visitors lined up to pay fifty cents each to climb to the top of it, where ten people at a time could fit around the balcony.

A giant painting of the conceptualized finished statue was put on display in New York, and photographs of the painting were carried in newspapers across the country, allowing the Statue of Liberty's image to seep into the American psyche a good ten years before she was anything

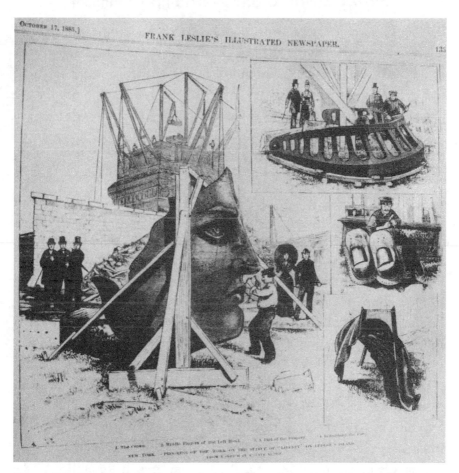

Figure 5.5. The illustrated press helped spread the popularity of the Statue of Liberty long before it was completed, as evinced in this illustration from *Frank Leslie's Illustrated Newspaper*, October 1885, courtesy of the National Park Service.

more than just an arm, a torch, and an idea. The newfangled illustrated newspapers like *Harper's Weekly* and *Frank Leslie's Illustrated Newspaper* disseminated the image of the Statue of Liberty across America to people who would never see her in person. From the beginning, the American people responded to her on a personal level, seeing in this female form of Liberty what they most wanted America to resemble.

Congress's Begrudging Approval Slowly Builds to an Overriding Optimism

Back in Paris in 1877, it's surprising that Bartholdi and Laboulaye were not more discouraged over the lack of substantial support coming from the United States. Some editorialists in the United States lambasted the idea of accepting a gift that came with requirements to pay for the pedestal and permanent upkeep. Cynical politicians compared it to the Trojan horse and suggested that only New Yorkers should be required to pay for it rather than all taxpayers, since only New Yorkers would appreciate it. As a whole, the United States was entirely too focused on its own concerns, such as the tangle of westward expansion, fighting the Indians, speculating on railroads and commerce, and the simmering labor disputes, for any enthusiastic support to rally behind an expensive venture proposed by a group of foreigners. The dedicated group of Franco-Americans backing the campaign in the United States managed to push through congressional approval to take over the old military fort on Bedloe's Island, in the form of a congressional joint resolution of 1877, but the public was by no means fully onboard as of yet.

The crowned head of the Statue of Liberty was ready for public display in time for the Paris World Expo of 1878 and traveled by open cart through the streets of Paris from the foundry to the Universal Exposition, past cheering throngs of Parisians. What they shouted when they saw her emphasizes the point that she was modeled upon the images of *La Republique* for the Second French Republic. As she passed them in the streets on the way to the expo, they gathered to hail her, shouting *"Vive la Republique!"*[28] Bartholdi and Laboulaye's Lady Liberty is hardly a symbolic Libertas, after all. She has none of the traditional symbols to identify her as Libertas: there is no cap, no staff, and the broken chain has almost disappeared under her foot. It might have been more accurate to call her *La Republique Éclairant le Monde*. The French people certainly thought so.

Fancy Fundraisers, Eiffel Secures Liberty, Thousands of Measurements

Seemingly impervious to the doubt and ridicule coming from the United States, Laboulaye and company pushed ahead with construction and a steady stream of fundraising events, public spectacles, and unveilings. The Statue of Liberty was created piecemeal in sections, and at the many galas celebrating every landmark of completion, the statue committee would take the opportunity to speechify. The speeches extolled the friendship between France and America, but there was always the underlying promotion of French national unity. There were lotteries, banquets, and even a cantata composed in her honor. In 1882, Bartholdi hosted select guests, including several journalists, for a fancy dinner party inside the newly completed knee of the statue. The elegant dishes were hoisted up by pulleys about four stories high to a platform inside.[29]

In chapter 13 we review the fortuitous addition of Gustave Eiffel to the team in 1880, when the original engineer designing the interior support structure suddenly passed away. Eiffel scrapped the initial plan, which probably would not have worked anyway, and designed what could be described as a miniature, crooked Eiffel Tower in the center of the hollow statue, upon which molded sheets of copper would hang. The molded copper sheets were hammered into place over wooden molds, and the entire process was repeated over and over again, as Bartholdi enlarged the statue three times in wood and plaster. Each time the whole was divided into sections requiring more than nine thousand measurements per section to ensure that they would fit proportionately together. From the middle of downtown Paris, as Lady Liberty gradually rose to tower over the city, she gave the impression of a giant new idea rising up out of the old guard. This was exactly Laboulaye's goal: to create a symbol that would both link his fellow Frenchmen to the

Figure 5.6. The Statue of Liberty was originally constructed in downtown Paris and made an imposing sight towering above the city skyline. This engraving listing the foundry of Gaget, Gauthier, and Company, where she was constructed, also shows cross sections of the statue, revealing the iron trusswork tower inside. Photo: Manhhai.

nobility of past ideals while also inspiring faith in the new republican ideals for the future.

The Statue Becomes La Américaine

The statue was finished in Paris in time for an official gift-giving ceremony on the Fourth of July, 1884, with the U.S. ambassador to France as the top dignitary present to receive it on behalf of the United States. It then stood in pause mode for almost a year as its builders waited to hear from the American fundraising committees about progress on the pedestal. Construction on the pedestal, which is almost as tall as the statue itself, had begun in 1884, but ground to a complete halt later that year when funds ran out. Finally in 1885 the statue was disassembled and packed into 214 crates and shipped to New York, where the crates would sit, exposed to the sun and rain, neglected and unpacked for months, near the stump of the unfinished pedestal.

This last indignity is what inspired Joseph Pulitzer to launch his final campaign to raise the pedestal funds, as previously mentioned. Pulitzer used this opportunity to poke fun at the wealthy New York politicians who could, each of them individually, as Pulitzer put it, for the price of one opera singer or ballet dancer, donate the remaining funds needed.

Bartholdi made one more worried trip to New York in 1885 to inspect construction on the pedestal and to be sure his instructions were followed in reassembling the statue. Fortunately for his peace of mind, he left before workers finally started unpacking the crates. As they did so, they found that some pieces were labeled incorrectly or the numbers were rubbed off, and they had to sometimes guess which ones went where.[30] In Paris, construction workers had used a scaffolding surrounding the entire statue, but in New York, with the pedestal underneath preventing a scaffolding, the workers hung from points above on the armature and then crawled around outside like ants. Sometimes they would hoist a section to the top, only to discover it was the wrong one. Amazingly, there were no casualties.[31]

Lady Liberty Inspired the First Ticker Tape Parade

The official inauguration date for the Statue of Liberty was supposed to be July 4, 1886, but more construction delays pushed it back to a rainy day in October. Despite the weather, the excitement of "Bartholdi Day" prompted the first spontaneous throwing of ticker tape out of office windows as the parade marched down Wall Street toward the harbor. Despite all the negativism in the United States in the years preceding this event, on October 26, 1886, Bartholdi's true-believer optimism and salesmanship were infectious. On that day there was agreement between rich and poor, black and white, immigrant and capitalist, all appreciating the higher beauty, and the higher ideal of liberty that this artwork only attempted to imitate. The overpowering love of freedom animated all.

This unblemished rapture faded quickly, however, and in 1893, Bartholdi made his final trip to the United States, concerned about reports that the lighting for the statue was inadequate and that it was already falling into disrepair. In fact, during its first twenty years, the statue *was* neglected, in part because it represented the end of an art form that had started to feel old-fashioned almost as soon as it was unveiled, especially in the rapidly modernizing new century. In 1901, President Theodore Roosevelt, whose father had been one of Lady Liberty's earliest supporters and a founding member of the Franco-American committee in New York, made the important decision to give up on turning the Statue of Liberty into a lighthouse. Roosevelt transferred authority for the statue's upkeep to the War Department, where it stayed until President Franklin Roosevelt transferred it to the National Park Service in 1933.

The original congressional approval to accept the statue had been obtained only because the committee promised that she would be a practical, functioning lighthouse rather than simply decorative art. For years, the engineers in charge tried very hard to make that impractical promise work. Steam-engine turbines were used first to generate electricity, but they required the ironic and expensive importation of freshwater to the island every day. Despite all the many ideas tried, including slicing large windows into the torch to allow more light to pass through, no one could ever get more than a glow to emit from the lady. In 1916, Woodrow Wilson celebrated her thirtieth anniversary during his campaign for reelection with the slogan Let There Be Light. This kicked off a nationwide fundraising campaign and substantial renovations that finally provided the kind of floodlighting that Bartholdi had wanted all along.

Liberty Becomes the Mother of Exiles and an American Icon: 1890–1986

The selection of the neighboring Ellis Island in 1890 as the new site for the processing of immigrants ensured a steady stream of millions of weary and tempest-tossed travelers over the next thirty years seeing the Statue of Liberty as their first impression of new hope. Neither Bartholdi, Laboulaye, nor Emma Lazarus, who wrote the poem "The New Colossus," were aware that Ellis Island would give the Statue of Liberty this permanent new identity. The Statue of Liberty as a mother welcoming all comers with unconditional love has firmly entered American mythological folklore, even though the truth is that U.S. immigration policies have been anything but welcoming at times, following the changing tides of economic and political ideologies of any given moment (figure 5.7, p. 138). The 1882 exclusion of Chinese immigrants was the first blatantly biased immigration law, but many more would follow after that "golden door" began to close in 1921. At the beginning of the twentieth century, quotas were imposed to restrict immigrants from "undesirable" countries in an attempt "to preserve the ideal of American homogeneity."[32] The mythic identity of the Statue of Liberty as welcoming any and all "huddled masses yearning to breathe free" has proved much more durable than the truth.

Another contributor to Lady Liberty's mythic identity is the commercial exploitation that has hounded the Statue of Liberty down through the years. The corporate-logo festooned spectacle that was her one hundredth birthday, celebrated on the Fourth of July, 1986, with Presidents Reagan and Mitterand presiding, was right in line with the way she's been an easy prop for admen all along. Coordinated by Chrysler CEO Lee Iacocca, fundraising for her renovation and repairs proceeded at a firecracker pace. Following in the footsteps of Joseph Pulitzer, appeals were made to schoolchildren and Boy Scouts. Just as in the original construction, some of the fundraising came from the general public, and some from the elite, who paid for corporate sponsorship opportunities and high-priced entry tickets to the final events. Official corporate sponsors included Nestlé, Oscar Mayer, Coca-Cola, and Chrysler, who all paid handsomely for the right to tie their product to the Statue of Liberty's official image in their advertising and packaging. Commercial as it was, the project was a success, though not without its own set of scandals and embarrassing firings.

Figure 5.7. This editorial cartoon published in 1892 in the *New York Evening Telegram* shows that the Statue of Liberty was not identified as a welcomer of immigrants until many years later. By 1890 anti-immigration activism was spreading as the rising flood of millions of new people crowding the cities spread disease and unsanitary conditions. National Park Service.

The New Torch Sparked a New Reputation

One of the most lasting outcomes of the 1986 renovation was the complete replacement of the original torch, metaphorically enabling Liberty's light to once again shine as the conscience of the nation. The original flame on the torch had suffered considerable abuse over several attempts to get more light out of it, and the patchworked relic can be seen today in the museum housed inside the pedestal of the Statue of Liberty. The original flame was replaced with a new flame gilded in gold leaf and lit at night with floodlights, something Bartholdi had suggested as far back as 1893.

Another positive outcome of the renovation and advertising hype of 1986 was a new sense of sincerity and refinement granted to the old gal. Her reputation as an icon had suffered in the iconoclastic 1960s and 1970s during the civil unrest that tended to mock all symbols of the traditional past. Satirizing the lady in the American press had been common in the statue's earliest days, especially when the project was still just an idea and it took so long to get that pedestal built. But after the Statue of Liberty was featured in propaganda posters to raise money for World War I Liberty bonds, her image remained nearly sacrosanct for decades. Artists of the 1960s challenged everything, and those upset with the imperialistic choices our nation's leaders were making started depicting her in the most compromising of positions. The spit and polish job for her one hundredth birthday party in 1986 allowed her another chance to shine through the layers of pollution that had collected over her. The red, white, and blue fervor stirred up by her facelift, complete with hundreds of tall ships in the harbor and a fabulous show of fireworks, reaffirmed patriotism as only Ronald Reagan could do.

Liberty Means Something Different to Everyone

Her creators called her *Liberty Enlightening the World* and said they hoped she would inspire what they considered the American ideal of liberty to spread throughout the world. Laboulaye predicted in 1876 that a hundred years hence, at the bicentennial celebration, "we shall

Figure 5.8. The Statue of Liberty has inspired replicas and imitations all over the world. One of the most moving was the thirty-three-foot-tall papier-mâché model erected by student protestors in Tiananmen Square in 1989. The Chinese students called her the "Goddess of Democracy," and although the tanks rolled over her a few days later, she has been re-created in several reproductions around the world, including this bronze memorial in Washington, D.C. Photo: James Wasserman.

then be only forgotten dust . . . but this statue will remain. It will be the memorial of this festival, the visible proof of our affection."[33] Hundreds of committees creating replica statues of Liberty around the world have worked through the same kinds of challenges that faced Bartholdi and Laboulaye with the original—obtaining cooperation of state and local authorities and raising money through fundraisers—because they believed in the inspirational power of this image. Clones of *Liberty Enlightening the World* have inspired a belief in the higher nature of humankind in Argentina, Australia, Austria, Brazil, China, Ecuador, France, Germany, India, Ireland, Israel, Japan, Malaysia, Kosovo, Mexico, Norway, Pakistan, Peru, the Philippines, Singapore, Spain, Taiwan, Ukraine, the United Kingdom, and Vietnam. The Boy Scouts of the 1950s made sure that at least one replica of the Statue of Liberty was in every state of the Union. The people of France have several, too, including the most famous reproduction, which is just down the Seine from the Eiffel Tower.

As Americans we have grown up knowing her as the Statue *of* Liberty, as the embodiment of our national ideal of liberty. The original French, on the other hand, saw her as Liberty *doing* something, and gave her a name that emphasizes the action of enlightening. Considering her original title, *Liberty Enlightening the World,* we can see that she is actively lifting her torch as she strides forward with rays actively emanating from her crown. She takes these actions not just for America, but for the whole world. The interpretations of both titles leave out the materialistic goals of some of her biggest cheerleaders, as well as mask the truth of unequal distribution of liberty, but this gloss should not have a lasting effect on the archetypal message that her colossal form contains. And that message is: action is required. Taking action to be educated and enlightened are the keys to maintaining a republican society where all can be considered equal under the law.

6

Behind the Statue of Liberty Is Her Earth-Mother Indian Queen

Hollywood has made a star out of the Statue of Liberty, and mostly by showing epic scenes of her destruction. The penchant for imagining her demise dates back to nineteenth-century cartoons in publications such as *Puck* and *Judge* where she was merciless lampooned in editorials showing her broken, falling over, aged, and decayed. Today she's a convenient prop in big-budget disaster movies because she has such an immediate connection with the viewer. Seeing something happen to her is felt as if it were happening to the collective "us." When we see her half-submerged in ice in *The Day After Tomorrow,* for example, or flooded over in the film *A.I. Artificial Intelligence,* or decapitated by a tsunami in *Deep Impact,* or buried in sand in the iconic *Planet of the Apes,* we are reminded that we all live together on one planet. She is transformed from a symbol for America into a symbol for Earth People.

We are focusing on the environment in this chapter because of what we learned when we investigated one of the Statue of Liberty's ancestors known as the Indian Queen. The Indian Queen was the earliest allegorical female used by the Europeans to represent America; indeed, she was generally referred to simply as "America." When we are not referring to her as the Indian Queen in this chapter, however, we will refer to her as Lady America, in order to distinguish between the land and the lady. From the 1500s on, her image adorned many of the maps and travel literature of the day. Full-bodied, mostly naked, and intimidating, the Indian Queen was an artist's invention from the European age of conquest intended to depict the bounty and mystique of the Americas.

As such, she provides an access point by which to review the relationship between the United States and the Native Americans from the perspective of both the environment and the image of the female in art. It also leads to contemporary connections between women and the environment, where we found women all over the world taking the lead in creating sustainable environmental policies in response to the coming environmental upheaval. This trend makes sense as women in developing countries, together with the Indigenous cultures worldwide, are the first people being affected in a personal way by climate change right now.

Seeing the resemblance between the Indian Queen and a form of the Earth Mother, we looked into the field of study known as eco-feminism, which allowed us to consider the Indian Queen on a whole new level: as playing right into the erotic imagery and metaphor of the land that paved the way for the domination paradigm later to consume this continent. The Indian Queen was used to describe the New World as a woman, and as both virginal and ripely sexual: whatever worked to invite sexual conquest. In this way, images of the Indian Queen helped set the stage for centuries of Euro-American domination of both the land and of women.

The Statue of Liberty and Native Americans

To fully appreciate the Statue of Liberty as a symbol of the United States of America, we need to acknowledge that the Americas were populated by distinct nations and civilizations before any Europeans landed. Both the history and the present of the Indigenous people belong in our collective future. The Indian Queen's complete lack of ethnic verisimilitude led us to examine real Native Americans, and in particular, their tradition of viewing the Earth in female terms. Native Americans see female spirits throughout nature, from their creation stories to the food they eat. In addition, their reverence for women has led to an entirely

Figure 6.1. A baroque version of the Indian Queen shows her astride an alligator with a cornucopia in the foreground. Detail from a fresco mural *Apollo and the Continents* by Giovanni Battista Tiepolo in the Würzburg Residence palace in Germany, dated 1752–1753.

different relationship with the land in comparison to the domination-warrior pattern of the Europeans. Rather than as a maiden to be subdued, Native Americans see the Earth as a mother to be honored.

We will look at how the history of contemporary Native Americans can teach us a lot about surviving climate change. Despite many attempts to exterminate their entire lineage, the Native Americans are still here. They are a most resilient people. They are not a people of the past; they are a living people with real contemporary problems and goals,[1] and finally their numbers are beginning to rise. They have survived forced migrations and adaptations to different and harsh environmental and climate conditions, microbial genocide, and, in the modern era, environmental colonialism. Sadly, their particular environmental health concerns will soon be global health concerns, as the pollution damage that is currently disproportionately impacting the outlying reservations continues to spread worldwide to impact us all.

Indigenous cultures that live in relationship with the Earth also tend to accept death as an inevitable and ceremonial part of life, compared to the irrational fear of death prevailing among those of us raised in the Abrahamic religions. Learning to live in relationship with the Earth and seeing her as a mother could help many of us to prepare for our own peaceful transition. If the climate has already passed the tipping point toward complete upheaval, then the inner work of preparing to face death is just as important as the outer work of being activists for political change and weaning our energy system off fossil fuels.

We suggest the Statue of Liberty as a new inspirational symbol to focus the attention of Americans on the environment. Long before the Revolutionary War, in the decade or so before any action was taken, the symbols of Lady Liberty and the Indian Princess helped inspire the crucial revolution in the mind—that hard to define, slow-growing change of one person at a time that gradually becomes a shift in public opinion. Maybe today Lady Liberty and the Indian Queen can help inspire us to a new revolution in the mind: one that changes our current societal belief that we have the right, or some would say the liberty, to dominate the land. Globally, right now, the responsibility to change that dominator belief weighs most heavily on the conscience of Americans, and that's because of a thing called thermal inertia, which we will discuss further at the end of this chapter. Basically, thermal inertia is about lag time. As we learned from professor of communication and Native American studies Bruce Johansen, the superstorms and increasing heat that we are experiencing on the Earth right now, today, are the result of the excess carbon dioxide and other emissions pumped into the air *in the 1960s*—and the majority of that came from the United States. Because today we are only pumping out more emissions than before, it is guaranteed that our grandchildren, fifty years from now, will be dealing with even greater climate calamities.

The Psychological Implications of Growing Up Believing the Earth Is Our Mother

"People seem to innately understand who mother is," says Bruce Johansen. Psychiatrist and activist Jean Shinoda Bolen put it this way:

Figure 6.2. *Mother Earth* by John Kahionhes Fadden. A Native woman with flowers, cattails, and strawberries in her hair, and holding soil, with growing corn in her cupped hands. Fadden says, "The Earth, among traditional Haudenosaunee/Iroquois and other Native nations, has the persona of a female, as does the moon." Photo: John Kahionhes Fadden.

"The Great Mother is a part of the bedrock of the psyche." Even in the patriarchal Greek mythology, first there was Chaos and then there was Gaia, the Earth. "Whether you're looking at Mongolia, or the Greeks, or the Incas," said anthropologist Jack Weatherford, "they associate the bounty of the Earth with a female mother who gives this bounty to her children."

Among some of the dialects of the Anishnaabeg of northern America, the word for "woman," translated literally, is "an Earth that walks," as history and comparative religion professor Jordan Paper told us. Different ecological situations created different religious traditions in the Americas, but they share in common an active relationship with their deities or spirits that are all around them in nature. The Anishnaabeg do not need to go to a special cathedral or temple to worship; they are in a worshipful state just walking through the woods. "When we speak of the Earth Mother it is literally the Earth," says Paper. "It's understanding the world itself as sacred—every aspect of it."

Female figurines and cave art in the shape of women have been found all over the Americas, similar to those found in Old Europe. In the Americas archaeologists have uncovered female images carved out of bone and tusk in the north, and fashioned out of gold and silver in the south. Christopher Columbus reported seeing female figurines on his very first voyages, saying they were identified by the Natives as the female spirit of the cassava plant.[2] Female spirits and ancestors are generally related to a local subsistence food source and have names like Corn Mother, Potato Mother, Buffalo Woman, and so on. The Coca Mama is sacred to the Andes region, where the coca leaf is chewed throughout the day to alleviate the rigors of high-altitude living.

Introducing the Indian Queen

The Statue of Liberty does not resemble an Earth Mother in any traditional way, but her ancestor, that voluptuous Indian Queen, certainly does. Regardless of the reverence for Earth as a mother among Native Americans, however, the European artists designing the first female allegory to stand for America were not likely trying to make this connection when they created the Indian Queen. Nor does the nickname of Indian Queen have any resemblance to living Native American women. Calling her Indian simply repeats Columbus's error, but as we noted earlier, there was nothing remotely resembling a monarchy in the Americas, so calling her a queen is also completely inaccurate. The powerful women encountered by the first Europeans were assumed to be queens, blind as the Europeans were to the elevated status of women overall among the Native North Americans. While we can appreciate the Indian Queen for her strength of character and enjoy this whimsical disorientation, the greatest relevance we found was how she led us to a new appreciation of the contemporary Native women of the Americas.

Maps are the earliest places where the Indian Queen appears in print as a representation of the New World. She is usually depicted in a tropical setting surrounded by parrots, palm trees, and the exotic and newly discovered animals reported by the explorers working their way across South America. Her feathered headdress and adornments match the early descriptions of the Tupinambá of Brazil,[3] but her facial features are decidedly European. Flemish engraver and publisher Theodor de Bry became famous at the end of the 1500s for his travel books about the Americas, though he never traveled there himself. De Bry based his publications on the accounts of explorers of present-day Virginia and northern Florida, and made liberal changes both to the text and illustrations. Like other publishers of similar material of the time, they exaggerated and interpreted in order to heighten appeal to the European audiences who devoured the travel literature as a form of erotica.[4]

European audiences couldn't get enough of this exotic woman who was both alluring and menacing at the same time. Improvements in mass printing helped spread the image of the Indian Queen, but the live performances and pageants in which she starred must have made a truly indelible impression on the illiterate. During the 1600s and 1700s, extravagant parades were common in cities throughout Europe where they were orchestrated for visiting nobility. During these pageants and tableaus real women were directed to act out the roles of allegories and virtues as if they were stepping out of paintings. Hundreds of musicians and floats would pass by costumed vignettes featuring a fierce Lady America carrying a bloody club, interacting with the other four corners of the world (figure 6.3). There was Asia with her beautiful silk robes, incense, and spices, and Africa, a dark-skinned, regal beauty with an elephant headdress. Always the most exalted was Europe, with rich robes and gems and surrounded by objects representing learning.

Still clearly depicting themselves as the most advanced and superior culture, Europeans had at least expanded their former concept of the tripartite world into what they now called "the four corners of the world." The allegorical four corners were called out to show how all the world paid homage to the honored guest.[5] They were also popularly painted as murals on church walls to show universal appeal, and they appeared on dining ware and tapestries in the homes of the wealthy as a sign of status. The allegorical female they added to this grouping for

Figure 6.3. The four corners of the world depicted as allegorical women was a popular motif appearing in tapestries, murals, fountains, porcelain, and live performances. This version is from the 1603 edition of *Iconologia* by Cesare Ripa, a book owned by many of the founders of the United States. Note the symbols of wealth for Europe in the top left, and how Asia, top right, and Africa, lower right, are more fully clothed, while America in the lower left is mostly naked.

the Americas resembles an Earth Mother in her nakedness and her display of fecundity and strength. That this combination of female power was threatening to Europeans is seen in Lady America's ever-present ax, club, or bow, and sometimes in the partially gnawed human limbs that surround her. Many of the engravings of the day featured cheery background scenes of mutilation and cannibalism, generally led by women, as if it were a common occurrence for the more hapless explorers to end up in their cooking pots.

The Indian Queen Says, "Come Up and See Me Sometime"

The other allegorical females standing for countries or continents were also sometimes depicted partially naked, but Lady America is the only one whose nakedness was a central identifying characteristic.[6] Comparing the land to a naked woman meant that both were under the control of male domination. "In a sense, to make the new continent Woman was already to civilize it a bit," said literary critic Annette Kolodny, "casting the stamp of human relations upon what was otherwise unknown and untamed."[7] The proliferation of prints of the Indian Queen effectively shaped our cultural understanding of both the Americas, and Native American women, for several centuries.

The continent was described in terms of opening her arms to welcome the Europeans, and sexual metaphors enticed more investors and more colonizers. Dozens of accounts from the late 1500s through the 1600s were collected by Kolodny in her book *The Lay of the Land,* where she shows that they alternate between describing the land as nurturing mother and enticing vixen. Walter Raleigh's *Discovery of Guiana* (1595) called it "a countrey that hath yet her maydenhead, never sackt." Robert Johnson's *Nova Britannia* (1609) claimed they were "ravisht with the . . . pleasant land" and the new continent as a "Paradise with all her Virgin Beauties." And John Smith's *Description of New England* (1616) described the land like a virgin, "her treasures hauing yet neuer beene opened."[8] From the earliest explorer texts through the era of westward expansion, the metaphor of sexual conquest was entangled with terrestrial conquest.

The descriptions of the New World as a paradise continued long after the colonists' reports of the harsh realities of survival were understood. Learning to adapt to life outside of European towns proved to be full of suffering for the colonists. Most of the Jamestown colonists of 1607, and more than half of the Pilgrims in New England in 1620, for example, would be dead before their first winter was over. Kolodny shows how the universal yearning for paradise, or at least for relief from the crushing poverty of so-called civilized Europe, was strong enough to override the reports of distress from the earliest settlers. Eroticized language and metaphor were continually renewed for the next several hundred years as the seemingly limitless frontier of the West reasserted these dreams of ravishing "empty" land until there was no more frontier left.[9]

The explorers' accounts read like promotional literature, as if to invite travelers to come to the land where sex was free and easy, as Indigenous history professor Joy Porter told us. Amerigo Vespucci's letters reported that Native women were "very desirous to copulate with us Christians."[10] One of our favorite engravings demonstrating this mingling of terrestrial and sexual conquest is Johannes Stradanus's *America* dated around 1575–1580 (figure 6.4, p. 152). In this scene, an overly clothed Amerigo Vespucci surprises a naked America from her slumber in a hammock. In front of the obligatory scenes of human limbs being munched on in the background, Vespucci clutches his scientific astrolabe and leers down at America. As Early American English professor Edward Gallagher described it, the male is about to dominate the female, Europe is about to dominate America, and science is about to dominate nature. "The desire to fornicate meshes with the duty to subjugate. America will be woo'd and subdued with the sword. Unlucky America."[11]

When we showed the Marten de Vos design of Lady America from about 1595 (figure 6.5, p. 153) to Professor Jordan Paper, an expert on both Asian and North American Indigenous peoples, he suggested it was an attempt to illustrate the European concept of an Amazon. The ax looks European, he thought, but the bow looks more East-Asian, "meaning the artist was apparently combining many cultures." The reason the biggest river in the world is named the Amazon is because explorers were always trying to relate their discoveries to something

Figure 6.4. *Amerigo Vespucci Awakens a Sleeping America* circa 1575–1580 by Johannes Stradanus, engraving by Theodor Galle. Notice the scenes of cannibalism in the background. National Gallery of Art.

from classical mythology like the Fountain of Youth, or Cities of Gold, hoping to outrank claims of other explorers and fund future trips. One of the earliest Spanish explorers reported back that he saw bands of fierce warrior women along the shores as he explored the mighty river in Brazil. Historian Max Dashú confirmed there were several legends from this region about the "Women-Living-Alone, the Women-Without-Husbands, or the Masterful-Women,"[12] but it was fear and misunderstanding of women's power in the Americas that inspired Europeans to call Indigenous women "Amazons." The distortion of the image of Indigenous women, as in the Indian Queen, was actually another manipulation of art in the service of empire building, says Dashú. This explains why the Indian Queen is often seen with her foot resting on a decapitated head. She's been used as propaganda from the beginning.

Figure 6.5. *America*, as engraved by Adriaen Collaert II circa 1595 after a design by Marten de Vos. The Indian Queen is riding an absurdly enormous armadillo, an animal indigenous to the Americas, apparently drawn by someone who had never seen an armadillo. In the background are scenes of fierce fighting, and on the left someone is roasting a human leg while another person prepares more legs for the meal.

The Naming of America

Because the Indian Queen is officially named America, we decided to look a little more closely at the origins of this word "America." You might think you know this one already: North and South America are supposedly named for one of Columbus's rival explorers, Amerigo Vespucci. Vespucci is traditionally given the honor, because he was alleg-edly the first European to realize that they were not exploring India or China, but rather a landmass previously unknown to Europe, or a "Novus Mundus" as he called it.

But did you ever wonder why they chose Vespucci's *first* name for the honor? Using the first name of an honoree for a place was reserved for monarchs, as in the state of Georgia being named for King George II, whereas the state of Washington was named for George Washington. According to this custom, we should be living in something like the United States of Vespuccia.

A compelling theory explaining this discrepancy is that the name America was already being used to identify the location, and that those who first used it in print linked it to Amerigo merely as a soundalike connection. The connection of the name to Vespucci first appeared in the *Cosmographiae Introductio,* a translation of the four voyages of Vespucci printed in 1507. The phrasing in the introduction can be interpreted as if the writer was already familiar with the name America and was trying to link it with Vespucci because they were publishing the travel journeys of Vespucci, and a big claim like that would help sales. Using the Latinized version of Vespucci's first name, the writer says, "I do not see what right any one would have to object to calling this part after Americus, who discovered it and who is a man of intelligence. . . ."[13]

If the name America was being used to identify the landmass before this publication, where did it come from? The theory popularized in the late 1800s by geologist Jules Marcou relates how Columbus and the early explorers reported on a mountain region and tribe in present-day Nicaragua called Amerrique. Marcou noted that Columbus mentions in his logs that the Carib Indians wearing gold indicated it came from the nearby Amerrique region. Explorer John Cabot drew a map in 1497 that included the name Amerrisque in the Nicaragua region.[14] If a location sounding like "America" was rumored to be a source of the gold they sought, then naturally the name would have spread by word of mouth among sailors returning to Europe.

Explanations for where the name came from don't stop there, however, and other theories include the English merchant Richard Amerike, who funded John Cabot's voyage in 1497, as well as Mayan, Viking, and

African words that sound similar. While as yet there is no way to prove these theories, we are partial to the idea that the name America has Native roots, as does so much else that developed into Euro-American culture.

The Indian Queen Ruled an Empty Paradisiacal Wilderness

When naming or describing this new land, Europeans were just as handy with the mythmaking. The English colonists' reports are full of surprise and delight at discovering landscapes that seemed preternaturally designed just for them to resemble English parks. They preferred the divine providence version of this explanation over acknowledging that they owed their survival to finding so many abandoned Indian villages with cultivated fields ready for planting nearby. The fiction that the land was a mostly unpopulated wilderness was crucial to the mission of the European conquest, as we learned from art historian Vivien Green Fryd. Romanticized concepts of the noble savage that turned into the Vanishing Indian allowed Euro-Americans to avoid addressing the reality of the Native people's lives.

Estimates vary widely on Native population before contact, but even the lowest estimates give a death toll due to disease as around 90 percent after the initial contact with the Spanish explorers.[*15] Early explorers like Giovanni Verrazzano, who explored the East Coast of North America in 1524, and Thomas Harriot, who was part of an exploration of present-day Virginia in 1585, described dense population centers up and down the coast.[16] They reported crowds of people, not the emptiness described by the Pilgrims upon arrival just a few decades later. Explorers in Harriot's time noticed that just days after their European

---

[*]"Population History of Indigenous Peoples of the Americas" at Wikipedia reports on one low estimate for South America of 37 million people in 1492 (including 6 million in the Aztec Empire, 8 million in the Mayan States, 11 million in what is now Brazil, and 12 million in the Inca Empire) reduced to 9 million in 1650. Estimates for North American populations range from 2.1 million to 18 million before contact, reduced to around 1 million.

expedition left a village, the Native people began to die mysteriously. Warfare, slavery, and massacres certainly played their part in the demise, but the overwhelming majority of the Native American population was killed by diseases inadvertently carried by the earliest explorers. It's debatable whether the European colonists would not have abandoned their plans to settle in North America—as the fearsome Vikings had done earlier—if they had arrived to face the full force of the Indian population defending their territory.

The Statue of Liberty and the Vanishing Indian

The Statue of Liberty was created over a time period immediately after the Civil War in 1865 through 1886, an era when the United States experienced enormous changes in attitude, social aspirations, expansion of the frontiers, and the development of the industrial complex. It was a time when the U.S. policy toward Indians grew increasingly violent, as did the U.S. policy toward land use in terms of the expansion of the frontier. One might even say that the U.S. policy of relating to the Indians paralleled the U.S. policy relating to land use. The Statue of Liberty's unveiling year of 1886 is the year that Geronimo surrendered, marking the end of the official U.S. military campaign against the American Indians in the Southwest. The completion of the cross-continental railroad in 1869 had led many to advocate a new, and more selfish, definition of American liberty, demanding the unlimited freedom to expand, to conquer the frontier, and, in effect, to ravish the virgin soil. All these ideas got tangled up in the beliefs about America's Manifest Destiny and were coming into being at the same time the Statue of Liberty was being born.

The attitude toward nature was also beginning to shift again by the time Auguste Bartholdi made his five-month sojourn through the states by rail in 1871. Bartholdi sent his mother early precursors of the tourist postcard from Vernal Falls and Mirror Lake in Yosemite, following the growing trend of describing the natural world as a tourist destination. Writing about the enormous beauty of California and describing a long and dusty stagecoach trip he endured just to see Sequoia Park,[17] Bartholdi was participating in a movement that led in 1890 to legislation that advocated for the preservation of large areas of land in the National Park system. Proponents like John Muir started writing about enshrining the wilderness and creating sanctuaries of protected lands as parks.

We learned a lot about these shifting concepts of wilderness as a place to be dominated or a place to be preserved from Joy Porter in her book *Land and Spirit*. Porter warns against the seductive notion of wilderness, saying she thinks it is "actually quite a dangerous concept." It is not beneficial to suggest "that land exists outside of man's historical relationships," she told us. For America's "natural cathedrals" to be made tourist destinations, first of all, American Indian peoples had to be dispossessed. Yosemite was a shockingly beautiful place when the Europeans first explored it, because Native Americans had cultivated it to be that way for thousands of years. Second, when industrialization's soulless and corrupt cities started making people sick, many turned to nature to seek a transcendent experience away from community.

Figure 6.6. Thomas Crawford's 1854 *Progress of Civilization* in the pediment over the entrance to the east side of the Capitol and the visitor center. This detail shows the action to the right of the allegorical America. She points to "progress" in the form of the frontiersman chopping at a tree stump, followed by a Native American child, and a woman next to a grave (obscured here)—with the Native American man in the classic Vanishing Indian pose. Author photo.

"Basically the wild becomes this crystallized version of what we haven't got, and if we haven't got peace of mind we look for it outside of civilization," said Porter.

The Euro-Americans told themselves a myth about westward expansion being part of their destiny, carved out of the savage wilderness by purehearted pioneers like Daniel Boone. Images of the ax, the tree stump, and the plow run rampant in the artwork of this time as the exploding population of Euro-Americans and new immigrants surged westward. The plow even appears in the state seals of New Jersey, Pennsylvania, and Maryland. These images of the tree stump, the frontiersman, and the Vanishing Indian all contributed to the nationwide dream version of history. In reality, however, the frontier expansion was fostered by land speculators much like the subprime mortgage flippers of today who started the recession. Banks held the mortgages, speculators flipped the properties, and greed pushed that "Westward Ho!" expansion.

Euro-Americans on the frontier either deliberately ignored or didn't see value in the evidence they encountered of sophisticated Native American communities. Instead, they wrote praises to the Creator for giving them what they believed was a beautifully preformed land that was created just for them. Ruins of cities indicating complex social structures and expansive trade routes crisscrossing the continent, like Cahokia near St. Louis, were dismantled for materials.

Part of the Euro-American blindness to Native American achievements lies in the Native Americans' ability to prosper in "symbiotic equilibrium" with the elements. Jack Weatherford details the Native Americans' mastery of the controlled burn, for example, used variously to keep wildfires at bay, enhance soil nutrient value, encourage the best tree growth, and assist in hunting and managing wildlife. Structured burns also allowed for the older trees to grow taller, which made them better suited for the Indians' canoes, and later allowed for the Europeans to launch a technological revolution in the shipping industry with ship masts taller and stronger than any found in Europe.[18] The amount of organized forest control going on by the Native Americans before contact with Europe is indicated by what happened when the human population on this continent declined by 90 percent after 1492. The trees grew back with such a vengeance that climate scientists today have pinpointed a correlation to Europe's Little Ice Age (mid-1500s to the early 1800s). When the people controlling the forests died, the massive new tree growth in the Americas consumed so much carbon dioxide that the ability of the atmosphere to trap heat was affected, and Europe grew colder.[19]

Native American sophistication in agricultural science is easier to see. Mohawk Douglas George-Kanentiio tells about the "Iroquois agriculturalists who were able to maintain the fertility of their farmlands and enhance crop yields over many years without using chemical additives."[20] The Native Americans did not view themselves as separate from or returning to nature as a place. Their cosmology provided them an inclusive, familial relationship with nature, a view that our Euro-American perspective has difficulty absorbing.

Earth and Female: Sacred or Evil?

Another blind spot preventing the Europeans from grasping Native American achievements was, as mentioned earlier, their inability to appreciate the female portion of divinity. The first European explorers came to the Americas having been raised to believe that there is only one God, and he was male. In their world, only men led religious services, so when they tried to interpret Native rituals and ceremonies, they ignored anything led by women as irrelevant. This belief caused them to discount or misinterpret not just half of the participants but also half the Native spirit world, which is female.[21] Missionaries reported primitive cultures with no religion at all, or when they acknowledged a religion they labeled it devil worship. Eventually Native religious ceremonies were declared illegal, meaning that continued adherence by the Indians to their spiritual customs was used as another excuse to justify imprisonment and cultural genocide.[22]

The gender equality among Native Americans is not always readily visible to Western eyes, even today. For example, the caves or huts where the women would sequester themselves for four days during their menstrual flow were identical to the huts used by the men for vision quests.[23] During these vision quests, Native Americans reaffirm their connection to the spirit realm, and as Professor Paper told us, the women would fast and have vision quests on a monthly basis regulated by their menstrual cycle. They were sequestered during menses because their spiritual power was believed so great at that time that it could overwhelm the hunting power of the males. When a girl had her first period, or menarche, she was considered somewhat dangerous, because she was deemed to be a woman coming into her power who had not yet learned to control it. When Indigenous women are asked why they don't participate in the elaborate dances and rituals designed for men to achieve power through connection to the Earth Mother, they say the women don't need to go to that much trouble because they already have power. From Paper's experience with fasting and vision questing among Native Americans, he has observed "that it is much easier for females, in general, than it is for males to enter trance. Males often need a lot more ritual preparation than females do. I've known females who need no rituals whatsoever to enter a functional trance."

By insisting there is only one deity, one sacred locus, and one sacred gender, monotheistic traditions cut out half of creation. Disregarding the complementary pair of Mother and Father creators working together, as is common in creation stories around the world, the result is opposition. "Sky becomes heaven, and the opposite of heaven is hell," said Jordan Paper. "Earth is not just desacralized. Earth is, and the female is, made to be evil."[24]

The ceremonies and creation stories of the Native Americans were inclusive of the female gender and continually reaffirmed and reinforced the powerful identity that Native American women enjoyed. Their menstruation rituals were misinterpreted by Europeans, of course, based on Judeo-Christian standards. Judeo-Christians also required the sequestration of women during their menstrual flow, but not out of respect for the life-affirming power of women. Euro-American upbringing taught that menses made a woman unclean, and the community needed to be protected from her defilement.[25]

Women's Action Essential
for the Environment

Numerous studies by groups like the World Health Organization have determined that Indigenous women and women in developing countries are more in tune with the changes in nature and climate than men are. Women are also the first to be adversely impacted by human-induced weather changes. The majority of food farmers in the developing world are women, and women are almost exclusively the primary water carriers.

Figure 6.7. *Corn Woman* by John Kahionhes Fadden. "The sustainers, the Three Sisters, corn, beans, and squash, have a female identity. All living things come from a female, a mother, and all things in our immediate surroundings come from the Earth Mother, the trees, grasses, animals, birds, the works," says Fadden. Photo: John Kahionhes Fadden.

In drought-prone areas where hotter temperatures are drying up water sources, some women walk eight to ten hours a day for their family's water supply.[26] Of the developing nations, the World Bank noted that "women play an essential role in the management of natural resources, including soil, water, forests and energy . . . and often have a profound traditional and contemporary knowledge of the natural world around them."[27]

International welfare agencies have recognized that putting women in charge of environmental decisions or giving them control over their own property, as is happening in the poorest areas of India, leads to more sustainable solutions. Banks in Indonesia began implementing the innovation known as the micro-loan, which is a small amount of money intended to buy something like a sewing machine or a goat that is capable of generating income for a family. Jean Shinoda Bolen reported to us that in the beginning these micro-loans were given out equally to men and women, until the different ways that the loans were applied and repaid were observed. Men tended to buy things to improve their social status, whereas women bought the sewing machines or the goats and then paid the loans back. Today, she tells us, more than 95 percent of micro-loans go to women, and further, small circles of women are now used as a form of collateral, insomuch as they keep each other responsible for paying back the loan. When one woman repays her loan, the next one is eligible, an example of how in different ways around the world, women form circles, knowing that together they create a larger effect.

Caring for women and girls is intertwined with caring for the environment, said Native American activist Winona LaDuke when she presented an appeal on behalf of Indigenous women around the world. Addressing the United Nations, LaDuke emphasized responsibility, saying that, in her Anishnaabeg tradition, women are "the manifestation of Mother Earth in human form."[28] Native American women are calling on other women to challenge historical precedents, to reclaim and "ultimately be in charge of our own destinies, our own self-determination, and the future of our Earth, our Mother."[29] It's not that women are better than men, but that when partnered equally with men, humanity moves forward faster.

Women in power could save the environment. This statement might seem simplistic, yes, but that's what is borne out by statistical studies. Female members of the U.S. Congress, overall and regardless of party, vote in favor of environmental protections more often than their male peers. This is according to a 2010 study titled "When Women Lead" from Rachel's Network, a philanthropy group advocating environmental stewardship and women's leadership.[30] Supporting organizations that support women has the furthest reach in creating social change, because when women are supported, the conditions improve for everyone—in terms of poverty, the environment, and social justice.

Pachamama at the UN

LaDuke demanded, What gives international corporations the right to override the Indigenous people's ancient responsibilities to the Earth? Decisions about land use are not being made by the people who are affected by those decisions, because corporate money is currently assigned the highest power on Earth. "What law gives that right to them?" she rails. Corporate money is "historically acquired immorally, unethically, through colonialism, imperialism, and paid for with the lives of millions of people, or species of plants and entire ecosystems." What gives this money the right to overrule the self-determination of future generations? Certainly not the law of Mother Earth.

As an entity, Mother Earth herself is gaining some political authority in South American countries with high populations of Indigenous people. Some of these countries are exploring innovative attempts to free their natural resources from international corporate control. In Ecuador, where 40 percent of the population is Indigenous, a Constitutional amendment was drafted giving legal rights to Pachamama, the spirit of the Inca who represents a World Mother or Mother Earth. The Pachamama amendment gives people the authority to petition on behalf of the Earth by recognizing her right to a healthy future.

In Bolivia, where 62 percent of the population is Indigenous, they called on their ancestral obligations to protect Pachamama and drafted a petition to the United Nations titled the Law of the Rights of Mother Earth. In the Amazon, the Pachamama Alliance was formed to create sustainability and protect the Indigenous people and their way of life. Women and the Indigenous and the poor are not only more vulnerable to climate change but are also more valuable in finding solutions to it. As the ones most immediately affected by climate change and environmental abuse, their ideas and solutions for change may hold the key to humanity's survival on this planet.

Relationship, Reverence, and Reciprocity

Like most Euro-Americans today, we grew up with a romantic notion of Native Americans as a noble but doomed people. Learning today how they prospered in complex cities dating back to the Middle Ages, and mastered cross-continental trade and travel, is thrilling, and provides an exquisite realization of what was lost through our mythologized version of history. Jack Weatherford's anthropological work gives us a new appreciation for how much of what we take for granted today, around the world, was first cultivated by the Native Americans. If we tried to summarize all these discoveries here, it would turn into a really long list, so instead we say go read Weatherford's books, *Indian Givers* and *Native Roots,* where he details these contributions in a lively narrative and makes the people responsible for them come alive. Weatherford takes care to reveal how each of his subjects is relevant to today's living Native cultures before discussing how they influenced the world in the past. One chapter has him surrounded by rifle-toting rebels in Central America, and the next having an epiphany on Machu Picchu as he tours the modern Peruvian agricultural station where the scientists are attempting to replicate the sophisticated agricultural techniques of their Inca ancestors.

We do not suggest that the Native Americans' intimate regard for the Earth can simply be adopted into a Western paradigm, but with effort, we could create a new paradigm to include the sustainable approaches of both cultures. The sense of reciprocity and relationship with the Earth is an essential missing element that the Indigenous people mastered and that Euro-Americans have a hard time grasping.

Meanwhile, we can individually work on integrating into our consciousness the sense of belonging to the Earth.

The planet "is a living, conscious entity," Kanentiio emphasized, "a
being in her own way. There is no separation between humans and the

Figure 6.8. *America* in the transitional stage between Indian Queen and
Indian Princess, printed in England in 1771. She's tamer and fairer now, but
she's still accompanied by an alligator and tropical foliage. Title page of *A
Collection of Plans of the Capital Cities of Europe, and Some Remarkable
Cities in Asia, Africa, & America*, John Andrews, London. Library of Congress.

planet on which we walk." According to Indigenous tradition, humans are in a relationship with the Earth that could dissolve at any time if one doesn't maintain their side of the bargain. "It is a dynamic relationship," said Jordan Paper. "We're given certain freedoms," said Kanentiio, "but with that come certain obligations," and one of these is to show reverence and thanks for the gifts of bounty from their mother the Earth. According to Kanentiio, the Iroquois, or Haudenosaunee, don't see current conditions as climate *change,* but more like "climatic revolt."

Ceremonial Reciprocity and Playing Indian

Generation after generation, the Native Americans have maintained a conscious relationship with the Earth through endless ceremonies of thanksgiving arranged to keep them mindful of their custodial position. "Everything we do," said Oneida Joanne Shenandoah, "from planting, to birthing, to sending someone on their journey to the spirit world, has to do with song and celebration." Kanentiio added, "The Haudenosaunee believe the Earth contains all the things necessary to live in peace and happiness so long as humans adhere to the laws of nature. Our elaborate ceremonies are meant to remind us of our obligations . . . and to respect all living things."[31] Reciprocity and offering gifts like tobacco to the Earth in frequent ceremonies keep them mindful of the gifts the Earth spirits give to them. Revolt follows from "human beings taking her gifts without adequate thought and gratitude," he said.

Some environmentally minded Americans, after waking up to how damaging our consumer lifestyle is on the environment, decide to "turn Indian" and return to the land. This new age trend is fueled by a romantic version of a Native American utopia where weekend shamanic workshops provide a way to suppress cultural guilt while completely ignoring the needs of contemporary, real Indians. If we are to learn anything from the Native American ways, we as the Euro-American culture first need to repair our relationship with Native Americans, and that starts by recognizing they are still a relevant and living part of us. The colonial imperialism of our ancestors continues to shape how we relate to Native Americans today, making them understandably hesitant to accept the requests for collaboration from non-Native activists and environmentalists. In all previous exchanges of information over the centuries, the Indians have been strip-mined, literally and culturally. Learning to live like an Indian today means learning to address the issues that plague contemporary Native American society. These issues include alcohol and drug addiction, suicide, poverty, and endless legal battles over sovereignty and land use.[32] We must be careful not to follow the historical domination pattern that exists between our cultures and our tendency to see something we like about Native American ways, and just snatch it. We must learn to respect the humans behind the Native culture and be careful to address their problems for lasting, constructive effect.

Bruce Johansen has been our guide on this subject, much as when he tutored us years ago on his and Don Grinde's vanguard scholarship regarding the influence of the League of the Iroquois on the founders when shaping the U.S. government. Johansen is a highly motivated and prolific academic who has also published widely on the science of global warming, with a special emphasis on how climate change and pollution are affecting Native people. Johansen showed us how Native people living in the Arctic are predicting how climate change will impact the rest of the world in the near future: rising temperatures are forcing them to adapt ancient ways and relocate entire villages.

Her Body Is a Proving Ground

Native American women are the least understood and most repressed subset of people in the United States today, thanks in part to the cultural misunderstandings of Native women we inherited from our founders, as well as deliberate misrepresentations like the Indian Queen. When the Native Americans were pushed into the reservation system and relocated to the least desirable lands, where their former ways of subsistence hunting and fishing were no longer feasible, many ended up joining the wage economy of the Euro-Americans. They assimilated into the patriarchal hierarchical culture, much to the detriment of the elevated role of women in their society. Industrialization of the Western world then surrounded the reservations and polluted their air and water, resulting in incommensurate numbers of cancer and other degenerative diseases among Indians,[33] particularly among women. Inuit women of the Hudson Bay region have the "highest levels of breast milk contamination in the world," reports Winona LaDuke, with heavy metals and PCBs at "contamination levels up to 28 times higher than the average of women in Quebec, and ten times higher than that considered 'safe' by the government."[34] Penobscot women of the upper Great Lakes near the paper mill industry there similarly discovered their breast milk has become toxic, reports Bruce Johansen.[35]

Native elders have been predicting for centuries that the European paradigm of domination and control would result in the collapse of sustainability. The twenty-first century has brought Native American women to the forefront of action on behalf of Mother Earth like never before. The Idle No More movement of Native American activists opposing the anti-environmental trend in the Canadian parliament was started around a kitchen table by three Native American women. They brought their ceremonial round dance to shopping malls and other public locations via social media flash mobs, and the idea caught on quickly with non-Natives protesting the Keystone XL Pipeline. As Native Americans put their Moccasins on the Ground in active protest, non-Native environmentalists began eyeing the sovereignty of Native land as a hopeful strategy to prevent retrogressive developments such as new cross-continental pipelines that will increase instead of decrease the amount of carbon in the atmosphere.

Look to the Native Americans

A study of Native American health is, for all of humanity, a foreshadowing of our future if we remain on the current course we've charted toward climatic revolt. The drug abuse, alcoholism, and high suicide rates on Native American reservations are usually explained as the fallout of centuries of broken treaties, forced migrations, and generations of mind control in Indian boarding schools where children were beaten and abused in order to kill the Indian inside. But Bruce Johansen brings to light another reason for the social dysfunction on reservations that has skyrocketed since the 1960s, and that is the unmanageable health problems of the Native communities that live there. Natives are suffering disproportionately from cancer, birth defects, and circulatory illnesses that have risen as much as 600 percent in some regions since 1975.[36] It's a neocolonial irony that the U.S. government pushed the Natives onto the poorest land during the Indian Removal, only to later discover that land was actually valuable in terms of fossil fuels and precious metals that were discovered underground. Extraction of these resources, particularly uranium and coal, has been devastating for the health of American Indians.

The remoteness of their reservations also attracts corporations looking for locations "away from people" to dump dangerous waste. The Western Shoshone Nation has the dubious distinction of being able to call themselves "the most bombed nation on the planet," because more than 650 atomic weapons have been detonated on their land in military tests. Those who live even farther out in the extremities of nature, such as the Inuit in the Arctic, are some of the first communities forced into migration as a result of man-made climate change. The melting of the permafrost and the ice cover is happening earlier and earlier each year, completely upsetting the interspecies balance and shortening hunting seasons, making the animals more desperate and dangerous. While some villagers are fighting off the polar bears that are suddenly invading their settlements, others are watching their entire villages erode into the sea.

We could talk here about the need to reduce global coal power use by 80 percent if we want our grandchildren's generation not to go hungry as a result of excess heat sterilizing crops.*[37] Or we could discuss the need for us to break our addiction to airplanes, or at least stop the subsidization of the airline industry to such an effect that it discourages innovation in fuel types. But distressing facts about the environment have not been motivational when countered by emotional appeals, especially when those counterarguments are couched in terms of protecting

---

*This is already happening in the breadbasket of America, as Bruce Johansen reported from Nebraska. Summers are sometimes so hot that crops become sterile.

the *liberties* of the so-called American way of life. Americans have been misguided to believe that their liberties as consumers are at stake, when really the liberties we should be curtailing are those of the carbon companies to make endless profits. If facts are what you need, however, we highly recommend Bruce Johansen's *Global Warming Combat Manual,* written so well that it is both frightening and enjoyable to read at the same time. For now, the public relations investments made by carbon companies like ExxonMobil[38] have seeded enough emotional doubt in public opinion to paralyze any effective, progressive policy. For now, American legislators remain convinced that protecting the free trade liberties of the corporation are more important than protecting future generations from any environmental damage that results from this unregulated liberty.

The Cornucopia of America and Preparing for Climate Upheaval

The fledgling U.S. government identified itself with the horn of plenty, or cornucopia, an Earth goddess symbol dating back to pre-Hellenic Greece. The cornucopia is seen together with the goddess of Liberty in the state seals of North Carolina, New Jersey, and Wisconsin (figure 4.5, p. 97); it appears with the allegorical females Victory, Grief, and History in the Peace Monument outside the U.S. Capitol; Ceres and the cornucopia are paired in the Brumidi fresco on the interior of the Capitol dome. Outwardly, the founding artists used the cornucopia to state that this country was overflowing with agricultural bounty and would be a commercially successful trading partner with the rest of the world. Inwardly, this symbol links us back to Gaia and Demeter/Ceres. The connection of the United States to Demeter through the cornucopia on our national insignia can be particularly instructive as we contemplate the coming environmental upheaval.

The mystery schools where Demeter was thought to prepare souls for a peaceful passage to the afterlife flourished in Eleusis for more than a thousand years. The pre-Hellenic versions of the myth of Demeter and her daughter Persephone as told by Charlene Spretnak

Figure 6.9. The cornucopia appears in this British print in front of a Native American woman, and together they symbolize America. She is greeting the seated Britannia, with her shield and lion by her side, while a goddess named Concord looks on. Titled *Britain, America, at Length Be Friends*, this etching and engraving appeared as the frontispiece of the *London Magazine*, 1774. Library of Congress.

in *Lost Goddesses of Early Greece* shed some clues on the Eleusinian Mysteries and how they psychologically prepared initiates for passage to the afterlife. The elements of kidnap and rape were added to the saga of Persephone much later, in what appears to be a reference to the culture of patriarchal domination that followed. The original version of this myth features Persephone and Demeter as maiden/ mother aspects of the same Earth goddess in charge of the seasons and agricultural bounty. The maiden aspect of the goddess voluntarily descends to the underworld for several months a year to teach the deceased how to find peace in the afterlife. When she returns topside, the Earth has renewal in spring again. The Earth Mother both gives all things life and welcomes them back into her womb after death.[39] No matter what spiritual path they follow, people facing the coming environmental upheaval in the near future would benefit from following the example of Demeter and Persephone by preparing themselves emotionally and spiritually for transition.

We Got Us into This Mess

As we have noted, the United States is largely responsible for the current state of global warming, and that is because of a chain of geothermal circumstances known as thermal inertia. It takes about fifty years for the carbon dioxide and methane that humans add to the environment to turn into heat, and from this perspective, the pollution growth in China and India is still too young to impact current global warming trends. Fifty years ago, the United States was leading other nations of the world in carbon emissions and energy consumption, and as the exemplar of an advanced civilization, ever since then our wasteful habits have spread around the world. Today the United States continues to produce far more carbon emissions per person than any other country in the world. As a nation, we have the moral responsibility to lead the way to a new energy future, because we have led the way to the energy present where now the whole world teeters on the verge of climate catastrophe. "It's already in the pipeline," said Johansen, referring to the emissions that will result in more warming in the future. "I mean it's already there. If we don't get a handle on this, it's going to be too late. It may be too late now."

The Statue of Liberty is a symbol of change. America has thrived on change, and right now, it is more essential than ever. Of course we mean the radical, practical changes the climate scientists are calling for, but more importantly, change is needed in our minds and hearts. We contend that more women in power will accelerate the transition from what Zohara Hieronimus named the death economy into a caring economy, where life is the first priority. Instead of living *on* the Earth and dominating and exploiting it like an empire for our pleasure, we must accept that we are *one* with the Earth. Recognizing where these metaphorical connections between dominance over women and over nature entered our language as illustrated by the Indian Queen can help us today as we struggle to shift our mind-set to one of sustainability.

Can we change the perception that we have the right to unlimited consumption into a feeling of responsibility to all Earth creatures? Can we outgrow the concept of American exceptionalism and join the community of the world? If the Statue of Liberty instills in us a sense of national pride, can we channel that into a revolution of our values regarding the Earth and our energy usage? As Americans we chose a goddess to be our guiding principle. If we can learn the compassionate connection of the goddess to be gained from this insight on a national scale, then the next American revolution could be the energy innovation revolution needed to save the planet. Let's change, America.

7

How the Statue of Liberty Became the Whore of Babylon

Now there's a chapter title you won't see in most other books about the Statue of Liberty! Casting the Statue of Liberty as the Whore of Babylon comes from a set of conspiracy theories that interpret the Statue of Liberty along radically different lines than we do. Though most of our academic friends point to the ahistorical support provided for wild allegations like these, and advise us to ignore them as paranoid delusions, we take these conspiracies quite seriously. First of all, they represent the periphery of a much larger attack on religious freedom in the United States. Second, concluding that the origins of the Statue of Liberty were evilly inspired is an offshoot of the claim that *all* goddesses are Satanic.

The problem with claiming that all goddesses are Satanic is that it's then used to justify the attack on women's rights. That may come as a surprise, but that's what we found: the conspiracy theories about the Statue of Liberty as the Whore of Babylon are tied up with the argument over a woman's right to control her own reproductive cycle. We have taken on the mission of exposing these kinds of half-baked conspiracy theories, and we believe one good reason to do so is because they contribute to the ongoing offensive against female empowerment.

"The Statue of Liberty is the beast mother of all harlots Isis,
Ishtar, Lucifer . . ."

—www.godlikeproductions.com/forum1/message1480519/pg1
(accessed February 6, 2015)

Studying conspiracy theories is like studying folklore: they both give clues to what a group of people are thinking as they try to make sense of their world. When we began looking behind the scenes of history for the secret life of Lady Liberty, we discovered a number of areas in the history of the United States that made us uncomfortable to examine. The same thing holds true when we looked a little more closely at these conspiracy theories—some of which are just silly outright lies—about the Statue of Liberty. They may appear as harmless fringe suppositions by a group of zealots, but behind them we found a burning hatred that is being manipulated by a politically savvy group of right-wing ideologues whose agenda includes the dismantling of the women's rights legislation achieved in the past few decades.

Most conspiracy theories about the Statue of Liberty usually allude to the Christian nation myth. If anything serves as a giant reminder that the United States was not founded as a Christian nation it's the Statue of Liberty in all her pagan goddess enlightened glory. The French politicians and artists who created this work modeled it after the artistic choices of the Revolutionary generation, as their goal was to symbolize what they saw as the particularly American version of liberty. The founding artists, of course, did not include any Christian symbolism in their official insignia. In fact, the Revolutionary generation deliberately did *not* identify themselves as a Christian nation. Instead they chose symbols of the Enlightenment to decorate their new nation, which is why we see so much architecture and so many mythological figures from Greek and Roman antiquity. They chose symbolism that they hoped would inspire a sense of *union through reason* in the collective identity of the new republic.

"These statues of 'liberty' are in reality representations
of Queen Semiramis."

—www.jesus-is-savior.com/False%20Religions/Illuminati/illuminati_exposed-part_2
.htm (accessed February 6, 2015)

In this chapter we will look into the particular American fascination with conspiracy theories and what that reveals about our collective fear of the "other." The use of the term "Whore of Babylon" is a good example of how an obscure biblical reference has been reinterpreted by successive generations of fanatical Christians to demonize one outsider group after another—from Jews, to Pagans, to other Christians. We'll trace the fear of the Goddess back to a most unusual interpretation of Eve and the serpent in the Garden of Eden, and we'll pick apart some of the better-known conspiracies about the Statue of Liberty to learn what they reveal about America's current psychological condition. We will examine allegations of a Masonic connection to the creation of the Statue of Liberty and why this particular group of others creates such fear among conspiracy theorists. And finally, we'll consider some modern-day conspiracies that are quite real.

Extremist Christians and Fear of the Other

Featured in this chapter are two defenders of religious liberty from whom we learned a lot: Pagan priestess and founder of the Lady Liberty League, Selena Fox, and research psychologist and author Mark Koltko-Rivera. Both of them helped us come to terms with the label of "Christian" when discussing the people who revile the Statue of Liberty as a demon. Fox prefers the term "extremist fundamentalists," or even more appropriately, she suggests the label "demonologists," because, although they purport to be Christians, they seem to be more interested in finding Satan lurking in disguise everywhere than in following Christ's example of loving thy neighbor as thyself.

Koltko-Rivera uses the terms "extremist Christians" and "religious bullies," and his insights were very helpful in understanding why extremist Christians are so uncomfortable around the image of divine female power. People entrenched in the pattern of male domination tend to label any deviation from the patriarchal norm as threatening, and therefore, Satanic. "Spiritual fascists" is another term he uses, saying they insist that "'the other' is just to be crushed." This insistence on no compromise is what has the current Republican Party so locked up. And it is exactly the kind of religious extremist mind-set that the framers of the U.S. Constitution were aiming to keep out of political service. Compromise is essential in a land that is based on self-rule and is designed to protect religious freedom.

It is not so much the opinions of a group of extremist Christians that we are worried about, as it is the well-funded group of right-wing militants who manipulate them. The evangelical believer has been turned into an effective voting bloc, and emotional speeches made in mega-churches about conservative values can turn out huge numbers of voters. Throw in some references to the demons infesting liberal politicians or our national icons, and the conditions are set for no compromise. Who would want to compromise with a demon?

"The flaming torch atop the Statue of Liberty is a Luciferian symbol of Antichrist's victory over Jesus at Armageddon! . . . The Illuminized French Freemasons who created the Statue of Liberty created it to shout the message . . . that America was to lead the world into the New World Order and that Lucifer was going to control the entire endeavor."

—Promotional description of the film *American Goddess: Lucifer's Torch* by Mike Hoggard, at www.cuttingedge.org/detail.cfm?ID=2315 (accessed February 6, 2015)

The Statue of Liberty is strong enough and flexible enough as a symbol to have withstood more than 130 years of changing public opinion. Ugly allegations have been thrown at her from the very beginning, and she's still standing tall, inspiring millions with her pure message. In contrast, Liberty's children are the ones who need defending from seductively emotional theories like these, and that is why we are taking the time to expose the fallacies in these allegations—to help the uninformed avoid being manipulated through the emotion of fear.

A generation of the Internet has turned us into easy targets for fear-mongering. Spreading the idea that the Statue of Liberty was created as a demon in disguise will create a fear of *too much* liberty, to the extent that these true believers would *welcome* an authoritarian control from a hierarchical patriarchy. What truly concerns us about the growing popularity of the demon-hunting version of Christianity is their very real political reach.

The Fall of Eve and the Suppression of the Oracular Serpent of Wisdom

The foundations for demonizing the Statue of Liberty go all the way back to the folklore of the Fall of Eve. We learned from cultural historian Riane Eisler that the story of Adam and Eve and the serpent starts to make sense only when seen in terms of one culture taking over another. Sumerian and Babylonian mythology predate the Hebrew scriptures, and much of the book of Genesis was copied from these earlier creation stories. Ancient cylinder seals from Sumeria dating to 2500 BCE show this scene that was familiar all over the Near East: a Tree of Life surrounded by a female, a male, and a serpent, all of them divine.[1] Before canonical Judaism, the tree was sacred to the Goddess, the snake was sacred to the Goddess, and the Tree of Life was often a symbol of the Goddess herself. The serpent as a symbol of the powers of regeneration and rebirth goes back as far as the Neolithic in artwork showing a snake coiling around both the womb and the phallus. The scene around the Tree of Life in those Sumerian cylinder seals shows the Goddess with her consort sitting one on either side of the Tree of Life. They offer the tree and the serpent, or the understanding of the regeneration of life, to the viewer.[2]

When the Hebrew priesthood reinterpreted this story to fit their canon, the female pictured next to the Tree of Life was no longer depicted as a goddess and a giver of life and understanding. Now she was not only a mortal woman but also the one blamed for bringing death as a punishment to all other mortals. When Yahweh took the place of the Creator Goddess, the female divine was rejected. The myths tell of

Figure 7.1. Pre–Hebrew scriptures version of Adam, Eve, and the serpent. Rendering of a Mesopotamian cylinder seal, circa 2200 BCE. This scene is prevalent in art of this time and appears to show a god and a goddess seated on either side of a tree to which they are gesturing, always with a serpent nearby. Rendering by Amy Ford.

the new supreme male god banning any association with earlier symbols of the Goddess.[3] Eisler always wondered about that word "henceforth" in the punishment allotted to Eve for her curiosity about the tree. It was decreed that henceforth women would have pain during childbirth and no control over conception. "Henceforth" implies that before then women *did* have the means and the understanding about how to control conception and ease the pain of childbirth. "That story only makes sense in terms of a cultural shift, doesn't it?" she asked. These interpretations of the Fall of Eve have been used ever since by church fathers to control the behavior of women.[4]

The abundance of female figurines found all over the world from as far back as thirty thousand years ago demonstrates that a reverence for a divine female dominated human consciousness for millennia. This changed about five thousand years ago when archaeologists mark the dawn of so-called civilization with the advent of the written word. At this time there was also a shift in mythological patterns, and sky-warrior gods began predominating. Neurosurgeon Leonard Shlain suggested that it was the invention of the alphabet itself that rewired human brains to become linear and left-brain oriented, and simultaneously facilitated the rise of the domination paradigm that wiped out the goddess-worshipping cultures.[5]

Original Sin and Women's Rights

The concept of original sin wherein all of humanity is born corrupt as a result of sexual desire and the Fall of Eve is not in the Hebrew interpretation of the Garden of Eden. Nor is it in Jesus's teachings. The idea of original sin developed as another way for the Roman church fathers to divide membership between the orthodox and the questioners. The doctrine of original sin started with Bishop Augustine about four hundred years after the birth of Jesus Christ. Augustine's writings about his struggle with his own sexuality and self-doubt—and his dismal view of human moral capacity that we are all born sinners—was adopted by the Roman Church when they declared that the only way to salvation from original sin was to be baptized into the "official" church. The Romans refined this philosophy to the point where the church began teaching that human beings cannot be trusted to govern themselves because of this inherently sinful nature. Only a divinely selected emperor or king was qualified to make decisions for the public.[6]

Politicians today who follow the evangelical Dominionist theology talk in similar terms about sexuality, as though it were the root of all trouble. Dominionists hold that women must remain subject to the rule of men, because Eve succumbed to the devil's temptations in the Garden of Eden and God then punished all women for eternity. Because of this original sin, women cannot be trusted with any important decisions, especially those about contraception, sexuality, or their health. These decisions must be legislated for their own protection.

The Hebrew Goddess

The Hebrew religion flourished for centuries in a region where intensive goddess cults surrounded them. It would be illogical to think they "remained immune to them," says historian Raphael Patai in his

Figure 7.2. *Adam and Eve in America* by Theodor de Bry, 1590, published in *A Briefe and True Report of the New Found Land of Virginia* by Thomas Hariot. This engraving demonstrates both how the Europeans considered the Native Americans as living in a Garden of Eden in America as well as how the evil power of temptation was female—note that the upper portion of the snake in the tree is shaped like a woman. Library of Congress.

seminal work, *The Hebrew Goddess.* "Yet this is precisely the picture one gets when one views Hebrew religion through the polarizing prisms of Mosaic legislation and prophetic teaching."[7] Archaeological excavations have uncovered female figurines of the goddesses named in the Bible by the ancient Hebrews, such as Asherah, Astarte, Anat, and the Queen of Heaven,[8] and so many goddess depictions have been uncovered that some have glibly concluded that "Yaweh had a wife." It seems clear enough that the earliest Hebrew tradition included the worship of this female divine figure common to all the Semitic people. As Max Dashú told us: "The shared goddess name, with known phonological shifts, shows how ancient she is. The Ugaritic goddess is named *Athirat,* paired with *El; Asherah* is the Hebrew name, paired with *Yah* (though the oldest biblical passages also used *El,* which simply means god), and the eastern Semitic Babylonians had *Ashertum."*

"Ashtaroth = Whore of Babylon = Aphrodite = Libertas = the
Statue of Liberty!"

—vaticannewworldorder.blogspot.com/2012/11/statue-of-liberty.html
(accessed February 6, 2015)

Patai's work shows that the Hebrews officially incorporated these female deities from their Canaanite neighbors into the Jewish temple, on and off, over several generations. We know this based on the many references in the Hebrew scriptures to the judges ordering these statues to be removed. Asherah is mentioned dozens of times in these texts, usually in the sections of the Bible written by the set of authors that scholars have identified as the Deuteronomist, or *D.* Asherah was often worshipped as a tree, or likened to a tree, and her groves were sacred, making her sound like a Mother Nature goddess. In the King James Version of the Bible, in fact, her name was consistently mistranslated as "a tree" or as tree images. The segments in the Bible that urge the cutting down of her sacred groves were written during and after the psychic loss of exile experienced by the Jewish people in Babylon. Many scholars have concluded that during this painful time of exile the authors of these texts were looking for reasons to explain or place blame for the nation's punishment. From this time forward, Judaic texts began to establish firmly that Yahweh was the one and only god, and a jealous and vengeful one at that. The veneration of other gods or goddesses would no longer be allowed.

This is the time when the second creation story was added to Genesis. The older version has a plural Creator fashioning man and woman at the same time and in *their* image. This new later version tells of a male god creating woman out of the body of man as an after-thought, to keep him company. The serpent or the symbol of oracu-lar power of the Goddess was now demonized,[9] and Israelites were instructed to kill every man, woman, and child if they revered any goddess.

With this version of the creation story, humanity was banished from a nature idyll into a world of rocks and thistles. Metaphorically, the instinctual connection to nature as a mother was severed at this point. It can be interpreted that when Yahweh cursed Adam and Eve, he also cursed the Earth, because the Earth itself was considered by many to be the Goddess.[10] Creation myths from around the world tra-ditionally consider nature and the world as sacred. But the interpreta-tion of the Hebrew creation myth reversed that concept by banishing humans out of the garden and into the world, described as a cursed ground, hard to cultivate and full of thorns, where man would work to *subdue* it. Communication and Native American studies profes-sor Bruce Johansen told us that the Indigenous people don't have any banishment from an original utopia in their stories. They believe they still live in the original garden. Adam and Eve, on the other hand, were forced into this harsh place, which we think of today as Earth, as punishment because they listened to a serpent (an ancient goddess symbol) and ate from a tree (an ancient goddess symbol). Man must now sweat and toil in nature, and woman is made his virtual slave. For her greater fault of tempting him, she loses the knowledge and control over when and how often to conceive. The knowledge of con-traception gradually disappears, as the resulting dangerous and pain-ful labors are explained as woman's eternal punishment for the sins of Eve.

"That is a demonic idol right there in New York harbor. . . .
It's a statue of a false goddess, the Queen of Heaven. We don't
get liberty from a false goddess, folks. We get our liberty
from Jesus Christ, and that Statue of Liberty in no way glorifies
Jesus Christ. . . . We practice idolatry in America in ways that
we don't even recognize."

—John Benefiel, self-appointed apostle of the New Apostolic Reformation
and advisor to politicians like Rick Perry, from a sermon in August 2010,
http://goo.gl/vK6qmJ (accessed February 6, 2015)

Another viewpoint entirely on the Fall of Eve is provided in
Kabbalistic studies as reported by Zohara Hieronimus, where the Tree
of Life is related to a pictogram of the human spiritual and material
makeup. Hieronimus compares the Tree of Life to a ten-dimensional
map or guide for becoming self-managed co-creators again. The Fall is
not interpreted in Kabbalistic teaching as a banishment from a place,
but from the ease of having everything provided. Eden is a state of
consciousness, not just a place. Similar to the teachings in the ancient
Hindu Vedas, the Fall is seen as a descent from a more developed spiritual aptitude where thoughts manifested physical perfection. Humanity
descended to a lower consciousness of matter in order to challenge the
free will to choose good in all thought, speech, and action. Without
effort, the individual would not have the opportunity to grow, or to
individuate.

The Whore of Babylon

The Whore of Babylon is one of the weird creatures described in the last
book of the Christian scriptures, that collection of troubling visions, the
book of Revelation. Written soon after Rome's destruction of Jerusalem
in 70 CE, its author is thought to be a Jewish Christian named John of
Patmos, who described in nightmarish terms his pain over being exiled
from his home. Religion professor Elaine Pagels told us there were several equally strange books of Revelation written around the same time,
some not discovered until the Nag Hammadi library was uncovered in

the 1940s. They all employed a similar use of code to avoid trouble with the Roman authorities. The authors all appear to be equally outraged at the fall of Jerusalem and wrote graphic descriptions of the punishment they were sure their vengeful God would inflict on Rome in retribution. Pagels described these writings as, "anti-Roman propaganda that drew its imagery from Israel's prophetic traditions."[11]

A common substitute for Jewish writers when criticizing Rome was Babylon, which to them symbolically stood for the empire that had six hundred years earlier exiled the Jewish people—and then suffered a terrible defeat. Adding the word "whore" to "Babylon" was the writer's way of saying that Rome was unfaithful to God. Pagels and other biblical scholars agree that the monsters John described in his Revelation are real people, with their identities coded by gematria. For example, "the most obvious calculations" for 666 "indicate that the 'number of the beast,' spells out Nero's imperial name," said Pagels.[12]

Christianity grew from being a persecuted minority into the religion of the Roman Empire. Over the centuries, John's vengeance visions were reinterpreted again and again, with Babylon being used to describe various new opponents. As early as 300 CE, Bishop Athanasius redefined the whore and beast of John's vision to mean Jews and pagans, as well as other Christians who did not adhere to the new orthodoxy under the Roman administration.[13] Demonizing the opposition has been a common tactic in organized Christianity ever since.

At the outset of the Protestant Reformation, the entire Catholic Church itself became known as the Whore of Babylon, with some of the first Lutheran Bibles ever printed including engravings of a monster-woman labeled as the pope.[14] Archaeologist Marija Gimbutas believed that the transmutation of the Goddess into a negative image was accelerated by the Christian Church. "This is really Christianity's doing," she said in a 1992 interview. "They demonized the one who was the most powerful. . . . The Goddess who rules over death and regeneration . . . became the witch. . . . In the fifteenth and sixteenth centuries, which are critical for this change, she became a Satan, a monster."[15]

"Only Jews and Christians worshiped a single god and denounced all others as evil demons," said Elaine Pagels in her book *The Origin of*

Figure 7.3. Medieval woodcut showing the Whore of Babylon and the seven-headed beast. Penn Provenance Project.

Satan. The concept of the oneness of the Creator was not uncommon among other pagan religions around them, but "only Christians divided the supernatural world into two opposing camps, the one true God against swarms of demons," she continued, "and none but Christians preached—and practiced—division on earth."[16] Though Christ said love your enemy, extremist Christians are more concerned with classifying people into the saved and the demon possessed. As Selena Fox put it, "My understanding, having been raised Southern Baptist, is that Jesus is about love, love your neighbor as yourself. It did not have an opt-out clause. It did not say love your neighbor as yourself except if they are Pagan."

One of Our Chief Founding Myths

Paranoia about conspiracies is part of the fabric of American history. There is no need to go point by point through the various conspiracy claims about the Statue of Liberty and debunk them all, because we know that for every straw doll we knock down, some fearmonger will put up another one. Because that's what it's all about: inciting fear. Groups that promote fear and hate are not unique to America, of course, but paranoid conspiracies are tied into American history in a peculiarly intrinsic way, as we learned from Arthur Goldwag in *The New Hate: A History of Fear and Loathing on the Populist Right*. There is a sameness across time and space, about the complaints of haters, which date as far back as the Illuminati panic that almost blocked Thomas Jefferson from becoming president. For example, the anti-Islamic speech of today sounds similar to the anti-Semitic speech of the 1930s. Linking the Statue of Liberty to a plot by the New World Order to take over America uses the same references as the conspiracy writers who opposed Franklin Roosevelt's New Deal.

Goldwag turned us on to Richard Hofstadter's influential *Harper's Magazine* essay, written at the end of the Red Scare, called "The Paranoid Style in American Politics," later published in book form. Despite the changing bogeymen, Hofstadter concluded that right-wing thinking inclined to conspiracies shared three hallmarks.

1. Someone is trying to undermine capitalism and substitute socialism or communism;
2. Political leaders are secretly members of the conspiracy and are secretly working to undermine American interests;
3. There is a network of agents of this conspiracy spread all over the country, working to make changes at all levels of society.[17]

"Lady Liberty (Enlightening/Illuminating the World), The Godess [sic] of Reason, The Queen of Heaven—and Her Anti-Christ Cult of Reason (aka "Synagog [sic] of Satan")—now led by America (Occultic Mystery Babylon)—is the Whore/Prostitute/Woman who rides the Beast."

—http://beforeitsnews.com/prophecy/2014/02/outrage-national-guard-marked-with-satanic-luciferan-cult-symbolism-by-us-government-jaw-dropping-videos-2458692.html (accessed February 6, 2015).

The accusation that the Statue of Liberty is the Whore of Babylon is usually followed by the lament that America would still be a Christian nation if it were not for these "others" infiltrating American society. Claiming that the United States was designed to be a Christian nation is one of America's "chief founding myths," says law professor Steven Green, because it provides a sense of important specialness and a conviction that we are the chosen people in the chosen land.[18]

The idealized Christian nation described by the conspiracy paranoids, however, more closely resembles the theocratic government of violent intolerance practiced by our Puritan ancestors than it does the Revolutionary generation. An irony of the Christian nation conspiracy is that the United States was founded with the explicit intention of dissolving this past control of the church over the government.

A further irony of lauding the sanctimonious Puritans as a model for behavior is that the rabid intolerance practiced by various Muslim sects in the Middle East today is akin to what lay at the very root of the English colonies in America. Our Puritan ancestors used Christian excuses to massacre Native American children; hang fellow Christians, Baptists, and Catholics; and torture their women as witches. When the Quakers came to town in the 1650s, their elevation of women to preacher status made them seem even more heretical to the Puritans. The Puritan government began to lose power in the 1690s, and that was when they simultaneously began to turn against their women with a paranoid witch craze in which 80 percent of those accused were women.[19] The extremists today wishing America would return to being a Christian nation are desirous of that same dominating top-down control as practiced by our Puritan ancestors in the family, in society, and in government.

The element of real concern regarding the Christian nation myth is that those advocating it have the power to make lasting changes. A recent Texas board of education ruling deleted everything from the curriculum about the separation of church and state and replaced it with sources that say divine providence guided the founders to create laws based on Christian principles. Steven Green reports that on the advice of American history revisionist David Barton, anything that "contradicted a view of American exceptionalism was gutted from the standards."[20]

The Conspiracy against the Statue of Liberty and American Self-Identity

Conspiracy theories about the Statue of Liberty all say that she was deliberately designed to symbolize meanings that are the opposite from what her creators told us. They say her creators lied about what she stood for and thought it a grand joke that most of us (except those in the know) swallowed it. A supposed source of clues that the Statue of Liberty hides secrets in her symbolism is provided by counting the number of prominent members of her building committee who were Freemasons, or pointing out that the Masons held a cornerstone laying ceremony for the pedestal. Selected dates of events during the Statue of Liberty's construction, together with selected measurements of height and angles, are analyzed astrologically and numerologically to further prove their conclusion that she is seducing us to the dark side. Using numerology or astrology to speculate on why there are seven rays in the crown or why certain dates were chosen for certain ceremonies can be worthwhile, and we've done it ourselves.[21] But when your speculations point you to interpretations that are completely at variance with the stated claims of the artist, you must also provide a good deal more corroboration to document that the artist was lying.

If you were surprised to hear that some people believe the Statue of Liberty is the Whore of Babylon, just do an Internet search using any word synonymous with "secret," together with the term "Statue of Liberty," and you will be presented with hundreds of thousands of hits. Some of the accusations contained on these websites are featured in the boxed quotes throughout this chapter. These kinds of titillating conspiracy theories have exploded on the Internet, in part due to the thrill of the reveal. People who are new at analyzing symbols are especially vulnerable to faulty interpretations, because the emotional surprise of one big reveal after another is addictive, and most of us haven't studied enough history to spot immediately how far off base they are.

Figure 7.4. An Internet search for the words "secret" and "Statue of Liberty" will reveal hundreds of sites like these claiming she is the devil.

Conspiracy Theory Number One: Fear of the Other, Fear of Being Displaced

We turned to research psychologist Mark Koltko-Rivera to try to understand the mind-set of conspiracy theorists who believe illogical claims. As Koltko-Rivera explained, the wild-and-wooly faction of conspiracy theorists doesn't have to spend much energy to explain when bad things happen in the world, because they already know who is to blame. There is no need to compare complex social factors in the economy or even the role of accidental chance as causative agents behind any threat to the status quo. "Conspiracy theories allow people to avoid the difficult work of educating themselves, participating in the democratic process, and creating real social change," said Koltko-Rivera. "Why bother? You can blame it all on some external scapegoat, and that's easier than the gritty work of trying to fix the world."

Minorities and suppressed classes are the traditional scapegoats, and advocates for civil rights for any minority have had to defend themselves through the ages for trying to uplift these convenient "others." According to this line of thinking, the status quo is God's will, and to change the status of minorities or suppressed classes threatens to bring God's destruction on society as we know it. For example, Benjamin Franklin's invention of the lightning rod was considered heretical because it interfered with God's will to express displeasure through electrical storms. Extremist Christians quoted Bible scripture to the abolitionists to argue that slavery was a God-ordained institution and should not be challenged. The same critics simultaneously used scripture to claim that woman suffragists of the mid-1800s were heretics for challenging the standard belief that women were subservient. The 1852 National Women's Rights Convention was declared Satanic just because they dared to discuss the issue of women wearing pants! These same arguments of heresy and God's will are used today against all issues related to women's rights.

Haters are usually not motivated by evil intentions, so much as by pain and fear of further loss, according to Arthur Goldwag. Being white and Protestant used to open doors automatically, but with white male Protestants no longer the dominant class by number, they are feeling these advantages slipping away.

Conspiracy Theory Number Two: Fear of Egypt, Fear of Catholics

Our current set of conspiracies positing that the Statue of Liberty is the Whore of Babylon are direct descendants of the Catholic-bashing that grew popular in the United States in the mid-1800s as a xenophobic reaction to the waves of immigrants moving in and creating job rivalry. Anti-Catholic writers, suspicious of the Catholic reverence for the mother of Jesus, proffered the notion that Mary was just one in a long line of masks for a single female demonic figure. As the anti-Catholic attacks on Mother Mary filtered down into mass consciousness and became a more generalized fear of the goddess as Satan, names used for this invented composite goddess included the Whore of Babylon, Jezebel, Semiramis, Diana, and the Queen of Heaven.

The majority of today's popular conspiracy writers claiming the Statue of Liberty is the Whore of Babylon don't bother to use footnotes, but those who do list Alexander Hislop as their main reference source. Hislop's 1850 anti-Catholic book, *The Two Babylons: Papal Worship Revealed to Be the Worship of Nimrod and His Wife,* used copious footnotes to share a nevertheless ill-informed view of the Babylonian culture, arguing that the Catholic religion was modeled on Babylonian idol worship. Quoting Hislop gives modern conspiracy writers "a veneer of scholarship with all its footnotes and interesting references," says Koltko-Rivera. Hislop postulated a Christian world view all the way back into pre-Christian times and named Semiramis as the original Babylonian queen who invented goddess worship— a complete fantasy. It is Hislop who, in his attempt to prove that Catholicism is based on pagan idol worship, determined that all goddesses are one and the same.

"As Hislop shows, Isis is the Egyptian name for the Babylonian goddess Ishtar, who is also the same as Athena (Greece), Minerva (Egypt and Greece), Astarte (Syria), Cybele (Rome), Ashtoreth (Israel), and Diana (Ephesus). This statue of the pagan Madonna, the Statue of 'Liberty,' is a statue of this same ancient pagan 'Queen of Heaven,' the wife of Nimrod, or Semiramis!"

—William F. Dankenbring "Is the Statue of Liberty Pagan?" http://yahushua.net/
babylon/liberty/pagan_statue.htm (accessed February 6, 2015)

Other than the Whore of Babylon, Isis is the next most frequent candidate for the goddess-figure revealed in these conspiracies as the true inspiration for the Statue of Liberty. We already reviewed how sculptor Auguste Bartholdi studied colossal Egyptian art with great attention, traveling there extensively as a young man, and noting that it "had a very considerable effect upon my taste for sculpture."[22] Much is made of Bartholdi's failed attempt to sell a lighthouse statue to the leader of Egypt several years before the Statue of Liberty project got off the ground, because the mysterious aura of Egypt gives paranoids a wide field for speculation. Although his Suez Canal design was in the form of a peasant woman (figure 7.5, p. 194), these paranoids go out of their way to create some nefarious connection between it and the universal goddess form Isis.

The lighthouse design Bartholdi planned for the Suez Canal was never intended to be Isis, however, but instead a symbol of progress, in reference to the newly installed electricity and the modernizing mission of the khedive—lighting the way for progress—for his country. Bartholdi appealed to the ego of the khedive, but as discussed earlier, he was still turned down, and the project never got past the clay-model stage. Years later, Bartholdi found himself forced to deny that New York's Statue of Liberty was ever offered first to the government of another country. While disingenuous to say the two statuettes were not related, he was telling the literal truth in that he never offered a statue "of liberty" to Egypt. To them he proposed a commercial venture and a statue "of progress." As Bartholdi said, "The Egyptian affair would have been purely a business transaction." This was a big difference to

Figure 7.5. Reproductions of the study maquettes Bartholdi made for the Suez Canal statue, *Egypt (or Progress) Bringing the Light to Asia*, which was never commissioned. "Progress Lighting the Way" was a very common theme in international statuary of the time. On display at the Liberty Island Museum. Author photo.

Bartholdi, who described his Liberty project as being "a pure work of love."[23]

The physical similarities between the two statue models for Egypt and the United States have provided endless hours of speculation for conspiracy theorists trying to prove that the Statue of Liberty is a calling card for the Illuminati world-domination plot. These are pretty loose connections, to be sure, but here lies the kernel of truth behind some of the wildest claims on the Internet "revealing" the Statue of Liberty as having a secret past as a statue of Isis.

"The Statue of Liberty's torch represents englightenment [*sic*]
and the fire of prometheus [*sic*] or Lucifer."

—MarkDice.com: http://goo.gl/9K7TQZ (accessed February 3, 2016)

Conspiracy Theory Number Three: Fear of the Enlightenment = Fear of Light = Fear of Freemasons

Conspiracy theories about the Statue of Liberty usually start by analyzing her light symbolism. By means of innuendo, a poor grasp of the Bible, and the weakest of logic, they link *all* light symbolism to Lucifer, the light-bearer, and thus to Satan. There's an entire subculture out there attempting to prove that Lucifer is the guiding spirit of the Freemasons. According to them, anything even remotely touched by a Freemason becomes proof of a grand scheme of Satanic world domination. When you equate light with evil, laughs Koltko-Rivera, "the logical consequence is we should all stumble around in the dark! That's just crazy."

A television show on the History Channel called *Decoded,* purporting to reveal the secret symbolism of the Statue of Liberty, featured a speaker who went as far as to say that the Statue of Liberty "should be torn down and taken to a scrap heap," because it is the Illuminati's "huge idol dedicating this country to [Lucifer] and showing that they rule here." On a subsequent Internet posting, after apparently receiving a lot of flak on these statements, the speaker partially recanted, saying, "I don't think it is 'evil' or should be torn down."[24] He stood by everything else he said, however, including all the historical inaccuracies about the statue and his conclusion that she was designed to "represent Satan" to "Masons and Illuminati who are in-the-know."

"The Statue of Liberty is just another Brotherhood symbol
highlighting the lighted torch of the illuminated ones,
the Luciferian Initiated Elites."

—http://enominepatris.com/occult (accessed February 11, 2015)

One thing missing from most conspiracy theories about the Statue of Liberty is any mention of her creator, Édouard de Laboulaye, revealing the poor scholarship of most of these theorists. A devout Catholic, Laboulaye was never a Freemason. Yes, it's true that the torch is a symbol of wisdom used by Freemasons, but of course it's also used as a symbol of wisdom by a lot of other groups, too, including both Jews and Christians. Yes, it's true that Auguste Bartholdi, the artist who Laboulaye commissioned for his project, became a Freemason the year they launched the official fundraising efforts for the Statue of Liberty, but, as we review in chapter 5, this was a good ten years after he had conceived of a lighthouse statue in the form of a woman. Yes, it's true that the symbolism of Freemasonry parallels that of the Age of Enlightenment and the idealism of the American Revolution, but Laboulaye and Bartholdi actually selected the torch and the crown of light to symbolize the conservative political goals of Laboulaye's new constitutional republic *in France.* The crown of light and the tablet of law are both Laboulaye additions, and thus have no ties to a Freemasonic influence.[25]

This is another thing missing from most Statue of Liberty conspiracies: the popularity and meaning of these symbols to her contemporaries in France. We already included several examples from French art of the same era that also depict robed women, the torch, and the crown of light. None of these features were original to Laboulaye's statue. The torch was also commonly being used at the time as a symbol for the age of electricity or progress,[26] and the crown of light was lifted straight from Christian religious icons and would have been interpreted by contemporaries as a sign of piety.[27]

Many conspirators bandy about the phrase that the Statue of Liberty was a "gift from the Freemasons of France to the Freemasons of America." While that is clearly not true, it would be closer to the truth to say that she was a gift from the millionaires of France to the millionaires of America, as we review in chapter 5. It is also true that Freemasons were involved at every stage of the Statue of Liberty project, but that's like saying Episcopalians were involved at every stage of the project. The Masons were so widespread and so influential in villages and towns, among the middle class, the prosperous merchant class, the liberals and conservatives, that "these were the people you wanted to ask for money for the Statue of Liberty," Statue of Liberty librarian Barry Moreno told us. It was not until after Bartholdi visited the United States that he joined the Freemasons, when he realized that being a member of this fraternity would help fundraising in both countries. The more you read about Bartholdi, the more it becomes clear that he was an excellent marketer, and he saw colossal statuary as his ticket to ensuring his name in history.

Freemasons were indeed attracted to Laboulaye's Statue of Liberty project and helped enormously with the fundraising. But their interest in the project was all about the concept, not the form. As Koltko-Rivera said, "The *form* of the symbolism of the Statue of Liberty itself has absolutely nothing whatsoever to do with Freemasonry. If there is anything Masonic about the symbolism of the Statue of Liberty, it is in the *concept* of individual liberty and freedom of conscience." Adding that Freemasonry bans all discussions of specifics regarding the nature of the divine being, Koltko-Rivera concluded, "There really is no goddess imagery in Freemasonry as such. No goddesses at all are singled out for praise or veneration or worship of any sort whatsoever among Freemasons." We should add that we interviewed Mark Koltko-Rivera not only because he is a research psychologist well versed in the appeal of conspiracy theories, but he is also a Freemason who has written extensively on the history of this community.

The Statue of Liberty's Contemporaries Were Not Threatened by Her Paganism

Among Laboulaye and Bartholdi's contemporaries, aside from some of the Catholic leaders of New York, there was no protest over American Liberty being depicted as a pagan goddess. Unlike today, the general populace back then understood that in the modern age such statues are symbols of abstract concepts, not objects of worship. The keynote address at the unveiling ceremony in 1886 was followed by a doxology, with Episcopal bishop Henry C. Potter performing the benediction.

Figure 7.6. Medieval woodcut of the Whore of Babylon together with the pope astride the seven-headed beast. This cover of an anti-Catholic pamphlet from 1546 blames the pope for disseminating false teachings instead of the true gospel. Penn Provenance Project.

The bishop gave "thanks for the lofty memorial which had been reared by the friendship of two great nations."[28] Except for a few editorial writers in the *American Catholic Quarterly Review*,[29] Liberty's contemporaries were not threatened by her paganism as today's extremist Christians are.

Protestant church leaders of the 1880s became some of the Liberty goddess's biggest supporters after Joseph Pulitzer's publicity campaign and even offered their churches as collection points for the fundraising.

Ministers wrote editorials praising the statue as exemplifying the land where there was freedom of worship.[30]

Conspiracy Theory Number Four: Fear of the Goddess = Fear of Women

The most recent group to jump on the conspiracy bandwagon to call the Statue of Liberty "the Whore of Babylon" is a politically influential new wave of zealotry known as the New Apostolic Reformation. They practice a form of Pentecostalism known as Dominionism, a belief that *man* was created to have *dominion* over all the Earth. One of their leaders, Peter Wagner, is preaching irrational fear among his followers by convincing them that they are the particular targets of this female Satan figure, the Great Whore of Babylon.

Wagner has convinced millions of Americans that "the Goddess" has a personal vendetta against them because they are "Bible Christians," a term they use to distinguish themselves from the other Protestant denominations that they consider too liberal, and especially from Catholics and Mormons. The Wasilla Assembly of God Church, where Sarah Palin was a member for twenty-five years and where she received a special anointing to protect her from "witches," follows this Dominionist line of preaching, with their particular concept of the evil goddess composite named Jezebel.

"The Government of the United States of America is not in any sense founded on the Christian religion."

—1797 Treaty of Tripoli, one of the very first international treaties entered into by the new United States and signed by President John Adams

---

The increase of attack rhetoric against the goddess coming from the religious right today does correlate to the rising power of women since the women's movement of the 1970s. Historian Max Dashú says religious conservatives invoke God's will in opposing women's liberation, "because they insist on the supremacy of the masculine principle, and that's how it's all mythically encoded for them." She describes their sermons about the Statue of Liberty or Jezebel or the Whore of Babylon as "a war of symbols . . . against everything that is modern and liberational. They treat female divinity as the ultimate symbol of evil."

According to this theory, any goddess or any "uppity woman" from any part of the world is conflated with this overarching female personification of Satan. It doesn't matter if she is a big-breasted, pregnant fertility goddess of the Neolithic, or an athletic, virginal hunter goddess of ancient Greece. If she's a female connected in any way to power or to the divine, she is identified as this female version of Satan. Woman must remain subservient to man to achieve salvation, meaning women with power must be evil. On the conspiracy websites that talk about the occult origins of Lady Liberty, Oprah Winfrey is often listed as the living incarnation of the Whore of Babylon. Not only is Winfrey a very powerful woman, she's also a very powerful Black woman interested in alternative spirituality and individual empowerment. This combination makes her especially threatening to those whose goal is to return America to the patriarchal theocracy they call a Christian nation. The title Whore of Babylon is also attached to the trendiest Hollywood and pop music starlets whose sexy photos parade across the screen while the narrator points to symbols and gestures that prove the stars are under the spell of the Satanic Illuminati. While it may be easy enough to show how our culture is flooded with images of torches, rays of light, owls, and eyes, in order to then conclude this repetition is deliberately controlled by a secret group of "others" with nefarious intentions requires a lot more than simply documenting the repetition of popular symbols.

All fundamentalist groups have as a main goal the repression of women. As Riane Eisler put it, "Whether for Hitler's Germany, Stalin's Soviet Union, Khomeini's Iran, the Taliban of Afghanistan, or so-called religious fundamentalists of all stripes—for them a top priority was, and still is, pushing women back into their 'traditional' place."[31] Social commentator Stephan Schwartz said, "The Theocratic Rightists' position, be it Christian, Jewish, or Moslem, is remarkably consistent across the globe: women are dangerous to men sexually, and need to be controlled." Even though the approaches are different, Theocratic Rightists all agree that women "should not have the right to control their bod-

Figure 7.7. Access to safe options for a woman to determine for herself when and how often to bring a child into the world is a liberty denied individuals within a patriarchal hierarchy. Here cartoonist Joel Pett makes the point with humor. Used with permission.

ies, and their place in society should be circumscribed."[32] In the United States, the pushback against women's rights to reproductive freedom has increased enormously since the Affordable Care Act of 2010. Thirty states have made it more difficult for women to make their own considered decisions on the emotional and physical well-being of bringing a child they may not be able to afford into this world.

Women's Rights Lead to Health and Prosperity

The extremist Christians' fear of the goddess translates into fear of an empowered woman, which, it turns out, is actually counterproductive to their own health. Giving a woman control over her reproductive cycle is key to pulling her family, and by extension, her country, out of poverty. "The first thing women do in developing countries when they have even the tiniest measure of wealth beyond absolute subsistence," says Schwartz, "is to seek birth control. They understand that family wellness and prosperity require moving beyond animal fecundity."[33] Schwartz was the first to introduce us to the statistical inversion between the proclaimed values of conservative voters and the actual health of the constituencies where they live.[34] He quotes from the statistical compilations showing that when public resources are spent on educating girls and women about reproduction there are fewer teen pregnancies and young women wait longer to get married, resulting in a lower divorce rate. If abortion is the issue and if preventing abortion is the goal, then preventing pregnancy is the logical extension. But in states where conservative social values predominate, there is no funding for education or contraceptive support, making the unwanted pregnancy rate higher, especially among teens.[35]

In states where social conservatives argue for the rights of the *unborn* children, they withhold funding from programs that aid the *living* children. Children in red states are far more likely to be neglected, abused, or murdered by their own family members than in blue states. "America has more child abuse than any other industrialized country in the world," says Schwartz. "We're number one. Much of the reason for our number one position is revealed when one examines state level data. Red Texas has four times more child abuse per capita than Blue Vermont."[36]

"[N]o one would be more zealous than myself to establish effectual barriers against the horrors of spiritual tyranny, and every species of religious persecution. . . . [E]very man, conducting himself as a good citizen, and being accountable to God alone for his religious opinions, ought to be protected in worshiping the Deity according to the dictates of his own conscience."

—George Washington, letter to the United Baptist Churches in Virginia
(Baptists were a persecuted minority at the time), May 10, 1789

Real Conspiracies to Worry About

Conspiracy theories are worth watching because they are often launched by groups that feel disenfranchised against those with more power, and that watchdog effect can help keep excess in check. Sometimes conspiracies are necessary and for the good. How far would the American Revolution have progressed, for example, if it weren't for the secret planning and correspondence of the Sons of Liberty and others?

There are any number of real conspiracies going on right now, and quite a few from the past that have had a tremendous impact on the course of history. Dedicated conspiracy hunters could perform a true public service if they were to turn their attention to researching how to expose the big banks that are currently conspiring to fix international lending rates and undermine financial regulations. They could be dogging giant corporations like Monsanto that are conspiring to deny consumers the freedom of making an educated choice about genetically modified foods. Instead, they spin their wheels looking for clues in popular culture to prove the existence of a secret cabal of men descended from the Bavarian Illuminati of the 1780s.

Other recent real conspiracies include the so-called spontaneous formation of the Tea Party, wherein lobbyists who worked for Big Tobacco conspired with the Koch brothers to formulate a "grassroots" political movement, with an agenda preset to target the science of climate change and restrictions to corporate interests.[37] These same lobbyists are now working for Big Plastic and spend their time swearing in court that the BPA from plastic in our food supply is not harmful to our health.[38]

An example of a factually flawed conspiracy that caused massive repercussions for millions of people is *The Protocols of the Elders of Zion,* a book that was published as an anti-Semitic hoax in the early 1900s in Russia as a justification for the bloody pogroms against the Jews. *The Protocols* details an imagined Jewish conspiracy of world domination and was quoted a few decades later by Adolf Hitler to legitimize his own persecution of the Jews. The book had already been thoroughly and completely exposed as a hoax by then, yet it continues to be used by radicals all over the world today to justify anti-Semitic violence.

The Evangelical Conspiracy
for World Domination

Dominionists are as extreme in their hatred of symbols of "the other" as are the fanatical Muslims criticized for pulling down the ancient statues of earlier cultures and destroying the sites of archaeological excavations. Like Islamic extremists, the Dominionists believe "the other" is not just to be feared, it is to be crushed. Dominionists come right out and say they are working on a conspiracy for world domination. Koltko-Rivera counts off for us, from their own mission statement, what they call the "Seven Mountains": "They specifically want to dominate religion, family, government, arts and entertainment, media, business, and education. If that isn't a conspiracy to dominate the world, what is?" They also preach in a language of spiritual warfare, which incites violence. These people have now targeted the Statue of Liberty—and all goddess statues in the official artwork of the United States—as symbols of the great female expression of Satan, the one they call "the Whore of Babylon"—the one who must be destroyed.

"It does me no injury for my neighbour to say there are twenty gods, or no god. It neither picks my pocket nor breaks my leg."

—Thomas Jefferson, *Notes on the State of Virginia*

As we worked on this book, the New Apostolic Reformation orchestrated a political religious crusade of prayer and hate speech targeted directly at the goddess. Called the DC-40, it advertised in slickly produced videos on the Internet using blood-drenched rhetoric that the female version of Satan was leading this country astray. They called for changing the name of the District of Columbia to the District of Christ, and replacing the goddess of Freedom statue that crowns the Capitol dome with a Christian cross. Selena Fox described it as an "attempt to turn the United States of America from a religiously diverse, pluralistic society, into one that would be a monoculutre, a particular form of political Christianity." An enormous amount of negative energy was expended by people who call themselves Christians, imagining violence and destruction raining down on the symbolic goddesses in the nation's capital, as well as on the liberal politicians whom they consider to be possessed by demons. Fox was particularly disturbed by their attack on Columbia, who represents an inclusive spirit of America. "This is an attack on the basic freedoms upon which our country was founded," she said.

The Republican Party has discovered how easy it is to manipulate evangelical believers into turning out to vote in massive numbers. Evangelicals were enormously helpful in getting George W. Bush elected both times, and their lobbying influenced the confirmation of conservative Supreme Court justices Samuel Alito and John Roberts. The belief of the New Apostolic Reformation, that man was created to have dominion over the Earth, has also contributed to stalling any serious political efforts to mitigate man-made climate change. Dominionists are taking the longest to come around to being environmental stewards, because they are so offended at the challenge to their belief that God placed man in the dominant position on Earth that they refuse to consider the interconnectedness of all life. What is lacking is a reverent attitude that life is sacred in nature, and as Max Dashú put it, reverence for the Earth is what is important, not what god or goddess you believe in.

A More Macho Jesus

Some evangelical leaders in the United States identified a new mission in the 1930s and '40s: to influence politics and create dominion. Jeff Sharlet documents in his book *The Family: The Secret Fundamentalism at the Heart of American Power* how a more aggressive version of Christianity was crafted deliberately to appeal to politicians. Leaders of this movement preached images of a more macho Jesus who believed in building up military defense. By the 1950s their secret political movement had grown so powerful that President Eisenhower, whose election was guaranteed by their support, began attending their prayer breakfasts and assisted in adding "one nation under God" to our Pledge of Allegiance and "in God we trust" to our coins. Neither of these evangelical statements had been on any government issue before the 1950s, though today many people point to these mottoes as proof that the United States was founded as a Christian nation.

"In this . . . Land of equal liberty it is our boast, that a man's religious tenets will not forfeit the protection of the Laws, nor deprive him of the right of attaining and holding the highest Offices that are known in the United States."

—George Washington, letter to the members of the New Church in Baltimore, January 27, 1793

The presidential elections of 2008 and 2012 drew these extremist Christians into the national spotlight as never before, with headlines like Texas governor "Rick Perry's Pastor Calls Statue of Liberty a Demon." Perry and Palin are among many Republican hopefuls who have affiliated with the mega-churches preaching Dominionist philosophy. Mike Huckabee, Ron Paul, Newt Gingrich, Ted Cruz, Michele Bachmann, and Bobby Jindal have all proclaimed their socially conservative values in front of these crowds and have received their financial backing in return. Arthur Goldwag says that politicians who support the "new hate" of these groups during election season, ironically, almost always revert to the corporate agenda as soon as they are elected, shipping all those jobs they promised overseas and putting into place measures that will harm the very people who supported them. With enough politicians infected by the Dominionist mind-set of no compromise, the end result will be stagnation in Congress. Politics is compromise. It doesn't work unless you can find common ground with your opposition to make compromise and move forward.

Allow Room for the Goddess

Misinterpreting scripture in order to conclude that all goddesses are one big whore-monster is part of an anti-female agenda that yearns for some idyllic version of 1950s America, where masculine white men were decidedly in control, and women stayed home. It may be hard to believe, but behind all this crazy talk about the Statue of Liberty, we

Figure 7.8. Suffragists wore the costume of the Statue of Liberty during their demonstrations for the woman's right to vote. This woman was identified in the paper only as Mrs. David O'Neil at the 1916 Democratic National Convention in St. Louis. Women's History Collection, Division of Social History (Political Collections), National Museum of American History, Smithsonian Institution.

discovered a fear of women's sexuality and women's power. Demonizing the female principle means more than demonizing women, however. It means demonizing everything stereotypically connected with women, including the qualities of nurturance and intuition when expressed by men. Those stuck in the patriarchal paradigm cast caring and creative men as weak, meaning men who develop their nurturing sides are also targets for ridicule.

In a nation that was founded to protect religious freedom and freedom of speech, anyone should be allowed to say that the goddess, or the Statue of Liberty for that matter, is the Whore of Babylon if they choose. However, when those same people turn around and say that religious freedom in this nation does not apply to anyone other than members of their particular brand of evangelical Christianity, then that's a problem. The Statue of Liberty reminds us that we all have the freedom to ask questions. Who you are and why you are here should not be just a matter of blind belief. You can and should discuss the ideas you have accepted since you were a child. You can and should challenge your assumptions, and that includes the folklore of your religion—especially if it does not allow room for the Goddess.

8

The Black Statue of Liberty

There's another rumor on the Internet announcing that the creators of the Statue of Liberty were racist because they changed the face of the statue to be European when it was originally supposed to be a freed slave woman. Like all good rumors, this one contains just enough truth to add resonance to the story, while adding fabrications that sadly deflect the reader into misplaced feelings of outrage over a racial injustice that never occurred. The basic premise of this claim is that Bartholdi originally designed the Statue of Liberty as a freed slave woman but then changed the face after folks in the Southern states objected. That is completely untrue, but unfortunately, this misdirected call for justice is obscuring the connection that the Statue of Liberty really does have with the fight for abolition and the U.S. Civil War. The intricacies of how she was inspired by abolitionist tendencies and the Union victory take a little more time to explain than the usual Internet rumor, however, and we will attempt to do that in this chapter in the larger context of a discussion about the dichotomy of American liberty.

This dichotomy of American liberty comes down to its unequal application and can be summed up in the person of Thomas Jefferson. Years ago, anything Thomas Jefferson said was just fine with us, as we were focused exclusively on his brilliant, descriptive dream of an enlightened republic and the separation of church and state. But now we look at him and wonder how history's most eloquent prophet of liberty could

remain a slaveholding aristocrat to the end of his days. How could someone compose such moving words on liberty as a right of the individual,
and then turn around and advocate Indian removal by luring them into
debt in order to obligate the selling of more tribal lands?

We were also inspired to look into the religion of the enslaved
Africans and their descendants and how it contributed a special understanding of "Goddess in the New World." The ancestral spirits from the
Yoruba tradition that followed the slaves across the ocean from West
Africa syncretized with Native American and Catholic traditions into a
manifestation of the female divine that is uniquely American. We also
studied what some of the newly freed Black Americans thought of the
Statue of Liberty as it was being built through the Reconstruction era
after the Civil War and into the Gilded Age. Studying this period of
history introduced us to the dilemma of liberty versus property and the
right to make a profit. The connection of the Statue of Liberty to slavery also led us to discover a real conspiracy to keep Black Americans out
of the artwork of the Capitol.

A Very Bitter Joke

"For Black Americans the Statue of Liberty is simply a very bitter joke,"
said writer James Baldwin, "meaning nothing to us."[1] Congressional
delegate Eleanor Holmes Norton disagreed, saying that attaching negativism to the 1986 renovation of the Statue of Liberty was not in her
interest. "The liberty notion is stirring to anyone . . . [and] American
symbols should not be taken to be the property of a particular group of
our heterogeneous society," she said, concluding that "the ironies of the
symbols have to be embraced."[2] Yoruban priestess Aina Olomo described
African Americans' complicated relationship with the Statue of Liberty
in terms of her religious practice and what she calls "a national soul
that evolves as part of the cultural experience." When she is in a foreign country, she explains, she "will respond when someone steps on my
national soul. I may not necessarily be a Republican or a Democrat, or I
may not necessarily agree with . . . some of the great heroes of our time,
but . . . it's sort of like a knee-jerk response . . . when that national col-

lective energy responds to something that is very deep in our psyche." In her experience, African Americans feel no special affinity for the Statue of Liberty because they consider it a symbol for the immigrants who came to this land looking for opportunity. Her ancestors came here as someone else's property, bought and paid for, and as such, a symbol to welcome immigrants would have no resonance.

Black Americans' opinions of the Statue of Liberty run the gamut today, just as they did when it was new. Fundraising for the statue began during the post–Civil War era and continued on through the ensuing violent clampdown, especially in the Southern states, as the old white power reasserted itself over Black Americans' newly won rights. During the fifteen years it took to create the Statue of Liberty, the United States was a place of the Ku Klux Klan and mob killings, where the first Black men elected to political office were pressured out or murdered. Lynchings of Black men increased from several hundred a year in the 1880s into the thousands by the end of the century.[3]

Suffragist Ida B. Wells took on lynching as her personal cause, and her investigative reporting brought the subject the notoriety it deserved, debunking the popular misbelief that most lynchings were punishment for black-on-white rape. She took on the formidable Frances Willard of the Woman's Christian Temperance Union for adding to the problem with Willard's slur that Black men were more prone to rape, especially when intoxicated, and therefore Southern white women needed the vote to protect themselves.

In W. E. B. Du Bois's autobiography, he wrote about his first glimpses of the Statue of Liberty in 1894. He recounted as they floated past it, he overheard a little French girl on the boat describing the statue as having "its back toward America, and its face toward France." To him, this was a perfect metaphor for how liberty had turned its back on so many people who called themselves Americans. This dissonance between the symbolism of the Statue of Liberty and the reality of life for Black Americans converged on Easter Sunday in 1906 in Springfield, Missouri, when three Black men were lynched from a bandstand where a replica Statue of Liberty rose above them.

"'Liberty enlightening the world,' indeed! The expression makes

Figure 8.1. An editorial illustration in the *St. Louis Post-Dispatch*, April 17, 1906, showing the Gottfried Tower in Springfield, Missouri, where three Black men were lynched on a bandstand with a replica Statue of Liberty above them. Library of Congress.

us sick," said one editorial writer for the *Cleveland Gazette,* a periodical read predominantly by African Americans, in 1886.[4] Many African American newspapers did include positive reports on the fundraising campaigns for the pedestal,[5] as well as the celebrations surrounding the statue's unveiling, but others could see only the giant hypocrisy. Referring to the ongoing struggle to provide more than a glowworm of light from the torch, the *Cleveland Gazette* editorial continued, "Shove the Bartholdi statue, torch and all, into the ocean." Liberty should not be lit "until the 'liberty' of this country is such as to make it possible for an industrious and inoffensive colored man in the South to earn a respectable living for himself and family, without being ku-kluxed, perhaps murdered, his daughter and wife outraged, and his property destroyed."

Racism: Made in America

After reading various Black Americans' opinions on the concept of American-made liberty portrayed as a Euro-American female, we were led to the realization that racism is an artificially constructed concept—and how it was, essentially, made in America. In the Mediterranean during the Roman Empire, anywhere from 40 to 80 percent of the population was enslaved, and slaves came in all colors, meaning African slaves were just one group of many. Discrimination wasn't based on the color of skin: all slaves were considered subhuman. In the earliest days of colonizing North America, as we learned from Howard Zinn's *A People's History of the United States,* it was much the same. The distinction was drawn between rich and poor, not black and white. Black indentured servants as well as whites worked off their time allotments and then were freed. Many of them, both black and white, were beaten and horribly abused, and some had their contracts sold from master to master, leading to a lifetime of servitude, again for both black and white.

When British colonization began in earnest, the majority of people coming over, of all colors, were traveling as indentured servants. As they earned their freedom, and new servants replaced the old, a new and rapidly expanding class of poor and struggling people appeared. The privileged few at the top grew increasingly nervous about being so outnumbered. Their greatest fear was the threat of riotous hordes rising up to challenge their authority. And that's exactly what happened. Zinn's book describes dozens of uprisings like Bacon's Rebellion in Virginia in 1676 where poor whites and poor blacks worked together with farmers and frontiersmen to overthrow the governor of Virginia. This rising disquiet prompted the implementation of racial segregation laws.[6]

Racism was not natural in the interaction between the blacks and whites of the working poor of the colonies. Blacks and whites lived and worked side by side until gradually laws were instituted discriminating against blacks and rewarding poor whites, especially in terms of capturing runaway servants and slaves. In the very early days of the colonies, blacks and whites intermarried, blacks hired whites, whites left property to blacks, and black planters even bought African slaves. But by the end of the 1600s, new laws began restricting the interracial socialization. It became illegal for blacks to employ whites, for example. A 1705 law passed in Virginia and Maryland made it against the law for a black man to strike a white man. Blacks could no longer hold office or testify in court.[7]

A white middle class was being created as a buffer and a wedge to prevent the poor classes of all colors from banding together to address common complaints. Racism was deliberately encouraged through "class scorn," rewarding the whites in minor ways to make them feel superior, Zinn says, and limiting the opportunities for free Blacks. When the population of blacks grew to outnumber whites, orphans and convicts were rounded up in England and shipped over to even the numbers. Rebellions continued to flare up regardless, and by 1760, Zinn counted eighteen uprisings against colonial governments and six specifically black rebellions.[8] Around 1765, the rebellious energy of the lower classes was masterfully refocused toward England as the common enemy of them all. Through the use of images of Lady Liberty and the rhetoric of liberty for all, even whites who held no property began to feel united with the upper class in a land of opportunity. Soon after the war, the number of whites entering servitude dropped precipitously,[9] indicating they bought the promise dangled before them of individual liberty for all.

Liberty versus Property

We learn in school that the decades leading up to the Civil War were all about the conflict over slavery, but in fact the subjects of most concern were property and capital and how to hold on to them as the populations of laborers and immigrants rose. Laborers and immigrants were always in the majority in Euro-American settlements, and as soon as the Revolutionary War was over, these propertyless classes began agitating. They had fought for independence, they argued, so they should also have the right to vote and participate in self-governing. Uprisings like Rhode Island's Dorr Rebellion in 1841 resulted in most state constitutions dropping the requirement of owning property in order to vote, but

Figure 8.2. *We Came to America* by Faith Ringgold, acrylic on canvas, painted and pieced border. A Black Statue of Liberty holding a baby lights the way for the ecstatic naked slaves rejoicing in the water while a slave ship burns in the background. Faith Ringgold copyright 1997, used with permission.

just for native-born citizens. The property restriction remained in effect for immigrants much longer, one of the minor concessions Zinn points to where small liberties like these were given out to just a fraction of the population at a time in order to divide and elevate them just a bit above the grumbling masses. The result was a growing middle class that gained just enough freedom to feel superior to the poor. Hopeful for their own future, they were much less likely to participate in a riot against the gentry. The thinking was that the poor would defend the rich if given enough freedom to hope that one day they might be one of them.

As the Civil War approached, more people started talking about liberty in terms of property.[10] The fading idealism of the Revolutionary generation, whose favored phrase had been "Liberty and Independence," was being replaced by a new motto: "Liberty and Prosperity." Slaveholders in the South were growing increasingly hostile about defending their own liberty from what they perceived as tyranny in the form of laws restricting their rights as property owners.

Speaking in Baltimore in 1864, Abraham Lincoln poignantly articulated how the notion of liberty could be so bewildering. He compared the liberty of the sheep, who did not want to be eaten, to the liberty of the wolf, who wanted to eat them.

> The world has never had a good definition of the word liberty, and the American people, just now, are much in want of one. We all declare for liberty; but in using the same word we do not all mean the same thing. With some the word liberty may mean for each man to do as he pleases with himself, and the product of his labor; while with others the same word may mean for some men to do as they please with other men, and the product of other men's labor. Here are two, not only different, but incompatible things, called by the same name—liberty. And it follows that each of the things is, by the respective parties, called by two different and incompatible names— liberty and tyranny.[11]

When the framers of the Constitution protected the liberty of the slaveholders over the liberty of the slaves, they must have known that some people's pursuits would jeopardize other people's happiness. The resulting mutually exclusive definitions of American liberty that developed meant that during the Civil War images of the American Liberty goddess were popular on both sides of the conflict. In the North she was seen freeing slaves, and in the South she fought against the tyranny of the federal government. Southern women dressed as the Roman goddess Libertas and posed for photographs flanked by Confederate soldiers, bayonets crossed overhead, while in the North Thomas Nast launched his career drawing cartoons of Columbia-Liberty weeping over the grave of a Union soldier or casting a ballot for Abraham Lincoln.

Figure 8.3. *Rather Die Freemen Than Live to Be Slaves* proclaims the African American soldier to the Columbia-Liberty goddess supporting the regimental flag of the 3rd Regiment United States Colored Troops. Photo card of painting by David Bustill, circa 1860–1870. Library of Congress.

The disconnect between liberty and property persisted after the abolition of slavery. The second industrial revolution that followed the war brought the inclination to think of liberty in terms of unrestricted trade. "Liberty and Commerce" became the slogan, and the heroes of the day were business titans whose investments built the new infrastructure of capitalism. Advertisers began unabashedly attaching patriotic symbols to all kinds of products as the repeated connection between liberty and commerce fed into the growth of the giant corporation era, where profit was the only motive.

The Real Connection between Slavery
and the Statue of Liberty

One of the wisps of truth behind the rumor that the Statue of Liberty used to be a freed slave woman is the sympathy that those who designed her felt for the abolitionist movement and Union cause. Édouard de Laboulaye, the mastermind behind the Statue of Liberty, was an impassioned abolitionist, writing as early as 1840 that slavery was not only evil but also would make the republican form of government unsustainable. He was especially active in the abolitionist movement between 1848 and 1852 during France's Second Republic when, for a brief time, slavery was outlawed in France and in all the colonies in the French Empire. At this time, Laboulaye and his colleagues talked enthusiastically about ending slavery on the face of the Earth. Laboulaye formed the French Anti-Slavery Society in 1865, and his wife, Micheline, headed the women's division, collecting clothes and donations for the newly freed slaves in the United States. In 1867, Laboulaye organized a congress of international abolitionist societies in connection with the Paris World Expo, and it was there that he and sculptor Bartholdi met Khedive Ishma'il Pasha of Egypt, whose name will come up yet again as we reveal another morsel of truth in the Black Statue of Liberty rumor.

According to Bartholdi, the first suggestion to create a statue "of Liberty" was made by Laboulaye at an 1865 dinner party he held at his home near Paris to celebrate the Union victory in the United States. This genesis of the Statue of Liberty idea has been questioned by some historians, because it was not reported until twenty years after the event, and then only in Bartholdi's rather self-serving biography of the statue. In it, Bartholdi described an illustrious group of French abolitionists who decided to create a medallion to present to the widow of Abraham Lincoln because they wanted her to know that not all of France had supported the Confederate South as their emperor Napoleon III had done. In describing the medallion they declared that President Lincoln had upheld the republic without "veiling the Statue of Liberty." Perhaps this was the seed that Bartholdi is referring to as prompting them several years later to attempt the creation of an actual statue of Liberty.

Laboulaye was honored by many Americans for his very vocal support of the cause of the Union with his writings that were published in both France and in the States. There can be no doubt that in the minds of his contemporaries when the project first began, the Statue of Liberty was related to the successful end of the Civil War. They talked about giving Liberty the task of healing the wounds of war,[12] and even as late as 1886 at the New York dedication ceremony, there were several mentions of the abolition of slavery. By this time, however, the meme that Lady Liberty was a birthday gift in honor of the 1876 centennial had become more popular. The slavery connection was already receding into the background, and by the time the immigration overlay was added to the statue's interpretation in the twentieth century, it had almost completely faded away.

The National Park Service commissioned an official inquiry into the Black Statue of Liberty rumor in the year 2000. Led by Rebecca Joseph, the investigators concluded that Bartholdi himself seems to have been mainly apolitical, and more interested in the project in artistic terms and how he could make his reputation on it. When he made his exploratory tour of the United States in 1871 to gauge interest in the project, he used letters of introduction that Laboulaye and company had given him, which provided Bartholdi with access to some of the most prominent abolitionists and Northern industrialists in the country. Joseph noted that Bartholdi was recorded as making "frequent references to race-related subjects" at these meetings, though these references sounded more like what Laboulaye suggested he should say rather than strongly held personal beliefs.[13] Ultimately the NPS report concluded that there is no truth in the rumor that Bartholdi's Statue of Liberty ever had anything but a traditionally Roman face.

We will take one final look at rumors before we move on to a real conspiracy about the exclusion of Black Americans in government-commissioned artwork. Conspiracy theorists trying to claim that the Statue of Liberty used to be a Black woman will often bring up the mistaken idea that the statue used to be an Egyptian woman. As we reviewed in the previous chapter, the most that can be said accurately in this regard is that the designer of the Statue of Liberty had conceived of an earlier statue of an Egyptian woman. Now, an Egyptian woman would not be what most people have in mind when they hear that the Statue of Liberty used to be a Black woman, but conspiracy theorists are famous for grasping at straws.

As we discussed in chapter 7, the study maquettes that survive from both the Suez Canal proposal (figure 7.5, p. 194) and the Statue of Liberty (figure 9.1, p. 235) do resemble one another, but Bartholdi was careful to distinguish between them, indicating one was a commercial venture and the other a work of inspirational art. There was no sense of liberty about the peasant woman proposed to hold the light in Egypt, and in fact, her human counterparts would probably have been drafted into the army of forced labor that ended up digging the massive canal.

Blacks Segregated Out of America's Mythic Dimension

It's ironic that falsehoods have to be concocted to connect the Statue of Liberty to slavery, when the connection is clear enough already. And no conspiracy rumors are needed when just a few hundred miles south, in Washington, D.C., there was a true conspiracy to remove images of Black Americans from the artwork of the U.S. Capitol. We learned a great deal about this subject from art historian Vivien Green Fryd in her groundbreaking book *Art and Empire: The Politics of Ethnicity in the U.S. Capitol.* Fryd shows that it's as if Black people didn't even exist during this time in our history. Only a handful of Black people can be found in all the murals and statuary decorating our nation's Capitol, and they are always marginalized as slaves lurking in the shadows. Fryd says that excluding African Americans from these works of art eliminates them "from the realm of our mythic identity in the U.S. Capitol building." One clear example of the deliberateness of this decision can be seen in the changes forced on the designer of the *Statue of Freedom* on the Capitol dome, which we review in chapter 11.

Native Americans, on the other hand, the other group with a problematical skin tone at the time, are featured much more prominently and frequently in the Capitol artwork, but not without a catch. In

Figure 8.4. This 1792 painting demonstrates the early abolitionist movement in the new United States, arguing that the newly won liberty should be extended to slaves, too. Samuel Jennings was commissioned by the Library Company of Philadelphia, a group with anti-slavery inclinations, to create a painting showing *Liberty Displaying the Arts and Sciences, or the Genius of America Encouraging the Emancipation of the Blacks*. Slaves bow at Liberty's feet, while in the background more slaves dance around a maypole.

the mythic identity of the U.S. Capitol Building, Native Americans are always depicted in the form of the Vanishing Indian—melancholy, or dying, or near a grave. Indians were allowed to "take on mythico-historical associations," says Fryd, "unlike blacks, because blacks reminded Americans of the pro-slavery and anti-slavery arguments that were the basis of the United States until the end of the Civil War."

The artwork of the Capitol was created mostly in the era leading up to and including the Civil War, when Euro-Americans were trying to convince themselves that they had a Manifest Destiny to bring culture and Christianity to the uncivilized people of the world. Through artwork and literature, they described the Indians as doomed to either complete assimilation in the Euro-American culture or to eventual extinction. The Vanishing Indian trope encouraged many enthusiasts with the best of intentions to swoop into Native cultures and remove their sacred objects to museums for so-called safekeeping. Winona LaDuke writes poignantly of this in her book *Recovering the Sacred* in which she recounts how even genetic material from the living was gathered for research without permission, and ancestors' bones were dug up and removed, to be reconstructed as skeletons in museum displays.

Fryd told us of two statues that were so offensive to American Indian activists that they were permanently removed from the stairway entrance on the east side of the Capitol when the entrance was expanded in the 1950s. Greenough's *The Rescue* and Persico's *Columbus's Discovery of America* had been on prominent display since 1837 and, until the twentieth century, had suited most Americans' tastes just fine. One depicts a bloodthirsty savage attacking a frontier family, and the other shows an Indian maiden cowering in submission as an armored Columbus strides ashore.

The Rescue was permanently damaged in the move, and today both works languish forgotten in storage. But as offensive as they are in terms of being provided without any context, Fryd believes it was a mistake to remove them. She would have preferred they be kept on display as documentation of the changing attitudes of the United States, because at one point these statues were used to promote what was thought to be the predestined nature of westward expansion. "If you pretend that didn't happen," says Fryd, "if you erase it, then you are sanitizing our history, and that's incredibly problematic. You're pretending that this history didn't happen, that our Congressmen didn't commission these works of art."

It's important to examine the portions of our history that make us cringe, especially in regard to our evolving sense of human rights and equal justice. Having objectionable statues like these on display—with the appropriate explanation on the plaques and from the guides—would help future generations see more clearly the paths we as a people have chosen, paths that have led us to where we are today.

Abolitionists versus Suffragists

Historically there is a direct connection between women's rights and civil rights. Women, of course, are also largely missing from the original artwork in the U.S. Capitol, except in the guises we discuss throughout this book. They are either idealized allegorical embodiments of the virtues, or they are saintly mother figures, pictured in the one and only approved role for women. The official woman suffrage movement in the United States began as an offshoot of the abolition movement, much as the second wave of the women's movement of the 1970s can be credited as being an offshoot of the civil rights movement. During both of these protest movements, women volunteers showed up to help and were told to either sit in the balcony or go make the coffee, but most of all, keep quiet.

This challenge to women's authority, and to their mental ability to help those less fortunate, led women of both generations to a newly raised consciousness. They must organize a separate movement to open up opportunities for women. For the first few decades of the nascent woman suffrage movement, in the 1840s and 1850s, abolitionists and women's rights activists worked side by side, men and women together, on both causes.

As the Civil War loomed, most woman suffragists willingly laid down their advocacy work to assist with the war efforts. But as soon as the war was over, when they tried to resume their activism, they found a wedge had been driven between these two disenfranchised groups. Those advocating for Black Americans were pitted against those working for women's rights, decreasing the effectiveness of both of their campaigns.

Many women insisted that the same civil rights coming for ex-slaves be granted simultaneously to women, but factions within the abolitionist movement disagreed. They called it "the Negro's hour," and worried if woman suffrage was pushed at the same time, suffrage for the Black man might be jeopardized. At the first annual meeting of the American Equal Rights Association in 1867, Sojourner Truth, a former slave, prominent suffragist, and abolitionist said, "If colored men get their rights, and colored women not theirs, the colored men will be masters over the women, and it will be just as bad as it was before. . . . I am for keeping the thing going while things are stirring; because if we wait till it is still, it will take a great deal to get it going again."[14]

When it came time to draft the Fourteenth Amendment to the Constitution, which was designed to eradicate the three-fifths clause and grant full citizenship to freed slaves, someone craftily inserted the word "male" into the language. Then just to be sure, they repeated it three times, making it very clear that full citizenship was being withheld from Black women. It was the first time gender was mentioned in the federal Constitution,* and women's rights activists were furious. They argued that it effectively turned females into noncitizens.

Former slave Frederick Douglass initially joined the women's rights activists in opposition to the Fourteenth Amendment, but later switched his support. He said at the 1868 meeting of the Equal Rights Association that "the government of this country loves women. They are the sisters, mothers, wives and daughters of our rulers; but the negro is loathed. . . . The negro needs suffrage . . . for his own elevation from the position of a drudge to that of an influential member of society."[15]

When the Fourteenth Amendment passed, women realized that their only option was to get their own Constitutional amendment. Elizabeth Cady Stanton predicted that if "male" was introduced into the U.S. Constitution, it would take them a century to get it out, but she was wrong. It's actually taken longer, because the Equal Rights Amendment, which would prohibit discrimination on the basis of gender, has never passed. Ask most young people today if women have equal rights guaranteed in the U.S. Constitution, and they will mistakenly say yes. "We talk about exporting women's rights," historian Sally Roesch Wagner told us, but "the world looks at us and says, well, we have a greater proportion of our leadership that are women than you do, and we guarantee women equal rights."

---

*Voting laws in some of the early colonies allowed female property owners to vote. Gradually, state constitutions inserted the word "male" into voter rights, meaning that until the Fourteenth Amendment, the gender discrimination against voting came from local state legislation, not the Constitution.

It bears repeating here that the United States currently ranks 71 on a list of 190 countries in terms of percentage of women in the national legislature, with approximately 19 percent of the U.S. Congress composed of women.[16] Many women's rights activists point to the Nordic countries as an example for how legislation and quotas are necessary to increase the number of female leaders in the United States. Gender equality has been legislated into both the home and society in many northern European countries, and today approximately 40 percent of the positions in their respective governing legislatures are held by women.

The United States missed the chance for a second American Revolution at this point in history. If the series of Constitutional amendments designed to protect newly freed slaves after the Civil War had included women, Wagner says it would have been truly revolutionary, because finally the Constitution would have guaranteed equal rights for everyone. The original Constitution contained slavery as a foundation principle of the United States government, and "the revised Constitution, after the abolition of slavery," said Wagner, "contained sexism as a foundation principle of the United States government."[17]

The betrayal felt by many woman suffragists by their former allies in the abolition movement brought ugly emotions to the surface and revealed embarrassing streaks of racism and xenophobia. Elizabeth Cady Stanton in particular has been called out for her racist language, but she was by no means the only one saying that educated white women deserved the vote before freed slaves and illiterate immigrants. Carrie Chapman Catt, who inherited leadership of the suffrage movement from Susan B. Anthony and went on to found the League of Women Voters, used nativist language that was just as offensive, advocating that women needed the vote to achieve white supremacy.

Often criticized as elitist, toward the turn of the century suffragists began to reform their own movement and found common ground with labor organizers during the Progressive Era. Activists like Jane Addams joined the suffrage cause and encouraged women to bring their mothering tendencies out into the community to aid the poor. The efforts of suffragists, labor unions, immigrants, peace activists, and other progressives coalesced under several common goals, such as ending child labor and creating better conditions for working women.

Liberty and the Slave Religion

The question of why Black women were singled out for discrimination in the Constitution returned us to one of our original questions about the Goddess in the New World. In chapter 10 we look at the symbolism of the "dark mother" and how it played into the fear peculiar to Western society of women's life-giving power. This led us to study the African traditions brought over to this country by the slaves, which included venerating their ancestors and goddesslike entities. Slaves and their proud descendants in North America reflect some of their ancestors' African traditions, as evinced by the experiential approach they employ in Christian worship today. Like the Native American traditions, African traditions place more emphasis on experience than on dogma. Dancing and drumming are so integral to their worship that some say they dance their religion.

In the Southern Hemisphere of the Americas the religious experience of slaves retained much more of the original African influence than it did in the North. This difference is explained by a number of factors. Most notably, the North did not have a constant re-Africanizing from new slaves in the form of the millions upon millions of newly kidnapped Africans arriving year after year in the South. The number of Africans imported directly into North America was far lower, meaning the Yoruba-based practices coming over from West Africa were not continually reintroduced like they were in the South, and were gradually forgotten. In North America, especially in the northern colonies, blacks were more integrated in Euro-American society when compared to the large concentrations of Africans working and living together on the South and Central American mines and plantations. Their isolation in the South from the Euro-American population facilitated the continuation of their private religious traditions.[18]

Finally, Catholic religious practices of South and Central America, which featured holy relics of ancestors/saints, candle lighting, votives,

Figure 8.5. Yemonja is often depicted wearing blue and white and appearing much like the Virgin Mary, as in this photo from New Year's Eve, 2007, in Brazil. Photo: FrancoBras.

altars, and above all the Virgin Mary's appeal as a mother goddess, resonated better with African traditions than did the dour and image-hating Protestant religious practices of the English colonies. The only part of North America that developed a strong Yoruba tradition was New Orleans, resulting from the large wave of immigrants who fled there from the Haitian slave revolt of 1804.

Unlike slaveholders in Catholic South and Central America, many slaveholders in Protestant North America initially resisted converting their slaves to Christianity. They struggled with a moral puzzle: perhaps it was somehow wrong to hold a fellow Christian in bondage. Second, there was the fear that once baptized, slaves would become more rebellious upon hearing the doctrine that all men are created in the image of God. Thus, in the slave quarters of the North a curious mixture of magic and religion flourished side by side, much like the folk magic traditions that continued in the Protestant English colonies.[19] Slaves used what they remembered from their African traditions and developed intricate forms of conjuring to accommodate Christianity within their supernatural beliefs. Magical charms and hexes helped these oppressed people both resist and also endure the harshness of their reality and were integrated into their religious beliefs.

Slaves in North America were attracted to the Protestant revivalist movement known as the First Great Awakening in the 1730s and 1740s, in part because the preachers evangelized about a personal religious experience with the Holy Spirit that often included ecstatic dancing and emotional calling out. When converted, however, slaves continued to have a strained relationship with Christianity. "Religious slaveholders are the worst," said Frederick Douglass in his autobiography, observing how the sanctimony was used as a "covering for the most horrid crimes,—a justifier of the most appalling barbarity . . . —and a dark shelter under, which . . . the most infernal deeds of slaveholders find the strongest protection."[20]

Yemonja Crossed the Ocean to Protect the Slaves

Most African slaves imported to the Americas came from areas in West Africa where they practiced a set of spiritual beliefs called Yoruba. Yoruba spirituality includes reverence for ancestors as well as forces of nature called orishas, and today it is ranked as the eighth most popular religion in the world. This global appeal of Yoruba is due in part to how well the African religious practices were retained and absorbed into the

Figure 8.6. In Brazil, millions gather on beaches to honor Yemonja through ceremonies involving offerings to the sea. Petitioners gather to launch votives in boats full of flowers, mirrors, candles, and dolls to their ocean goddess. They ceremonially carry these statues to bathe them in the ocean for good luck. February 2013. Photo: Bahia Notícias.

local traditions in the Americas and then syncretized with Catholicism. Blended practices like Voudoun, Candomble, and Santeria have wide appeal among those who resonate with nature-based religions. In South and Central America, the curious result is that millions of people decorate their religious regalia with Native American feathers while praying for fertility and good fortune to a divine female named for an African water deity who, when she appears in human or mermaid forms, looks a lot like the Virgin Mary.

When we asked Yoruban priestess Aina Olomo which of the Yoruban orishas, or divine entities, she might compare to the Statue of Liberty, she named Yemonja. Yemonja began as a freshwater river deity in Nigeria and then transformed herself into a saltwater great mother goddess of the sea. Merged with the sea, Yemonja is too large to come inside the church, said Olomo, adding that "Yemonja was not Christianized or syncretized; instead, the Virgin Mary was Africanized."

Because Yemonja transformed her mythology and became someone else, Olomo sees her as "the one most closely aligned to an African concept of liberty and a future after enslavement."

Olomo tells of countless reports of mermaids and other visions of Yemonja seen from the crowded ships on which kidnapped Africans were making the ocean crossing, taking heart that she was crossing with them. The packing of humans on slave ships was notoriously intolerable, and especially so for pregnant women. Imagine giving birth while chained to corpses stacked row by row in eighteen inches of space, covered in filth. To these tormented people, the sea became their only hope for freedom, as that way led back home.

Followers of Yoruba spirituality are required to show respect to their orishas. Orisha is not a word one would translate directly into "god" or "goddess," Olomo explained, comparing them rather to a force of nature. "It is the natural world that allows itself a human experience as a consciousness selected for worship or an archetype." Some orishas who manifest in human psychology are fire, some are air, some water, and so forth, and each power of nature has its own divine consciousness. "Through the orisha psyche," she said, "the human race experiences and has access to the sacred." Similar to the instructions we hear regularly from the Native Americans, the orishas demand that "we must love, honor, and respect all elements of nature and this planet."

Olomo compared this demand for respect for this overwhelming awesome power to what would happen if one walked out into a stormy sea farther than one could stand. It wouldn't matter to the storm if you are a good person or a bad person. It is just doing its thing. "How we care for the planet influences the depth of our divinities' receptiveness and the amount of their divine energies that they send to us," concludes Olomo.

Any tradition that affirms ancestor veneration as Yoruba spirituality does, ties people together with both their future and their past in a constant reminder that *we are one.* Olomo calls a human being "a collection of all the genetic codes stored in their blood," including everything internalized by the family preceding them. She sees her job

Figure 8.7. Yemonja is remembered as a mermaid who crossed the ocean, protecting her captured followers on slave ships, and transforming herself so she could stay with them on these distant shores. Photo: Toluaye.

as an individual to add to that ancestral compilation. "Your experiences join the collective information and you add to the continual process," she said. We are all responsible to the past as well as to the future. The long periods of incarceration their ancestors endured has also conferred African Americans with a unique commitment to freedom.

Modern Descendants of Yemonja as the Statue of Liberty

A force of nature could be a descriptive term for the stereotype of the black mother in U.S. culture today: they are tough, no-nonsense, and can intimidate even the most imposing of men, especially when their children's welfare is at issue. Today, many of their children are victims of the profit-driven War on Drugs, which has resulted in far higher incarceration rates per capita in America than anywhere else in the world, with an overwhelming majority of imprisoned nonviolent drug offenders being African Americans.[21] One in every one hundred Americans today is behind bars,[22] giving our nation a new snarl to unravel in the challenge between liberty and privilege.

Sometimes, in connection with that Internet rumor that the Statue of Liberty was originally an African woman, there will be reference to a strong woman poem we love called "Black Statue of Liberty" by spoken-word artist Jessica Care Moore. Its female narrator strikes us as a descendant of a force of nature like Yemonja. Quoting just a few lines here should make it clear why we believe discovering this poem almost makes the spreading of that inaccurate rumor worthwhile.

> *I stand still above an island, fist straight in the air*
> *Scar on my face, thick braid in my hair*
>
> . . . .
>
> *I'm a symbol of freedom, but I'm still not free*
>
> . . . .
>
> *I sweep crack pipes out of school yards*
> *nurture my man when times are hard.*
> *So, where the hell's my statue?*
>
> . . . .
>
> *I can bake cookies, bear babies, preside over revolutions*
> *Get rings out of tubs, wear a suit, sport baggy jeans,*
>   *slick my hair back*
> *Or tie it up in braids.*
> *My aura is unafraid.*
> *So, no statue in the big apple can mess with me.*

*I am the walking, talking, surviving, breathing,
    beautiful
Black Statue of Liberty.*[23]

From being rejected as a "bitter joke" to being accepted by the national soul, the Statue of Liberty proves that she is not the property of a particular group in our amalgamated society. Embracing the ironies of this particular symbol through its many interpretations and conflicts over American liberty allows us to view the history of the United States in a way that includes the histories of the persecuted peoples of this nation. Real Black women are a powerful force not to be trifled with. Focusing on empowering their inclusion in society so that their needs and solutions can contribute to the America of change should be what comes to mind when we hear any rumors about a Black Statue of Liberty.

9

The Statue of Liberty and the Secrets of Mary

Imagine the Statue of Liberty with her hip thrust out in a provocative pose and her breasts clearly defined. No, we're not describing the famous Mae West impersonation of the Statue of Liberty from her movie *Belle of the Nineties,* but instead sculptor Auguste Bartholdi's first test models, or maquettes, he produced while working on Liberty's design conception. These early statuettes were decidedly more feminine than the one we're used to—though not nearly as buxom as Ms. West's version.

The psychological ramifications of the masking or displaying of the female form is a debate that has long raged in art history. In this chapter, we will look into some of that scholarship as we use imagery of the Virgin Mary to compare what we learned about the body hidden underneath all that drapery on the Statue of Liberty. The sexualization of the female form in the art world of the mid-1800s in France does play into the design of the Statue of Liberty, but Bartholdi's changes to the posture of his Liberty were made more to improve the aesthetic value of the gigantic statue when seen from a distance, rather than to downplay her sexuality.

The design of the maquettes for the Statue of Liberty did indeed grow more conservative as the models progressed under the influence of Bartholdi's mentor and partner on the project, Édouard de Laboulaye.

Figure 9.1. An early design study for the Statue of Liberty by Auguste Bartholdi. The left hand was to hold a broken chain, which Bartholdi moved to underneath her feet when he realized it would be too small to be seen from a distance. Photo: Musée Bartholdi, Colmar, reproduction copyright C. Kempf. Used with permission.

Laboulaye's own motives help illustrate the dilemma presented to women of that time in terms of defining their sexuality. Laboulaye was intent on disassociating their project from the sexually charged Marianne-Liberté of the French Revolution, whose partial nakedness and disarray were interpreted as riotous and unlawful. Ultimately, however, Bartholdi came to the conclusion that a straight body worked best because flat, linear proportions created a more regal impact and assisted the impression of movement that viewers perceive while floating past her on a boat.

The Goddess of America

Connecting the Statue of Liberty to the Virgin Mary started when we searched the Internet for the term "Goddess of the New World" and found "the Virgin of Guadalupe." What's this? A Marian apparition in Mexico is colloquially known as the Goddess of the New World? We knew we had to learn more. Actually, the Virgin of Guadalupe's official title from the pope is "Mother of the Americas" or "Patroness of the Americas," but no matter what you call her, the Virgin of Guadalupe has surely inspired millions with a liberating message.

Depicted on a five-hundred-year-old burlap canvas as a brown-skinned Native American woman in the traditional pose of the Virgin Mary, the painting of the Virgin of Guadalupe is classified as a Black Madonna, even though she has little in common with that genre of mysterious artwork from Europe's Middle Ages, which we feature in chapter 10. She falls into more of a subset of the phenomena that we call "the Brown Madonnas." Brown Madonnas were icons of Mary made to appeal to the Native Americans and African slaves, and the success of these images at creating unity between opposing cultures was phenomenal. Nicknamed La Morenita, or "little brown girl," the brown-skinned woman in the Virgin of Guadalupe painting is the lowest of the low when it comes to ranking suppressed peoples, and this is one of the reasons she's so popular—anyone can relate to her, especially the downtrodden. When Mexico fought to separate from Spain in 1810, the leader of the fight for independence carried an image of the Virgin of Guadalupe on his banner, as did the leaders of the 1910 Mexican Revolution.

Figure 9.2. The Virgin of Guadalupe in Mexico is known as the Goddess of the New World and has inspired millions with her liberational message.

The legend of the Virgin of Guadalupe helped convert millions of Natives to Catholicism in the first few decades of the Spanish conquest of the Aztec Empire, and while some would interpret that to mean that her image aided in their domination, among Mexicans she is seen as a liberator used by reformers and revolutionaries. "The impact of Mary's appearance as Guadalupe was tremendous," says author Sally Cuneen, because "the indigenous people became convinced that the Virgin did not have the same attitude to them as their white oppressors."[1] The painting of the Virgin of Guadalupe itself is recorded in historical documents long before the legend explaining its miraculous creation. It was just thirty years into the Spanish conquest, in 1556, when the painting is first referred to in writing as the subject of some controversy within the church because the Natives were attributing miracles to it claiming it was an image of their old Aztec mother goddess. This process of encouraging adherents of older Earth-based religions to recognize Christianity as something familiar and comforting is called syncretization, and other factions within the church have capitalized on it through the centuries as a means of conversion. But in this case the first mention of the painting is from Franciscan friars who were concerned that encouraging the Natives to believe that the image depicted a female Aztec deity in disguise meant they were bringing false idols into the church.

The legend that grew up to explain the painting's powers is very similar to those told about the origins of the Black Madonnas in Europe. On the hill of Tepeyac not far from downtown present-day Mexico City, close to a recently destroyed temple to the Aztec mother goddess, an apparition of the female divine appeared to a recently converted peasant. She identified herself to him as Tonantzin, and her message to him was that she would remain the "mother of you all" in this new form. Do not to be afraid, she told him, speaking in his native tongue of Nahuatl. "Am I not one of you?" She wanted the location marked again with a shrine holy to the mother, and the peasant dutifully hurried off to the bishop to put in her request. The bishop, of course, dismissed him without belief, but the peasant didn't give up. Back and forth between his lady on the mountain and the bishop he went, and on the third visit, he discovered mysterious roses blooming on the mountain even though it was the middle of winter. The lady said they were to prove the divine nature of her appearance to the bishop. She arranged the roses in the peasant's tilma, a burlaplike cloak made from cactus fiber, for him to carry back, and when he unrolled the cloak for the bishop they were both astonished. The imprint left behind was a clear image of the Virgin Mary, looking very much like Mary of the Immaculate Conception, complete with crescent moon under her feet and support offered by angels. The painting on the tilma has been declared miraculous by the Catholic Church, and though the many scientific tests performed on the cloth might say otherwise, one thing is for certain: it's truly miraculous that this simple cactus-fiber cloth has not deteriorated in almost five hundred years.

Why Is She Named Guadalupe?

Something else mysterious about the Virgin of Guadalupe is where that name came from. It seems most likely that the name came over with the Spanish conquerors as reference to a town in the Extremadura region of Spain. Bolstering this theory is the famous Black Virgin of Guadalupe, a tiny black-faced Virgin Mary statue that has been enshrined in Spain since the 1300s. Columbus is said to have prayed at this Black Virgin's shrine before he left on his first voyage, and also forced several of his Indian captives to return with him there to give thanks for his safe return afterward. The conquistador of Mexico, Hernán Cortés, was born in the Extremadura region, and he and his crew of soldiers and sailors would surely have been familiar with the Spanish Black Virgin's shrine.[2] It's logical to assume that when a painting of a brown-skinned Madonna in Mexico began attracting attention because of the miraculous cures it was said to bestow, that the name for one Black Madonna was simply transferred to the other.

Another compelling theory has the name Guadalupe originating from various stems of words in the native Aztec language, lending support to the belief that the Natives venerated this image because they believed it to be their native mother goddess secretly wearing a Mary costume. The theory goes that the Natives would refer to this image using any of several suggested phrases in Nahuatl such as "serpent goddess," or "the one who crushes or treads on the serpent,"[3] or versions of Coatlicue, the name of the Earth Mother goddess. These names sounded similar enough to "Guadalupe" to Spanish ears, and thus the association to the Black Virgin back home in Spain made the name stick.

Though some in the church vehemently protested the finessing of this legend to facilitate conversion of the Indigenous people, eight million Aztecs converted to Christianity over the next few years. The brown-skinned Virgin of Guadalupe helped unite Aztecs and Spanish as one people, under the "merciful mother of all of you who live united in this land." The belief in her message likely saved millions of Native people from torturous deaths at the hands of the Inquisition that was beginning to spread its tentacles throughout Mexico and South America. Today, the shrine built where the brown-skinned Nahuatl-speaking lady appeared and claimed to be the mother of us all is the most visited Marian shrine in the world. More than twenty-two million pilgrims descend on the town each year to slowly march in processional up the mountain to her shrine. Her following is so strong that in 2002, Juan Diego, the peasant who was added to the legend many years after it was first recorded, was canonized as the first Indigenous American saint by the Vatican—even though there is no real record of his existence.

Brown Madonnas Holding White Children

Unlike their Black Madonna counterparts in Europe, the pigmentation of the Brown Madonnas in the Americas is quite clearly a connection to the Native and Black Americans. A shrine to another Brown Madonna, the Virgin of Regla in Cuba, is located at one of the initial drop-off points for African slaves, which adds another layer of syncretization to this image. Yoruban priestess Aina Olomo described the Virgin of Regla as "a mask that the power of Yemonja was hidden behind during the early days of slavery." As we reviewed in the previous chapter, Olomo explained how through this guise, a notion of liberty was retained within the spirituality of the West African ancestors of the Yoruba people despite their enslavement and how they were affected by the African holocaust, or *maafa*. The enslaved Africans were able to recognize in the Virgin Mary elements of the spirit of Yemonja who they believed had crossed the ocean with them to protect her "children," or followers.

Like the Virgin of Guadalupe in Mexico, the Virgin of Regla in Cuba has a traditional European Black Madonna counterpart in Europe, a tiny black statue discovered in the 1200s and enshrined in a port city of Spain, where she became a patron saint of sailors. Unlike the Virgin of Guadalupe, the Virgin of Regla in the Americas is usually seen holding a Christ child. Notably, this is a pale-skinned child being held by a dark-skinned woman. This image of dark mothers with pale children is popular in Central and South America, referencing the many mixed-race children resulting from the domination culture. As Olomo recounted, however, sometimes the mulatto children of the master and the slave were lighter because of rape, of course, but sometimes also because of love and mixed marriages, which were more common in South America than in North America. The image of a divine mother and child with different skin tones reminded them that this divine female was the mother of everybody; she accepted all of them. Just because they were the master's children didn't mean the mothers didn't love them, Olomo reminded us. A similar theme can be read into the brief trend in early United States artwork depicting the Euro-American Liberty goddess as protecting a dark-skinned child who is often wearing feathers. The message of these pairings was that the American Liberty goddess may have rejected the Indian Princess costume, but her motherly influence would safeguard all her children no matter what they looked like.

The Spanish conquistadors brought the Virgin Mary to the Americas believing she would help them conquer and convert the people in the new land. Instead, the Indigenous recognized Mary as being in the same class as their mother deities and began decorating her images with corn and bean plants, much as they had for Tonantzin. Mary has a long history of being interpreted as a nature goddess in disguise. Peasants across Europe did the same thing, following the same patterns of worship that they had adhered to for centuries to honor, say, a Celtic spirit of the well, even after the church renamed the spirit as a saint or the Virgin Mary. In the Americas, where she also took on the darker skin tone, Mary became a friend to the oppressed and a reconciler of cultures, affirming at least a small part of the Natives' human dignity and spirituality.

The Statue of Liberty has also been decorated lovingly with corn plants. At the 1885 world's fair in New Orleans, the Statue of Liberty was reproduced entirely out of corn, hay, and grain,[4] creating a symbolic mash-up of the female agricultural spirits honored by the Native Americans and the patriotic pride being exported by the United States. This towering Corn Mother–Liberty demonstrated the deep-seated love for the image of Liberty and the tendency to associate the female divine with symbols of sustenance. Though not done deliberately, the creators of this corn figure of Liberty were echoing the tradition of the Native Americans, who regularly acknowledged the gifts of corn from the bounty of Mother Earth through ceremonial gestures of reciprocity.

The Maternal Aspect in the Statue of Liberty Was Recognized

Today, the Statue of Liberty is widely perceived as a universal mother figure, especially as the "Mother of Exiles," but this motherly perception did not attach itself to her until several decades after her creation. The reasons for the lasting success of the Statue of Liberty are many, including location, timing, and simplicity of form, but it's her matronly dignity that truly won our hearts, says Statue of Liberty librarian Barry Moreno. Jungian psychiatrist Jean Shinoda Bolen compares the Statue of Liberty to Kwan Yin and calls her America's Goddess of Compassion, based on her nurturing persona in welcoming tired and poor refugees. As such, Bolen says, the Statue of Liberty is the perfect compassionate symbol for those uplifting moments when the United States comes to the aid of other countries after natural disasters or wars.

She is a noble symbol that draws people into a cohesive group, making her a positive influence, as even cynical historian Albert Boime had

Figure 9.3. This statue of Sacagawea and her child is one of several additions to the National Statuary Hall in the Capitol Building that allow for prominent female and Native American and African American citizens to be part of the history of our nation as revealed in its artwork. As a brown-skinned woman succeeding in a traditionally male position while retaining her maternal strength, Sacagawea was adopted by suffragists as a role model. Author photo.

to admit. People need unifying symbols, and the Statue of Liberty has surpassed all the other attempted mother-goddess substitutes, such as the American Liberty goddess or Columbia, and the male personifications of Uncle Sam or Yankee Doodle. None has endured as powerfully or evoked such emotion as the Statue of Liberty, and part of that is due to her resonance as a mother.

The maternal aspects of the Statue of Liberty are deeper than the accidental association with the moniker Mother of Exiles given her by the poet Emma Lazarus. Roman Libertas was always depicted as a matronly woman, says defender of religious liberty and Pagan priestess Selena Fox, and if you are wondering who her children are, just look in the mirror. We are all Liberty's children, says Fox, and this relationship should remind us that liberty is "a two-way street. . . . That we are the progeny of American Liberty means we must pay attention to American liberty," she says. Just because liberty is at the foundation of this nation, doesn't mean we can take it for granted. "We must constantly pay attention to liberty, guard our liberty, and work to keep liberty alive and well."

The cross-cultural appeal of the Statue of Liberty has been explained as coming from the timeless symbols of law and order that keep her from feeling firmly rooted to any one particular time or nation. We contend, however, that the driving urge to create the countless replica Statues of Liberty all over the world is explained more by the ability of all Earth People to relate to her as a mother figure than as a figure of law and order. The wash of motherly welcome felt by millions of immigrants was a shared emotional experience that was retold over and over as those immigrants spread westward through the country. Starting about twenty years after the Statue of Liberty was unveiled, many of those millions began coming from Catholic countries and naturally related their overwhelming feelings of joy at seeing the Statue of Liberty with the transcendent experience they associated with venerating the Blessed Mother. Today thousands of tourists each year make a pilgrimage to the Statue of Liberty, where, as author Marina Warner explained, they can enter her body much like a pilgrim entering an ancient Neolithic earth chamber. Earth chambers like Newgrange in Ireland were designed to resemble parts of female anatomy that humans could walk into, symbolically returning them to the universal mother.[5]

Mary Syncretized with the Great Mother Goddess

Relics and traditions dating as far back as the Paleolithic era point to the veneration of a great goddess together with a male consort or son—divine couples or families that worked as a unit. These longstanding mythological patterns were hard to give up when Rome made Christianity the state religion and insisted upon the most unusual Hebrew tradition of a singular masculine Creator God. As Christianity converted the followers of the Earth-based religions of Europe, the desire for a mother figure or goddess continued to reassert itself in creative ways, the most accepted of which was the veneration of Jesus's mother. Mary has had limited success as a substitute Mother Goddess, however, because she never achieved divine status. The organized church deemed that she was forever lesser to the Trinity, making her, in a sense, the goddess demoted. Regardless of the limitations, she provided a portal through which the church could fill the need for mother-comfort while growing increasingly patriarchal and misogynistic. "This is how we wind up with the Virgin Mary and many, many saints," historian Max Dashú told us. They are "mythic carriers for an enormous freight of older ancestral heritage that is the divine woman, the ancient goddess."

When one is able to acknowledge that religious customs and practices blend together in favor of endorsing the dominating culture, it is clear to see that the legend of a divine resurrected savior born from a virgin mother has several precedents in earlier pre-Christian traditions. The legend of Jesus's miraculous birth parallels tales of many heroes in the older Greek, Egyptian, Babylonian, and even Native American mythology that include human mothers effecting divine incarnation.[6] The legend of Cybele and her son/consort Attis closely mirrors the tale of Mary and Jesus, as do the legends of Isis and Osiris/Horus, and the Greek myths of the resurrected Dionysus born of a mortal mother and divine father. In a complicated path, Christianity as we know it today, says Dashú, is a Hellenized Romanization of Judaic teachings. "They were modeling Christianity on the Roman Empire" in terms of structure, she pointed out. "Even the terminology; *diocese*, for example, is a Roman imperial administrative term."

As the Roman Church conquered various cultures, Mary took on the symbolism of the earlier goddesses of these cultures. She assumed the dove of Ishtar, the grain of wheat from Spica Virgo, and the starry mantle of Aphrodite Urania. Her feast days were celebrated on former feast days of mother goddesses, like the Feast of the Annunciation assigned to the feast day of Cybele.[7] Statues of the Egyptian goddess Isis seated with Horus on her lap were sometimes literally painted directly over to become the Virgin Mary and the Christ child.

Figure 9.4. Many statuettes like this one of Isis nursing Horus were later painted over to appear as Mary with the baby Jesus. Circa 680–640 BCE, Walters Art Museum, Baltimore, Maryland. Photo: Jeff Kubina.

Catholics are quick to point out that Mary is not divine and they do not *worship* her as a female divinity. They merely acknowledge her holy status as the Mother of God and note how that role gives her a special ability to intercede on their behalf with God. In the early 300s, when Christianity shifted from being a persecuted religion to becoming the official practice of the Roman Empire, the new Roman Church hierarchy faced a steep challenge to convince the populace to give up their old gods and goddesses. In 431 they convened in the town of Ephesus, near present-day Turkey, to debate whether Jesus was man or God or both. The decision of this council impacted Mary's status as well, as it was here that the bishops crowned her with the official title of Blessed Mother, or Theotokos, which translates literally as the bringer forth of, or she who birthed God, or Mother of God.

In the pre-Christian world, Ephesus was the center of Diana/Artemis worship, and her impressive temple there was declared one of the Seven Wonders of the World. This wonder was destroyed by a Christian mob just a few years prior to the Council of Ephesus where Mary was raised to Mother of God status. Declaring Mary the only mother figure permitted by the new state-church, allowed her to rival and eventually suppress the remainder of Diana/Artemis worship in this area. Interestingly, the famous statue of the many-breasted Artemis formerly housed at this temple was depicted in late Roman images with a black face and hands, a pattern followed by the Black Madonnas discovered in the Middle Ages. The Phrygian Earth Mother Cybele is also linked to this location, and is also frequently depicted with a black face. In another curious loop back to the Statue of Liberty, Cybele's son/consort Attis is generally portrayed in artwork wearing that same Phrygian cap, which later became so controversial in the iconography of Lady Liberty in America.

There's Something Missing about Mary

The Virgin Mary can only partially fill the longing that humanity has for a Mother Goddess, however, because she does not allow women to experience their full power. The organized church promotes Mary based on her alleged ability to transcend the carnal sexuality of real women, and as eternally virgin, she is unattainably pure, far above the average woman. In fact, her blessed roles are mutually exclusive: real women cannot strive to be both a blessed virgin and a blessed mother at the same time. In some pre-Christian traditions like the Greek, goddesses were often described in triune aspects as maiden-mother-crone, acknowledging the different phases of a woman's life. The Roman Christian church orthodoxy taught that to be complete a woman must be a mother like Mary, and this conundrum was translated into the doctrine that to control conception was a sin. With Christianity condemning the ancient art of contraception, women faced an unending cycle of perpetual childbirth, along with the early death that so often accompanied it. Fear of pain and death pushed many women to choose the unnatural life of celibacy, cloistered away from life in a nunnery.

The myths of the Virgin Mary have blended with our understanding of who we are as sexual beings. As humanity seeks new methods of relating, we would do well to remember that the submissive and eternally virgin aspects of the Virgin Mary were the creation of sexually repressed men. Her myth was promoted by the church fathers as a counterpoint to Eve, whose sin condemned all women. Mary was dubbed the new Eve, the model for a redeemed humanity with her obedience to God's will, but women were still cursed as the weaker sex. It was God's will that childbirth had to be a punishing, painful experience, and any action taken to alleviate that was still considered a sin.[8]

When not interpreted through the lens of women's rights, on the other hand, the lofty and sublime standards of the Virgin Mary inspired many great achievements, particularly in the arts. "The eternal womanly draws us upward," said Goethe,[9] acknowledging how the Virgin Mary became a powerful muse. This is evidenced in soaringly beautiful Gothic architecture dedicated in her name, inspired poetry and music, and some of the most exquisite artwork in the world. Variations on the name Mary for girls and places exploded in popularity in the Middle Ages,[10] as Mariology reached new heights.

Figure 9.5. The Mystical Body of the Church was seen by Hildegard of Bingen as a powerful woman emerging from white mountain peaks, with a golden-petaled flower opening from her chest. The figure in the center is thought to be the Virgin Mary, described by Hildegard as the Sister of Wisdom. From the *Liber Scivias*, copy of the former Rupertsberg Codex, circa 1180; St. Hildegard's Abbey, Eibingen, Germany. From a collection compiled by the Yorck Project.

Glorifying the Beloved Lady

The status of women rose for a brief period in Europe through the glorification of the "Beloved Lady" while many men were away at the Crusades. The quest for this ideal woman coincided with the quest for the Holy Grail, and together they sparked a rejuvenation of spirituality in the 1100s.[11] Especially prevalent in southern France, this resurgence of interest in the divine female is preserved for us in the work of the troubadours. Eleanor of Aquitaine held a Court of Love, where the woman was exalted, establishing what cultural historian Riane Eisler would call "a period of partnership resurgence." The church's new advocacy for a greater veneration of the Virgin Mary made the 1100s a high point for women in

Christianity. Marina Warner described it as a time when "every soul's potential in relation to a benevolent divine providence" was celebrated, something that "would never be achieved again."[12] Hildegard of Bingen (1098–1178) was a remarkable example of how an effective woman took advantage of the only education available to her at the time, found in the church, and then set about influencing world events. Not only did her correspondence advising popes and kings determine their political actions, but her mystical writings about the transcendent state achieved by contemplating the figure of female wisdom still inspire today.

Interest in hermetic discovery traditions such as the Kabbalah and alchemy also disseminated throughout Europe in this same time period, and a verbal synchronicity, sometimes referred to as the green language or the language of the birds, developed to conceal these heretical ideas from the church. Much of what the troubadours wrote in their contemplation of a divine female force was in this language of the birds, turning it into a kind of code. For example, they wrote about the Church of Amor, which could either be the Church of Love, or the opposite of the Church of Rome (Amor is Roma spelled backward). If anything was more heretical to the Catholic Church of the Middle Ages than giving women equal status in the church, it was talk about a female divinity. The idealization of the woman would soon be put down by the infamous Inquisitions, the first of which was actually launched against a Christian sect, the Cathars, that practiced gender equality by allowing women to be priests, teachers, and healers.

How Mary Magdalene, the Apostle to the Apostles, Became a Prostitute

In approximately 1050 CE, at least two churches in southern France began claiming they had relics of the bones of Mary Magdalene. The legends about Mary Magdalene as the secret bride of Jesus can be traced to this same location, where they tell of Mary Magdalene continuing with the preaching of Jesus's secret teachings and living out the rest of her years in a cave. The Cathar Christians of southern France may have picked up on this legend and incorporated it into their teachings.

However, the only evidence connecting the Cathars with the claim that Mary Magdalene and Jesus were romantic partners derives from anti-Cathar sources, so it may have been invented to discredit them.[13]

Made popular by the bestsellers *Holy Blood, Holy Grail* and Dan Brown's *DaVinci Code,* the legend has Mary Magdalene, sometimes together with Lazarus and several others, sometimes just herself or her children, landing in southern France after fleeing the Holy Land in a rudderless boat. This French legend of the Magdalene's story joined the other manifestations of the female archetype that came out of the high Middle Ages, and was quite a role reversal from her former reputation as the fallen woman assigned to her in previous centuries.

The smear campaign against Mary Magdalene actually began as Roman Christianity turned on the gnostic Christians, as we review in chapter 10. As with just about everything else the Romans did, their version of Christianity was well organized and hierarchical. When they sat down to choose the texts they would classify as official, they diminished those that spoke of women leaders and prophesiers, and of Mary Magdalene as the leader of the early Christians. A few references to women leading the church slipped past them, nevertheless, and made it into the official canon, such as Romans 16:7, for example, when Paul talks about his coworkers and fellow evangelists including the outstanding apostle who is senior to himself, a woman named Junia—but most of them didn't make the cut. The negative values about women that were promoted by the bishops of the Roman Church of later centuries were not shared by Jesus himself.

In the first four hundred years after Jesus's death, as the bishops banned women from even speaking in church, the numerous mentions of Mary Magdalene in the four accepted gospels presented them with a problem. The bishops tried to discredit any mention of her as spiritual leader and were confounded by the descriptions of her as a participant at the center of the action with Jesus, particularly at the crucifixion and resurrection.*

---

*Mary Magdalene was one of the first to witness the risen Christ, according to all four gospels, and *the* first according to John. See Matthew 28:1–10; Mark 16:1–20; Luke 24:1–12; John 20:1–18.

The question was: How could they diminish the role of a woman who was called the apostle to the apostles by the early Christian gnostics and who was so obviously held in high esteem by Jesus himself? The answer: Turn her into a prostitute. By the sixth century CE, Roman bishops were reinterpreting scripture to establish Mary Magdalene as the repentant whore. Nowhere in any of the four gospels is she referred to as a prostitute, so they attached her name to the unnamed woman accused of adultery, and the unnamed woman who anointed Jesus's feet and then massaged them with her hair. This construct of the penitent whore fabricated by the church became very popular among Catholics. Many sinners found hope in the Magdalene's repentance, as they struggled to uphold the unattainable purity of the Virgin Mary.

The Magdalene's special relationship with Jesus, including the secret teachings he allegedly passed down to her alone, was recorded in the gnostic gospels, which remained mostly buried until 1945. It's theorized that other surviving glimmers of these gnostic versions about Mary Magdalene's leadership role in the early church somehow found their way to southern France in the eleventh century, sparking these legends. Whatever caused the renewed folk interest in Mary Magdalene and her relics and teachings at this time, her renewed popularity was likely the spur behind the organized church launching its own new promotion of the Virgin Mary as the new Eve.

Male and Female, He Created Them

Two of the most prolific suffragists from the mid-1800s were determined to expose how the teachings of the organized church were the main lever of the oppression of women through the centuries. Resolute in their insistence that no lasting reform to women's rights would occur until the role of women in official Christianity was addressed, Elizabeth Cady Stanton and Matilda Joslyn Gage were ostracized by the mainstream suffrage organization for these beliefs. This was a splintering of leadership that hobbled the campaign for woman suffrage for decades. Author of *The Woman's Bible,* Elizabeth Cady Stanton declared that "every form of religion that has breathed upon the earth has degraded women."[14] Author of *Woman, Church and State,* Matilda Joslyn Gage insisted, "The story of Eve was not peripheral to Christianity; it was its corner stone; for, without the doctrine of the fall, and the consequent need of a Savior, the whole Christian super-structure drops into nothingness."[15] The basis for the oppression of women, in other words, was the church, and furthermore, the basis of the church itself was the oppression of women.

Gage wrote extensively about how the "belief in a trinity of masculine gods . . . from which the feminine element is wholly eliminated," was the central error to which all degradation of women could be traced. She pointed to the older account of the Creation in Genesis (not the later revised creation story that added that bit about the rib) where male and female were created equally by a Creator God who was referred to as a "them." Genesis 1:26–27 in the New International Version of the Bible says, "Then God said, 'Let us make mankind in our image, in our likeness'. . . . So God created mankind in his own image, in the image of God he created them; male and female he created them." Gage interprets this as "the simultaneous creation of man and woman," where the text "plainly recognizes the feminine as well as the masculine element in the God-head, and declares the equality of the sexes in goodness, wisdom and power."[16]

Both Gage and Stanton were outraged when their colleague Susan B. Anthony proposed merging the National Woman Suffrage Association the three of them had cofounded with the ten times larger Woman's Christian Temperance Union headed by Frances Willard. Gage objected so much that she resigned and started her own progressive group of liberals, who were aligned in their goal of maintaining the wall of separation between church and state. Stanton stayed on, but not without embarrassing the majority by speaking out against Willard's goals to attain a Constitutional amendment naming Jesus as head of the government, requiring mandatory prayer in schools and reintroducing religious tests for public servants.[17] Gage was shunned and spent the final years of her life isolated from her friends of forty years. Her fall from favor was essentially over her insistence on advocating for wider social causes like prison reform, labor reform, and reproductive rights.

Her group of reformers was considered so radical that her mail was intercepted by the government, and she was denounced from the local pulpits.[18]

Fear of the Sexually Emancipated Woman

A hundred years later, the so-called third-wave feminists who became active in the 1980s and 1990s pushed even harder against the church-influenced teachings prescribing the proper place for women, and one of their main platforms was an attempt to reclaim some of the language. What does it mean to be a whore, and why is it such a slur, they asked? "Riot grrrls" of the punk rock scene were known to scrawl the words "cunt" and "whore" on their exposed flesh as they battled for respect in the mosh pits. The SlutWalk is a recent trend where feminists march in response to accusations that rape victims are the ones to blame rather than their attackers. If a woman wants to own the identity of being a slut, or exercise her liberty to dress as provocatively as she chooses, then why should words degrading her sexual choices be derogatory? As Black Madonna expert Ean Begg told us, the word "whore" in Old English just meant "darling." It stood for a woman free to be herself; a whore doesn't belong to either a husband, or a father, or the church. Looking at it not too literally, the whore is the woman who is free on her own, and is making up her own mind.

Free in her own mind as an independent woman is what extremist Christians today will try to put down with the label of whore. We found another odd parallel here to the Statue of Liberty. Maybe it's true for all works of art starring a woman, but apparently people just can't resist wondering who the real model was for the piece, and whether she was a prostitute. What does this reveal about our public perception of women and the female body? In the case of the Statue of Liberty or the *Statue of Freedom* on the Capitol dome, what does it reveal about our public perception of American liberty that we constantly hear the giggling rumors that, underneath the robes, there is a woman for sale?

We heard this for ourselves when attending a talk by Cokie Roberts on her books about women of the American Revolution. We asked her

Figure 9.6. The Libertas Americana medal was designed by Benjamin Franklin in 1783 to recognize the assistance of the French in winning the Revolutionary War. The profile of Liberty with the pole and cap behind her was copied for the first coins minted in the United States in 1792, though the unbound hair, which can symbolize sexual emancipation, was soon coifed in later designs. Photo: CentPacRR.

in front of the audience if the women of that time talked about the discrepancy between allegorical women being used to represent a liberty that these real women themselves did not enjoy. Ms. Roberts seemed to misunderstand our question, and instead reduced the audience to snickering by saying that the *model* for the *Statue of Freedom* was certainly someone they talked about, because she was a woman of some scandalous reputation. This allegation appears nowhere in the news reports or documents of the time, according to *Statue of Freedom* researcher Katya Miller, who thinks that the model was the sculptor's wife, Louisa Ward Crawford, who served as his model and muse. That Ms. Roberts would deflect a question into this territory because she knew it would get a laugh and enable her to move to the next question simply proves our point. Why is this aspersion so tempting to cast?

The Statue of Liberty Is Not a Prostitute Either

The question of comparing the Statue of Liberty, or other allegorical women related to her, to prostitutes has been pondered in feminist literary criticism and art history analyses for years, and the considerations are deeper than we can do justice to with this brief summary. Literary critics have argued that in the iconography of the age, uncontrolled sexuality in women was interpreted as a threat to property, law, and order. The self-possessed woman, with the life-giving power that men subconsciously fear, threatens the line of succession in the patriarchy and the very foundation upon which their myths are based. It's this threat that makes folks come out with the whore epithet against the powerful and self-possessed Lady Liberty.

Historian Maurice Agulhon is the expert on the symbolism of Marianne in France wherein their female images of Liberty include a freer expression of sexuality, and wherein the symbolism of the state has changed radically following upheavals in France's government every twenty years or so. Agulhon observed a well-established tradition to besmirch popular uprisings by claiming "the role of the goddess of Liberty can only be played by a woman of 'easy virtue.'"[19] Architectural historian Marvin Trachtenberg closed his popular book about the Statue of Liberty by comparing her to a prostitute. "For a fee she is open to all for entry and exploration from below," he said.[20] Feminist critic Kaja Silverman looked at the Statue of Liberty's access more in terms of the Oedipal quest. If everyone secretly yearns to return to the safety of the womb, inside the mother, even without seeing her as sexual, the Statue of Liberty fulfills this sensation, says Silverman. On the outside the Statue of Liberty appears maternal, but upon entering the inside, the visitor finds metal trusswork and molding, an imposing monument to form and structure—nothing reminiscent of flesh and blood.[21]

All these theories aside, the basic fact is that the Statue of Liberty is enterable because Bartholdi was cashing in on the latest craze of his time. Everyone was creating taller and taller structures, especially in conjunction with the competitive world's fairs, and visitors were flocking to the new attractions to climb the dizzying heights. The original Ferris wheel was designed for the 1893 World Columbian Exposition in Chicago, the Eiffel Tower for the Paris World's Fair of 1889. Bartholdi designed windows into Liberty's crown for the express purpose of enabling visitors to enjoy the view from above. The public got its first chance to climb inside her head when the head and shoulders alone were sent to the world's fair in Paris in 1878. The torch and arm had already delighted climbing visitors when it was sent to the Philadelphia World's Fair in 1876, and ticket sales for both were used to help pay for the construction of the rest of the body.

Was the Model for the Statue of Liberty a Prostitute?

The much-debated question of who modeled for the body of the Statue of Liberty might never be answered, and it's quite possible the answer is no one. Pierre Provoyeur in "Bartholdi in His Context," one of his essays in the book *Liberty: The French-American Statue in Art and History,* says it "seems certain that no preparatory anatomical study was done: there is none in the Inventory of 1914 or in the Musée Bartholdi." The artistic trends of the time were to cloak the body in drapery, and in essence that is what we have for the body of Lady Liberty: only drapery.

Just as it's believed that the sculptor's mother may have been the model for the face of the Statue of Liberty, others think that Bartholdi used his future wife, Jeanne-Emilie, as an artist's model for the body. The dates of the maquettes don't match up to when he allegedly first met his wife, however, so this is unlikely. Jeanne-Emilie does have a rather sketchy past, and it's possible she was working as an artist's model in 1871, and also that Bartholdi met her on his first trip to the United States that year. Christian Blanchet and Bertrand Dard in their book *Statue of Liberty: The First Hundred Years* say Bartholdi almost certainly met Jeanne-Emilie on that 1871 trip, but that he did not create the maquettes for the statue until after he returned to France during those five years before he met her again, so she could hardly have been his model.[22] Barry Moreno tells us the records show Bartholdi did not meet her until his second trip to the United States in 1876. He married her later on this same trip, though speculation remains that he may have arranged this second meeting to give their relationship a sense of propriety.

Moreno called Jeanne-Emilie "a woman who unfortunately told a lot of lies about her background." This includes her lying about her age, saying she was thirty-two at the time of her marriage to Bartholdi, when she was really forty-seven. She was five years older than Bartholdi, and ended up serving as another maternal figure for this man who had a strong mother-fixation. But according to Moreno, Jeanne-Emilie was a devoted wife and caretaker, living in the shadow of Bartholdi's mother, Charlotte, who also lived in the home with them, and to whom Bartholdi remained loyal. When he wrote his mother about Jeanne-Emilie from the states he described her as originally coming from a respectable family in France, but she had no money and was now working for her living as a companion to a French Canadian woman. The stern Charlotte was skeptical of the new wife at first, but she was eventually won over when the couple returned to France.

The Statue of Liberty, like Mary, Is Simultaneously Virgin, Mother, and Whore

Pointing out that the Statue of Liberty was a metaphorical woman-gift from one nation to another, Barbara Babcock draws a comparison to the tradition of nations giving women to each other as a form of diplomacy. Giving the daughter or sister to be married into the monarchy of another country was the only lasting cement of many peace treaties. For many of the years preceding the Statue of Liberty's completion, France and the United States had been embroiled in a bitter tariff trade war, and the industrialists on the Franco-American fundraising committees may have considered their Liberty as a sort of peace offering to the flow of commerce.[23] The note struck at all the fundraising banquets emphasized the economic and commercial ties between the two countries, and

Figure 9.7. The Bartholdi family enjoying a musical evening at home around 1890. Auguste and his mother, Charlotte, at the piano, and his wife, Jeanne-Emilie, looking at the camera. Charlotte was known to be a talented pianist. Photo: Musée Bartholdi, Colmar, reproduction copyright C. Kempf. Used with permission.

the day after the official unveiling ceremonies in New York in 1886, a delegation of officials from France was feted at the New York Produce Exchange. In his speech the president of the exchange focused on "commerce that lights the torch and flames of liberty and is the power of civilization."[24]

Like the Virgin Mary, Mary Magdalene, and the Brown Madonnas of the Americas, the Statue of Liberty has filled many roles for many people. Among Bartholdi's own nicknames for his creation were his "Big Girl," his "Daughter Liberty," and "My American." Her most popular nicknames among her American fans of the twentieth century were "Miss Liberty," emphasizing her young, virginal qualities, and the "Mother of Exiles," emphasizing her nurturing, welcoming qualities.

Because of these parallels, some feminists have complained that the Statue of Liberty is just one more way men have asserted their feminine ideal and the virgin-mother paradox in an attempt to control women's sexuality. The heavy drapery obscuring her body and life-giving parts is compared to the patriarchal trend to control female sexuality. Laboulaye's metaphor for liberty controlled by law is interpreted as contributing to the societal control of women.

Learning about the many archetypes of female divinity can move us beyond the "dichotomy of virgin/whore, mother/lover that afflicts women in patriarchies," says Jean Shinoda Bolen. One example of this is found in the mysterious poem discovered among the Nag Hammadi gnostic texts called "The Thunder, Perfect Mind" in which the speaker moved beyond dichotomy and embraced all archetypes at once. The reader is exhorted to aspire to a divine female power through a series of opposing statements such as "I am the whore and the holy one. I am the wife and the virgin. I am [the mother] and the daughter . . . I am knowledge and ignorance. I am shame and boldness. I am shameless; I am ashamed. I am strength and I am fear. I am war and peace. Give heed to me. . . . I am compassionate and I am cruel. Be on your guard!" That about sums up how impossible it is to accurately describe in words the figure of divine female wisdom.

Likewise, the Statue of Liberty has been described along every ray of the spectrum, from virgin to mother to whore, and like the Virgin Mary has been considered a liberator of women by some, and as a participant in women's suppression by others. Images of the Statue of Liberty and the Virgin Mary provide comfort to millions, but it is not just their mothering welcome that allows us to compare them. In addition, both are held sacred by people from different religions, and both are multicultural in their appeal across national and state boundaries. As characters in mythology, they represent different aspects of every human being, and appreciating them in these deeper contexts—while tuning in to the divine female power of the Statue of Liberty—can lead us to discover what is missing in the human condition.

10

The Liberty to Choose
What to Believe

After reviewing several other areas wherein symbolism has been used to conceal female power and female divinity, it's encouraging to learn that the philosopher behind the Statue of Liberty was a feminist. The Statue of Liberty was not designed overtly to symbolize women's rights, of course, but she has been read that way by some feminists, while others have seen her as just the opposite. We turn our attention now to the France of her creators, where we found many other flexible symbols of female allegory like the Statue of Liberty who have been adopted by opposing forces and appreciated in a variety of conflicting ways.

Allegorical women in France are more earthy and sexually charged than those in the United States. France's allegorical female is named Marianne, and she is usually depicted wilder than the American Liberty Goddess, though in fact she has gone through just as many transmutations from maiden to vixen and back again as the Liberty goddess has in America. Looking for how these permutations relate to real women, we discovered that the French Revolution is credited as the beginning of the international woman suffrage movement. The first protest march on Versailles was led by women who then continued on as instrumental organizers throughout the years of revolt. Analyzing the many faces of Marianne led us to the symbolism of Joan of Arc and how she can also be compared to the Statue of Liberty.

After examining the Brown Madonnas of the Americas, we now go further back in time to wonder what the Black Madonnas, predominantly found in France, were hiding. This question led us back to the Cathar Christians and what this ascetic group of healers trying to model themselves on the life of Christ did to upset official Christianity so much that the pope said, "Kill them all." By comparison, this, in turn, led us to a further examination of the secret gnostic gospels that also celebrated a female divine power and welcomed women leaders in the very early church. Considering that the Statue of Liberty is a figure of enlightenment and female divinity, we can see that she is one of a long line of descendants from these other mysterious and powerful divine females, including these from the Christian tradition.

The Statue of Liberty's Philosopher Was a Feminist

When we say the creator of the Statue of Liberty advocated women's full participation in society and law, we're not talking about the sculptor Auguste Bartholdi, but rather his mentor, Édouard de Laboulaye. Most chroniclers focus more on Bartholdi when talking about the genesis of this statue, because he was more out front on the project. He assumed most of the responsibility for selling the idea to the public in the United States, for example, but Bartholdi himself was quick to say that Laboulaye was the initiator of the idea and the collaborator on the design. Laboulaye was the first to suggest that the statue should be a gift to the United States after the Civil War. He was the first to say that the monument should be in the design of La Liberté. He was the first to create fundraising groups both in France and the United States, with both groups being comprised of his personal friends from the upper-class intelligentsia and politically moderate circles. He provided Bartholdi with crucial letters of introduction to influential people in the United States who would give the project effective vocal support.

Laboulaye came out very early in support of women's rights. In 1843, even before the Seneca Falls Convention of 1848, which was the first organized woman's rights meeting in the United States, Laboulaye published a historical study in France on the legal status of women. Together with his wife, Micheline, they were active in the abolitionist movement in France and internationally. Micheline was a sort of scholar herself, publishing a biography of Joan of Arc in 1877. Laboulaye presided over a banquet in France for the national organization for woman suffrage in the 1870s right in the middle of the fundraising for the Statue of Liberty, meaning both the Statue of Liberty and women's rights were on his mind simultaneously.

Bared Breasts versus Covered Breasts

Laboulaye made frequent references to the painting by Eugène Delacroix—depicting the July Revolution of 1830 and called *Liberty Leading the People*—in order to describe what he did *not* want his Liberty to look like. The most obvious difference between the two images of Liberty is that in Delacroix's painting Liberty's dress is falling off. Both of her breasts are entirely exposed, which in French art and politics of this time meant that this was a radical Liberty. The law-and-order-loving Laboulaye wanted no association with this symbol, which he believed would corrupt the conservative influence he was trying to portray with his respectably clad Liberty.

In France an artist's decision about whether to expose Liberty's breasts worked as a sort of key to proclaim his political leanings. Simplified, that interpretation was: exposed breasts meant you symbolized the radical Left, and covered breasts meant you were a moderate or conservative. Art historians have filled volumes interpreting the meanings of exposed breasts through the ages. Marina Warner devoted an entire chapter in *Monuments and Maidens: The Allegory of the Female Form* to the "slipped chiton," or the classically draped garment, and what it means in various grades of slippage. "Adapted to political imagery," she said, "the exposed breast denoting the wild thing can also mutate her into . . . a matron and nurturer, and a type of the protective state."[1] One breast exposed, according to French historian Maurice Agulhon, was interpreted as the innocence of nature or the life-giving of a mother.[2]

The Delacroix painting fell out of favor soon after it was completed

Figure 10.1. *Liberty Leading the People* by Eugène Delacroix is an example of a Liberty that Laboulaye expressly said he did *not* want his Statue of Liberty to resemble. The exposed breasts can symbolize the radicalism of the political Left.

in 1830, when a new monarchy resumed control and revolutionary images were stored away. Another reason this controversial painting did not see permanent display in the Louvre until the 1870s, says Warner, was that Delacroix depicted a woman who was sexually emancipated, muscular, and of the people. Raising the flag in her huge hands, she reveals a scandalous hint of armpit hair. It was revolutionary to depict Liberty/Marianne as a real woman.[3] Warner says the contemporary critics mostly complained that Liberty looked dirty and unseemly. It was rumored that Delacroix was trying to reproduce in painting the tales of real women, often prostitutes, who rallied troops from the tops of barricades during the July Revolution of 1830,[4] an act that must have become something of a French tradition. Victor Hugo wrote of witnessing a similar scene during the 1848 revolution, when two different women climbed to the top of a barricade, pulled up their skirts, and taunted the soldiers to shoot their life-giving parts, which they did.[5]

Symbologist David Ovason gave us quite another interpretation of Liberty's uncovered breasts in Delacroix's painting. He said the uncovered breasts here have to do with honesty and the subject's willingness to be completely open, or bare, with the viewer. In this depiction, "it's not so much Liberty guiding the nation, as it is honesty," Ovason said, "for at last this underlying rabble has risen with this feminine idealism in its being." With the purity and inspiration of the honest feminine ideals, the rabble was able to rise up and sweep aside, temporarily in this case, "the opposing monarchical forces and the opposing forces of the church."

Breasts are important to the Statue of Liberty insofar as they are practically absent from consideration. The Statue of Liberty's breasts are no more than a modest outline underneath all that classic drapery. Though interpreted as sexual repression by some feminist critics, the Statue of Liberty's lack of exposed flesh was a political statement Laboulaye was intent on making.

Marianne's Breasts and Their Many Meanings

Stereotypically, French people are famous for having far fewer sexual hang-ups than Americans, a fact attributed to that Puritanical streak from America's English ancestors. This difference comes to life when looking at images of Lady Liberty in America compared to images of Lady Liberty in France, where she is often named Marianne. Just like Lady Liberty, who had several costume changes during the American Revolution, in France Marianne has different features and degrees of undress depending on which faction was in power and which was in revolt. The thing about Marianne, though, is that she's always wearing that Phrygian cap. Without the provocative cap she is instantly transformed into a promoter of stability and is renamed La Liberté or La Republique or even La France.

Maurice Agulhon is the authority on the figure of Marianne and wrote three volumes tracing her changes through the various French regimes. When her image first appeared around the time of the French Revolution, looking very much like a demure French maiden wearing the symbols of the Roman goddess Libertas, she was given the nickname Marianne because it was the most popular girl's name in France at the time. Marianne was a popular name, of course, because girls were being named in honor of the Virgin Mary and her holy mother, Anne.

Figure 10.2. Versions of Marianne showing her in traditional costume and in various stages of partial nudity and fierceness. Library of Congress.

The revolutionaries in France were far more vicious in their attack on the establishment than their counterparts in the American Revolution, though they were inspired by many of the same philosophies of the Enlightenment. In France, where the monarchy and the organized church were tightly interlaced, as the revolutionaries pulled down the symbols of one, they also pulled down the symbols of the other. To replace religion, they founded the Cult of Reason, and in establishing their new government, they tried to completely remove all traces of Christianity from the state. They replaced statues of Mary and the saints in Notre Dame with statues of Marianne/Libertas. They designed elaborate ceremonies that, although modeled on Christian rites, featured real women and girls dressed as La Liberté and Raison. They preferred to use real women, they said, because they did not want to promote idolatry in any form, and because real women were considered more radical.[6] In 1793 the first anniversary of the new republic was celebrated with leaders drinking publicly from water streaming from the breasts of a statue called by contemporaries both *Nature* and *Isis,* and later having a processional pass a giant statue of Liberty from which thousands of doves were released.[7]

Personifying the nation as a desirable female has always helped men bond and feel unified, and images of women were everywhere in the French Revolution.[8] As the violence increased and morphed into the Reign of Terror, images of Marianne/Liberty grew increasingly aggressive and more disheveled in response. Joan Landes in *Visualizing the Nation* said that the harpylike caricatures of the real women who were leading the French Revolution helped people deal with the concern over their world being turned upside down. The inversion of gender roles was just as terrifying to some as the violence, and as the terror was controlled, images of Marianne returned to the more traditional, modest look. Warner believes that the swings in public opinion between "accepting woman as an active agent of change or desiring her to remain a passive source of strength" contributed to the two distinct classes of female liberty they used: either virago or matron.[9]

"Oh Liberty, what crimes are committed in thy name?" cried Madame Roland, pausing on her way to the guillotine to bow at the

statue of Liberty in the Place de Révolution. Many who had publicly
advocated woman suffrage in national elections, like the Marquis de
Condorcet and Olympe de Gouges, were killed in the Reign of Terror.
Although the first stirrings of the international woman suffrage movement are attributed to the French Revolution's reforms in voter rights,
and women were active agitators and organizers of the rebellion, the
National Convention of 1793 abolished all societies of women and continued to deny them the vote. Surprisingly, women in France would not
earn the vote until 1944.

Joan of Arc to the Rescue

In the hundred years following the French Revolution, the French
people cycled through monarchy, revolution, anarchy, and republic
in what seemed like an eternal cycle of overthrowing the establishment. The people were desperate for some form of stability and
civility, and Laboulaye considered his Lady Liberty project the solution. *La Liberté Eclairant le Monde* would be a symbol of the balance achieved by rejecting both monarchy and anarchy. The radicals
had appropriated Marianne as their symbol; the moderates around
Laboulaye had elected Libertas. The remaining faction of royalists
and clerics found they needed a new allegorical female to symbolize
their own opposition to the naked sexual liberality in the artwork
of the radicals. The Virgin Mary had been associated with the
monarchy in the past, but as the government had moved away from monarchy to parliamentary government, she was no longer a perfect fit
for the traditionalists.

Joan of Arc rode in to take her place as the conservatives' female
personification. Joan of Arc was never intended to be a symbol for
all the people of France. She was adopted solely as the darling of the
clerical-monarchical party, and was used to encourage the French
women of the privileged classes to be pure as sisters of Joan, and to be
satisfied in their limited role of child-rearing. In a similar way during
and after the American Revolution, Joan of Arc was used in America
as a rallying symbol to inspire women's patriotism and participation in

boycotts. She appeared in a 1798 play in the United States titled *Female Patriotism,* with her visions showing her the republic and women's new role in it as Republican Mothers.[10]

Joan of Arc remained a popular national symbol in France, and in the early 1900s, she was noticed by British suffragist Christabel Pankhurst, who had fled to France to avoid arrest for her activism in London. Pankhurst interpreted Joan in quite a different way from the monarchists of Laboulaye's generation and selected her as a symbol of a strong woman challenging authority and standing for a righteous cause. While the French noblemen of the mid-1800s had been attracted to Joan for her allegiance to the king and her devotion to a church-state, the suffragists were attracted to her bravery in the face of entrenched masculine power.

Good symbols will do that. If they have multiple layers, they can represent many things to many people, much as the Statue of Liberty has done. British suffragists began using the armored Joan of Arc in their symbolism (figure 10.3, p. 270), and when visiting Americans Alice Paul and Lucy Burns studied with the famous Pankhurst family, they adopted many of their tactics. Some of the British suffrage symbolism came home with them to the United States, including the armored Joan of Arc, which was first used by the more militant branch of the U.S. suffragists, but later morphed into a generic herald or an angel-like figure (figure 12.6, p. 326) that appealed to a broader spectrum of women.

In art, Joan of Arc is another example of female allegory representing different things to different people. Because she was officially considered a radical, and therefore anathema, by the church until the twentieth century, Joan could also be placed in this class of female symbolism we are considering as wisdomkeepers concealed by the church. What we mean by that is Joan was willing to listen to what she considered an *inner knowing,* or her voices, which she described as coming from a female divine source: she called them St. Catherine and St. Margaret. Joan of Arc also prayed to a Black Madonna known as the Lady of Miracles in Orléans in 1429, one of at least twenty-five Black Madonnas later destroyed by Protestant mobs in the 1500s.[11]

Figure 10.3. Joan of Arc inspired the royalists of Laboulaye's generation, as well as the militant suffragists in the United Kingdom and the United States, as seen here on the cover of *The Suffragette*, a publication of the Women's Social and Political Union (WSPU), edited by Christabel Pankhurst. Illustration by Amy Ford.

Bartholdi and the Black Madonna

As we evaluated the Statue of Liberty, we looked for historical examples of other symbols of freedom embodied in the form of a woman to help us understand what these allegories mean for real women symbolically, sexually, and politically. That is why we now turn our attention to the Black Madonnas; they can be seen as a symbol of the secret power of the female divine that is suppressed by the Christian Church. One connection between the Black Madonnas and the Statue of Liberty is their purposefully androgynous features.

As mentioned earlier, there is some supposition that Bartholdi may have modeled the face of the Statue of Liberty after his mother. Art historian Albert Boime suggested something far more radical, however: that Bartholdi modeled Lady Liberty's face after his father figure, Édouard de Laboulaye. Even our librarian friend at the Statue of Liberty, Barry Moreno, agreed there is a resemblance when Laboulaye's portrait is compared with a close-up of Liberty's facial features, especially the prominent lower lip (figure 10.4, p. 272). But Moreno believed, and we agree, that Bartholdi would not have made the sentimental error of using the features of *any* real person for a colossal statue that he was striving to give that "impassable glance," which "ignore[d] the present" and was "fixed upon an unlimited future." Trying to make his statue as timeless as the monuments in Egypt, Bartholdi deliberately crafted an androgynous face and gave it a far-off gaze, because these are the tools of the artist to associate a colossal concept, like liberty, with eternity.

Like the Statue of Liberty, the Black Madonnas are described as having a slightly fierce expression and rather androgynous facial features. Black Madonna researcher and Jungian analyst Ean Begg talked about conscious androgyny as the goal for all humanity. He compared the Black Madonna to a woman who has completely integrated her *animus,* or masculine psychological qualities. This transformation makes her quite a powerful entity, as someone able to speak with authority while still relating compassionately to everyone. "The Black Virgin is about a new relationship between men and women," he told us.

In Europe, "Black Madonna" is a term used to describe roughly

Figure 10.4. Bronze bust of Édouard de Laboulaye, the father of the Statue of Liberty, created by sculptor Auguste Bartholdi. Replica on display at the Liberty Island Museum. Compare this face to figure 2.4. Author photo.

three hundred statuettes and some paintings that appeared, with a high concentration in southern France, from the late 1100s until approximately the 1400s. Physically, most of the Black Madonnas are small, only a few feet high, and the majority are made of wood. They are not all alike, but many of them share the pose known as the Throne of Wisdom, wherein the Madonna sits, straightbacked, looking straight ahead, and the Christ child sits in the same position, facing forward on her lap. It's as if the Madonna is the Throne of Wisdom (Sophia) herself. Their hands are often disproportionately large, which is a trait also seen in Cathar art, and usually it is just her hands and face that have darkened, not her clothing. (There goes the theory that they are turning dark from candle soot or age!)

The reasons for the blackness of the Madonna's skin tone are not as obvious here as they seem to be in the Americas, where their darker skin tones assisted in the conversion of the Natives. There are dozens of theories explaining why European artisans started to color their Virgin Mary statues black. However, the theory we would like to focus on here is that they were created to symbolize the dark or hidden teachings of the church, which revolve around the female divine. Black can be the color of concealed secrets, and Black Madonnas may have symbolized, to their creators, a hidden wisdom within the church that had to do with Mary, or with the female divine, in general. Using Jungian terminology, the Black Madonnas represent the dark mother within us all, guiding us through the darkness of death and the unknown. They represent our shadow self once it has been integrated by the larger personality.

Sometimes candle soot is indeed the cause of the blackness, but Begg calculates that in at least fifty cases, the dark coloring was a deliberate intention of the artisan who fashioned the original statue. More revealing is that even in instances when candle soot was determined to be the cause and was cleaned off, as in Einsiedeln in Switzerland, the surrounding villagers demanded the black coloring be restored. Black Madonna statues are loved fervently by their devotees, who have been known to leave behind their crutches, along with countless stories of miraculous cures that have resulted from praying at their shrines.

The Black Madonna Is the Earth Mother

Legends describing where the Black Madonnas in Europe came from were referred to when we told the origins of the mysterious painting of the Virgin of Guadalupe in Mexico. One day a peasant stumbles upon, or is led by mysterious forces to, a site that was formerly sacred to an ancient goddess. There he discovers a little statue in a stream, a cave, a well, or sometimes even lodged in a tree. Often nearby there is a site of some incredible natural phenomenon, like a sharp mountain ridge or a fantastic gorge. Because these Black Madonnas are often found near sites holy to the pre-Christian goddesses, another theory relates their dark color to the color of earth itself. When you combine the dark color of earth with the symbol of the mother, you get Earth Mother.

The theory goes that folks wanting to continue practicing their ancient goddess veneration would cloak an acceptable Catholic image around her to avoid being punished by the church. The Black Madonnas are well known for their special assistance in women's health and reproductive issues as were many pre-Christian goddesses. Another of the Black Madonnas' specialties is freeing prisoners, just like our old friend the Roman goddess Libertas.

Though skeptics will point to logical explanations for the odd coloring of the Black Madonna, devotees prefer the supernatural explanations and claim this holy mother who is dark asserts herself at times when people need guidance through the darkness. Ean Begg believes the Black Madonnas began to appear in the Middle Ages because the archetype needed to manifest at that time. They appeared following a period of psychic loss, after Europe had lost Jerusalem in the tragedy of the Crusades, and society was turning inward to more spiritual explorations. According to this line of thinking, this same archetype needs to manifest in our own time, because after centuries of church suppression and historical neglect, Black Madonnas began to appear again after having been rediscovered in the twentieth century. Following another period of psychic loss after World War II, books about the Black Madonnas started coming out and multiplying quickly, shrines were cleaned up, and pilgrimages suddenly grew popular again.

Some researchers have connected the Black Madonnas to the Cathar Christians, suggesting that they were created as a symbol of their underground, or symbolically dark or hidden, church. Some of the anti-Cathar literature of the period claimed that the Cathars spoke of a Mother-Father God, a sure way of getting yourself burned by the Inquisition.[12] Anti-Cathar literature also claimed that the Cathars were promoting the story of Mary Magdalene bringing Jesus's secret teachings to France. This leads to some theorizing that the Black Madonnas are depicting Mary Magdalene herself, who may have been dark-skinned, or again using black to symbolize "hidden," meaning Mary Magdalene is the hidden, or suppressed, power within the church. Sometimes the legend includes a dark-skinned companion or servant of the Magdalene who arrived with her on the shores of France in that rudderless boat,

Figure 10.5. A typical Black Madonna statue is this one from Montserrat in Spain, where she is seated straightback like a chair, and the child likewise, who is sitting on her lap as if she is the Throne of Wisdom itself. Photo: Csiraf.

and who may have been her daughter with Jesus in disguise. This companion is described as a dark-skinned Egyptian named Sarah, and today Sarah is considered the patron saint of the gypsies and depicted as a Black Madonna. Every year the Romani people of southern France carry her dark statue in processional to be bathed in the sea, in an identical ritual performed in Mexico and South America in honor of the dark Virgin of Regla and Yemonja.

Cathar Christians and Women

Most of what is known about the specifics of Cathar Christianity comes from their enemies who were trying to justify their extermination of entire towns and cities. The original teachings of the Cathars were burned along with tens of thousands of the practitioners themselves—men, women, and children together—on the orders of the pope. This is where the infamous quote "Burn them all—God will know his own" comes from. This sect of Christians, also known as Albigensians, followed a Christian reform tradition apparently imported from the region of present-day Bulgaria. The Cathars' goal was to return to the original version of Christianity. As such, they foreswore the wealthy, pompous trappings of the Roman Church, and through ascetic poverty, preaching, and itinerant healing, they sought a mystical union with the cosmic god.

From what we can gather, Cathars believed that the material world was a version of hell, and thus did all they could to alleviate the suffering of others while here. They believed all souls were trapped in material flesh, and because all souls were the same, they did not differentiate between men and women striving for mystical union. Women were preachers and healers and leaders in the Cathar Church, though they generally didn't travel. Cathars are often compared to the early gnostic sects that ran into conflict with organized religion in the four hundred years following Christ's death. Both Cathars and gnostics intermingled mystical aspects of Judaism and Christianity; both believed that the inner or higher wisdom was reserved for the elect few; and both encouraged women as well as men to be teachers, believing women equally capable of creative direct experience with the divine.

Just why these beliefs bothered the pope so much that he instituted a crusade against his fellow Christians is tangled up in the politics and greed of those advocating the suppression of this sect. The
Cathar piety would have been embarrassing to a corrupt and ostentatious clergy, but it seems that the Cathars' gnosticlike beliefs of a direct
union with God and their general equality of women were considered
the truly dangerous, heretical threats to the church. From 1209–1229,
Pope Innocent III launched what is called the Albigensian Crusade,
offering Cathar lands and holdings to any French nobleman who took
up arms against the communities and towns where this sect flourished.
To root out any stragglers remaining after the brutal massacres, the very
first medieval Inquisition was launched, with the Dominican Order
sanctioned to use torture and death to obtain confessions of differing
opinions, that ultimate danger to the church: heresy.

Translated literally from the Greek, "heresy" means "to choose."
For the next several hundred years, the Inquisition violently beat into
people that to choose one's own beliefs outside of the orthodox program
was justification for agonizing punishment and death. Starting with the
Cathars, but soon to include Jews, Moors, Anabaptists, and wisewomen
using herbs to alleviate the pain of childbirth,[13] practically everyone was
in danger of being labeled a heretic and thrown into the fire. Known as
the Burning Times, millions were burned for the sin of heresy. Most of
those accused of witchcraft were women, but most of them, like Joan
of Arc, were not burned as witches. They were actually put to death for
being heretics.

One of the classiest results of the U.S. Constitution was the asser-
tion of religious freedom. That citizens of the new United States were
legally protected to *choose* whatever spiritual path they wanted to follow was truly revolutionary. The Statue of Liberty and the similar versions of the American Liberty goddess with which the Revolutionary
generation dotted their landscape are clear reminders that the United
States was not established to be a Christian nation. The founders did
not identify their mission with Christian symbolism, not even disguised Christian symbolism, as in hidden under a black skin tone. The
U.S. founders, and Bartholdi and Laboulaye after them, symbolized

Figure 10.6. This is one of the first drafts for the United States Great Seal created by Pierre-Eugène du Simitière in 1776 under the direction of Franklin, Adams, and Jefferson. It included Liberty with her pole and cap, wearing an armored breastplate, and Justice with her scales, carrying a sword. The eye of Providence oversees everything. The people of this new nation were free to choose what to believe, as ensured several years later by the Constitution's radical break in abolishing the long tradition of requiring anyone elected to public office to first swear an oath of religious loyalty. From *The Eagle and the Shield*, published by the U.S. State Department.

this nation as an enlightened goddess because the people here were free to *choose* what to believe.

Freedom to Choose What to Believe

The world of biblical scholarship owes a great debt to Professor Elaine Pagels, who brought the translations of the gnostic gospels to popular readership in her 1979 book *The Gnostic Gospels,* one of the top one hundred books of the twentieth century, according to Modern Library. Pagels joined our *Lady Liberty Radio Interview Series* to talk about that book, as well as her more recent books, including *The Origin of Satan* and *Revelations*. From her we learned that the foundation of what we consider today the Orthodox Church has at its core the denunciation of heretics. Before the Christian Church was Romanized, it was made up of a wide assortment of bickering sects that followed whatever interpretation they chose.

We use a small *g* when talking about the gnostics, because as Pagels showed us, the people we call "gnostic Christians" were actually several different groups of people with many different beliefs. It is not a proper noun characterizing one group of people, but rather the name reflects what these groups shared in common with one another: the belief that direct experience or an inner *knowing*, or *gnosis*, of a religion was more important than dogma. They talked about a Father and a Mother God, with the mother aspect of God balancing the more aggressive male side, but they also added that allusions to gender were only metaphor, because God is neither male nor female.[14]

The material about the Cathars, Mary Magdalene, and the Black Madonnas all lead back to this earlier version of Christianity wherein women and the divine female were welcome. One of our initial questions when looking at the Statue of Liberty as a goddess was: What is it about the concept of goddess or female divinity that makes those of us brought up in the Euro-American, Protestant religions react with suspicion or fear? Suffragist Matilda Joslyn Gage had a good answer to that. "People are trained to believe what the church teaches, without examining for themselves," she said.[15] As a rule, we are not taught to think for ourselves. Most practicing Christians today still don't know about the gnostic gospels, or their example of how women in the early church were free to experience their own full potential. The Statue of Liberty should remind us all to think for ourselves, ask questions, find out who we are and why we're here, and most importantly, examine why we believe what we believe.

The so-called gnostic gospels are a series of parchments and scroll fragments that were contemporaneous to, or in some cases predate, the four gospels of the Christian scriptures. Most of the texts were discovered in the deserts of Nag Hammadi in Egypt starting in 1945. They turned out to be the ones voted as heretical by the early Roman church fathers who burned everything they disagreed with. The bishops did such a good job of burning and banning and otherwise destroying the writings of their opponents that a false history developed—of a golden age of the early church where everyone was in harmony. There were a few mentions of heretics in the writings of these church fathers, but what the heretics actually believed was not fully understood until just the past few decades. The Nag Hammadi library texts are rare survivors of the purge, and they bring to life the many conflicting groups that followed Christ's teachings in the first few centuries after his death.

The translation and testing of these hidden gospels was subject to much political debate, delaying the publication of most of them until 1975. Even today, they have yet to make more than a ripple in public consciousness or make any changes in organized religion. The texts include the Gospel of Mary Magdalene, the Gospel of Judas, the Gospel of Philip, the Gospel of Thomas, and some beautifully strange poetry. Pagels said that although the various groups of gnostics disagreed with each other on almost everything, they all seemed to agree that the story of Adam and Eve and the serpent had been grossly misinterpreted (their version cast Eve as the wise one), and that women were as equally capable of achieving mystical union as men. According to his earliest followers, Jesus came as a guide to *enlighten,* not as the arbiter of sin and repentance.[16] They taught that it was possible to heal and be like Jesus if they followed the secret teachings reserved for only the trusted few. This striving to become a perfected being like Jesus was one of the main objections of their contemporaries. Those who advocated that Jesus *was* God called it blasphemous for others to strive to become *like* him.

The Throne of Sophia

A good portion of the texts of the gnostics concerns their unique understanding of the female aspect of divinity, the Sophia, or wisdom, sometimes referred to as the bride of Christ. The school of Jewish mysticism known as Kabbalah also highlights a feminine presence of God called the Shechinah, described as the indwelling presence of God that fills all life-forms. She is present everywhere.[17] Both the Sophia and the

Shechinah were seen as intercessors between humanity and the divine. The familiar images of the Virgin Mary seen bathed in a ray of light are depictions of this Holy Wisdom or Holy Spirit in direct communication with her. When the gnostics talked about Sophia, they were referring to the wisdom of spiritual freedom and its method of attainment.

Wisdom is the liberation from our ignorance of who we are and why we're here on planet Earth, and it comes from the divine spark, or the soul, which is Sophia. The Statue of Liberty is crushing a chain under her foot, which could symbolize the chain that binds us to the physical world. To break free of it and achieve balance, one needs the wisdom that comes from immersing oneself in prayer (talking to the deity), meditation (listening to the deity), and service to others (acting for the deity). In astrological terms this is summed up in the sign of Virgo, the divine woman, which is the essence of service to others. Feminine and masculine principles are not separate entities; they are two halves that require the other to create a whole, as in sending and receiving. When one or the other dominates, then all of creation is thrown out of balance.

What is clear in the banned gnostic texts is that Jesus favored Mary Magdalene above all the other apostles, gave her special instructions, and expected her to lead the church when he was gone. By elevating the female, Jesus was balancing his male energy. It is not unusual for religious mystics to describe their transcendent experiences in sexual terms, and perhaps that metaphor was being employed when the gnostic gospels talk about Jesus kissing Mary Magdalene. A whole cottage industry of speculation about their sexual union has grown up around that mention of a kiss, but it very well could have been a metaphorical description of their union in spirit, and the reason he handed down the more advanced teachings through her.

Where Did We Get the Idea that Christianity Was Anti-Women?

Many of the gnostic churches were led by women, they listened to women as their chief prophets, and even enjoyed women performing the sacraments and baptisms. In so doing, they were following a radical new pattern that had been established by Jesus himself. Jesus's teachings were all about compassion, caring, nurturing, nonviolence, and partnership. He instituted a revolutionary break with the gender-segregated traditions of his Jewish background by assembling men and women together, side by side, praying with them, eating with them, working with them, and teaching them at the same time as men.[18] Strong women were attracted to his following and were strengthened by their association with him.

Women raised in the Christian tradition today are not taught to value themselves based on Jesus's approach to gender equality. Instead the church reinforces the weak and evil nature of women and their need to be submissive to men, opinions that entered the Christian canon from a long string of misogynistic church fathers such as Irenaeus (circa 130 CE), Tertullian (circa 155 CE), Athanasius (circa 296 CE), and Augustine (354 CE). Tireless in their zeal to stamp out any evidence of the gnostic questioners, when they identified the standard twenty-seven books of the Christian scriptures, they left out the ones that praised female partnership. It's unclear whether they hated women because the gnostics allowed them to lead, or if they hated gnostics because they allowed women to lead, but what *is* clear is that Jesus didn't have any of these issues. Woman-hating did not come from Jesus, it came from these guys.

Nowhere in any other culture is there such mortification of the body and shame associated with the life-giving parts. Matilda Joslyn Gage called this teaching "the most grievous wrong ever inflicted upon woman," and that degrading woman's moral pride created this "loss of faith in one's own self, and disbelief in one's own right."[19] Taken to its extreme, this shame of the body has led to laws barring women from breastfeeding their babies in public. One of the most primal creation miracles that chemically prepares the baby for later life and hormonally helps the mother deal with stress is outlawed because old guys like Tertullian wrote about their hang-ups with women. In his treatise "On the Apparel of Women," Tertullian declared that men were not responsible for their lust, because women had the duty to veil and cover themselves completely or else they were to be blamed for his sin.

Resurgences of Female Power Are Followed by Crackdowns

The point of all these history lessons, and our attempts to relate them to the Statue of Liberty, is the understanding that we can use her as a reminder to tend our own liberties. Women in the Western world have certainly made great strides toward gender parity in the past few decades, and yet, while there's still a long way to go, we must be ever mindful of the swinging pendulum of social opinion. Previous eras that we discussed, when women's power rose briefly, have been crushed by backlashes in the form of the Inquisition, or an almost complete erasure of the gnostic texts. As long as the domination paradigm persists, whenever women's power is on the rise, humanity risks reprisals capable of pushing it back into even darker ages.

The gospels that were kept out of the Bible proclaimed that to

Figure 10.7. Joel Pett is following something of a cartoonist's tradition by using Lady Liberty to symbolize the conscience of the nation. In this panel she reminds us to tend our liberties and keep Uncle Sam in check. Sam in the cartoon world often represents the more selfish, controlling material desires of the nation. Used with permission.

know oneself was the way to know God—that inner gnosis, or knowing, was the path to union with Christ.[20] In Luke 17:21, Jesus says
that the kingdom of God is within you. Awakening to this realization
that the cosmic mind is working through you, and through everyone,
connecting all of us together sounds like the discoveries coming from
quantum physics where the observer affects the observed. Everything is
related and connected on some deep and as of yet untapped level. We
all have male and female aspects within us. The challenge is to unite
them into a cohesive whole, to be symbolically androgynous like the
Black Madonnas—or like the Statue of Liberty—to achieve the wisdom
of balance.

11

Armed Liberty

Freedom Acquired through Bloodshed

D id you know that there is a second statue of Liberty in America? She holds the position of honor as the crowning pinnacle on top of the U.S. Capitol dome, and from high on her perch she overlooks every congressional deliberation below. The State Department officially calls her the *Statue of Freedom,* but we believe the name originally given her by her sculptor is more appropriate: *Armed Liberty.* The exchange of Lady Liberty's floppy Phrygian cap for the war helmet of Minerva reveals a great deal about race relations in the United States during the time of her creation, right in the middle of the Civil War. In addition, the compromises behind the three major changes in the design of the *Statue of Freedom* show us where the leaders of the time were headed with their ideas on how to Americanize the world. They also caused us to wonder about the popularity of Minerva in American art and what influence this warrior goddess archetype has had on America's self-identity.

The transformation of the Capitol dome statue from a gentle, olive-branch-toting female allegory of peace into a heavily cloaked, boot-wearing gal sporting the war helmet of Minerva introduced us to the complication of adding armor to the American Liberty goddess. What does it say about America's founders that, second only to Lady Liberty, they were most attracted to Minerva, the Roman interpretation of this so-called motherless goddess of war, who is known in literature as always coolly "siding with the male in all things"?

We will start with the *Statue of Freedom*'s special connection to slavery, and how she's reached out to speak to peace-activist women. And finally, we will go way back to look at Minerva's surprising secret pre-Hellenic history, which will shed some light on the psychological analysis of the archetype of Athena in today's powerful women.

The *Statue of Freedom* in the Civil War

The African slave connection to the *Statue of Freedom* on top of the U.S. Capitol is a well-known bit of trivia. A bright and talented enslaved man named Philip Reid was responsible for saving *Freedom*. We even know how much he was paid for the job: $41.25, this according to his May 16, 1861, pay voucher retained by the Architect of the Capitol. Because he was a slave, all the wages he earned while he was hired out for the Capitol job would have gone straight to his owner, with the exception of what he was paid for working overtime, on the day of rest, Sunday. That's the amount recorded on the pay voucher where he signed his name with an *X*. He got $1.25 a day for thirty-three Sundays.

While Reid was keeping the fires burning under the molds at the Maryland foundry where the statue was to be cast, the story goes that he watched carefully and learned what the more skilled workers were doing. When it came time to cast the bronze, the Italian immigrant workers trained to handle the job decided to strike to demand higher wages. The owner of the foundry refused to give in to them, and instead put the slave Reid to work to figure out how to fit the molds together and take over the more delicate part of the job. The success of the end result is evidenced by the bronze statue's having survived more than one hundred years of Washington, D.C., pollution before being taken down for its first restoration. Slaves of Washington, D.C., were emancipated in 1862, so Reid would have been a free man by the time the statue was installed on top of the dome in 1863, but there is no record of him witnessing the event.

The creation of the *Statue of Freedom* was part of an expansion project of the original Capitol Building that was deemed necessary to make room for the increasing numbers of congressional representatives being sent to D.C. from newly added states. The mammoth construction project went on for years, starting in 1850 and continuing right through the Civil War. When President Lincoln was asked whether the materials going into the construction of the new Capitol wouldn't be better served melted down as ammunition for the war, he said no. Continuation of the construction will signal to the people that the Union will survive after the conflict has ceased, he said.

Thomas U. Walter, the architect selected to design the new Capitol, created the iconic dome we all immediately recognize, and in his original drawings he sketched what he thought should be on the top of that dome: a statue of Liberty. Walter's sketch shows a traditional Liberty image of a robed female holding a pole topped with a Phrygian cap, which would have been clearly discernable from below as a traditional Lady Liberty. This was 1850, the same year as the passage of the notorious Fugitive Slave Act, requiring all law enforcement and government officials in the North and South to assist in the return of runaway slaves, one of this country's most egregious affronts on liberty that resulted in the kidnapping and enslavement of many free Blacks.

Former Mississippi senator Jefferson Davis served as secretary of war under President Franklin Pierce from 1853–1857, and he was tasked with overseeing the renovations on the Capitol. As a result, it is Davis's Euro-centric and pro-slavery prejudice that we see stamped all over the art of the new Capitol Building,[1] and nowhere is that more apparent than in the headgear for the *Statue of Freedom*. As the rapidly changing course of events would have it, by the time the statue was finished and being secured to the dome, war had been declared and slaveholder Davis was serving as the president of the Confederate States of America.

We are grateful to the work of Katya Miller for much of what we learned in this chapter, especially about Thomas Crawford and the *Statue of Freedom*, subjects of her forthcoming, definitive book. Crawford was an American who, since 1835, had lived in Rome, where he was trained in the high classical school of sculpting. He had already completed several other sculptures for the new Capitol when he was

Figure 11.1. Dr. Bob Hieronimus gives the peace sign outside the Capitol dome, where the *Statue of Freedom* watches over every deliberation of Congress. Notice that the Phrygian cap in this version of Lady Liberty has been replaced by Minerva's helmet topped with an eagle. Author photo.

awarded the commission for the Capitol dome's crowning statue. Crawford also designed the bronze doors for the eastern entrances to the House and Senate wings and the pediment sculpture for the Senate wing that includes the Vanishing Indian motif (figure 6.6, p. 157). He would go blind as he was finishing *Armed Liberty*, and she would be his last commission. Dead at the age of forty-three from a brain tumor, he would not be present to fret over the last-minute snafu with its casting. This was probably a blessing, given that his deathbed wish was for it to be cast in Germany, where he believed the most skilled craftsmen were.

A Whole Lotta Compromise Going On

Jefferson Davis was schooled in the classics at West Point, and he knew full well the meaning of the Phrygian cap in ancient Rome, where it was worn by slaves after they were emancipated. Imagery of the American Revolution was teeming with liberty caps, interpreted as a metaphor by the colonists for emancipating themselves from the tyranny of British monarchy. The liberty cap grew more controversial after radicals adopted it during the French Revolution, where it acquired a patina of violence. Davis saw the Phrygian cap as linked to both the riotous, uncontrolled anarchy of the French Revolution and the ceremony of freeing slaves in Rome. The combination of freeing slaves and violent uprisings together in one hat brought up for him the national obsession of any Southern gentleman of his time: the fear of slaves rising up in revolt. The last thing he wanted to add to the simmering tensions in the country was a symbol on top of the Capitol that could be read as an endorsement for the emancipation of slaves.

The letters back and forth between Davis, through the building supervisor, to sculptor Crawford document the radical changes that the statue experienced from the first design called *Freedom Triumphant in Peace and War* to the final result: *Armed Liberty*. When Crawford added the Phrygian cap to the second version, Davis objected, saying the cap's "history renders it inappropriate to a people who were born free and should not be enslaved."[2] Davis's explanation ignores the fact that more than half the population of colonial America had come to this continent as servants and were treated little better than slaves. Some were kept as virtual prisoners, and at least 25 percent of all indentured servants in the colonies died from the harsh treatment before their terms of labor came to an end.

The problem that faced Jefferson Davis was not a new one: How to depict the traditional Lady Liberty in a nation that condoned slaveholding? Davis's solution? Give her a war helmet. A veteran of the Mexican War, Davis envisioned Liberty as a warrior and wrote that liberty must sometimes be maintained through military force.[3] He was delighted at the addition of the globe under Lady Freedom's feet, which Crawford included in his second revision. Placing *Armed Liberty* on top of a globe, which they called the "American World," which was then placed on top of the Capitol, was a symbolic prediction that the United States would become an influencer of other nations, spreading Manifest Destiny outside its borders.[4] With these kinds of goals, substituting that controversial liberty cap with Minerva's war helmet made perfect sense.

Crawford had already compromised for Davis on an earlier statue of Liberty that he also designed to include the Phrygian cap. This one was to be included in the sculpture for the Senate east entrance of the Capitol that was to be a pair of goddesses called *Justice and Liberty.* The work is now called *Justice and History,* because when Davis objected to the cap, this time Crawford completely swapped goddesses. For the statue on the dome, he likewise compromised his initial designs, but then he added some unique flourishes to Minerva's helmet that ironically ended up making most people assume this statue was a Native American woman. Davis must have gnashed his teeth if he ever heard that interpretation.

The Phrygian cap is not entirely absent in Capitol artwork, though, and appears more than once in the Constantino Brumidi 1865 fresco on the interior ceiling of the dome, for example. This mural is up so high that people only know the details of it from the reproductions on sale in the Capitol gift shop, but the *Apotheosis of Washington* is a riot of goddesses and allegorical females and worth checking out just for that reason alone. You'll see helmeted Minerva representing science, and there's the red liberty cap on the heads of both Liberty and a figure labeled America.

Figure 11.2. Detail from the *Apotheosis of George Washington*, the 1865 Constantino Brumidi fresco on the ceiling of the Capitol dome. According to an 1897 history of the Capitol by George Hazelton, the figure representing Revenge holding the two torches is a portrait of Jefferson Davis, and the white-bearded fellow representing Tyranny is a portrait of Robert E. Lee. Architect of the Capitol.

There's also a cameo appearance by the *Statue of Freedom*, complete with her unique eagle-headed helmet. In Brumidi's painting she is labeled the Goddess of War, and she wears an intimidating expression as she rushes forth with her sword upraised, challenging the vices depicted in the form of old men labeled Tyranny and Kingly Power (figure 11.2). One of these old men looks suspiciously like Jefferson Davis himself.[5]

Why the Statue of Liberty Is Not Wearing a Phrygian Cap

In 1876 the creators of the Statue of Liberty were expressing just as much concern over the Liberty goddess's customary red headgear as Davis had, if not more so. Being French, they were even more aware of how the radical revolutionaries of that country had used what they called "le bonnet rouge" to foment rebellion. Édouard de Laboulaye made a moving speech at a fundraiser at the Paris Opéra in which he explained why he and Bartholdi replaced Liberty's traditional Phrygian cap with symbolism for light. To the French of the 1870s, to red-cap or not to red-cap was a clear political choice. The tens of thousands of radical revolutionaries executed for uprising during the 1871 Paris Commune had read a newspaper they called *Le Bonnet Rouge,* and their version of Lady Liberty was a muscular and disheveled Marianne who always wore the red cap.

Laboulaye despised the anarchy and violence of the commune, and, in fact, it was his reaction against the violence of the commune that finally pushed the Statue of Liberty out of the conceptual stage in their minds and into reality. In comparing their Liberty project to Delacroix's *Liberty Leading the People* (figure 10.1, p. 264), to show how his *La Liberté Eclairant le Monde* would represent an *American* Liberty, Laboulaye said, "She is not Liberty with a red cap on her head, a pike in her hand, stepping over corpses. Ours, in one hand holds the torch,—no, not the torch that sets afire, but the flambeau, the candle-flame that enlightens. . . . This . . . Liberty lives only through Truth and Justice, Light and Law."[6] By selecting a headgear normally reserved for monarchs—literally "crowning" her with light instead of the more radical Phrygian cap—the creators of New York's Statue of Liberty aligned themselves with the stability of a conservative government.

Why the *Statue of Freedom* Is Wearing Feathers

Returning now to D.C.'s version of Lady Liberty, when sculptor Thomas Crawford added eagle feathers to the helmet for the *Statue of Freedom,* he said he was referencing our country's Native American origins. But he didn't add just feathers—he added the entire head and talons of the eagle to her crown. He also changed the cloak she wore so that it was not the standard Greco-Roman drapery, but instead had a beaded fringed addition similar to some Native American designs. When the *Statue of Freedom* was taken down in the early 1990s for cleaning and repair, Rayna Green remembers hundreds of Native Americans making a pilgrimage to see her up close. "Indians recognized her as their girl," said Green, director of the American Indian Program at the Smithsonian Institution's National Museum of American History.[7]

The *Statue of Freedom* is a manifestation of all the controversies and compromises of the tumultuous times in which she was created. Her conception coincided with the publication of *Uncle Tom's Cabin,* which fired up the abolitionist cause. By the time she was completed and being raised to the dome by winch and pulley, it was 1863, the year of the Emancipation Proclamation. She is a melting pot with symbols for the disenfranchised entering into her story, and as such, she can be considered even more American than the Statue of Liberty. She was cast by a Black slave, she has Native American symbolism in her clothing, and her female form represents women—all groups combined in a symbol of freedom that was not granted to any of them. This multitude of "Others," as Fryd called them, "coalesced in Crawford's statue and in Davis's own vision of white superiority that he insisted be represented."[8] At her rededication ceremony in 1993, after the *Statue of Freedom* was restored, poet laureate Rita Dove described her by saying, "She is one of the many and she is each of us."

Freedom Speaks to Women

For decades, the full-size plaster model of the *Statue of Freedom* was stored away in a basement in the Smithsonian. Then one day in the 1960s, a spiritual Hawaiian woman received a mental message from what she called "the Lady of Freedom," that she wanted to be set free. Morrnah Simeona was sitting on the lawn of the Capitol, looking up at the statue on the dome far overhead, when she heard the voice of the statue asking if Simeona knew who she was. *Sure,* thought Simeona, *you're Pocahontas. No,* she was corrected, *I'm the Lady of Freedom, and from today on your work will be to set me free.* Simeona used her spiritual organization to begin fundraising for the restoration of the plaster model, and in 1989 she presented a bill to the Hawaiian House Committee on Intergovernmental Relations and International Affairs to recognize the *Statue of Freedom* as "a symbol of World Peace." Simeona was inspired to "rectify and release the past errors" of acquiring our nation's freedom through bloodshed, "so that the United States of America can experience a new birth of Freedom." She believed that "to initiate awakening in the people of our great country is Divine destiny—to bring Peace and Freedom to the world."[9] As a result of her activism, the nineteen-and-a-half-foot-tall plaster model now occupies a primary position in the middle of a wraparound staircase in the Capitol visitor's center, where visitors can see up close her long hair flowing down her back and the claws in the eagle talons hanging like earrings on either side of her helmet.

Interest in restoring the model soon transferred to interest in restoring the actual bronze statue, which was treated to a complete overhaul in 1993. Simeona had passed away in 1992, but around the time that the restored statue flew through the air, dangling from a helicopter headed back up to the dome, another spiritual woman was contacted in meditation. Katya Miller clearly heard the *Statue of Freedom* instructing her that more people needed to hear her message, and she's been working on a book on this subject ever since. That two separate peace-activist women felt guided by this statue to encourage more people to focus on her as the consciousness of the nation and a symbol for world peace, rather than as an armed Liberty dominating the American world, in our opinion, means that the archetype of the American Liberty Goddess is reasserting itself in our nation's consciousness. It's time for Americans to take responsibility for changing our patterns of domination. It's time for us to lead by example and set a new paradigm allowing enlightened liberty to bring about world peace.

Minerva and the Revolutionary Generation

Leading up to and during the Revolution, Minerva herself—not just her helmet—ran a distant second to Libertas as the most popular goddess in patriotic artwork. Usually Minerva is seen guiding Libertas or Columbia with her wise counsel. The Revolutionary generation was

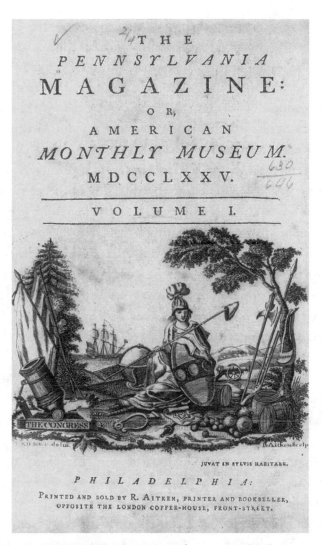

Figure 11.3. A pre-Revolutionary use of an armed Liberty standing for America on a magazine title page designed by Pierre-Eugène du Simitière, 1775. Library of Congress.

under the influence of the Age of Reason, and thus Minerva as the clear-headed goddess of wisdom was the obvious choice for much of the new insignia. Minerva was designed into the seal of the Academy of the Arts and Sciences in 1780, the seal of Union College in 1795, and into the name of New York's first daily newspaper, Noah Webster's 1793 *The American Minerva: Patroness of Peace, Commerce, and the*

Liberal Arts. In explaining their choice of this particular Roman goddess the founders described her as the Minerva of Peace and indicated that her sword was pointing downward. While Minerva is technically the goddess of war, the founders generally chose her because of her dual role as the goddess of wisdom. We'll cover in a bit how the seemingly contradictory nature of Minerva/Athena's many domains is explained by the pre-Hellenic versions of her myth.

Most of the founders were schooled in the classics and would have known Minerva in her Roman guise, which described her as her father's daughter who would "side with men in all things." This patriarchal-preference came from the Greek myth of Orestes, who murdered his mother, which has been read symbolically as the overthrow of the goddess-worshipping cultures. Athena was the deciding vote for acquittal of matricide at his trial, reaffirming her description as her father's daughter. Her creation story in the Greek myths, copied by the Romans, has Athena springing out of Zeus's head fully formed, in full armor. In other words, she was born of the male intellect and was considered motherless. Though usually abbreviated out of her story, Athena did actually have a mother. She was a pre-Olympian Titan named Metis, who was also a goddess of wisdom. Zeus turned Metis into a fly and swallowed her after impregnating her, because her children were prophesied to become more powerful than Zeus. That child, who indeed turned out to be more powerful than Zeus, managed to outwit his trickery and be born anyway!

In these Greco-Roman myths, Athena/Minerva is known as a cool strategist, and her battlefield advice to war heroes of mythology is legendary. She is also a patron of the arts and the creator of music, science, and invention. It is in this latter portrayal that she appealed to the founders of the United States. Minerva starred in the first opera ever written and performed in the new nation. Written by Declaration signer and designer of the American flag, Francis Hopkinson, the opera was called *The Temple of Minerva,* and the plot featured Minerva guiding the young Columbia-America and predicting a happy future for her if her sons would stand united. A Philadelphia newspaper described one of the performances just a few weeks after the final victory at Yorktown as being attended by the minister of France and his guests, General George Washington with his lady.[10]

The founders were attracted to Minerva, because education was key to their conception of peaceful self-governance. Translated into today's parlance: It's important to vote, but it's even more important to cast an educated vote. "We the people," in order to live up to our founders' ideals, are obligated to stay informed and choose the best options for long-term sustainability. Otherwise, our destination will be sidetracked by short-term special interests. The long-term foresight and wisdom of Minerva were suggested as ideals for the new nation.

Another big champion of the informed electorate was Édouard de Laboulaye, who advocated for universal public education as the foundation for a successful republic.[11] His multivolume *Histoire des Etats-Unis,* published in 1866 just as the project for the Statue of Liberty began, is described as the statue's literary equivalent, and in it Laboulaye uses the metaphor of America spreading its light to the world.[12] Laboulaye said, "Establish schools, and you chase away ignorance, crime and misery, and you diminish hatred, for you will make the country wealthy and great by the well being, morality and happiness of each."[13] He admired Benjamin Franklin's talent for using symbolism to inspire moral values in the public, seen as a necessity for sustaining a democratic republic, and hoped with this Statue of Liberty that they might also achieve something with "a far-reaching moral effect."[14]

Minerva and Manifest Destiny

If we've learned nothing else in our investigations, it's that the same symbols can inspire different people to work toward very different ends. When Lady Liberty picks up some of the symbolism of Minerva, she is an especially excellent example of this point. We asked historian Max Dashú why the Revolutionary generation almost always referred to this goddess of wisdom and war as the Roman Minerva instead of as Athena, the earlier Greek model. Dashú suggested that the founders were more attracted to the republic of Rome than the failed democracy of Greece, and reminded us that the Minerva we see in early colonial broadsides is distorted through

Figure 11.4. In the Constantino Brumidi fresco on the ceiling of the Capitol dome, Minerva is portrayed as the goddess of wisdom and invention, inspiring famous American inventors like Benjamin Franklin and Samuel Morse. Architect of the Capitol.

the lens of the *Interpretatio Romana*. Whatever goddesses from earlier cultures Minerva may be based on, Athena included, they were Romanized and reinterpreted to fit the motives of the Roman Empire.

An image of the armed female was used during the Roman conquest in a way that was repeated later by the colonizing European powers. Armies led by an armed female on their banner put a friendly female face over their domination, acting almost as a cloak of invisibility. European colonial empires adopted the armored female as a sort of mascot. She is depicted with spear upraised leading the troops in European colonial propaganda of the day. The armed female symbolized the combination of force and maternal care that they were trying to explain as necessary to "civilize" the Indigenous people, who were always depicted as backward in European colonies around the world. A similar tactic is used when referring to the Catholic Church as the mother church even while it subjugates women. Minerva was an especially popular image in expansionist Victorian England, where she had merged with the native Celtic goddesses to become the ever-armored Britannia.

Minerva's Secret Background

What most of us know about the Greek and Roman goddesses reflects coded patterns of adaptation for women in a patriarchal culture. So says Jungian psychiatrist Jean Shinoda Bolen, who points out that, after all, these myths were recorded at the dawn of the patriarchy, or what we call civilized history. But history does not begin with the Greeks. Those famous Greek myths about the doings on Mount Olympus recorded by Homer and Hesiod were based on earlier versions of similar stories. Many of them can be traced to the myths of older, matrifocal cultures that revered a great Mother Goddess. The stories about Athena and Minerva become much more interesting, and less contradictory, when their pre-Hellenic origins are added back into their story.

Studying the earlier counterparts of Athena and Minerva in Minoan Crete or Libya explains the split personality nature of her domain. We wondered how one entity could be the specialist in both wisdom and war, as well as the guardian of everything from household skills like weaving and carpentry, to inventions and science and music. Charlene Spretnak showed in her book *Lost Goddesses of Early Greece* that when the Greek myths we know from elementary school were converted from myths of earlier matrifocal cultures, they were altered to fit into the patriarchal pantheon, necessarily resulting in numerous contradictions.

Greek Athena evolved from a goddess in Minoan Crete, a highly advanced, matrifocal partnership culture, where she was independent, and where Zeus was her son-lover rather than the all-powerful father. This older version of Athena is perhaps one aspect of the Medusa, the serpent-headed woman derived from a culture where serpents were seen as a symbol of wisdom and renewal.[15] In the patriarchal Greek version of her story, Athena is responsible for killing the Medusa, which could be a symbolic rendition of the motherless daughter assisting in the killing of the old mother-centered culture and their snake prophets in favor of the new father-centered culture.[16] Author Karen Elias-Button shows how, in Minoan Crete, Athena (or Athene, as she is also known) may have been considered the daughter aspect of the Medusa, and says, "Seeing Athene and Medusa . . . in their rightful roles as daughter and mother, it is possible to interpret their story . . . as a woman's myth." Unlike the mother-daughter goddess pair Demeter and Persephone, in the paring of Medusa-Athena, Elias-Button says, the daughter has "superseded the 'mother,' and, as the embodiment of a differentiated feminine consciousness, has assumed the ascendant position."[17]

The Greeks changed Athena to emphasize that she was born of a man. The mother aspect of the Medusa is now defined as having serpents for hair, and cast as evil.* This correlates to the story of Eve and the serpent, which can similarly be translated as the overturning of a goddess-worshipping culture by a warrior-god culture. The formerly all-powerful daughter-figure Athena is shaped through these myths to prefer siding with men in all things.

There are other more ancient goddesses who can be traced through archaeological and linguistic evidence to be the forerunner of the Athena prototype. One example is the Libyan goddess named Neith, who is likewise described as the inventor of weaving and magic, hunting and war, and is also self-perpetuating and an all-powerful mother of the gods.[18] Minerva in Rome is a combination of the roles and legends of the Greek version of Athena blended together with a more ancient Etruscan goddess who ruled the arts and wisdom but had nothing to do with war. Both the Greek and Roman versions of Athena/Minerva are associated with the owl of wisdom, but in these earlier goddess depictions she is sometimes actually seen *as* an owl. This could be a reference to the bird-women goddesses of the Neolithic, when women, birds, and water were connected in hundreds of archaeological vessels in the shape of women with bird bodies and birds with women's bodies. The goddess in the form of a bird held the waters of life.[19]

---

*In *Monuments and Maidens,* page 112, Marina Warner credited Robert Graves for seeing the Medusa as the "goddess of matriarchy" and her destruction as "the historical memorial of her cult's eclipse," or as he put it: to record "the usurpation by Hellenic invaders of the Moon-goddess' powers."

Athena/Minerva in Power Today

We learned a lot from Jean Shinoda Bolen and her book *Goddesses in Everywoman* as we tried to understand the psychological influence on our national identity resulting from our founders' strong affinity with Minerva. Bolen related it to her therapy work where she uses the archetypes of the Olympian pantheon, suggesting that when a man or woman identifies too strongly with the Athena archetype, they would be well-served to focus more on the mystical and vulnerable and intuitive attributes of Artemis, Aphrodite, or Hestia, for example. Bolen's psychological insights have helped millions of men and women

Figure 11.5. Minerva appears on the U.S. army version of the Medal of Honor, the highest military honor that can be awarded by the U.S. government, presented to military personnel for extraordinary bravery in combat above and beyond the call of duty. Minerva also appears in the navy version of this award, but the Statue of Liberty is in her place for the air force version. Library of Congress.

empower and transform themselves, but her more important work as of late has been advocating for a United Nations Fifth World Conference on Women. She says she has taken this on as her personal mission, because she knows that no matter how much inner work we do to raise consciousness, without taking action and manifesting meaningful changes, women will remain second-class citizens.

The Athena archetype has served well for a majority of the women who first entered politics, making them shrewd enough, like Athena, to succeed in a man's world. Many female politicians and business leaders in the United States today fit the Athena pattern of being highly intelligent, perceived by others as cold and calculating, and excellent strategists, like chess players, with their eye on long-term goals. What many of these women are missing, and what the United States itself is missing—with its tendency to side with the patriarchy in all things—is the ability to connect compassionately with the mother archetype. Many women in leadership positions focus exclusively on the warrior aspect of Athena and end up following the same patterns of domination without compassion of the current patriarchal paradigm. Mentally unhealthy women can make as many bad decisions as mentally unhealthy men, of course.

A new generation of female leaders is realizing that they can change the system from within instead of conforming to it. New leaders of both genders are realizing that they do not have to negate their vulnerable, caring, and nurturing aspects in order to be effective. The pre-Hellenic versions of Athena/Minerva would indicate that women leaders can be independent, wise, and strong, while simultaneously functioning as daughters and sisters firmly rooted to the ancient mother.

Instead of celebrating powerful women who excel with life-giving properties, however, Hollywood and Madison Avenue have created a cool, kick-ass warrior woman to glorify. Cultural historian Riane Eisler sees as counterproductive these new female heroes achieving a form of dominator power by taking on the traditionally male qualities of combat and assassination. This is not male bashing we are talking about here. We are talking about rearranging our values so that the traditionally female qualities of giving life and of nurturing are seen as being just as heroic as the qualities of strength and courage that are manifested by

Figure 11.6. The cultural popularity of the Statue of Liberty as a symbol of America really took off with World War I propaganda posters like these. On the left, a Boy Scout hands a sword that reads "Be Prepared" to a muscular Lady Liberty who is wearing both Minerva's helmet and the crown of seven rays. On the right, she makes an emotional appeal to immigrants to conserve food as their duty to preserve freedom. Library of Congress.

our warriors. There are men who are very good nurturers and caregivers, of course, but most Americans are still being taught to condemn men in the role of the nurturer. It's perceived to be effeminate (as if that's a bad word) and weak, while women are encouraged to act like men to succeed. Maybe it would behoove us to recognize that both men and women should be encouraged to act "like women" to succeed.

Athena/Minerva and Lady Liberty

The look of the American Liberty goddess has changed since the Revolution, paralleling America's changing national self-identity.

Attaching armor and other domination symbols to the Liberty goddess symbolically condoned the dominator actions of the United States and the tendency to drift toward imperialism. We have let ourselves believe that domination is the only means to progress. "Once an Athena woman changes the way she thinks, her relationship to people can change," says Bolen.[20] America's changing national self-identity includes learning to balance these dominator traits with the nurturing and vulnerable caring traits that are chemically programmed within all of us.

Yes, we do need more women in politics, in business, the military, and law enforcement, but we also need men who are able to lead with compassion, too. Balanced human beings are willing to listen and to compromise. We say: If you find yourself faced at election time with a choice between a male and female candidate, and you've sufficiently educated yourself to believe they will be equally motivated by compassion, then yes, it's best to choose the woman, because reaching parity should be the long-term goal, and right now we have a long way to go to even up the numbers in Congress.

The Statue of Liberty has no armor, and she has too many liberational themes of enlightenment attached to her to have been used very often as a symbol of America's imperialism. She is related to Athena/ Minerva, however, through her emphasis on enlightenment in the form of education and the patriarchal law and order of control. We believe if Americans can focus on the Statue of Liberty as an American goddess and acknowledge the power of her nurturing qualities, our country will begin to act with more compassion on the world stage. We can learn from our nation's attraction to the armed female and the Minerva/ Athena archetype and use it to reconcile our own individual self-determination and independence with the full power of Lady Liberty. It's time to bring everyone's individual strengths to the table and reevaluate both our perceptions of powerful women, and the powers that we perceive as valuable.

12

Lady Liberty and Her Sisters

We Are One

S o far we have reviewed many of the female divinities of mythology and art that echo in the bearing and details of the Statue of Liberty. In this chapter we will use her torch to illuminate behind the lines of standard history texts until we can see some of the real women of the United States of America and how their lesser-known histories can be considered part of the secret life of Lady Liberty. The collective reaction of American women to the essence of liberty as it entered their hearts is part of what Bartholdi and Laboulaye were trying to symbolize with this massive female monument, and it is their perspective that we will consider here.

The history of women is the history of 52 percent of Americans, and yet so little of it is told in our school textbooks. We reviewed the elevated status of women in the Indigenous traditions in chapter 2 and the reverence for the female divine among African traditions in chapter 8. Here our focus will be on the lives of some of the Euro-American women, from the hardscrabble life of the colonial era, to the refinement of the Enlightenment and the disruption of the Revolution. As we'll see, the American Revolution changed the conditions for Euro-American women of all classes, from servants to aristocrats, just as the direct involvement of women, their ingenuity, and resourcefulness changed and shaped the American Revolution.

The framers of the Constitution were students of the Enlightenment and believed that through reason and altruism society could become virtuous and harmonious. They wrote copiously about how important virtue was to the success of their self-governing experiment, but "it would take the women to make that happen," said Cokie Roberts in her book *Ladies of Liberty*. It would take the women "to push and prod the country toward a more perfect union, to create the institutions that would shape our nation."[1]

As the twentieth century broke over the horizon, a new generation of activists, working under the shadow of the Statue of Liberty, shook the women's rights movement out of the doldrums into which it had fallen in past years. Using a strategic combination of symbolism and activism, they charged toward that goal of a Constitutional amendment. Sometimes they dressed up as the Statue of Liberty or Columbia, and later they actually became symbols themselves, inspiring others with their courageous actions and refusal to give up until they got the vote. We look at their effective use of unifying symbolism and how the lack of same, missing from the movement of a later generation of activists, worked against furthering the cause of women's liberty. All of these women could be called Liberty's sisters . . . but they were not the first.

Women Leading the Revolution

"Are not women born as free as men?" asked early patriot James Otis Jr. when he was denouncing the Stamp Act in 1765.[2] After reading this chapter, perhaps you will better remember James Otis Jr. not as one of the first to denounce the Stamp Act, but rather as "Mercy Otis Warren's brother." If anyone deserves to be called one of our founding mothers, it is Mercy Otis Warren, and we'll tell you why in a bit. Unlike Mercy, however, James Otis Jr. was one of the very few revolutionaries who also advocated for women's emancipation at the same time as declaring independence from Great Britain. As we have said before, most of the rest of the Revolutionary generation, women as well as men, were not ready to take on two revolutions at once and were willing to settle instead for fewer liberties being allotted to "the ladies"

Figure 12.1. At the beginning of the twentieth century young suffragists grew more active and organized parades and demonstrations where they often dressed as allegorical Ladies Liberty and Columbia. One of their main symbols, called the Herald, led the way forward with her trumpet. Library of Congress.

(as they called themselves), and over a much longer period of time.

We are grateful to many academic historians of the past several decades who have specialized in the field of American women's histories for making our mothers' ancestors come alive. Much of this chapter is based on the works of Carol Berkin, Linda Kerber, Edith Mayo, and Sally Roesch Wagner. Through their work we discovered that the American Revolution, though rightly criticized as incomplete in so many ways, was indeed revolutionary, especially for women—even though women were still not considered full citizens at the end of it. The revolutionary changes in the conditions for women were smaller and much slower in coming than those for propertied white men, making these changes harder to document, but they were still revolutionary for all that.

For one thing, opportunities for female education exploded after the Revolution, and girls started going to school for the first time. The civic duty of virtue assigned to women after the war inspired women to slowly but surely take to the streets and make America more benevolent. It's easy to fault the founding fathers for their grandiose talk about liberty for all when they really meant liberty for the privileged few. But it does seem that throwing off the king scared them less than allowing women to demonstrate power outside the home, even though both ideas were the result of centuries of conditioning.

And yet, the patriot men knew their political movement would not succeed without directly appealing to the women for help. They talked about convincing their wives that there was value in sacrificing material goods, and more, up to the point of putting their families in danger. "What many say is the greatest difficulty of all we have to encounter," said Christopher Gadsden, addressing the South Carolina assembly in 1769, "is to persuade our wives to give us their assistance, without which 'tis impossible to succeed."[3] To pay for the expenses of protecting the colonists during the French and Indian War, Parliament was taxing an ever-growing list of household items—everything from necessities to luxuries, including glass, lead, paper, paint, and tea. John Adams remembered how "every fireside, indeed was a theatre of politics,"[4] as the women and the households were drawn in to the war effort, whether they liked it or not.

Colonial women were the first tax protestors, says Sally Roesch Wagner, because their shopping decisions launched and enforced all of the boycotts against British goods. In the beginning, the boycott was the only option the patriots had to protest the onerous new taxes coming from Great Britain.[5] Today, we all know about the men who disguised themselves as Indians and dumped tea into Boston Harbor, but did we also learn about the women who, without disguise, signed their own names to a petition in Edenton, North Carolina, declaring their boycott of all imported British goods? We know of this petition because it was published with a scornful description and harpylike caricature in a London newspaper (figure 12.2). The simple act of declaring a political opinion in public opened these women up for all kinds of ridicule. The loyalists in the colonies especially lampooned the women, pointing to their female effrontery and predicting the patriot cause would be the

Figure 12.2. The women of Edenton, North Carolina, were satirized in the Loyalist and British press for expressing their independent thoughts and publicly signing a petition in 1775 to boycott all British goods. Notice how independent thought among women was predicted to lead to promiscuous behavior and the neglect of children (under the table). Library of Congress.

harbinger of a petticoat revolution—as if that was to be dreaded even more than war with the British! Nevertheless, other colonial women copied their examples, and women-led boycotts and public demonstrations spread. At one "tea party" in Wilmington, Delaware, the women gathered around a bonfire of tea.

As supplies grew scarce, hoarding was a natural reaction, and women grew even more vocal in their determination to assist the Revolution. Twenty women in East Hartford, Connecticut, marched in "martial array & excellent order" to demand "requisitions" of the sugar being hoarded by a shopkeeper.[6] In 1778, Abigail Adams wrote to her husband, describing a hundred or more women in Boston who marched to the warehouse of an "eminent, wealthy, stingy Merchant" who was rumored to be hoarding coffee.[7] To the amusement of the men watching from across the street, when the merchant refused to turn over his keys, the women restrained him "by the Neck" and then proceeded to unload the coffee into their carts and drive off. Women took it upon themselves to needle the local merchants to ensure conformity with boycotts. Other women wrote letters to the editor of their local paper, organized collection drives, and donated their jewelry to buy supplies for the army.

Women found many ways to demonstrate independent political thought, something previously unheard of. The Revolutionary generation had grown up being taught that women were weak and easily corruptible, and were to be shielded from the real world and from politics. Their job was to be a calming and moralizing influence on the real actors in society: men. Ben Franklin wrote to his wife that women should never meddle in politics, "except in endeavors to reconcile their husbands, brothers and friends who happen to be on contrary sides. . . . If your sex can keep cool, you may be a means of cooling ours the sooner."[8]

Before the American Revolution, women were considered no more than domestic servants—necessary but dependent, and sometimes a real nuisance. George Washington's dispatches from the front are littered with complaints about the women among the twenty thousand camp followers of that war, and how they "clogged every movement"[9] of the army—along with the dogs, chickens, and even some children who traveled with them.[10] Washington knew that having some women along on the military campaign was essential, for the washing and nursing, of course, and many of the women were wives of the soldiers. In addition to cooking, cleaning, and bandaging, women served as spies, soldiers, and couriers in Washington's army. Some brave souls even disguised themselves as men and enlisted. Many women preferred the dangers and half-rations of the battlefield to staying home, vulnerable to the swath of destruction that was the wake of any traveling army.

Mercy Otis Warren and Abigail Adams Expressing Independent Thought

The strong women of the colonial era and the Revolutionary generation are chronicled in many great biographies, and we have included a very short section of a few of them in the back of this book. Just two were selected for highlighting here to show how the societal shift to accept women with independent political thoughts began with individuals one by one challenging tradition within their own spheres of influence. Both Mercy Otis Warren and Abigail Adams contributed to the raising of consciousness that women and men have equal mental capacity and should have equal opportunities for education. Yet, both were also first and foremost good mothers and conformed entirely to the restrictions of their expected roles.

Mercy Otis Warren is a name we should learn in elementary school right along with Paul Revere and Samuel Adams, because her opinions and writings were just as influential as theirs in launching the independence movement and recording its mythology. Her intellect and opinion were highly regarded by the entire Revolutionary generation, including the famous founders whose writings have been analyzed ever since by pundits searching for the origins and influence behind their new ideas. Mercy Otis Warren was the origin and influence behind many of their new ideas. She was a regular correspondent with John Adams, Patrick Henry, Thomas Jefferson, and just about all the leaders, and they took her advice seriously. She grew up in Massachusetts in a politically active family, and her father and brothers led the earliest protests in Boston against the tyrannical extortion of the British. She married another patriot leader, James Warren, and he continued to encourage her to use her mind, while she assisted him in his political career. They hosted gatherings of the radical Sons of Liberty in their home, where Mercy Warren helped Sam Adams develop the idea for the Committee of Correspondence, the network of communication set up between the rebels in the various colonies.

Balancing her writing career with raising five sons, she never challenged the notion that motherhood was her most important role, and perhaps that is why she was accepted as a successful writer.[11] The popular plays and satires she wrote urging rebellion were both entertaining and effective propaganda, and she was the first person to perceive liberty as an "inherent right."[12] She urged her friends Thomas Jefferson and John Adams to be bold and begin the debate for independence. Though her pre-Revolution works were published anonymously, after the war she began publishing under her own name, including one of the first histories of the American Revolution. This very popular three-volume set titled *History of the Rise, Progress, and Termination of the American Revolution* published in 1805 featured her strong, and sometimes quite biased, opinions about the various leaders of the day, some of which became cemented as fact in our mythological history.

Warren and her close friend Abigail Adams both had curious minds and unusual encouragement from their families to exercise them and express their ideas. The correspondence between Abigail and John Adams is legendary. She served as advisor, confidante, and informer for him from the beginning of the conflict through his presidency. Most discussions about women in the Revolution include a reference to Abigail's entreaty to John to "remember the ladies" when the men set about creating the new government independent from England. She was recommending the colonists break the tradition of using English common law codes that legally bound women as subjects of men. In that letter she says he knows as well as she does that sensible men like himself know they are happier when they respect their wives as "friends" rather than relating to them in a "master and servant" dynamic. "Why, then," she asked him, "not put it out of the power of the vicious and the lawless [men] to use us with cruelty and indignity with impunity?"

John's answer was a somewhat flippant dismissal about how women already had the power to rule their husbands, and if given any more power, the men might become completely subject to the "despotism of the petticoat." He acknowledged how critics of the

Revolution were even now fretting over how their calls for independence were filtering down to dangerous notions of liberty among disobedient schoolchildren, servants, American Indians, and Black slaves, but chuckled that her letter was the first to suggest that *women* might want a slice of this liberty pie, too. Her final letter to him in this exchange gently calls him out for being a hypocrite, and warns him that "arbitrary power is . . . very liable to be broken," noting that women had it in their power to nonviolently "throw both your natural and legal authority at our feet."[13]

Republican Motherhood after the Revolution

Abigail Adams was not the only one who drew the parallel between the struggle of patriot men fighting for the right of self-determination with Great Britain and the legal codes that held women under a similar tyranny of laws. When the colonists declared themselves independent from the king and capable of self-government, a few of them recognized

Figure 12.3. Florence Noyes made a striking figure as a Liberty/Columbia, complete with Phrygian cap, in front of the Treasury Building during the March 3, 1913, suffrage parade in Washington, D.C. Careful to select symbolism that would appeal to the majority, early twentieth-century suffragists included allegorical, robed females familiar from the nation's past in support of woman suffrage. Library of Congress.

that the very injustices they complained about were the same as those they enforced in their laws against women. Thomas Paine, for one, pointed this out. He was an admirer of British women's rights activist Mary Wollstonecraft, and published (but didn't write as is commonly misreported) "An Occasional Letter on the Female Sex." After the Revolution, he made himself quite unpopular by continually talking about how many different groups of people were not permitted to express the rights contained in the Declaration of Independence.

After women participated in the war effort in such noble and effective ways, a new role was clearly needed for them, and one was deliberately created via sermons and newspaper editorials. Historian Linda Kerber dubbed this new role "Republican Motherhood" and described it as a new assignment for upper-class women of the new American states. The framers of the Constitution believed that the future of the republic depended upon the moral character of its citizens, and that charge was entrusted to the mothers. Although not granted any rights in the Constitution, American women were granted a civic duty to be good Republican Mothers raising good patriot sons. Republican Motherhood could almost be described as a "fourth branch of government," says Kerber,[14] its role was so essential to the success of the patriots' experiment in republican ideas.

Virtuous citizens, it was believed, were necessary to run the government selflessly for the benefit of the whole. Leaders must be classically educated, morally superior to withstand the temptations of the material world, and willing to sacrifice personal goals. In embodying the concept of the Republican Mother, women were encouraged to continue the personal sacrifice at which they had excelled during the war, and also to forego any hope of personal freedom or independence, because these qualities were reserved for the male sphere.

Republican Motherhood Meant
More Girls Could Go to School

One of those slow-burning revolutionary changes for women resulting from the American Revolution was that when women were assigned the civic duty of raising virtuous patriots, it was necessary to educate them to a level where they could become competent teachers. Before the war, if a woman received any education at all, it was from private tutors or indulgent family members. Many of the women of the Revolutionary generation were raised by fathers who were influenced by the Enlightenment philosophy that every human has the capacity to reason and develop moral standards. Changes in attitudes about educating girls were slowly beginning to be felt even before the war, and some fathers were allowing their daughters to sit in on tutoring sessions given to their sons.[15] But for the most part, before the Revolution, it was considered pointless and a waste of time and money to educate girls.

Opponents worried that the mental strain on women would stunt their nurturing abilities and lead to a nation of abandoned children. It was also predicted that increased intellect in a woman would lead to moral depravity.[16] Women's brains were thought to be inferior, and as daughters of Eve, women were also considered morally weak. Most men believed it was their duty to do the thinking for the women in their lives and shelter them from the evil world by deciding for them what was best. Before the war, women in the early colonies did not have the role of responsible caretaker in the family. Fathers were responsible for ruling the family, and wives and children, both considered legal property, were completely dependent on their husbands and fathers.[17] Women who challenged authority were seen as disruptive to the very fabric of society, putting the whole colony at risk.

Between 1780 and 1830, the literacy rate among women jumped from half of that of men to about equal.[18] Female academies popped up all over the country, and reformers like Benjamin Rush, Emma Willard, and Judith Sargent Murray eventually swayed public opinion enough to support the idea that educating women, at least up to a certain point, was good for the nation. Declaration signer Benjamin Rush was the leading advocate for women's education in the new republic, saying, "one cause of the misery of many families, as well as communities, may be sought for in the mediocrity of knowledge of the women. They should know more . . . in order to be happy themselves."[19]

Education introduced girls to the modern world, though the subjects

Figure 12.4. Readers in the United States had their first taste of Mary Wollstonecraft's book *A Vindication of the Rights of Woman* in excerpts published in the *Lady's Magazine* in 1792, accompanied by this frontispiece showing Liberty with her pole and cap receiving a scroll reading "The Rights of Woman." The kneeling figure presenting the scroll is labeled as the genius of the *Lady's Magazine*, and the figure behind them as the genius of emulation. Library of Congress.

available for them to study were still severely constrained. Women were not taught the classics, for example, given that subject was considered necessary only for navigating the political world, and thus necessary only for men. Emma Willard scandalized the nation by teaching anatomy at the first school for women's higher education, which she founded in 1821.

But although the curriculum was limited, at least women's education was becoming valued as having purpose, even if that purpose was still confined to the home and family. Like Mercy Otis Warren, Judith Sargent Murray was accepted as a professional writer probably because she also remained a good role model for Republican Motherhood. In addition to raising and educating her children and many nieces and nephews, she wrote influential essays like "On the Equality of the Sexes," which was published two years before the more famous work *A Vindication of the Rights of Woman* by Mary Wollstonecraft in England.

Wollstonecraft lived a life that seemed tailor-made for the opponents of female education who predicted that the more a woman increased her intellect the more of a moral degenerate she would become.[20] In addition to advocating for reforms in women's education and legal status, Wollstonecraft was a practitioner of what was called free love, a feminist term from the 1700s and 1800s that today means something quite different. Women's rights advocates and other reformers argued that love should not be subject to legislation, as in the restrictive marriage and divorce laws, and that all humans had the freedom to love anyone they chose. Wollstonecraft was not married to the father of her first child and lived together with the father of her second child before she married him. She and other reformers believed that romantic and sexual freedom were as relevant to independence as educational and domestic freedoms, but her scandalous reputation eclipsed the impact of her philosophy, and her legacy was not resurrected again until the twentieth century.

Spiritual Movements Provided Leadership Roles for Women

Under a patriarchal system, women are held to different moral standards than men. As cultural anthropologist Sherry Ortner put it,

"Male-defined structures represent and conceptualize their unity and status through the purity of their women."[21] The conformity or nonconformity of women is interpreted in terms of threat or stability to the social fabric. The story of one of the first female religious dissenters in the English colonies, Anne Hutchinson, is a good example of how women with too much power outside the home were considered a special threat to the community.

In the early 1600s, Hutchinson objected to the state control of religion in the Massachusetts Bay Colony much the same way her fellow Puritan Roger Williams had done five years earlier. But her banishment included a special denouncement of her as a woman for upsetting the natural order and the hierarchy of the colonial magistrates. Her actions that seemed most threatening to the magistrates were holding popular women's circles with sixty to eighty women gathered to hear her interpret the sermons and scriptures they'd heard on Sunday.

Other women must have been inspired by her example, because after she was banished to Rhode Island the records show that other women continued to challenge the church-state authority and were also put on trial and excommunicated for infractions like singing too loudly or questioning how old a child should be when baptized. Women who challenged the church-state were seen as especially threatening to the status quo, because they were considered dangerously seductive.

Throughout Euro-American history, women have carved out special leadership roles in religious and spiritual movements. This tendency only increased as literacy rates rose. Regarding the Second Great Awakening of the 1830s to 1840s, historian Gordon Wood said that as the country became democratized, it also became evangelized. People strove to republicanize their churches, much as they had done with their government.[22] Hierarchies were challenged, and more common people took to itinerant preaching. Women responded in large numbers to the new style of evangelizing, and churches started taking on more political causes as the moral rectitude that women had been trained in turned into missionary urges to share benevolence with those less fortunate. Many women left their homes for the frontiers to teach and try to convert Native Americans to Euro-American customs and religion.

Others concentrated on joining the all-male abolition societies and lent their energies to ending human bondage.

Mother Ann Lee was an early leader of a church, arriving in New York from England with twelve Shaking Quaker followers just before the American Revolution broke out. Lee was considered a prophet by her followers and claimed many visions and revelations throughout her life, including the radical notion that men and women should be treated equally. She and her devotees eventually built a flourishing community of villages that multiplied through Pennsylvania and Ohio, and their well-made, simple Shaker furniture is a sought-after antique today. Other women following spiritual messages founded utopian communities experimenting with new standards and establishing the United States as a haven for spiritual expression where women could assume positions of leadership.

After the psychic losses of the Civil War, many people turned to spiritualism for comfort, and again women found a special niche for leadership. Several successful spiritual movements that grew to international membership were founded by women, like Mary Baker Eddy's Christian Science and Helena Blavatsky's Theosophy. Author Mitch Horowitz demonstrates how Helena Blavatsky helped spark the 1960s civil rights movement in the United States by showing how Martin Luther King Jr. was influenced by Ghandi, who in turn was influenced by Blavatsky's Theosophy, which he credited for helping him formulate the philosophy of nonviolent protest.[23]

America the Benevolent

Republican Motherhood and the new educational opportunities and benefits it brought were initially restricted to the elite, as are most social revolutions at the start. It was the more affluent and educated women, those who could afford to do so, who took the extra education they were offered and walked out of their homes and into leadership positions in the community. They started by organizing and leading public schools for immigrants, slaves, and the poor, given the consideration that literacy was becoming imperative for everyone in the increasingly industrialized postwar world. In the first few decades of the 1800s, women tested the waters and gradually swelled the ranks of reformers and educators, becoming practiced organizers and speakers on subjects like reforming health care and sanitation, abolishing slavery, women's rights, sexual and reproductive freedoms, and reforms in the treatment of the mentally ill, prisoners, and debtors. In many ways, the education of women led to that more perfect union the founders described in the preamble to the Constitution.

Nurturing qualities are certainly not exclusive to women, but nurturing qualities had been up until now firmly rooted in the women's sphere. And until the American Revolution, women had been completely restricted to the home. Now, humanitarian-minded people of both genders began speaking about injustice in the community at large. The children and grandchildren of the Revolutionary generation still held dear the values of liberty, but they were determined to spread them out to more people. In the colonies prior to the Revolutionary War, fewer than one hundred benevolent societies had been formed. Between 1787 and 1817, more than fourteen hundred aid societies were established, with Americans rushing to the aid of slaves, widows, orphans, and immigrants. They went to work as missionaries, temperance workers, and peace advocates. With benevolent societies springing up everywhere, the young United States of America, after the Revolution, acquired a reputation for being one of the kindest nations in the world.[24]

It was slow going, of course. It took decades for women to convince themselves and the community to overcome the taboo against women speaking in public. Those who led by example, such as the suffragists from the mid-1800s, were vilified by hecklers who threw rotten vegetables at them and threatened the women with violence and death. Women speaking in public on any subject were seen as a threat to the social order, and that made a lot of people react very defensively. America the benevolent also struggled against the deep undertow of profiteering and expansionism that characterized the Jacksonian era, defined roughly from the late 1820s until about 1850. The belief that education and natural philosophy could bring about social change through reason was dwindling as industrialization became the more common goal.

Suffragists and the Symbolism of Motherhood

Although the concept of Republican Motherhood gave upper-class women a civic duty and a chance at an education, the role also limited a woman's sphere of influence to the home. Advocating for more choices and educational opportunities for women clashed headlong into the entrenched belief that without morally superior women serving as the backbone of the home and family, society would simply crumble to ashes. Politics was considered corrupt, and women were to be protected from its corrupting influences. Yet, running reform movements had multiplied the reasons women wanted to get the vote—now they were inspired to help others. Moreover, leading these reform movements had given many women great managerial and public-speaking experience.

Women activists who came of age under the shadow of the Statue of Liberty, post 1886, changed the debate about suffrage. To learn about suffrage symbolism, we turned to Edith Mayo, curator emeritus in political history at the Smithsonian's National Museum of American History. We found that more than anything else, the symbolism of motherhood was used effectively by both sides of the argument, both for and against women's entry into the political sphere.

The early decades of the suffrage fight had been conducted mainly with words, meaning imagery supporting women's political suffrage didn't really exist much before the twentieth century. Before then leaders were focused on educating others to their cause and wrote reams of words to convince a suspicious public that, not only did women possess keen intellects, but that change would be good for everyone. The mainstream suffrage organizations actually agreed that women were morally superior to men and used this as another reason why women should be voting. They emphasized motherhood and duty and showed how women had special skills and instincts that would enable them to sweep house and clean up politics. They also used comic renditions of children to express—from the mouths of babes—the inequities of the situation for their mothers. Suffragists of this era worked very hard to calm the fears of the opposition by reassuring them that woman suffrage would not upset traditional gender roles or lead to a weakening of the social fabric.

The problem with using the mothering and moral uplift angle as the reason to win the vote is that it gave most women only that one role in which to see themselves, even *after* they won the vote. Nevertheless, the younger women activists of the early twentieth century, eager to turn education into agitation, also decided to turn motherhood symbolism to their advantage. The younger women continued to use the approach that women's excellence at domesticity would have a cleansing effect on politics and assured opponents that the women's sphere wasn't necessarily changing, just expanding from the home to include the whole community as home.

Votes for Women

These three little words succeeded at uniting the young and the old and the various factions of woman suffragists who were arguing over priorities. Everyone agreed that improving conditions for women started with earning the right to vote, but when Susan B. Anthony orchestrated the narrowing of the focus so singularly on suffrage, many of the other social conditions women were fighting to change, such as divorce and custody laws, property rights, and higher education opportunities, were effectively swept from view and delayed for decades more. The invention of the wearable slogan button in the late 1890s helped to unify the suffrage cause around this catchy phrase, while around the same time the imagery of the woman's rights movement also started to grow popular in the form of cartoons, postcards, and publications.

When most people think of woman suffragists, their minds conjure up images of white-haired ladies in Victorian dresses and granny glasses. Lost on anyone who didn't take a women's history class is the significance of the modern young women and their militant, disciplined activism that revitalized the stalled movement at the turn of the century. The imperious Carrie Chapmann Catt had inherited the leadership role of the National American Woman Suffrage Association (NAWSA) from Susan B. Anthony, and she continued with the conservative state-by-state approach of ratifying woman suffrage in state constitutions. In a way comparable to Édouard de Laboulaye, Catt and her colleague Anna

Figure 12.5. Woman suffragists were the first ever to organize protests outside the White House. This photo is labeled "College Day in the Picket Line," February 1917. When these women, who were dubbed the "Silent Sentinels" because of their silent protesting, decided to maintain their vigil even after the United States entered World War I later that year, they were attacked by opponents and jailed for disturbing the peace. Library of Congress.

Howard Shaw preferred the law-and-order approach. They chose symbols of justice and inclusion, and did not approve of rocking the boat.[25] Their insistence on maintaining proper, well-mannered codes of conduct meant that generations of activists had passed on, leaving women with very few results since organizing for women's rights began in the 1840s. By 1890 only a handful of western states and territories had legalized a woman's right to vote: Wyoming, Colorado, Utah, and Idaho.

Alice Paul Changes Tactics

Riding the tide of the Progressive Era for reform and modernization, Alice Paul, Lucy Burns, Harriot Stanton Blatch, and other young women like them ardently brought reform to the women's movement. Like the Sons of Liberty, who were willing to risk it all to start the

American Revolution, women from Alice Paul's generation (1885–1977) were willing to put their lives on the line to make change. The importance of Alice Paul to the passage of the Nineteenth Amendment cannot be overstated, and most Americans have never heard of her.

Paul and Burns met while studying abroad in England where both joined the suffrage demonstrations in London led by the Pankhurst family and the Women's Social and Political Union (WSPU). They participated in mass demonstrations, were arrested numerous times for disorderly conduct, and learned how to use the hunger strike to continue the protest while in jail. They bonded with each other over their frustration with the seemingly stagnant state of the women's movement in the United States, and in 1910, when they returned to the states, they were determined to shake things up. Elizabeth Cady Stanton's daughter Harriot Stanton Blatch was another who studied in England and brought the Pankhurst motto, Deeds Not Words, back to America.

When the corseted leaders of the NAWSA balked at the radical, "unladylike" suggestions for more public displays, Paul and Burns branched out and formed their own National Woman's Party (NWP), wherein instead of *asking* for rights, they started *demanding* them. They switched the focus from the state-by-state campaign, because they determined that pushing for a Constitutional amendment was the only viable long-term solution. Alice Paul organized a trained and disciplined cadre of women soldiers who turned into effective lobbyists and stump speakers in a day when women were still not able to speak in public without ridicule. Their effective use of symbolism, their pioneering first-ever picketing of the White House, and their switch to emphasizing the need for a Constitutional amendment pushed their cause to success.

When World War I broke out, unlike their past counterparts who had lain down their cause during the Civil War as a gesture of unity, the NWP decided to maintain their nonviolent protest of Silent Sentinels outside the White House. This demonstration was considered outrageously unpatriotic, and the women were physically attacked by opponents and arrested for disturbing the peace. Imprisoned at Occoquan

Workhouse, Paul led them on a hunger strike to protest, which the jailers tried to counteract with beatings and torturous methods of force-feeding the women. When news of their deplorable conditions was leaked to the press, President Wilson was shamed into agreeing to their release. Woodrow Wilson has gone down in history as the president who made the world safe for democracy, but his version of democracy did not give women any role but child-rearing, and most of his Southern Democratic Party members agreed.

They Turned Into Their Own Symbols

The image of the suffragist was transformed during this time, from one of a shrewish harridan to a young woman in modern dress unencumbered by corsets and bustles. The younger, more radical NWP distributed images of working women that appealed to progressives like themselves who were interested in more sweeping social reforms as well as votes for women. The image of the ideal woman of the age—called the Gibson Girl, with the hourglass figure and demure expression—was replaced by the smart, capable New Woman, who wore sensible clothing that did not restrict movement or cause fainting spells. Artist Nina Allender became the official cartoonist and illustrator for the NWP publication, the *Suffragist,* and hundreds of her drawings of educated, sophisticated young women turned these leaders of the National Woman's Party into symbols themselves, revitalizing the movement and inspiring others to follow them.

One of Paul and Burns's first effective attempts at shaking up the NAWSA was to organize a parade in Washington, D.C., for March 3, 1913, the day before Woodrow Wilson was to be inaugurated as president. Like Laboulaye, they knew that adopting familiar images of stability would link them to the past and pacify those afraid of change. Their pageants and parades were full of women dressed as robed female allegories marching in support of women's rights. This trend had also been adopted from the British suffrage movement wherein artist Sylvia Pankhurst designed an angel blowing a trumpet as the logo for their *Votes for Women* weekly journal. This angel evolved into an American

BROADSIDE

Price 2 Cents
Number 6

Published by the WOMEN'S POLITICAL UNION
WHEN EVENTS DEMAND

APRIL, 1911

THE TRUMPETER AWAKING NEW YORK

The trumpeter realizing all the achievements of the women of the past, bearing a banner which in the number of the stars emblazoned on it suggests the five States in which women have won political freedom, calls in bugle notes upon the women of New York to march on May Sixth in solemn protest against their continued disfranchisement.

MARCHING ON!

THROUGH THE AGES, when stirred by vital issues MEN HAVE MARCHED FORTH to beat of drum, marched with banners flying.

ings, of rights to our property, of rights to our children, of rights to our very selves, the women of yesterday gained for us. Our pioneers marched on, faces ever forward. They braved all things, and we harvest the fruit of their pain.

No woman who feels the duty to pass on to our

march will count as ten, for her self-reliance and determination will convince the disbelievers in her earnestness as naught else can.

"And Reason, that old man, said to her, 'Silence! What do you hear?'

And she listened intently and she said, 'I hear a sound

Figure 12.6. A 1911 broadside showing the Herald symbolism of the suffrage movement, published by Harriot Stanton Blatch's organization, the Women's Political Union (WPU). The WPU focused on the rights of working women and later merged with Alice Paul's group to become the National Woman's Party. The five stars on the flag represent the five states that had granted woman suffrage by 1911. Library of Congress.

version called the Herald, which resembles the Winged Victory goddess known as Nike to the Greeks. The Herald appealed to both the conservative NAWSA and the NWP, because it resonated with America's established standards of Columbia and Liberty.

The Herald, the Martyr, and the Mother

The winged Herald became the logo for the National Woman's Party, and Inez Milholland made her come alive when she dressed all in white and rode a white horse at the head of several suffrage parades. A trained lawyer, labor rights activist, and gifted speaker, Milholland died suddenly at the age of thirty from pernicious anemia and exhaustion. She collapsed in the middle of a speech during a speaking tour through the western states, and her last words uttered, "Mr. President, how long must women wait for liberty?" were well publicized. The NWP pushed for her memorial to be held in the U.S. Capitol, the first-ever honor of this kind for a woman, of which they took full P.R. advantage. "She was eulogized in symbolic terms," said Mayo, when they described her as "the flaming torch that went ahead to light the way, the symbol of light and freedom." The photographs of her riding a horse in flowing white

Figure 12.7. Inez Milholland dressed as the Herald to lead the suffrage parade in Washington, D.C., on March 3, 1913. Milholland would die unexpectedly three years later and become a martyr for the cause. Library of Congress.

robes, wearing a gold helmet and carrying a banner that read "Forward into Light," were produced as a poster and became adopted as the official logo and motto of the National Woman's Party. Inez Milholland had literally become the Herald.

Examples abounded showing early twentieth-century suffrage activists dressed as versions of the American Liberty Goddess. At the 1916 Democratic Convention in St. Louis the suffragists of the NAWSA organized a very ladylike gauntlet for the candidates to walk through on their way to the convention. They called it "the Golden Lane," and it featured suffragists lining either side of the road, dressed all in white with gold sashes, silently holding the banners of the suffrage group they represented. Midway along the route, the delegates passed a human tableau of several women dressed in Greek-style robes on the steps of the Fine Arts Building. The central figure was called Liberty and carried a torch (figure 7.8, p. 207). She was identified in the newspaper caption as Mrs. David O'Neil—we don't even know her first name—because the custom of the day was to identify women merely as extensions of their husbands. That same year, Woodrow Wilson's campaign for reelection featured a motor tour that included vaudeville star Claire Rochester dressed as the Statue of Liberty. She rode in a car with her Liberty Girls, who did double-duty by running around collecting contributions for the Let There Be Light electric-light illumination project for the Statue of Liberty.

Sometimes symbolism of the Statue of Liberty was used to proclaim women as the more enlightened gender. Placards advocating suffrage show allegorical females with a sunburst or halo behind them, and often these females carried a torch. Sometimes the illustrations indicated that the light was moving from West to East, as a reference to the state-by-state ratification effort that had found its earliest success in the western states and was slowly moving eastward. Their herald symbolized the herald of a new day, proclaiming "Forward into Light."

Feminists Alienating Mothers

As militant as they were about change, the suffragists in the early 1900s worked hard to make their symbols inclusive, which is in marked contrast to the iconoclastic symbols made popular by the militant feminists of the second wave of the women's movement in the 1960s and 1970s. Even though the various factions of suffragists in Alice Paul's generation disagreed on tactics, they all employed the theme of motherhood to their advantage. Many of the New Women encouraged the premise that women in politics would have a pacifying and salutary effect on society simply because they were women.

Second-wave feminists of the 1970s, who wanted to put forth images of equality, were annoyed by these turn-of-the-century notions that there was any difference at all between the genders. The assumption that one gender was naturally more pure or moral than the other was recast as a restriction on women who chose to be empowered beyond the role of motherhood. The goal of activists was to show that women were capable of accomplishing anything men could do, but many of them set about doing that by attacking the symbol of the devoted mother and homemaker. Unlike the symbolism employed by the suffragists of Alice Paul's generation, the imagery chosen by the women's movement of the 1970s did not resonate with the majority in the middle.

Edith Mayo believes the lack of compelling visual imagery hindered the passage of the Equal Rights Amendment (ERA) in 1982 and led to the subsequent decline in interest in the women's movement in the 1980s. Radical feminists of the 1960s and 1970s condemned the role model of the housewife, and the counteroffensive has been long and effective. Sounding much like the opponents to votes for women back in the nineteenth century, opponents to the ERA said that women's lib would lead to children being neglected, the sanctity of homelife being destroyed, and women taking over all the good jobs, putting men out of work. The images coming from the National Organization for Women spoke mainly to the radicals. Talking about motherhood as a role of strength, as we are doing in this book, made some activist women furious, and they had nothing but contempt for the early suffrage mothers. They bristled at historical discussions about Republican Motherhood and found allegorical women to be offensively limiting. Historian David Hackett Fischer

Figure 12.8. An illustration from *Puck* magazine in 1915 showing a robed female carrying a torch, with her cloak reading "Votes for Women." She is bringing *The Awakening* from the West to the East, indicating the eleven western states that had ratified woman suffrage in their state constitutions by this time. Library of Congress.

analyzed the challenge of symbolism during the second wave of feminism by showing how they emphasized the more elusive concept of equality for all,[26] as opposed to the concepts of liberty and justice for all that were emphasized by the early suffrage mothers. Agitation for *equality for all* is more likely to trigger the defenses of those in control of the status quo to fight back. Subtle but powerful differences: liberty and equality are not the same things.

The activists and agitators of the women's movement of the late 1960s struggled to design an appropriate symbol for their new movement. A double *X* in a circle was proposed, but failed to take off, and then Robin Morgan submitted the strike fist in a circle as part of the biological female symbol that was used to protest against the Miss America Pageant in 1969. The Statue of Liberty was also put forth, designed with an upraised clenched fist. Buttons with provocative slogans were pervasive throughout the women's protest movement, because

Figure 12.9. In contrast to figure 12.8 of *The Awakening*, this popular image from 1872 also used the image of a giant female allegory crossing a map. In this painting, she is usually called Columbia, and she is moving from the East, where there is light, to the West, which is in darkness, helping cement the belief that the United States had a Manifest Destiny to spread their version of civilization. This virtuous female is carrying a schoolbook and leading the way by stringing telegraph wires and forging a trail for the railways behind her. Native Americans and bison flee before her. *Spirit of the Frontier*, sometimes called *Westward Ho!*, was painted by John Gast and popularized in travel literature and engravings.

sharing an opinion on a button was often easier than confronting people directly. Still, the strike fist within the female symbol, when accompanied by rhetoric that devalued their role as mother, alienated many. The lack of sensitivity for the majority of women who were not activists or agitators, but simply homemakers looking for justice, has been suggested as one of the reasons the Equal Rights Amendment failed to achieve the supermajority required to pass.

Why the ERA Is Still Necessary
for Wonder Women

That we still do not have Constitutional protection against gender discrimination in the United States reveals more than a failure to find unifying symbols, of course. There is a larger cultural problem that historian Riane Eisler refers to as a society-wide devaluation of nurturing and caregiving because they are associated with women. As long as women are devalued, so will these traits of nurturing and caregiving be devalued. The so-called third wave of feminists, many of them daughters of the radicals from the 1970s, have inherited the activism and enthusiasm for change but are also working to open up the movement to address issues pertinent to all people of all economic and cultural backgrounds. The revised movement, in addition to its focus on workplace equity, is also welcoming to women, and men, who choose to stay home and raise their children. They are working to see the day when professional benefits can be earned for the kind of time and labor it requires to properly nurture a family—a situation already occurring in some Nordic countries.

With the various other measures that have passed in the past few decades designed to protect women from gender discrimination in the workplace and in education, some question why the fight for the passage of the ERA continues. The answer is easy: the only sure protection from gender discrimination is a Constitutional amendment. All other state and federal legislation that is now in place can be undone with new legislation. Religious ideologues gaining money and political power continually make a priority of dismantling legislation designed to protect women's rights, and until this discrimination is prohibited by the Constitution, all advances stand the risk of being reversed.

When talking about Lady Liberty's sisters, one more to mention would certainly be Wonder Woman, the red-white-and-blue-wearing superhero who is secretly an Amazonian princess named for the goddess Diana/Artemis. Her creator had feminist intentions when he created a strong female action hero for comic book readers as a role model for young girls in 1942. Actually, with her flag costume, Wonder Woman resembles more the Columbia of the early republic than a traditional Lady Liberty, but there have also been superheroes who look exactly like the Statue of Liberty, as well! There was the post–World War II Miss America and a short-lived Lady Liberty of the 1980s, but neither one made the lasting impact that Wonder Woman has—with her bullet-repelling bracelets and golden truth-serum lasso. *Wonder Women* is the title of one of a series of recent books reframing the discussion and the goals for gender balance by showing new perspectives for working women—from business and politics to law enforcement and education.

A New Symbol Is Needed to See Nurturing as Strong

Today's younger female leaders from the corporate and political worlds have sparked an encouraging trend that recognizes the value in the qualities traditionally marginalized as being feminine or women's issues. They are speaking up and pointing out, with the statistics to support them, that women's issues are really human issues, or economic issues affecting all humans—and that when corporations grow more flexible to allow for so-called women's needs, the whole corporation benefits. Everyone is more creative and more productive when all human needs are considered and valued. When men and women both get subsidized family leave to care for anyone from aging parents to young children, when childcare is provided on site, when pregnancy is not a detriment to career advancement, everyone benefits. The new female leaders are realizing that no one has to be a Wonder Woman, as Deborah Spar, Sheryl Sandberg, Mika Brzezinski, and others have realized. The smart ones have figured out that forming circles and working together to create change from within is much more effective, and satisfying.

Like the Statue of Liberty, the images and ideas of what constitutes a liberated woman continue to change. Issues confronting modern feminists are different from those confronting the upper classes and the educated early suffragists, and are different as well from those faced by the militant younger suffragists, or campaigners for the ERA and Title IX. Gone are the days when mothers were idealized as the saviors of virtue in this nation. Gone, too, are the days when mothers and housewives were belittled for giving the women's movement a bad name, as if they were not living up to their full potential. Coming soon are the days when mothers and fathers and all women and men who are caregivers and nurturers are respected as symbols of strength and authority. This time line of change has carried us forward from when women were property, to Republican Mothers, to bluestockinged intellectuals, to torch-carrying Columbias in parades, to today's feminists who are men and women, young and old, and every race under the sun. Today's feminists are working together to find a new symbol to identify us as Earth People in tune with the Earth as our mother, and with everyone and everything living on it as our relations, because we are all family when *Liberty for all* is the goal.

13

A Delightful Inconsistency

Feminists and Labor Activists on the Statue

The Statue of Liberty is incredibly flexible, both literally in her physical structure and also in her symbolic meanings. Her flexible ability to be interpreted in so many ways has added a confusing mantle to her mythological interpretation, so to reveal the secret life of Lady Liberty we began by unpinning the layers of propaganda and mythic assumptions that have been cloaked around her over the decades. We found that examining the history of any cherished national symbol too closely is bound to shatter illusions you didn't even know you had. When the treasured beliefs you had about a symbol are revealed to be propaganda, it can lead to questions about your own self-identity and national character. If your self-identity is tied to the myth of American exceptionalism, then it might feel like a kick in the gut to read some of these stories revealing selfish motives behind the Statue of Liberty. Most people probably imagine that the Statue of Liberty stands for all the good things that America is supposed to be—and we think so, too, even after this critical study. But in this chapter we will use the protest actions organized by women's rights activists at the Statue of Liberty to examine some of these delightful inconsistencies about Lady Liberty and how they actually contribute to her strength.

The propaganda attached to the Statue of Liberty succeeded so well that her image has assisted in gilding the history of the United States itself. When considering why she was created, most of us choose not to remember the glaring inequality between the classes in that time period and how little liberty was actually being experienced by most people in the United States. A new brand of hero was cropping up after the Civil War with the rise of the industrial tycoons. As they squabbled and bribed and monopolized to build the railroads and telegraph lines and other investments that modernized this nation, the country turned from agriculture to industry. Poor farmers joined immigrants flooding the urban areas. Tens of thousands of people found themselves virtually confined in sprawling slums and tenements. Orphans roamed the streets, and unchecked police brutality was the norm. Reconstruction in the South was met with intimidating violence to suppress the newly freed Black citizens, while woman suffragists nationwide were recoiling from the blow handed them when their fellow abolitionists compromised women right out of the Constitution. The policy of the United States toward the Native Americans grew more belligerent after the Civil War as Plains Indians resisted moving to reservations, and ex-military men needed jobs. Decades of broken treaties, massacres, and retributions escalated as Euro-Americans poured West, their numbers increasing exponentially as the new railway system took shape. In the East, labor organizers learned to use the strike to compel workplace safety improvements and then clashed with desperate immigrants brought in to break the strikes. It was hardly a place where a giant work of art in tribute to liberty seemed to fit.

Our Woman Liberty

After publishing *United Symbolism of America* in 2008, we thought we knew a lot about the Statue of Liberty, but it was not until we were introduced to historian Sally Roesch Wagner that we learned of the protest action against the Statue of Liberty staged by suffragists in 1886. Our mutual friend John Kahionhes Fadden of the Six Nations Museum in Onchiota, New York, referred us to Professor Wagner to further our research into Iroquois women's rights and how they influenced the early suffragists. We learned even more, however, from Wagner's fascination with suffragist Matilda Joslyn Gage and the creative activism Gage and her fellow suffragists devised as they fought to have their voices heard.

Most other sources that refer to the suffragist protest at the 1886 unveiling of the Statue of Liberty list an inaccurate reason for their motivation. The *New York Herald* newspaper report of October 28, 1886, inaccurately claimed that the suffragists were protesting because no women were invited to the VIP ceremony on Bedloe's Island. This was an error that would be repeated in multiple publications one hundred years later during the 1986 centennial celebration for the Statue of Liberty.[1] While certainly the women were greatly outnumbered by the men, there *were* several women present on the island as the wives of the important members of the fundraising committees. Additionally, several official groups of women marched in parades from Madison Square Garden through lower Manhattan, including at least two suffrage groups.

Women of this era were encouraged to believe that attending public events was dangerous and unladylike, and indeed there was such a crush of people on Bedloe's Island (today called Liberty Island) that even the VIPs were jostled. Railroad magnate and keynote speaker Chauncey DePew was observed helping Cornelius Vanderbilt with his bloody nose.[2] The *New York Times* gave a detailed report on the ceremonies that day, listing by name many of the women present, including Mrs. Clarence Carey, who grew restless during the long wait for President Cleveland to arrive and decided to climb to the top of the torch, "the first lady to accomplish this laborious feat."[3]

But Lillie Devereux Blake is the name we really want to emphasize here. A successful novelist who first earned her reputation as a journalist during the Civil War, Blake was president of the New York State Woman's Suffrage Association and of the New York City Woman's Suffrage League when the Statue of Liberty came to town. Blake was one of those creative activists with flair, and she decided that a staged protest at the Statue of Liberty's unveiling ceremony was an opportunity that they could not pass up. Despite having only four dollars in the association's treasury, her group determined they would raise the funds to rent a boat and join the flotilla. Her daughter Kate Devereux Blake recalled the scene many years later for a *New York Times* interview in 1915 when Kate returned to Bedloe's Island for a second suffrage protest. Back in 1886, she remembered that their boat included dignitary guests such as the governor of New Mexico and the lieutenant governor of Wyoming, two of the earliest states to grant women suffrage. Some organizational confusion placed the women's boat right at the lady's feet between two military ships. "The boat was brought up near the island," recalled Kate, "and my mother made her protest against the unveiling of the figure of a woman as Liberty in a State where women were not free." Speaking to close to two hundred supporters on their boat, she also pointed out that "Liberty, as well as the other virtues, were feminine."[4]

In her own written accounts of the day, Lillie Devereux Blake named her "our woman Liberty" and recalled feeling immensely moved to see, in the eyes of her fellow suffragists on the boat, a shining hope as the veil fell from the statue. The cacophony that followed—of cheers, boat whistles, ship horns, and crowd hurrahs from the island and on the shore—lasted for almost half an hour. "And over all this scene of animation," wrote Blake later for the *Woman's Journal,* "above the land, above the sea, towering far above the pigmy men at her feet, rose the majestic woman form, Liberty. . . . All this done by men in honor of a woman." The suffragists' official proclamation declared: "In erecting a Statue of Liberty embodied as a woman in a land where no woman has political liberty, men have shown a delightful inconsistency which excites the wonder and admiration of the opposite sex."[5] Blake was obviously touched, however, as were her fellow protestors, at the magnitude of the colossal Lady Liberty in front of them. In her *Woman's Journal* report the next month, she imagined the "silent lips of bronze" prophesying hope for women. It was worth all the effort, she said, to see their suffrage banner flying before "our woman Liberty," where she imagined hearing her say, "I am the embodied hope of the future, and the enthroned prediction of liberty for women."[6]

A year after staging the 1886 protest at the unveiling of the Statue of Liberty, Blake marched down the aisle at the one hundredth anniversary of the signing of the Constitution, disrupting the ceremony to

Figure 13.1. The Statue of Liberty in the classic Uncle Sam pose, when war bonds were renamed Liberty bonds during World War I. U.S. National Archives.

hand President Cleveland a protest letter regarding the "unjust interpretation of the Constitution in behalf of the women of the United States."[7] Wagner tells us that these events marked a turning point in the post–Civil War suffrage cause, as division within the ranks resulted in many of the more visionary radicals splitting off and forming new groups around this time. Blake had already spearheaded pensions for Civil War nurses and helped to found Barnard College in an attempt to establish equal education for women. These were causes she continued to be involved with throughout her life, as well as working to improve the lives of immigrant women.

Don't Disagree with Susan B.

The reason you probably have never heard of Lillie Devereux Blake is because she had a falling out with Susan B. Anthony. For years the official history of the woman suffrage movement was based almost exclusively on the multivolume *History of Woman Suffrage,* over which Anthony had editorial control in the final years as she outlived her collaborators. As Wagner put it, by the fourth volume, the woman suffrage movement was led almost single-handedly by Anthony, with assistance from Elizabeth Cady Stanton and occasional help from Matilda Joslyn Gage. Stanton's name and contributions were revived by feminist scholars in the 1970s, but Matilda Joslyn Gage, despite having served as the main writer and editor on the first three volumes of the *History,* is still largely unknown today. Not so among her contemporaries. The *Woman's Journal* in 1888 described Gage as "conspicuous, and united with Mrs. Stanton since the early days, and the three names, Stanton, Anthony and Gage, linked together in the authorship of 'The History of Woman Suffrage,' will ever hold a grateful place in the hearts of posterity."[8]

The disagreement that Gage, Stanton, Blake, and others had with Anthony was about focus. Anthony believed that success for women's rights lay in narrowing the focus of their arguments exclusively to winning the vote, while others wanted to continue a multipronged approach for more comprehensive reforms for women in society as a whole.

Anthony made the decision to merge their suffrage organization with the conservative Woman's Christian Temperance Union—believing that multiplying their numbers tenfold would bring them closer to the vote. Instead, it alienated her closest friends and collaborators, Gage and Stanton, who had both been vocal with their critiques of organized Christianity as the main cause of women's suppression. As the suffrage movement grew more conservative due to this merger, the more revolutionary reform activists were gradually written out of history.

Matilda Joslyn Gage was a mighty intellect who in the 1800s was talking about issues still dominating today's headlines, such as equal pay for equal work, female trafficking, and pedophile priests. Gloria Steinem has described her as a woman who was ahead of the women who were ahead of their time. Thanks to Sally Roesch Wagner, Gage's family home in Fayetteville, New York, has been converted into a museum, resource center, and leadership training foundation for young girls. Much can be learned at www.matildajoslyngage.org, including the surprising influence that this visionary suffragist had on the creation of L. Frank Baum's utopian world of Oz. Baum was Gage's son-in-law, and they lived in the same house while she was writing her *Woman, Church and State,* exchanging ideas with each other that may have influenced the plot for *The Wonderful Wizard of Oz.*

One more visionary activist we will mention is Belva Lockwood, someone who is not discussed outside of women's history courses but should be because she changed the legal status of women unlike any other. She was also the first woman to run a serious campaign for the U.S. presidency in 1884. The same year as the cornerstone was laid for the foundation of the pedestal for the Statue of Liberty, Belva Lockwood and her vice presidential candidate, Marietta Stow, were campaigning across the country to be elected to the highest office in the land even though neither of them could vote. Lockwood was a trained lawyer and had legally petitioned until she won the right in 1879 to be the first woman to argue a case before the Supreme Court. She drafted legislation that ensured equal pay for equal work, and in her later years she advocated for disarmament and international peace.

Lockwood was at the forefront of the battle against coverture, the

Figure 13.2. Light imagery was popular in suffrage paraphernalia of the early twentieth century, like this one showing Votes for Women in a sunburst being adored by a robed female. Torches, stars, and sunbursts were common, as was the motto Forward into Light. Women's History Collection, Division of Social History (Political Collections), National Museum of American History, Smithsonian Institution.

old English common law still practiced in the United States at that time, which declared that a married woman lost all her legal rights to personhood after she married. She was "covered" by her husband, who assumed all rights to her and her decision-making powers, because it was assumed that women did not have independent minds. They were as children, complete dependents. Married women could not sue in court, did not own any property, had no rights to their children in the case of divorce, could not keep the money they earned, or inherit property. Some judges refused to allow Lockwood to speak in the courtroom on the grounds that she was a married woman, regardless of the fact that she had been admitted as a member of the bar.

Despite these challenges, she grew her practice and specialized in cases related to the rights of women, Native Americans, and African Americans. A truly effective champion, Belva Lockwood broke down many of the legal barriers for women that prevented them not only from acting as attorneys but also from even being allowed to speak for themselves in a court of law. Up until her death, she continued advocating for the rights of women and international peace.

Women in the Hollow of Man's Hand, to Be Crushed at His Will

A footnote to the Belva Lockwood story connects us to the Statue of Liberty in a way that reveals with one sentence how degraded a status women held at that time. Although she did not campaign, there was one other woman who ran for president before Lockwood. Victoria Woodhull declared herself as a candidate for the U.S. presidency in the election of 1872, though unlike Lockwood, her name did not appear on the official ballot. Her declaration was more of a publicity stunt for her suffrage newspaper, and Woodhull was unable to focus on her campaign when her activism in another arena got her arrested and required her full attention. By exposing in their newspaper the adulterous affair of Reverend Henry Ward Beecher, a leading critic of free love, Woodhull and her sister were brought up on obscenity charges. These subjects were still considered taboo to write about, especially for women.

As mentioned earlier, in the nineteenth century the term "free love" was used by feminists to advocate for reform in areas such as divorce and adultery laws, reproductive rights, spousal rape, and homosexuality. During the Beecher-Tilton adultery trial, Beecher was represented by corporate lawyer William M. Evarts, who a few years later would be heading the fundraising committee for the Statue of Liberty pedestal. During this sensational trial in the early 1870s, however, Evarts argued that "women were not free, but were held in the hollow of man's hand, to be crushed at his will."[9] We wonder what progressive Emma Lazarus would have thought of that when Evarts pressured her to write what would become her famous poem "The New Colossus" for an arts fundraiser for the pedestal fund.

Some kind of cosmic irony must have been at work on the day of the Statue of Liberty's unveiling ceremony in 1886. Evarts was the final speaker at the dedication, and at the conclusion he was to signal the sculptor, Auguste Bartholdi, up above in the crown, to drop the French flag that was veiling her face. Due to an untimely pause that Evarts made while speaking, Bartholdi cut the cords too soon, and Evarts never got to complete his speech. The deafening horns, whistles, and cheers carried on so long that he eventually sat down, his opinions drowned out by the people's enthusiasm for Lady Liberty.

Hollowness and Flexibility

Social critic and art historian Albert Boime came up with the clever metaphor of a hollow icon to describe the Statue of Liberty. Of course, the Statue of Liberty is literally hollow inside, but Boime's metaphor also perfectly captures why the Statue of Liberty has succeeded so well as a symbol. "*Liberty* is literally an empty vessel," he says, "standing ready to be charged with fresh interpretation, an old bottle perpetually awaiting a refill of new wine."[10] Barry Moreno, Statue of Liberty librarian, agreed, and enumerated the many opposing causes La Liberté has been adopted to represent, including the right to have a monarchy as well as those wanting nationalism, for pro- or anti-mass immigration, for freedom of religion, and for crusaders against immorality—"any kind of idea you care to infuse her with," he concluded. "People have used her in ways from conservative to liberal and everything in between." Out of the one, come many, we might say. The Statue of Liberty is a multileveled archetypal symbol that allows for many different interpretations of her to appeal to wildly different causes.

The more one questions the myths that pass for American history, the more one finds careful constructions devised by the dominator class, with the objective of creating an agreeable public. Law professor Steven Green noted that without a common ethnicity or heritage, Americans rely on their myths to unite them and make them Americans. "Our founding myth gives us our identity, helps establish us as a common people, and distinguishes us from other peoples (such as the notion of American exceptionalism)."[11] Studying the secret life of Lady Liberty forced us to look behind these myths of American exceptionalism, as well as the myths that have been put forward about her creation.

An Eiffel Tower Inside

Anyone who has not made the tourist trek to Liberty Island to climb to the top for a view from the crown might assume that the Statue of Liberty is made of something solid, like marble, as most statues are. It might stand to reason that the winds whipping around the harbor of New York would require something very heavy to stand up to them, but it turns out just the reverse is true. Her very hollowness is what makes her strong. An engineering marvel of the day, the Statue of Liberty is composed on the outside of very fine sheets of copper, hammered down to the thickness of two pennies, molded into shape, and then hung in sections from a lattice-work steel pylon in the center (figure 5.6, p. 134). Liberty's "body" is essentially a very strong trusswork tower, secured deep into the ground amid tons of concrete. Thousands of thin metal rods poking out from this tower are attached to the molded copper sheets, which are fitted together to hang on the frame in the shape of the artwork. The outer pieces are not firmly attached to each other, allowing the molded pieces to almost float in place as temperature variants shrink and expand the copper skin. The thinness of the connecting rods allows them to act as springs and gives the sheets enough flexibility to adjust to the temperature. The hollow core and flexibility are the secret strength behind the statue's wind resistance, and metaphorically behind the symbol's longevity.

The engineer who devised this brilliant solution was Gustave Eiffel, who was not brought onto the project until 1880, after the original engineer, Eugène Viollet-le-Duc, passed away unexpectedly. Viollet-le-Duc had been a tutor of the young Bartholdi and was attracted to the Liberty project as a supporter of the political aims of Laboulaye's committee. His plan involved filling compartments with sand up to Lady Liberty's hips. According to architectural historian Marvin Trachtenberg, however, this probably would not have been successful over the long run. Eiffel was inspired to join the project more by the engineering-artistic challenge rather than the political message, and he devised a solution similar to the wind-resistant and elegant railroad bridges he was already famous for constructing over the rivers and gorges of Europe. Eiffel's personal passion was aerodynamics, and, following his success with his almost one-thousand-foot-high Eiffel Tower several years later, he would conduct hundreds of experiments in wind resistance, making some significant advances to the field of powered flight.

One of the reasons colossal artworks are so awe-inspiring is the curiosity that is piqued about how they were engineered. Viewing the interior of the Statue of Liberty, where one can see the imagination and integrity that are her strength, is just as inspiring as the moral uplift achieved by the view from outside. Author Marina Warner thinks she's almost more beautiful on the inside where the mystery of the internal structure is revealed. "She is mechanical, strong, . . . internally the sculpture ripples and flows more plastically than her resolute outer form would ever let one guess."[12]

A testament to the successful engineering of strength and endurance that supports Lady Liberty is the damage sustained on Liberty Island after Hurricane Sandy slammed through in 2012 with winds of more than eighty miles an hour. The year before the storm, as we worked on this book, the statue was closed for months for routine renovations, and we eagerly awaited its scheduled reopening in 2012 so we could visit. Just one day after it reopened, it was hit by the biggest storm in New York history, closing Liberty Island again, this time for almost a year. Yet the statue itself wasn't damaged. It was the brand-new visitor's center and the security screening facilities that took the hit, with docks and brick walkways tossed about like toothpicks. The statue and the pedestal weathered the superstorm and its winds just fine.

A Hollow History

The identity of the Statue of Liberty has likewise flexed and changed through the years as the buffeting winds of political and social opinion have shifted. As much as we'd love to believe the myth that the Statue of Liberty was designed with the lofty goals of welcoming the tired and the poor, it's not true. As we review in chapter 5, in many ways she was designed to promote a narrow set of business and political interests in France with the intention of bonding with the same conservative interests in the United States. What she became after Americans adopted her is another story, but that is indeed how she started out.

It was during the years after the U.S. Civil War that Laboulaye and friends over in France were coming up with the idea for a statue of Liberty. Their idealized version of *American* Liberty was ironically conceived amid the corrupt Grant administration in the United States, which was notorious for fostering an industrialization and mechanization boom that both chewed up the environment and eroded the public trust. Capitalism in the United States became the new master, and its goal seemed to be to enslave labor of any and all colors. Around America's centennial in 1876 the country was in transition from an agricultural to an industrial economy that was described by W. E. B. DuBois as "a new capitalism and a new enslavement of labor."[13] The problem now, pinpointed DuBois, was not race, but the unequal distribution of wealth.

When the crates holding the Statue of Liberty arrived in New York in 1885, the United States was even more divided than it had been during the Civil War. Labor leaders had just begun organizing protests, and with an anarchist element infiltrating their movement, their protests were growing violent. The excessive ferocity of the police in quashing these demonstrations was infamous and widespread. Early labor organizations were the first to adopt the Statue of Liberty as a mascot, long before the statue itself was completed. Her image had become well-known across the country as a result of the many associated fundraising campaigns, news reports, and advertisements that featured it.

To labor activists, liberty meant the release from the slavelike conditions under which the majority of Americans were working. To the capitalists who controlled these conditions, liberty meant the freedom to hire and fire at will and set wages as high or low as they chose. When "Liberty!" became a rallying cry for workers, and was used as the name of a popular anarchist newspaper, it had a dampening effect on fundraising efforts for the statue. The support of the powerful elite was needed for Bartholdi to convince Congress to approve of the statue venture, but initially the elite tried to kill the idea. And they very nearly succeeded.[14] To those in power, the thought of too much liberty was a frightening thing. With anarchists screaming "Liberty!" in the U.S. squares, some of the wealthy said a giant public tribute to liberty would appear to be endorsing the rights of the poor. The main financial backers of the statue project in France had been the standard patrons of the arts. In the United States, the growing class struggle between capital and labor, and the adoption of Liberty by the latter, put an end to that traditional route. This dissention caused that embarrassing yearlong delay between the arrival of the completed statue in crates from France and the completion of the fundraising to finish construction of the pedestal in the United States.

The erection of the Statue of Liberty in 1886 coincides with the year that organized labor really stood up for itself. During the four previous years there had been an average of 500 labor strikes per year involving about 150,000 workers. In 1886 those numbers tripled to 1,400 strikes in that year alone, involving more than 500,000 workers.[15] Just a few months before the statue's October inauguration, a deadly riot broke out in Chicago during a labor rights protest at Haymarket Square, and the excessive police violence that ensued resulted in several deaths. Biased reporting and a rounding up of the usual suspects from among the anarchists and socialists led to a sentence of hanging hurried through for seven labor activists, despite lack of evidence connecting them with any crime, and widespread belief that they were being framed. News about the Haymarket Trial was largely condemned as a mockery of justice by intelligentsia and progressives in both the United States and Europe.

The contrast between the Haymarket Trial and the upcoming patriotic celebrations planned in New York for the unveiling of the Statue of Liberty drew many prominent writers to observe the patent hypocrisy of an homage to liberty in a land where such blatant legal scapegoating could be condoned. Haymarket was referred to in different terms by railway magnate and New York politician Chauncey M. Depew in his keynote address at Liberty's unveiling. In his speech he listed the social inequalities of the day that in his opinion would eventually "work themselves out . . . without the aid of Kings and armies, or of Anarchists and bombs." Just as in France, the elite in this country saw their protection coming from "under the benign influences of enlight-

Figure 13.3. Lithograph issued by Currier & Ives in 1884 as part of their racially bigoted anti-immigration Darktown Comics series titled *Barsqualdi's Statue of Liberty Frightening the World, Bedbugs Island, New York Harbor*. The words on the book this woman is holding read "New York Port Changes," a commentary on the corruption of the harbor administration. The rooster is a symbol of France. Library of Congress.

ened lawmaking and law-abiding liberty."[16] In other words, Depew was claiming *this* statue of Liberty belonged to law and order, not to those bomb-throwing anarchists.

There are several other links between the Haymarket Affair and the Statue of Liberty that bring to light more of Liberty's delightful inconsistencies. First there was Henry George, a prominent activist for progressive change, whose bestselling book *Progress and Poverty* is said to have launched much of the reform of the Progressive Era. Among this book's admirers was Emma Lazarus, the poet whose words assigned a new identity to the Statue of Liberty as regards the plight of the immigrants. In the summer of 1886, the year the Statue of Liberty opened, there was a heated mayoral campaign being waged in New York City, where Henry George finished a close second to iron magnate Abram Hewitt. Abram Hewitt was the former U.S. congressman who, in 1877, had introduced the bill that led to the official acceptance of the Statue of Liberty as a gift, and he had continued to support the project as a sincere patron of the arts. Henry George, on the other hand, saw the Statue of Liberty as a symbol of the workingman. After he lost the election he vowed to his prolabor supporters, "We have lighted a torch whose fire they will not be able to quench."[17]

In New York that fall the wife of one of the activists convicted at the Haymarket Trial, Lucy Parsons, was on a speaking tour trying to raise money for an appeal for her husband, who was later hanged, even though he was not even present at the demonstration when the bomb was thrown. A powerful speaker and labor activist herself, and described by the Chicago police as "more dangerous than a thousand rioters," Lucy Parsons also did some campaigning for Henry George while she was in town. Disturbed by the rhetoric and buildup of preparations for Lady Liberty's unveiling, Parsons described her as "Liberty . . . for the rich and not for the poor." Parsons was a brown-skinned woman of Mexican, Native American, and African descent, and probably a former slave herself. She and her husband had fled Texas for Chicago, where their interracial marriage was more accepted. She wrote extensively for the anarchist and socialist newspapers and spoke on behalf of worker's rights all her life. In New York before Liberty's inauguration, she pointed to the "shops and factories where the working people are slaves."[18]

In contrast to Parsons's views, and in keeping with Lady Liberty's delightful inconsistencies, another famous radical revolutionary had the opposite reaction when she first saw the Statue of Liberty. Anarchist agitator and provocateur Emma Goldman, who later earned the nickname of the most dangerous woman in America, reported how tears welled in her eyes the first time she glimpsed the Statue of Liberty.[19]

Pulitzer on a Pedestal

We have already discussed Joseph Pulitzer's campaign to save the Statue of Liberty's pedestal by raising money for it from the public at large. Here we will elaborate a little on this Hungarian immigrant's rags to riches story and why he was really attracted to the project. Best known today for the journalism prize in his name, he arrived in the United States when he was seventeen with practically no money in hand. Recruited in Europe to fight in the U.S. Civil War, he grabbed at the chance for a new life in the states, where he slowly worked his way up to becoming a journalist and later a newspaper tycoon. In 1883 he bought the failing *New York World* from infamous railroad tycoon Jay Gould, and turned it around to become the largest newspaper in the country.

He struck it rich with circulation-boosting publicity stunts, many of which starred the trailblazing Nellie Bly. His idea was to add entertainment and shock value to the reporting of the news, but the novelty of a woman reporting from around the world also gave women a real-life role model in a time when the determined capabilities and mental acuity of women were not on high display. Later Pulitzer would add the first comic strips and enter into competition with William Randolph Hearst over who could produce the most sensational headlines and yellow journalism.

With an exuberant personality, Pulitzer had been drawn early on to politics, starting as a Republican, but switching to Democrat after realizing that graft was business as usual in the current Republican Party. At the time of his famous campaign for the Statue of Liberty, he was serving as a member of the U.S. House of Representatives from New York. The Democrats had just taken the White House, but the Republicans still controlled New York City, and also dominated the Franco-American Committee, which was responsible for building the pedestal for the Statue of Liberty. When the money ran out in the winter of 1884, and as the wind began to blow over the stub of a pedestal, Pulitzer seized the opportunity to shame the Republicans in charge. He started naming names in his newspaper of the wealthy Republican patrons of the committee, asking why they didn't each just write a check for the remaining one hundred thousand dollars needed. He inferred that they were stalling until the Republicans regained the White House so they could make the statue's completion a Republican victory and celebration.

Pulitzer's appeal struck the emotions of readers across the country, who responded by the thousands. His spin that Lady Liberty's foundation should not be built by the millionaires of this country, but by the people, saved Liberty from being created totally by and for the elite. Instead, in less than five months, Pulitzer was able to hand over to the pedestal committee the amount they needed to complete the job raised from the "dimes of the people, not with the dollars of the rich few."[20] Part of his promotional plan had been the promise to list every contributor by name in his paper, no matter how small the contribution. This public accounting feature was updated daily and provided the added bonus of ensuring there was no graft or loss of any of the funds.

Everyone Wanted to Be There

The enormous outpouring of support from the general public had a decisive effect on the Statue of Liberty's reputation. By the time of the dedication ceremony, everyone who was anyone wanted to be there, and from the rich to the poor, from labor to capital, everyone acted as if they had always supported the project and thought it was a marvelous idea all along. The government's veto of the request to fund the pedestal had ensured that individual citizens had to muster to complete the project. This public coordination effectively freed the statue from the changing moods of political officials, and allowed the American people to firmly declare they were adopting the French lady for themselves. Pulitzer sold the idea so well that the authorities were forced to accede to public opinion, and in the process he managed to leverage a subscription-boosting campaign for his newspaper and gain entrée for himself into the upper-crust society that had previously been denied to him. Pulitzer continued to prosper in high society, and later named his sailing yacht *Liberty,* a pleasure craft so big that later, during

World War I, the navy requisitioned it for use as a floating hospital.

As governor of New York and later as president of the United States, Grover Cleveland twice denied funding to the Statue of Liberty, calling it an inappropriate use of public money. He was a minimalist in government and needed to be convinced that the statue would have practical use before he felt comfortable releasing constitutionally approved taxpayer dollars to maintain it. The committee managed to convince him that the statue would function as a lighthouse—the first electric lighthouse in the United States, in fact. Having been cool to the project all along, Cleveland did not plan to attend the unveiling ceremonies in 1886, until he realized what a glorious spectacle it was going to be and changed his mind. In his speech that day, he emphasized that this Liberty was carrying not a weapon, but a torch that "illumined the way to enfranchisement," and that, joined by others around the world, she would soon truly be "Liberty enlightening the world."

On Bedloe's Island for the unveiling ceremony there was room for only several hundred VIPs, but lining the streets of Manhattan great swarms of people pressed together in the pouring rain to watch the parades—some estimate up to a million people turned out. The enthusiasm grew as the streets below were showered with ticker tape from the office windows on Wall Street. As darkness fell, and notice went out that the fireworks had been canceled due to the rain, the disappointed crowds were instructed to move along. Sally Roesch Wagner says what followed was so typical that it barely warranted a mention in the press. Overly zealous police encouraged the people to disperse by indiscriminately using their billy clubs, meaning people who had gathered to welcome Liberty to the United States were beaten for not leaving fast enough, causing a near riot. Several employees of the Unexcelled Fireworks Company had to be sent to the hospital.[21]

A Ladylike Appeal to Liberty in 1915

As noted above, even the suffragists who attended the unveiling in 1886 to protest the statue were moved by the sight of an enormous woman standing for liberty, and as their campaign for suffrage crept along, they too embraced her as a mascot. The next generation of suffrage leaders organized an "Appeal to Liberty" that started with a tableau at Bedloe's Island on the Fourth of July, 1915. Actress Margaret Wycherly dressed as the goddess of liberty and, surrounded by her attendants, read out their appeal at the foot of the statue in front of crowds of supporters and press (figure 13.4). According to the *New York Times,* "The sun came out brilliantly as the closing words of the appeal were sounded, and a band struck up the Star-Spangled Banner." One of the leaders of the event shouted up to the statue, "What says the Goddess?" and almost immediately the reply came floating down: "Votes for Women!" Later they took their message and costumed women on a Liberty float in a parade downtown, where the appeal was read out again several times by Wycherly. The appeal questioned, among other things, why

Figure 13.4. In 1915 suffragists organized another protest at the foot of the Statue of Liberty that included Broadway actress Margaret Wycherly in costume as the goddess of Liberty reading out their "Appeal to Liberty." At the conclusion, the reply "Votes for women!" came floating down from above. Library of Congress.

the "opinion of illiterate males" was valued at the voting booth, while that of "the 41,000 women teachers of the State" was not.[22]

A 1917 book by Alice Duer Miller titled *Women Are People!* included a poetic dialogue between the Statue of Liberty and a group of suffragists that summarized the hypocrisy many of them still saw in the statue.

> *I am that Liberty which all your brothers*
> *Think good for them and very bad for others.*
> *Therefore they made me out of bronze, and hollow,*
> *Immovable, for fear that I might follow*
> *Some fresh rebellion, some new victim's plea;*
> *And so they set me on a rock at sea,*
> *Welded my torch securely in my hand*
> *Lest I should pass it on, without command.*
> *I am a milestone, not an inspiration;*
> *And if my spirit lingers in this nation,*
> *If it still flickers faintly o'er these waters,*
> *It is your spirit, my rebellious daughters.*[23]

The Granddaughters Rising

When Matilda Joslyn Gage and Susan B. Anthony interrupted the celebration for the Declaration of Independence in Philadelphia in 1876 to present their Declaration of Rights of Women, Gage said they were doing it for future generations. They knew they might be arrested, and understood that their efforts would have little immediate impact. They were doing it, she said, "for the daughters of 1976, so they would know their mothers had impeached the government for its treatment of women."

Those rebellious daughters and granddaughters of these suffrage activists did indeed rise. In 1970, in honor of the fiftieth anniversary of the passage of the Nineteenth Amendment, women activists again headed out to the Statue of Liberty to enlist her in their cause. A famous photograph shows her towering over their protest banner, which looks like a caption for her stating: "Women of the World Unite!" (figure 13.5).

This protest action and media coverage helped launch what is known as the second wave of the women's movement. Jacqui Ceballos of the Veteran Feminists of America remembered it all started when Betty Friedan breezed through her New York chapter of the National Organization of Women (NOW) with the idea that a parade or a strike or "something big" should be planned to commemorate the fiftieth anniversary of women earning the right to vote. Ceballos volunteered her group to help, and with a shoestring budget they brainstormed on how to get the word out. Someone suggested they take over the Statue of Liberty as a publicity stunt, as other groups had done to draw attention to their social justice causes. A flyer advertising the Women's Strike for Equality on August 26, 1970, in New York City, featured a drawing of the Statue of Liberty holding up the female symbol with the strike fist instead of the torch. With a headline of "Statue of Liberty or Statue of Sham?" most of these protestors probably didn't even realize that they were echoing their grandmothers when they asked, "Isn't it ironic that the symbol of freedom in America is a woman, for no woman in America is free?"

Ceballos credits two of her committee members, Pat Lawrence and Marian Gannett, as the ones with the original idea to take over the Statue of Liberty. They were both professional artists and made several trips out to the statue ahead of time to take measurements for the banner and, after assessing wind velocity, determined a means of securing it. They used their large art studio to assemble two, forty-foot banners,

Figure 13.5 (opposite). Over the years, the Statue of Liberty has been the site of several protests for women's rights. On August 10, 1970, the New York chapter of NOW staged an action at the Statue of Liberty that included hanging a forty-foot banner proclaiming "Women of the World Unite!" from the statue's pedestal. They were trying to attract attention to their Women's Strike for Equality two weeks later, organized in commemoration of the fiftieth anniversary of the Nineteenth Amendment. Photo: Anne Hazlewood-Brady papers, Maine Women Writers Collection, University of New England, Portland, Maine. Used with permission.

the famous one saying "Women of the World Unite!" and the other listing August 26 as the date women should strike for equality, calling on New Yorkers to march down Fifth Avenue.

On the ferry ride over to the statue on August 10, 1970, Carole De Saram remembered how they wrapped the banners around their bodies, concealed underneath their clothes, and with about two hundred other women hiding picket signs, they made it across without detection. The press, arriving early, almost blew their cover, but the hovering media helicopter filming the altercation probably ended up saving them in the end. As the women tried to hang the banners from the pedestal, several park rangers charged out to stop them, and De Saram remembered being very worried someone might fall. Ceballos recalled pushing on the door to keep the guards out, and also recalled that when the mayor heard of the altercations, he called to tell the rangers to leave the women alone. On the ground, Marjorie De Fazio, who was there with her little children in tow, just remembered the eruption of cheers from the crowd when the banners were finally unfurled.

"I did feel in my heart a deep connection to the statue," said Mavra Stark, who was part of the distraction group on the ground. Stark felt confident that Lady Liberty was, "in effect, winking at me and all the women there. She was one of us, if only for a little while. I felt a reverence for her while protesting there, a deep respect for everything she meant to me. . . . I had never thought of her in feminist terms before, but I did at that point."

Women around the world apparently agreed with her, for the news-wire photos of Lady Liberty proclaiming "Women of the World Unite!" brought thousands out to march in New York City two weeks later. Coverage of the event also increased attendance at related sit-ins, teach-ins, and marches in other parts of the country. Marjorie De Fazio and Jaqui Ceballos both remembered showing up on Fifth Avenue with the fifteen or so women who had organized the march, still uncertain if anyone would come. They had a permit only to march on the sidewalks and started out tentatively, until suddenly thousands of people started to join them. Someone shouted to take the street, and the next thing they knew they were stopping traffic. Estimates say there were at least

Feminists Shifting Emphasis From Persons to Politics

By DEIRDRE CARMODY

The women's liberation movement — a massive behavioral revolution aimed at overturning the very structures of a male-dominated society—has entered a new stage of development. It is now concentrating its energies on legislative lobbying and politics.

Many women have passed through the movement's con...

women would hold the power and would have such choices as whether to bear children in utero or in test tubes—a world, in the words of radical feminist Robin Morgan, "which would make 1984 look like Mary Poppins."

The largest of the groups, the National Organization for Women (NOW), has about 20,000 members, and there...

(the first time either the Democratic or Republican party had given the job to a woman), and the convention passed a rules change that calls for a woman to chair the 1976 convention and every alternate convention thereafter.

"Women were the most together group at the convention." Representative Bella Abzug, New York Democrat, said the other day in a telephone interview from the Ladies Retirement Room ("I must do something about that name," she said) in the House of Representatives.

"We showed we could put something together politically," said Mrs. Abzug, who was defeated in the Democratic primary by Representative William F. Ryan. "I think that it's fair to say that what has happened in the last year or so is the first real political movement by women of any national scope since the suffrage movement."

There were some defeats for feminists at the convention, however, when their intensive backstage maneuvering failed to pass either the South Carolina challenge, which would have put more women in that state's delegation, or a pro-abortion minority plank. However, the fact that the emotional issue of abortion even reached the floor, despite the lobbying...

100 women liberate Miss Liberty

...Betty Friedan to awaken, organize and assert the vast political power represented by women."

Through its tax-exempt arm, Women's Education for Delegate Selection, the caucus held seminars around the...

...Fasteau, co-...ator of the women's rights project of the American Civil Liberties Union...

Figure 13.6. The "Women of the World Unite!" banner was carried at the head of the march down Fifth Avenue on August 26, 1970, when twenty thousand people took to the streets of New York, and other cities across the nation, with slogans like "Don't Iron While the Strike Is Hot." Women were agitating for fair treatment under the law, equal access to higher education and social institutions, and an end to discriminatory practices prohibiting unmarried women from owning property or even applying for credit cards. Montage of newswire reporting created by Hieronimus & Co.

twenty thousand marchers in total. The Statue of Liberty banner proclaiming "Women of the World Unite!" led the parade.

Earlier that day Betty Friedan and various other NOW members organized several other actions as part of the Women's Strike for Equality. They sat down to eat in male-only restaurants, and they distributed a parody newspaper at the *New York Times* to show the unequal manner in which journalists reported personal information in the news about women, but not about men. Other NOW members led protests at the Social Security administration where widows were denied pensions, and at divorce courts, advocating that the courts equalize the laws for women and men. Carole De Saram organized an action in a bank where she and a number of women waited in line and then politely asked to speak with a woman vice president. When informed that the bank had none, they created a scene saying they would withdraw their money and find a bank that promoted women to senior positions. Despite having won the right to vote fifty years prior, women were still being denied jobs, were excluded from some universities and private clubs, and could not buy property without the permission of their husbands. Husbands could still legally beat and rape their wives in most states.

Few Statues Are as Beautiful

Historian Max Dashú describes the Statue of Liberty as "beautiful," especially her face because it is not a prettified female stereotype. "The book of law, the torch she raises, she's very powerful." We realize that some veteran feminists object to representations of allegorical women as objectified virtues, but all of the women leaders we talked to shared a reverence for the Statue of Liberty, and recognized the unifying power of her symbolism for women.

In another ironic twist, it was the conservative leanings of her French creators that ensured the Statue of Liberty would be fully clothed and not objectified sexually. This nonobjectification is especially helpful as an alternative to contrast with the media saturation today of narcissistic icons touted as the ideals of female beauty and power. Promoting a celebrity culture leads to consumerism, and the female body is alluring, so it is used to sell everything. Ads are designed to make women feel they are lacking something if they don't measure up, and this has programmed women to think of themselves as nothing more than an imperfect body. Don't accept it when the media says they are just giving us what we want with these oversexualized versions of women. They are giving us what *advertisers* want, and that includes the qualities we use today to define a beautiful woman.

The inconsistency of Lady Liberty's appeal stems from her symbolism being strong and flexible enough to speak to both labor and business, anarchists and jurists, immigrants and xenophobes, women and men—in fact, anyone and everyone who desires the liberty to pursue one's own beliefs. "The Statue of Liberty belongs to everyone," said veteran feminist Carole De Saram. "She's not a symbol of just one ethnic or economic class. She's everybody."[24] Because she is also a woman, however, we see her as a special inspiration for feminists, both male and female, and as a symbol of change. The Statue of Liberty is an inconsistency, it's true, but just as our suffrage mothers said, she's a delightful one.

14

The Statue of Liberty as a Symbol for the Future

The Statue of Liberty was created for a particular set of people, with a particular set of goals, at a particular time in history. That she broke free from these goals to become a transformative symbol for individuals all over the world, and remains so more than one hundred thirty years later, testifies to the strength and flexibility of her symbolism. Around the world, we are individually becoming one with Lady Liberty as the enlightening power of individual liberty breaches the confines of history. Her success is explained by various theories, with some saying it's due to her simplicity, others her size or her location. In our opinion, the ancestral circle of strong women and goddesses that she embodies also plays a part in her international appeal.

No longer is Lady Liberty restricted to the role defined by statesmen—that of the perfected woman symbolizing morality with the aim of controlling people within the law. With this book, we offer the Statue of Liberty as a new symbol for strength through compassion. If a notion as universal and powerful as liberty can be accepted in a female form tells us anything, it would be that the female form is powerful enough to contain it.

And yet, standard history continues to teach that patriarchy and domination are the norms of civilized history. Instead of learning about the many matrifocal cultures of the past or those that continue to today,

362

we are taught that history did not begin until Sumer and then moved westward through Greece and Rome to Europe, and then onward to the pinnacle of America in one long line of "civilized" nations. That this misconception continues is not due to a lack of data. There is plenty of data showing not only that partnership between the sexes has been the norm in the past but also that women are effective leaders. It's not the lack of data, but rather the misinterpretation of the data that has led to the common assumption that male-domination is the way things have always been and the way nature intended. The European imperialism and the racial biases attached to these assumptions are engrained in our understanding of who we are, and they continue to mislead us today, especially in our relations with Native Americans and the environment.

The New American Revolution

We need another American Revolution—this time for the so-called environmental problem—or how we choose to govern ourselves will be wiped away in importance in place of brute survival. What we found in researching this book is that revolutions generally represent a rising up against the domination paradigm toward a more partnership-oriented system. Every revolution starts with human compassion, wanting to right an injustice. We believe it's time for all of us individually, one at a time, to throw off the yoke of consumerism that the American plutocracy continuously reinforces as the American Dream. Throw off the corporate-driven consumer mind-set that drives you. Remember, one of the motivating factors of the original American Revolution was the impetus to throw off a corporate monopoly and prevent corporations from completely controlling all public decisions—in that case, it was the East India Company controlling decisions about tea. America is the leader in pollution and in generating the consumer mind-set around the globe through our entertainment and fast-food industries and military interventions. It is this mind-set that is killing the planet. It's time for Americans to take responsibility and uproot the belief that man was created to have dominion over the Earth and to be in conflict with nature. Today this outdated belief is on course for annihilating the human race

Figure 14.1. The *Statue of Freedom* on a three-story-high mural in downtown Baltimore as conceived by Dr. Bob Hieronimus. Her skin tone in this interpretation makes her unquestionably a Native American. Detail from *We the People*, 2013. Photo: Stuart Zolotorow.

altogether, and we must change, or the Earth will change it for us.

Social movements start when lots of little people make lots of little decisions. Gradually, little acts of resistance and change multiply until more and more people copy them. All of us can and do make a difference in the little choices we make every day and in the little acts of compassion we spread through our lives. There is a physical change that occurs in our hearts when we activate our inherent altruism, when we give to the homeless, when we hug a stranger in need, when we come to the aid of disaster victims. When Americans tap into this power as a group, they can be a truly powerful force for change. Responding to others in need, we forget the boundaries that divide us in everyday life.

The founders of the United States surrounded themselves with goddesses, but almost no one interpreted these artworks as inspirations for real women to find their individual power. When women finally did break into the man's sphere, they found themselves forced to fit into the male patterns of strength in order to compete, instead of tapping particular female strengths. Nevertheless, the United States has always been a spiritual country, and many policy changes have been motivated by spiritual movements, especially when the Great Awakenings republicanized Americans' approach to church worship. The new American awakening we are calling for here will get a great boost when organized religion learns to revere the Earth as sacred, and stops preaching that man was placed here to dominate nature. Until then, it is unlikely that any significant advances will be made to mitigate gender inequality or the coming climate revolt.

We Are the Ancestors, We Are the Seventh Generation

It should be apparent by now that one of the significant differences between this book and other books about the Statue of Liberty is that we accept the notion that cosmic or divine forces play a role in shaping events. Though we tried to stick mainly to the academic approach of reporting only on material that has been fact-checked, we accept that there are plenty of things in this world that cannot be explained by rational facts. Secular academics will rule out anything that sounds like divine synchronicity or the hand of God or Goddess as an explanation for why certain people were in the right place at the right time. Yet even they will acknowledge there was something of a perfect storm ridden by the Revolutionary generation that resulted in the most radical of all social movements the world has ever seen.

This is not to say we acknowledge a manifest destiny of "progress" in the march westward nor, by any means, that everything that the American Revolution accomplished was positive. Rather, we're saying that all living beings are connected by vibrational energy fields and by the air we breathe, and that that connectivity has something to do with the way social movements operate. We don't understand how a collection of little actions by a few people become massive shifts in beliefs and practices population wide, but we do acknowledge the possibility that some positive cosmic forces are behind it.

According to the great mythologist Joseph Campbell, we do have the ability to change the future by where we place our focus. "We are the 'ancestors' of an age to come," he said, "the unwitting generators of its supporting myths." Focusing on nurturing and caregiving as actions of power and strength today will lead to that reality in the future. "In a very real sense," Campbell concluded, "this is a moment of creation."[1]

We have the same responsibility today to our sons and daughters, and yes, even unto the seventh generation, as the Native Americans teach. In 1876, when suffragists challenged the one hundredth birthday celebration of the Declaration of Independence, they said they were staging the protest not for themselves, but for their daughters. Ten years later, the women's rights activists who protested at the inauguration of the Statue of Liberty in 1886 quickly adopted her as a symbol for the future they were working to create—a future of empowered and liberated females. Lillie Devereux Blake imagined the Statue of Liberty saying, "I am the embodied hope of the future, and the enthroned prediction of liberty for women."[2]

Except for a brief, starry-eyed period right after the Revolution, Americans have followed the reductionist scientific model, believing that everything and everyone is separate, and that in order to survive

Figure 14.2. Editorial cartoonists like Pulitzer Prize–winning Joel Pett of the *Lexington Herald-Leader* of Lexington, Kentucky, juxtapose Lady Liberty and Uncle Sam to symbolize the conflict between the nation's compassionate nature versus its oligarchical tendencies. Used with permission.

we must compete and dominate. Our founders were incredibly optimistic in believing that their Revolution would create a new type of man, one who was motivated by reason and a virtuous eagerness to serve and improve the community for the benefit of all. The Marquis de Lafayette described the new nation as a "temple of freedom [that would] ever stand as a lesson to oppressors, an example to the oppressed, a sanctuary for the rights of mankind!"[3] That they didn't succeed in creating such an enlightened society is partially explained by their disregard for the leadership abilities of the female half of humanity and the special talents they bring to finding creative solutions.

Where Are Your Women? .

Conducting this genealogical research to find the ancestors of the Statue of Liberty, we gained new perspectives on an American history full of female role models who combined strength with compassion. The so-called goddesses of the New World who we review in this book, from the Indian Queen to the Brown Madonnas, are related in terms of advocating an appreciation of life on Earth as sacred and worth protecting.

We invite you to ask everywhere, "Where are your women?" in the same way that the Native Americans challenged the colonists, the Cathars challenged the pope, and the second-wave feminists challenged the bank presidents. But that question also implies the partner question: "Where are your men?" In this we mean, Where are the men who are embracing their own strength of the inner goddess and honoring the power of the women in their lives? We are not only looking for the women who will step up and lead the world into a new future of balance and partnership. We are also looking for the men who will welcome them and make room for them at the top. Co-creation is what the future needs, when humanity can truly exist as "we the people," and working toward it will bring a new symbol to light.

The Earth People Prayer

We are not just the people from the United States of
    America.
We are not just the people from the East or West Coasts
    of America.
We are not just the people from the Eastern or Western
    Hemispheres of the planet.
We are People of the Planet Earth.
We are Earth People.

BOB HIERONIMUS

That old Earth People prayer summarizes the new identity of oneness we must secure as we face environmental upheaval in our near future. A shift to caring for those around us will be crucial to survival, and learning to focus on sharing resources, being kinder and more helpful to each other and to animals and the environment now will improve our collective chances. Let's try to remember that American liberty was founded under the assumption that humanity was inclined to benevolence and predisposed to be of service to others—just as the

Figure 14.3. The Indian Princess presenting universal symbolism including the pyramid with the eye in the triangle from the U.S. Great Seal. *One People, One Planet* mural by Dr. Bob Hieronimus, Baltimore, Maryland, 2009. This painting was produced together with Justin Williams and Karly Fae Hansen during a live musical performance of Telesma. Author photo.

contemporary research into oxytocin and related hormones is scientifically bearing out. Our founders encouraged virtue in the symbols they chose, and the enlightened Lady Liberty encourages us to look inward for the source of enlightenment within our souls, to the bright spark that connects us to the divine creator and to one another. The Statue of Liberty could point us to a second great Enlightenment—not one of reason this time, but one of consciousness. This would be an age of awareness that we are all Earth People, that we belong to the Earth, and we are related to all living creatures on it.

Scandals and corruption are ever-present in our culture, and Americans have always been and will always be protesting against them. Despite uncovering quite a few embarrassing features about American history in the making of this study, however, we ended up feeling even prouder of the people we call Americans, and even more inspired by the original intentions of the founders of this nation, as incomplete as the execution of these intentions may have been. In the end, the most hopeful part of living in this country is that America is a place of change—and change means hope. By focusing renewed attention on the Statue of Liberty as the American goddess, we hope to return attention to the virtues of American liberty that were formerly restricted to the so-called women's sphere and fully embrace them in a future of American liberty based on partnership.

We look forward to a future where life is valued from the start, and education and support are provided to all people so they have the liberty to shine to the best of their abilities and fullest potential. It's what Alice Paul and Mercy Otis Warren wanted. It's what Édouard de Laboulaye and Auguste Bartholdi wanted. It's what George Washington and Ben Franklin wanted. The future definition of American liberty, as the liberty to do good and improve the world for others who will come after us, will outshine the liberty to make personal profit and gain. If we believe in this future, we can bring it about by living it in our own lives right now. We are all connected, which means changing our own lives can change the world. Because we are all one. We are all Liberty's children.

Guest Biographies

The *Lady Liberty Radio Interview Series*

As we collected the research that went into this book, we reorganized our ongoing radio program, *21st Century Radio,* for several years in the early 2010s to create a Lady Liberty interview series. We interviewed goddess history experts, Native American scholars and wisdom keepers, art historians and experts in related fields, and quoted from these interviews throughout this book. This appendix provides biographies of the participants in the *Lady Liberty Radio Interview Series* who are featured most prominently.

Ean Begg

Jungian analyst, writer, and lecturer Ean Begg read modern languages at Oxford and later studied at the C. G. Jung Institute in Zurich where he gained a diploma in analytical psychology with his thesis on *The Lord of the Rings.* He has lectured widely and appeared on numerous television programs, notably the six-part BBC series *Is There Something After Death* and the BBC's *C.G. Jung Centenary Program,* both of which he compiled and presented. His written works include the influential 1986 book *The Cult of the Black Virgin; Myth in Today's Consciousness;* and *The Trail of Merlin,* as well as several other books coauthored with his wife, Deike Begg, including *In Search of the Holy Grail and the Precious Blood* and *On the Trail of Merlin: A Guide to the Western Mystery Tradition*. They live in London. www.DeikeBegg.com.

Jean Shinoda Bolen, M.D.

An internationally known Jungian analyst, active workshop leader in the women's movement, and the author of several books, Jean Shinoda Bolen was recently named a distinguished Life Fellow of the American Psychiatric Association. She is a former clinical professor of psychiatry at the University of California at San Francisco and a recipient of the Pioneers in Art, Science, and Soul of Healing Award from the Institute for Health and Healing. She is a diplomate of the American Board of Psychiatry and Neurology, and with her trailblazing book *Goddesses in Everywoman,* she has been an influential force in the women's spirituality movement for the past few decades. Her current assignment is to encourage the calling of a United Nations Fifth World Conference on Women. www.5wcw.org.

C. Sue Carter, Ph.D.

A biologist and behavioral neurobiologist, C. Sue Carter is an internationally recognized expert in behavioral neuroendocrinology and was the first person to identify the physiological mechanisms responsible for social monogamy. She holds a Ph.D. in zoology from the University of Arkansas, and when we talked to her she was on the faculty of the College of Medicine at the University of Illinois at Chicago as professor of psychiatry and codirector of the Brain-Body Center. She is also a Fellow of the American Association for the Advancement of Science. Her research program is geared to understanding the social behavior of mammals, specifically how it pertains to the development of various mental illnesses such as autism, schizophrenia, anxiety, and depression. Carter studies social bonding, male and female parental behavior, the social control of stress reactivity, and the social control of reproduction, learning much from the socially monogamous prairie vole. She is currently the director of the Kinsey Institute and Rudy Professor of Biology, Indiana University, Bloomington.

Max Dashú

Historian Max Dashú founded the Suppressed Histories Archives in 1970 to document women's history from an international perspective. Her aim is to restore women to cultural memory, and she has collected some fifteen thousand slides and twenty thousand digital images toward this end. She has presented hundreds of slide shows at universities, community centers, bookstores, schools, libraries, prisons, galleries, festivals, and conferences around North America. Extensive research on matrifocal, or what Dashú calls "mother-right," cultures and the origins of domination have made her an expert on ancient female iconography. The archives present multitudes of forgotten women who were nevertheless influential to history as founders, chieftains, Clan Mothers, shamans, priestesses, healers, medicine women, physicians, athletes, warriors, rebels, educators, scientists, and much more. She challenges the idea that this knowledge is the sole preserve of academic specialists, and uses images to teach and make female heritages accessible to a broad range of women, both inside and outside of academia. She has published two DVDs, "Women's Power in Global Perspective," and "Woman Shaman: The Ancients." Her forthcoming book is *Witches and Pagans: Europe 700-1100.* www.SuppressedHistories.net.

Riane Eisler, J.D., Ph.D. (hon)

Riane Eisler is president of the Center for Partnership Studies and the author of *The Chalice and the Blade; Sacred Pleasure; Tomorrow's Children;* and *The Power of Partnership.* Eisler is a social scientist, attorney, and author whose work has influenced the fields of psychology, education, religious studies, economics, political science, women's studies and complex system management studies. She is the recipient of many honors, including the Humanist Pioneer Award, and membership in the World Commission on Global Consciousness and Spirituality. Her latest book, *The Real Wealth of Nations: Creating a Caring Economics,* details what each of us can do to shake ourselves out of the dominator model of society and move us forward to a more just and sustainable partnership society. www.rianeeisler.com, www.caringeconomy.org, www.centerforpartnership.org.

Nancy Jo Fox

Nancy Jo Fox is a former member of the faculty and administration of the New York School of Interior Design. She was coordinator of the certificate program where she taught color and advanced color theory, a course she created. She is an author, interior designer, lecturer, and avid collector of folk art, antique toys, and fox items. She is a member of the American Society of Interior Designers, the International Furnishings and Design Association, and the Inter-Society Color Council. She is featured in the Gold Book and *Who's Who in Interior Design in America*. She is a graduate of Duke University, B.A. Art History, and has her master's in American folk art from New York University. She worked extensively with the Museum of American Folk Art in New York City, from where her curated show, Liberties with Liberty, a collection of antique and modern folk art, toured all over the United States, and then toured internationally with a poster exhibition. The companion book to the show, *Liberties with Liberty: The Fascinating History of America's Proudest Symbol* published by Dutton in 1986, is one of the most widely quoted books on the evolution of the symbolism of the Statue of Liberty.

Selena Fox

Selena Fox graduated cum laude with a bachelor's degree in psychology from the College of William and Mary in Virginia and received a master's in counseling psychology from the University of Wisconsin, Madison. She is currently a consultant on religious diversity to federal and state government agencies and private institutions. Reverend Fox is senior minister and high priestess of Circle Sanctuary, a Wiccan church and Pagan resource center and nature preserve. A psychotherapist and independent scholar in Pagan studies, folklore, ecopsychology, and environmentalism, she is currently involved in a number of interfaith endeavors that bring together people of different spiritual and philosophical backgrounds. After several successful legal battles to maintain religious freedom for Pagans in the United States, she renamed Circle Sanctuary's Religious Freedom Network the Lady Liberty League. www.CircleSanctuary.org.

Vivien Green Fryd, Ph.D.

Vivien Green Fryd teaches American art from the colonial period to the present, as well as courses in nineteenth-century European art, methods in art history, American studies, and gender studies. She is the author of *Art and Empire: The Politics of Ethnicity in the United States Capitol, 1815–1860* and *Art and the Crisis of Marriage: Georgia O'Keeffe and Edward Hopper.* Forthcoming are *Against Our Will: Representing Sexual Trauma in American Art, 1970–2014,* which is under consideration for publication at a scholarly press, and a new book, *Trauma Writing: Henry Ries' Photographs, 1946–2004.* She is the professor and chair of the Department of History of Art at Vanderbilt University.

Douglas George-Kanentiio ("Good Pine")

Doug George-Kanentiio is a member of the Bear Clan of the Mohawk Nation at Akwesasne in New York. A former editor of *Akwesasne Notes* and *Indian Time,* he is on the board of directors of the National Museum of the American Indian, and also serves on various committees of the Mohawk Nation in respect to land claims, taxation, and a number of other contemporary issues. An award-winning columnist, he has served as advisor, producer, and scriptwriter for national television documentaries on Iroquois subjects. He wrote regular columns for the *Syracuse Herald American* and *News from Indian Country.* His books include *Skywoman: Legends of the Iroquois* (coauthored with his wife, Joanne Shenandoah), *Iroquois Culture and Commentary,* and *Indian on Fire: A Voice from the Mohawk Nation.* www.hiawatha.syr.edu.

Bruce E. Johansen, Ph.D.

A tireless researcher who has literally changed history, Bruce Johansen is a professor in the School of Communication at the University of Nebraska, Omaha, where he teaches and researches environmental issues and Native American studies. He has written more than forty books, and even more chapters for inclusion in colleagues' books, more than three dozen articles in scholarly journals, more than one hundred book reviews, and scores of additional articles. Some of his books referenced here in this book include *Forgotten Founders; Exemplar of Liberty* with Donald Grinde; and *The Global Warming Combat Manual,* one of many books in which he documents the disproportionate effects of global warming and toxic pollution on Indigenous people and what we can learn from the Native Americans about respect and reciprocity.

Mark Koltko-Rivera, Ph.D.

Mark Koltko-Rivera holds the 32nd-degree in the Scottish Rite of Freemasonry, is a Masonic Knight Templar, and has written extensively on Freemasonry, psychology, and Mormonism. He received his doctoral degree in counseling psychology from New York University in 2000 and is the author of *Freemasonry: An Introduction* and *The Rise of the Mormons: Latter-day Saint Growth in the 21st Century.* He is the founder and creative director of Free-Masonic Media, which produces online educational videos about Freemasonry at www.freemasonschool.com. His personal website is www.koltkorivera.com.

Edith Mayo

Curator Emerita in political history, Edith Mayo worked for more than forty years as a curator and historian at the Smithsonian National Museum of American History (NMAH). A graduate of George Washington University majoring in American studies, she was a member of Phi Beta Kappa. At the Smithsonian NMAH, she actively collected for the museum's holdings in the areas of women's history, politics, civil rights, and voting rights, and she strongly advocated the importance of twentieth-century collecting in museums. Mayo was several times elected to the National Council of the American Studies Association and taught about material culture in a jointly sponsored course for the Smithsonian Institution and American Studies Department at George Washington University. She lectures widely on women's history and the First Ladies and serves as a distinguished lecturer for the Organization of American Historians.

Katya Miller

A United States Capitol Historical Society Fellow, Katya Miller is a graduate of the Design Department of the University of California, Berkeley. Since an early age she has practiced the art of metalsmithing, saying that she gradually learned to let the "metals speak her." For thirty years she has been producing cultural imagery through jewelry and video. Her jewelry designs sell in museums and catalogues nationwide and at CuturalImages.net. After a mystic encounter and direct command from Lady Freedom during a deep meditation, Miller spent the better part of twenty years collecting the story of this statue, which is being turned into a book with the working title of *Beloved Freedom: The U.S. Capitol's Top Secret.* Her publications on the Statue of Freedom for *The Capitol Dome* magazine, published by the U.S. Historical Society, can be found at www.LadyFreedom.net.

Barry Moreno

Barry Moreno is librarian and historian at the Statue of Liberty National Monument and in the Museum Services Division at the Ellis Island National Museum of Immigration in New York City. He is the author of *The Statue of Liberty Encyclopedia; The Statue of Liberty;* and *Statue of Liberty—Wonder of the World.*

Aina Olomo

Her Royal Eminence Aina Olomo is an ordained priestess and titled Yoruba chief who has practiced Yoruba spiritual traditions for more than thirty years. In the Republic of Benin and Nigeria she has been restored and recognized as a member of royal lineage. She is consecrated to the Yoruba fire divinity Sango, a head mother of ancestral societies, and an ordained interfaith minister. She describes herself as a spiritual activist, a Nu-African, and an indigenous Yoruba of the Western Hemisphere. She is committed to social change, empowering the divinity of the individual, interfaith sharing, and the spiritual advancement of the Yoruba theological concepts. Chief Olomo has published several essays and an award-winning book, *Core of Fire: A Path to Yoruba Spiritual Activism.* She is an instructor, lecturer, and convener of workshops and seminars.

David Ovason

David Ovason has written many books, which include *The Zelator; The History of the Horoscope; The Secret Symbols of the Dollar Bill; Nostradamus: Prophecies for America; The Secrets of Nostradamus; The Secret Architecture of Our Nation's Capital;* and *Shakespeare's Secret Booke.* The subject of the female archetype manifests in all of his books to some degree, though he would modestly profess he is no expert. We drew on his wealth of knowledge, gleaned from primary research in the leading libraries of the world and his enormous collection of occult and astrological artwork. This knowledge encompassed a mastery of several languages, arcane symbolism, and hermetic traditions. David Ovason had a unique perspective on the theme of duality and the feminine archetype and how they apply to the American psyche.

Elaine Pagels, Ph.D.

Elaine Pagels is the Harrington Spear Paine Professor of Religion at Princeton University and the author of several books on early Christianity. She earned her Ph.D. in religion from Harvard University as part of a team studying the Nag Hammadi library manuscripts. She is best known for her 1979 book, *The Gnostic Gospels,* which won the National Book Award and was named one of the one hundred best books of the twentieth century by Modern Library. Several other books that she has written have also been bestsellers and award-winners, including those referenced here in this book: *Adam, Eve, and the Serpent; The Origin of Satan;* and *Revelations: Visions, Prophecy, and Politics in the Book of Revelation.*

Jordan Paper, Ph.D.

Jordan Paper is a professor emeritus at York University in Toronto with an academic focus on religious studies, East Asian studies, and Indigenous governance programs. He is the author of *Native North American Religious Traditions: Dancing for Life; Offering Smoke: The Sacred Pipe and Native American Religion; The Spirits Are Drunk: Comparative Approaches to Chinese Religion; Through the Earth Darkly: Female Spirituality in Comparative Perspective;* and *The Deities Are*

Many: A Polytheistic Theology, among various additional titles, articles, and presentations.

Joy Porter, Ph.D.

Professor of Indigenous history at the University of Hull in the United Kingdom, Joy Porter's specialist subjects are Indigenous history, culture and literature, modernity, U.S. Freemasonry and associationalism, ethnicity and the environment, ethnicity and the world wars, and aspects of Canadian studies. Our interviews with her focused on her 2011 book, *Native American Freemasonry: Associationalism and Performance in America* and her 2012 book, *Land and Spirit in Native America.*

Joanne Shenandoah, Ph.D. (Tekaliwah-kwa, or "She Sings")

Joanne Shenandoah is one of "America's most celebrated and critically acclaimed Native American musicians of her time," according to the Associated Press. She is a Grammy Award winner along with multiple other awards for her music, including original compositions both traditional and contemporary, and a promoter of peace through music for planetary sustainability in trust for future generations. A direct descendent of the famed Oneida Chief Shenandoah, who was a friend and ally of George Washington, Joanne Shenandoah is a founding board member of the Hiawatha Institute for Indigenous Knowledge, a nonprofit educational facility based on Iroquois principles. In 2014 she served as co-chair for the Department of Justice Attorney General's National Task Force of Children Exposed to Violence. She has performed for such noted leaders as His Holiness the Dali Lama, Nelson Mandela, Huston Smith, Mikhail Gorbachev, and is celebrated with the honor of East-West Interfaith Ministry as "a bridge for peace in and among all cultures and spiritual traditions." The prestigious locations where she has performed include the White House, five presidential inaugurations, Carnegie Hall, the Vatican—St. Peter's Basilica, Madison Square Garden, the Parliament of the World's Religions, and Woodstock '94. www.joanneshenandoah.com.

Sally Roesch Wagner, Ph.D.

Sally Roesch Wagner is a feminist pioneer, speaker, and activist, and founder of one of the first college-level women's studies programs in the United States. She is also one of the first to receive a Ph.D. for work in women's studies at the University of California, Santa Cruz. She appeared in the documentary by Ken Burns *Not for Ourselves Alone,* and in the PBS special "One Woman, One Vote." Wagner is the founding director of the Matilda Joslyn Gage Foundation in Fayetteville, New York, and an adjunct faculty member at Syracuse University. She received the Katherine Coffey Award for outstanding service to museology from the Mid-Atlantic Association of Museums in 2012 for her development of the Matilda Joslyn Gage Center for Social Justice Dialogue. Her written works include *A Time of Protest: Suffragists Challenge the Republic; Sisters in Spirit: Iroquois Influence on Early Feminists;* and the introduction to the 2002 edition of Matilda Joslyn Gage's *Woman, Church and State.* www.sallyroeschwagner.com.

Jack Weatherford, Ph.D.

A cultural anthropologist who emphasizes the role of tribal people in world history, Jack Weatherford's most popular book was *Genghis Khan and the Making of the Modern World,* which turned in to an international bestseller published in more than twenty languages. He was awarded the Order of the Polar Star in 2007 by the president of Mongolia. His other titles that are referenced in this book are *Indian Givers: How Native Americans Transformed the World* and *Native Roots: How the Indians Enriched America.* Weatherford has taught anthropology at Macalester College in Minnesota since 1983. He graduated from the University of South Carolina in 1967 with a bachelor's degree in political science followed by a master's degree in sociology in 1972. He also received a master's degree in anthropology in 1973 and a doctorate in anthropology from the University of California, San Diego. He says that "we haven't yet discovered America," and until we acknowledge what parts of "us" are Native American, we will not really know ourselves.

Brief Biographies of a Few Female Leaders We Should Have Learned about in School

This appendix is intended as just a sampling to get you started. We urge you to look up the full biographies of these women and follow the trails to learn about even more inspirational women like them who are hidden behind the lines of standard history textbooks. Many famous notable women are not included here in this list because we briefly mentioned them earlier in the book itself.

Jane Addams (1860–1935) won the Nobel Peace Prize in 1931 for her work reforming social conditions for the poor, women, juveniles, and laborers. "Politics is housekeeping on a grand scale" is her famous quote, expressing the sentiment of many reformers who believed liberating women, with their particular domestic skills, and allowing them power outside of the home would improve the community at large.

Mary McLeod Bethune (1875–1955) pioneered education for Black children, established schools, and advocated for civil rights. She also became an advisor to President Franklin Roosevelt, promoting what education could do for Black Americans.

Elizabeth Blackwell, M.D. (1821–1910) was one of the first women to get a degree in medicine in the United States. Afterward, however, she could not find employment, so she founded a social welfare organization in order to be able to practice in her chosen field.

Lydia Maria Child (1802–1880) wrote many books, including an influential cookbook that was in almost every kitchen. Her first novel, about a Native American and a white woman, was also one of the first anti-slavery tracts in the country. In it she documented that the first enslaved people in this land were Native Americans, not Blacks.

Christine de Pizan (1364–1429), born in Venice, was the first professional female writer in Europe, serving as a court writer for French royalty. She wrote about women's rights in the late medieval ages and asserted the common humanity of woman. One of her most famous works, *Book of the City of Ladies,* described famous women who influenced history and used an allegorical female named Reason to argue that stereotypes about the weaknesses of women persist only because women were prevented from participating in society.

Tennessee Claflin (1845–1923) and her sister Victoria Woodhull created a sensation in the suffrage movement by advocating sexual liberation and dress reform. She was a founding member of the Wall Street investment firm Woodhull, Claflin & Company, one of the first Wall Street brokerage firms opened by women.

Cockacoeske (circa 1640–1686) was one of the female leaders of the Pamunkey, part of the Powhatan confederacy in the Virginia area. These are the people of the Pocahontas legend who kept the Jamestown settlers alive during their first winter of 1607. Cockacoeske herself was recorded in the Virginia colony history as a female diplomat who tried to negotiate terms with the British after the border disputes that led up to Bacon's Rebellion in 1675 when frontiersmen were pushing to expand into Indian lands. As leader of her people, she tried to work within the

British legal system to maintain peace and protect and strengthen their intertribal confederacy.

Female Leaders of the Early Christian Church (first four centuries, CE). As scholars like Elaine Pagels open up the field of biblical history, the names of the women who followed Jesus in leadership roles in his church are being revealed. They include Junia (first century), an apostle whom Paul described as superior to himself; Thecla (30 CE), a follower of Paul; Melania (325–410), who traveled freely as a holy pilgrim; and Prisca and Maximilla (late second century), who were leaders and may have been the founders of the Montanist Movement.

Deborah Sampson Gannett (1760–1827) was the first-ever woman to go on a public lecture tour in the new United States. In 1802 she thrilled audiences by recounting how she had disguised herself as a man and fought in the Revolutionary War. Inspiring though she was as a living example of the competence and aptitude of women, she worked hard not to upset the socially accepted gender role restrictions too much. She always began her lectures by praising the proper role of women as that of a wife and mother, insisting their chief responsibility was to shape the moral character of their men.

The Grimké Sisters (Angelina 1805–1879 and Sarah 1792–1873) were early abolitionists, despite being raised in wealthy, slaveholding privilege in South Carolina. In the 1830s they lectured against slavery and advocated for women's rights. They were sanctioned by their ministers especially for reporting on female slaves being raped by their masters, because it was believed that women should not speak about such things. They were the first women to defy the taboo against women speaking publicly against slavery.

Francis Ellen Watkins Harper (1825–1911) was a Black woman who had been born free in Baltimore. She supported herself from the age of thirteen, and in the 1850s she became involved in the abolition and woman suffrage movements, helping found the National Association of

Colored Women. She published the first novel by a Black woman and reported on the status of free Blacks and particularly the role of women rebuilding the South after the Civil War.

Clara Lemlich (1886–1982) was an organizer of working women and an early leader of the International Ladies' Garment Workers' Union. In 1909 she spearheaded a strike of twenty thousand New York garment workers, which was the impetus behind the unionization of many factories and the improvement of deplorable conditions for the workers, the majority of whom were women. Unfortunately for the women working at the Triangle Shirtwaist Factory, the reforms did not reach everywhere, and it was only a year later that that notorious building went up in flames, trapping and killing almost 150 women.

Edmonia Lewis (1844–1907) was a remarkable artist and a contemporary of Thomas Crawford and Auguste Bartholdi. An African American/Native American woman, she studied sculpting in Rome and gained recognition and large commissions for her neoclassical statues. Many of her most famous works feature the broken chains of slavery.

Jane McCrae (1752–1777) was a propaganda instrument cleverly manipulated to raise interest in the American cause, thereby helping to turn the tide of the Revolution. Her death scene was portrayed in paintings and written about by propagandists such as Joel Barlow, Philip Freneau, Mercy Otis Warren, and later James Fenimore Cooper. McCrae was a young Tory who was mistakenly killed and scalped by Native Americans allied with the British, and the colonial patriots seized on her violent death as a demonstration of the cruelty of the Native Americans. Many new converts to the patriot cause were created as a result of the death of Jane McCrae.

Lucretia Mott (1793–1880) was a preacher of the Quaker faith who sermonized against slavery and was one of the first woman suffrage activists. Together with Elizabeth Cady Stanton, she organized and coauthored the Declaration of Sentiments for the 1848 Seneca Falls Convention.

Eliza Lucas Pinckney (1722–1793) ran her father's vast South Carolina estate from the time she was a teenager. Given unusual freedom and education by her family, she experimented with the crops until perfecting an innovation in the cultivation of indigo, which led to indigo becoming one of the most lucrative exports of the colonies. Eliza Pinckney also raised her children to be active patriots. Two of her sons became influential leaders in the new federal government: Thomas Pinckney was ambassador to Great Britain and envoy to Spain and nominated for vice president in 1796; Charles Cotesworth Pinckney was a signer of the Constitution and nominated as vice president in 1800, and for president in 1804 and 1808.

Susie King Taylor (1848–1912) was a slave who learned to read in secret, escaped slavery, became a nurse in the Union Army during the Civil War, and continued teaching other Black people to read. After the war, she established several schools and taught many freed slaves to read.

Mary Walker, M.D. (1832–1919) wore men's clothing to serve as a surgeon during the Civil War and advocated her whole career against the unhygienic and restrictive requirements of women's fashions. For her bravery in venturing into enemy territory to treat the wounded, she was awarded the congressional Medal of Honor. She is the only woman to ever receive this, the nation's highest military honor, which was later revoked, only to be restored again in 1977.

Wetamo, or Wetamoo (circa 1635–1676) was a female leader of the Wampanoag warriors in Metacomet's campaign. She fought against the colonists in Rhode Island in what is known as King Philip's War.

Frances Wright (1795–1852) was a Scottish-born reformer who founded utopian communities to educate slaves and work toward abolition in the United States. She wrote about sexual freedom, birth control, interracial relationships, woman suffrage, and in defense of Native Americans.

Notes

Chapter 1. What Do We Mean by "The Secret Life of Lady Liberty"?

1. Trachtenberg, *The Statue of Liberty,* 15.
2. Boime, *Unveiling,* xiii.
3. Bolen, *Goddesses in Everywoman,* 20–21; and Baring and Cashford, *Myth,* 302.
4. Pellegrino, D'Amato, and Weisberg, "Gender Dividend."
5. Trachtenberg, *The Statue of Liberty,* 79.
6. Zinn, *People's History,* 9–10.
7. Dashú, "Meanings of Goddess."
8. Ibid.
9. John Adams's papers available online from the National Archives, http://goo.gl/gchFDE, accessed April 20, 2016.
10. Shlain, *Alphabet,* 407.
11. Sandberg, *Lean In,* 172.
12. The Dalai Lama quoted at the Vancouver Peace Summit in 2009.

Chapter 2. Where Are Your Women?

1. Inter-Parliamentary Union, "Women in National Parliaments Situation as of June 2015."
2. Pellegrino, D'Amato, and Weisberg, "Gender Dividend."
3. As quoted in Moore, Brooks, and Wigginton, *Transatlantic Feminisms,* 5.
4. The 1781 treaty negotiation speech: Report of Proceedings of a Commission Appointed by General Nathanael Green on 26 February 1781 to Conduct

Talks with the Cherokees, Nathanael Greene Papers, 1775–1785, folder 5, Library of Congress; Speech of Cherokee Women to General Greene's Commission, July 26–August 2, 1781; Nancy Ward Speech to the U.S. Treaty Commissioner (1781); Speech to the U.S. Treaty Commissioners (1785); and Cherokee Women to Governor Benjamin Franklin (September 8, 1787). As quoted in Moore, Brooks, and Wigginton, *Transatlantic Feminisms,* 180.

5. "Substance of the Speech of Good Peter to Governor Clinton and the Commissioners of Indian Affairs at Albany," Collections of the New York Historical Society, 1st Series (1814), vol. 2, 115, quoted in Beauchamp, "Iroquois Women," 87. Also found in Grinde and Johansen, *Exemplar,* 223.

6. Grinde and Johansen, *Exemplar,* 218–20; and Johansen, *Debating Democracy,* 119.

7. Mann, *Iroquoian Women,* 112; and Dashú, "Female Divinity in South America."

8. Dashú, "Meanings of Goddess."

9. Pemberton, "The Carvers of the Northeast" in *Yoruba: Nine Centuries of African Art and Thought,* eds. Henry John Drewel, et al. (New York: Harry Abrams, 1989), 210, quoted in Dashú, "Meanings."

10. Gage, *Woman,* 44.

11. Ibid., 43.

12. Moreno, *Encyclopedia,* 172.

13. Spiering, *Bearer of a Million Dreams.*

14. Kimura, "Men and Women Display Patterns of Behavioral and Cognitive Differences."

15. Fine, "Will Working Mothers' Brains Explode?"

16. Angier, "The Biology Behind the Milk of Human Kindness."

17. Carter, "Motherhood."

18. Ibid.

19. MacDonald and MacDonald, "The Peptide That Binds," 10.

20. Eisler, *The Chalice and the Blade,* 162; Wood, *Radicalism,* 147; and Berkin, *First Generations,* 27.

21. Eisler, "What's Good for Women Is Good for the World."

22. Ibid.

23. "List of Women CEOs of Fortune 500 Companies," Wikipedia.

24. Pellegrino, D'amato, and Weisberg, "Gender Dividend."

25. Bolen, "Why I Persevere in Advocating."

26. "Letter to Harry Burn from Mother," Knox County Tennessee Public Library, http://goo.gl/VzT9JK, accessed July 31, 2015.
27. Newton-Small, "11 Things You Don't Know About the Senate Sisterhood."

Chapter 3. What the Statue of Liberty Learned from the Indian Princess

1. Bartholdi, *Statue of Liberty*, 20.
2. Kammen, "From Liberty to Prosperity," 259; and Taylor, *America as Art*, xi.
3. Higham, "Indian Princess," 61; and Fischer, *Liberty and Freedom*, 234.
4. Fryd, "Hiram Powers."
5. Warner, *Monuments*, 273.
6. Fryd, "Hiram Powers"; and Moreno, *Encyclopedia*, 144.
7. Wood, *Radicalism*, 109.
8. Ibid., 61.
9. Holmes, *Faiths*, 56.
10. Ibid., 44.
11. Ibid., 47, 106.
12. Taylor, *America as Art*, x; and Higham, "Indian Princess," 50–52.
13. Higham, "Indian Princess," 53.
14. Day, "With Peace."
15. Honour, *New Golden Land*, 93.
16. As quoted in Honour, *New Golden Land*, 119–20.
17. Wood, *Radicalism*, 109.
18. Commager, *The Empire of Reason*.
19. Grinde and Johansen, *Exemplar*, 32–33.
20. Weatherford, *Indian Givers*, 138; and Grinde and Johansen, *Exemplar*, 142–68.
21. George-Kanentiio, *Iroquois Culture and Commentary*, 112–13.
22. Grinde and Johansen, *Exemplar*, xxiii, 93–109, 163.
23. Charles F. Adams, ed., *The Works of John Adams* (Boston: Little, Brown & Co., 1851), 4:292, as quoted in Grinde and Johansen, *Exemplar*, 200.
24. Foner, *Complete Writings of Thomas Paine*, 1:610, as quoted in Grinde and Johansen, *Exemplar*, 152.
25. Grinde and Johansen, *Exemplar*, 142–68.
26. Father Joseph François Lafitau, *Customs of the American Indians Compared with the Customs of Primitive Times*, eds. and trans. Williams N. Fenton

and Elizabeth L. Moore. 2 vols. 1724. (Toronto: The Champlain Society, 1974), I: 69, as quoted in Mann, *Iroquoian Women,* 182.

27. Allen, *The Sacred Hoop,* 39.

28. Day, "With Peace"; and Berkin, *First Generations,* 43–44.

29. Mann, *Iroquoian Women,* 20.

30. Green, "The Pocahontas Perplex"; and Allen, *Pocahontas,* 4.

31. Higham, "Indian Princess," 76–77.

32. Allen, *Pocahontas,* 18–21.

33. Higham, "Indian Princess," 76–77.

34. As quoted in Gschaedler, *True Light,* 29.

35. Laboulaye, *Histoire du Droit,* 241.

Chapter 4. Goddesses Were Everywhere

1. Wood, *Radicalism,* 165.

2. Fleming, "From Indian Princess to Greek Goddess," 66.

3. Higham, "Indian Princess," 55.

4. Fryd, *Art and Empire,* 157.

5. Kammen, "From Liberty to Prosperity," 272.

6. Wood, *Radicalism,* 230.

7. Grinde and Johansen, *Exemplar,* 210–14.

8. Taylor, *America as Art,* 14, 90.

9. Fleming, "The American Image as Indian Princess."

10. Higham, "Indian Princess," 62.

11. Kammen, "From Liberty to Prosperity," 263–64.

12. Fischer, *Liberty and Freedom,* 233.

13. Wood, *Radicalism,* 216.

14. Ibid., 215.

15. Ibid., 218.

16. Fischer, *Liberty and Freedom,* 135.

17. Ibid.

18. Fleming, "From Indian Princess to Greek Goddess," 64.

19. Higham, "Indian Princess," 74.

20. Fleming, "From Indian Princess to Greek Goddess."

21. As quoted in Kerber, *Women of the Republic,* 230.

22. Gschaedler, *True Light,* 81.

23. Joel Pett, interview by Dr. Bob Hieronimus, *21st Century Radio,* June 15, 2014.

24. Zinn, *People's History,* 57–58.

Chapter 5. Colossal Statuary Consists of More than Size

1. Bartholdi, *Statue of Liberty*, 33.
2. Moreno, *Encyclopedia*, 133.
3. Ibid.
4. Ibid., 32
5. Gschaedler, *True Light*, 6.
6. Ibid.
7. Ibid., 8.
8. Gschaedler, *True Light*, 30; and Berenson, *The Statue of Liberty*, 15.
9. Moreno, *Encyclopedia*, 134; and Dillon and Kotler, *The Statue of Liberty Revisited*, 6.
10. Moreno, *Encyclopedia*, 134.
11. Provoyeur and Hargrove, *Liberty*, 44.
12. Moreno, *Encyclopedia*, 33.
13. Bartholdi, *Statue of Liberty*, 36.
14. Trachtenberg, *The Statue of Liberty*, 81.
15. Gschaedler, *True Light*, 17.
16. Ibid., 20.
17. Ibid., 9.
18. Boime, *Hollow Icons*, 91.
19. Berenson, *Statue*, 36.
20. Moreno, *Encyclopedia*, 40.
21. Berenson, *Statue*, 24.
22. Bartholdi, *Statue of Liberty*, 20.
23. Silverman, "Liberty, Maternity, Commodification."
24. Blanchet and Dard, *Statue of Liberty*, 11.
25. Boime, *Unveiling*, 95, 100.
26. As quoted in Gschaedler, *True Light*, 42.
27. Provoyeur and Hargrove, *Liberty*, 30.
28. Blanchet and Dard, *Statue of Liberty*, 67–68.
29. Mitchell, *Liberty's Torch*, 150.
30. Ibid., 217.
31. Moreno, *Encyclopedia*, 64.
32. "Immigration Act of 1924," Wikipedia.
33. Bartholdi, *Statue of Liberty*, 57.

Chapter 6. Behind the Statue of Liberty
Is Her Earth-Mother Indian Queen

1. Lyons and Mohawk, *Exiled in the Land of the Free,* 12.

2. Paper, *Through the Earth Darkly,* 112.

3. Higham, "Indian Princess and Roman Goddess," 50.

4. Babcock, "Taking Liberties," 403.

5. Corbeiller, "Miss America and Her Sisters," 209.

6. Ibid.

7. Kolodny, *The Lay of the Land,* 8–9.

8. Robert Johnson's "Nova Britannia: Offering Most Excellent Fruites by Planting in Virginia. Exciting All Such as Be Well Affected to Further the Same" (London, 1609), 11; Walter Raleigh's "Discovery of Guinana" (1595) in Howard Mumford Jones, *O Strange New World: American Culture—The Formative Years* (New York: Viking Press, 1964), 48; and John Smith, "A Description of New England," in *Force's Tracts,* vol. 2, p. 9, as quoted in Kolodny, *Lay of the Land,* 4.

9. Ibid., 5.

10. As quoted in Gallagher, "America."

11. Gallagher, "America."

12. Dashú, "Female Divinity South America."

13. As quoted in Cohen, "Naming of America."

14. Cohen, "Naming of America."

15. "Population History of Indigenous Peoples of the Americas," Wikipedia. Original source: "La catastrophe démographique" [The Demographical Catastrophe] *L'Histoire* no. 322, July–August 2007, 17, accessed July 31, 2015.

16. Mann, *1491,* 50.

17. As quoted in Gschaedler, *True Light,* 31.

18. Weatherford, *Native Roots,* 40–50.

19. Powell, "Columbus' Arrival Linked to Carbon Dioxide Drop."

20. George-Kanentiio, *Iroquois Culture,* 78.

21. Paper, *Native North American Relligious Traditions,* 15.

22. Ibid.

23. Ibid., 12–13.

24. Ibid., 8.

25. Ibid., 94; and Christ, "Why Women Need the Goddess."

26. Kingsolver, "The Weight of a Falling Sky."

27. "Gender and the Environment," *The Global Development Research Center,* www.gdrc.org/gender/gender-envi.html, accessed March 21, 2015.

28. LaDuke, "The Indigenous Women's Network."

29. Ibid.

30. Rachel's Network, "When Women Lead."

31. George-Kanentiio, *Iroquois Culture,* 40.

32. Smith, "For All Those Who Were Indian in a Former Life."

33. LaDuke, "The Indigenous Women's Network."

34. Ibid.

35. Johansen, *Indigenous Peoples,* 368.

36. LaDuke, "The Indigenous Women's Network"; and Johansen, *Indigenous Peoples,* 373.

37. Johansen, *The Global Warming Combat Manual,* xx, xxii.

38. Exxon Secrets, "How ExxonMobil Funds the Climate Change Skeptics," www.exxonsecrets.org/maps.php, accessed March 28, 2015.

39. Spretnak, *Lost Goddesses,* 105–6.

Chapter 7. How the Statue of Liberty Became the Whore of Babylon

1. Baring and Cashford, *Myth,* 43.

2. Ibid., 490–99; and Eisler, interview by Dr. Bob Hieronimus, *Lady Liberty Radio Interview Series, 21st Century Radio,* March 20, 2011.

3. Baring and Cashford, *Myth,* 490.

4. Pagels, *Adam, Eve, and the Serpent,* 24.

5. Shlain, *Alphabet,* viii.

6. Pagels, *Adam, Eve, and the Serpent,* 145.

7. Patai, *The Hebrew Goddess,* 4.

8. Ibid., 19.

9. Baring and Cashford, *Myth,* 499.

10. Ibid., 495.

11. Pagels, *The Origin of Satan,* 16.

12. Pagels, *Revelations,* 33.

13. Ibid., 173.

14. Ibid.

15. Marija Gimbutas, interview by David Jay Brown, *Mavericks of the Mind,* www.mavericksofthemind.com/gim-int.htm, accessed April 20, 2014.

16. Pagels, *Origin of Satan,* 130.

17. Hofstadter, "The Paranoid Style in American Politics."

18. Green, "Understanding."

19. Berkin, *First Generations,* 41–46.

20. Green, "Understanding."

21. See the chapter on the Statue of Liberty in Hieronimus and Cortner, *United Symbolism of America.*

22. Bartholdi, *Statue of Liberty,* 36.

23. Gschaedler, *True Light,* 15.

24. Dice, "What Brad Meltzer's Decoded Missed."

25. Blanchet and Dard, *Statue of Liberty,* 47.

26. Provoyeur and Hargrove, *Liberty,* 30.

27. Blanchet and Dard, *Statue of Liberty,* 53.

28. "The Statue Unveiled," *New York Times,* October 29, 1886.

29. As quoted in Trachtenberg, *The Statue of Liberty,* 214.

30. Gschaedler, *True Light,* 115.

31. Eisler, "What's Good for Women Is Good for the World."

32. Schwartz, "The Vagina Battles."

33. Ibid.

34. Schwartz bases much of his work on Cahn and Carbone, *Red Families v. Blue Families.*

35. Schwartz, "Vagina Battles"; and Schwartz, "Social Values."

36. Schwartz, "Social Values."

37. Gore, "False Spontaneity of the Tea Party."

38. Dubose, "Producers of BPA."

Chapter 8. The Black Statue of Liberty

1. *Statue of Liberty,* DVD, directed by Ken Burns.

2. Lewis, "'Liberty's Gala Perplexes Black Patriots."

3. Raboteau, *Canaan Land,* 72.

4. Editorial, *The Cleveland Gazette,* November 27, 1886, 2.

5. Joseph, Rosenblatt, and Kinebrew, "The Black Statue of Liberty Rumor."

6. Hamilton, "Pocahontas"

7. Berkin, *First Generations,* 105–9.

8. Zinn, *People's History,* 59.

9. *Liberty! The American Revolution,* DVD, directed by Ellen Hovde and Muffie Meyer.

10. Kammen, *Spheres of Liberty,* 264–66.

11. Basler, *The Collected Works of Abraham Lincoln,* 7:301–2, as quoted in Kammen, *Spheres of Liberty,* 7.

12. Moreno, *Encyclopedia,* 57–58.

13. Joseph, Roseblatt, and Kinebrew, "Black Statue of Liberty Rumor."

14. Women in World History Curriculum, "Debating Conflicting Rights, United States, 1867–69."

15. Ibid.

16. Inter-Parliamentary Union, "Women in National Parliaments Situation as of June 2015."

17. Wagner, *Time of Protest,* 10.

18. Berkin, *First Generations,* 120–21.

19. Berkin, *First Generations,* 116–17; and Chireau, *Black Magic,* xx.

20. Douglass, *Narrative of the Life of Frederick Douglass,* 66.

21. Prison Policy Initiative, "States of Incarceration: The Global Context."

22. Pew Center on the States, "One in 100: Behind Bars in America."

23. *Black Statue of Liberty* (Live at the Apollo Theater), 1995, http://jessicacaremoore.com/portfolio-item/black-statue-liberty-live-apollo-theater, accessed June 10, 2015.

Chapter 9. The Statue of Liberty and the Secrets of Mary

1. Cunneen, *In Search of Mary,* 220.

2. Ibid., 222.

3. Warner, *Alone,* 390, citing Demarest and Taylor, 30ff.

4. Provoyeur and Hargrove, *Liberty,* 259, 270.

5. Warner, *Monuments,* 10.

6. Heiler, "The Madonna as Religious Symbol," 356.

7. Ibid., 352.

8. Gage, *Woman,* 414; and Warner, *Alone,* 338.

9. Campbell, *Mystic Vision,* 350.

10. Warner, *Alone,* 338.

11. Begg, *Cult of the Black Virgin,* 129; and Markale, *Women of the Celts,* 173–74.

12. Warner, *Monuments,* 184.

13. Beavis, "The Cathar Mary Magdalene and the Sacred Feminine."

14. As quoted in Wagner, *Sisters in Spirit,* 18.

15. As quoted in Wagner, *Matilda Joslyn Gage,* 41.

16. Gage, *Woman*, 484.

17. Wagner, *Matilda Joslyn Gage*, 46–47.

18. Ibid., 56–57.

19. Agulhon, "On Political Allegory," 169.

20. Trachtenberg, *The Statue of Liberty*, 196.

21. Silverman, "Liberty, Maternity, Commodification."

22. Blanchet and Dard, *Statue of Liberty*, 48.

23. Blumenthal, *France and the United States*, 167–80, as quoted in Glassberg, "Rethinking the Statue of Liberty," 3.

24. Moreno, *Encyclopedia*, 175; and Boime, *Unveiling*, 100.

Chapter 10. The Liberty to Choose What to Believe

1. Warner, *Monuments*, 282.

2. Agulhon, "On Political Allegory," 168.

3. Hobsbawm, "Man and Woman in Socialist Iconography," 122; Boime, *Hollow Icons*, 9; Trachtenberg, *The Statue of Liberty*, 67; and Warner, *Monuments*, 271.

4. Warner, *Monuments*, 271.

5. As quoted in Silverman, "Liberty, Maternity, Commodification," from Victor Hugo's *Choses Vues*, published posthumously in 1887.

6. Warner, *Monuments*, 286.

7. Schiebinger, *Nature's Body*, 175–79; and Gough, *The Terror in the French Revolution*.

8. Landes, *Visualizing the Nation*, 45.

9. Warner, *Monuments*, 282, 289.

10. Kerber, *Women of the Republic*, 104.

11. Cunneen, *In Search of Mary*, 206.

12. Baring and Cashford, *Myth*, 646; Beavis, "The Cathar Mary Magdalene and the Sacred Feminine."

13. Gage, *Woman*, 414; and Warner, *Alone*, 338.

14. Pagels, *Gnostic Gospels*, 49–59.

15. Wagner, in the introduction to Gage, *Woman, Church and State*, 20, quoting Gage from a review of the book *Woman, Church and State* in the Fayetteville *Weekly Recorder*, 1893.

16. Pagels, *Gnostic Gospels*, xx.

17. Hieronimus, *Kabbalistic Teachings of the Female Prophets*, 15.

18. Pagels, *Gnostic Gospels*, 61.

19. Gage, *Woman,* 40, 483.
20. Pagels, *Gnostic Gospels,* xix.

Chapter 11. Armed Liberty

1. Fryd, *Art and Empire,* 110.
2. As quoted in Fryd, *Art and Empire,* 193.
3. Miller, "An Appreciation of Thomas Crawford's Statue of Freedom."
4. Fryd, "Lifting the Veil."
5. Hazelton, *National Capitol,* as quoted in Fryd, "Lifting the Veil."
6. Laboulaye, "Speech at the Opera of Paris," April 25, 1876, as quoted in Blanchet and Dard, *Statue of Liberty,* 44; and Boime, *Hollow Icons,* 121.
7. Bayliss, "The Three Faces, All of Them Female, of Liberty."
8. Fryd, "The Statue of Liberty."
9. As quoted in Miller "Freedom Speaks through Us."
10. Anderson, "'The Temple of Minerva' and Francis Hopkinson," 166.
11. Moreno, *Encyclopedia,* 135; and Fischer, *Liberty and Freedom,* 370.
12. Moreno, *Encyclopedia,* 135; Trachtenberg, *The Statue of Liberty,* 82; and Boime, *Unveiling,* 87.
13. As quoted in Moreno, *Encyclopedia,* 135.
14. Bartholdi, *Statue of Liberty,* 17.
15. Baring and Cashford, *Myth,* 344.
16. Elias-Button, "Athene and Medusa."
17. Ibid.
18. Ibid.
19. Baring and Cashford, *Myth,* 14.
20. Bolen, *Goddesses in Everywoman,* 106.

Chapter 12. Lady Liberty and Her Sisters

1. Roberts, *Ladies of Liberty,* 394.
2. As quoted in Roberts, *Founding Mothers,* 49.
3. As quoted in Berkin, *First Generations,* 173.
4. As quoted in Kerber, *Women of the Republic,* 41.
5. Wagner, *Matilda Joslyn Gage,* 16; Berkin, *First Generations,* 172; and Roberts, *Founding Mothers.*
6. Berkin, *First Generations,* 180.
7. Kerber, *Women of the Republic,* 44.
8. As quoted in Roberts, *Founding Mothers,* 29.

9. Kerber, *Women of the Republic*, 57.

10. Berkin, *First Generations*, 187.

11. Kerber, *Women of the Republic*, 83.

12. Warren, *History*, 136.

13. Correspondence between Abigail Adams and John Adams is available online from the National Archives. See letters dated March 31, 1776 (http://goo.gl/H4XFDk); April 14, 1776 (two letters, http://goo.gl/7MeHED and http://goo.gl/jbWjaD); and May 7, 1776 (http://goo.gl/EYso5r).

14. Kerber, *Women of the Republic*, 11, 199–200.

15. Berkin, *First Generations*, 196–97.

16. Kerber, *Women of the Republic*, 225–26.

17. Berkin, *First Generations*, 34.

18. Kerber, *Women of the Republic*, 193.

19. As quoted in Kerber, *Women of the Republic*, 218.

20. Kerber, *Women of the Republic*, 225–26.

21. Ortner, "The Virgin and the State," 22; Babcock, "Taking Liberties," 402.

22. Wood, *Radicalism*, 331.

23. Mitch Horowitz, interview by Dr. Bob Hieronimus, *21st Century Radio*, October 18, 2009.

24. Wood, *Empire of Liberty*, 486–87.

25. Fischer, *Liberty and Freedom*, 449–50.

26. Ibid., 663.

Chapter 13. A Delightful Inconsistency

1. Wagner, *Time of Protest*, 151.

2. Gschaedler, *True Light*, 150.

3. "The Statue Unveiled," *New York Times*, October 29, 1886.

4. "Early Suffrage Protests," *New York Times*, July 11, 1915.

5. "They Enter a Protest," *New York Times*, October 29, 1886.

6. *The Woman's Journal*, November 1886 as quoted in Wagner, *Time of Protest*, 113–14.

7. As quoted in Wagner, *Time of Protest*, 127.

8. As quoted in the introduction to Gage, *Woman*, 8.

9. As quoted in Wagner, *Time of Protest*, 117.

10. Boime, *Hollow Icons*, 113.

11. Green, "Understanding."

12. Warner, *Monuments*, 6.

13. W. E. B. Du Bois, *Black Reconstruction*, as quoted in Zinn, *People's History*, 210.

14. Wagner, *Time of Protest*, 107.

15. Zinn, *People's History*, 270.

16. "The Statue Unveiled," *New York Times*, October 29, 1886.

17. As quoted in Boime, *Hollow Icons*, 133.

18. Ibid., 134.

19. Warner, *Monuments*, 13.

20. As quoted in Boime, *Unveiling*, 116–17.

21. *New York Tribune*, October, 29, 1886, 2, as quoted in Wagner, *Time of Protest*, 109.

22. "Women Ask Votes at Liberty's Feet," *New York Times*, July 6, 1915.

23. Miller, *Women Are People!* 87–88.

24. This section is based on interviews between Laura Cortner and Jacqui Ceballos on January 8, 2014, Mavra Stark on January 6, 2015, Carole De Saram on January 21, 2015, and Marjorie DeFazio on January 22, 2015.

Chapter 14. The Statue of Liberty as a Symbol for the Future

1. Campbell, *Goddesses*, xiv.

2. *The Woman's Journal*, November 1886 as quoted in Wagner, *Time of Protest*, 113–14.

3. As quoted in Kaminski, *Lafayette*, 101.

Bibliography

Adams, Charles F., ed. *The Works of John Adams*. Boston: Little, Brown & Co., 1851.

Aguila, Dani, comp. and ed. *Taking Liberty with the Lady, by Cartoonists from Around the World*. Nashville, Tenn.: Eagle Nest Press, 1986.

Agulhon, Maurice. *Marianne into Battle: Republican Imagery and Symbolism in France, 1789–1880*. Translated by J. Lloyd. New York: Cambridge University Press, 1981.

———. "On Political Allegory: A reply to Eric Hobsbawm." *History Workshop Journal* 8, no. 1 (1979): 167–73.

Allen, Paula Gunn. *Pocahontas: Medicine Woman, Spy, Entrepreneur, Diplomat*. New York: HarperCollins, 2003.

———. *The Sacred Hoop: Recovering the Feminine in American Indian Traditions*. Boston: Beacon Press, 1992.

Anderson, Gillian B. "'The Temple of Minerva' and Francis Hopkinson: A Reappraisal of America's First Poet-Composer," *Proceedings of the American Philosophical Society* 120, no. 3 (June 1976): 166.

Angier, Natalie. "The Biology behind the Milk of Human Kindness." *New York Times,* November 24, 2009.

America: The Story of Us. DVD. Executive Producers Jane Root and Michael Jackson, produced by Nutopia for History, 2010.

Arce, Enrique J. "Amerigo Vespucci and the Name America." *Inter-America* 1 (August 1918): 323–32.

Babcock, Barbara A. "Taking Liberties, Writing from the Margins, and Doing it with a Difference." *The Journal of American Folklore* 100, no. 398, Folklore and Feminism (Oct.–Dec., 1987): 390–411.

Babcock, Barbara A., and John J. MacAloon. "Everybody's Gal: Women, Boundaries, and Monuments." In *The Statue of Liberty Revisited: Making of a Universal Symbol,* Wilton S. Dillon and Neil G. Kotler, eds., 79–99. Washington, D.C.: Smithsonian Institution Press, 1994.

Bales, Karen L., Ericka Boone, Pamela Epperson, Gloria Hoffman and C. Sue Carter. "Are behavioral effects of early experience mediated by oxytocin?" *Frontiers in Psychiatry* 1, no. 24 (May 2011): 1–12.

Bangs, Herbert. "The Two Marys." *The Feminine Face of God: Searching for the Divine Mother in the History of the Western World.* Unpublished manuscript, December 21, 2009.

Baring, Anne, and Jules Cashford. *The Myth of the Goddess: Evolution of an Image.* London: Arkana/Penguin, 1993.

Barreiro, Jose, ed. "A View from the Shore: American Indian Perspectives on the Quincentenary." Special issue, *Northeast Indian Quarterly* 7, no. 3 (Fall 1990).

Barry, John M. *Roger Williams and the Creation of the American Soul: Church, State, and the Birth of Liberty.* New York: Viking Adult, 2012.

Bartholdi, Frédéric Auguste. *The Statue of Liberty Enlightening the World Described by the Sculptor.* Published for the Benefit of the Pedestal Fund. New York: North American Review, 1885.

Basler, Roy P. ed. *The Collected Works of Abraham Lincoln.* New Brunswick, N.J.: Rutgers University Press, 1953.

Bayliss, Sarah. "The Three Faces, All of Them Female, of Liberty." *New York Times,* July 2, 2000.

Beauchamp, W. M. "Iroquois Women." *The Journal of American Folklore* 13, no. 49 (April–June 1900): 87.

Beavis, Mary Ann. "The Cathar Mary Magdalene and the Sacred Feminine: Pop Culture Legend vs. Medieval Doctrine." *Journal of Religion and Popular Culture* 24, no. 3 (Fall 2012): 419–31.

Begg, Ean. *The Cult of the Black Virgin.* Asheville, N.C.: Chiron Publications, 2006.

Berenson, Edward. *The Statue of Liberty: A Transatlantic Story.* New Haven, Conn.: Yale University Press, 2012.

Berkin, Carol. *First Generations: Women in Colonial America.* New York: Hill and Wang, 1996.

Black Statue of Liberty (Live at the Apollo Theater). http://jessicacaremoore .com/portfolio-item/black-statue-liberty-live-apollo-theater, 1995. Accessed June 10, 2015.

Blanchet, Christian, and Bertrand Dard. *Statue of Liberty: The First Hundred Years.* Translated by Bernard Weisberger. New York: American Heritage Press, 1985.

Blumenthal, Henry. *France and the United States: Their Diplomatic Relations, 1789–1914.* Chapel Hill: University of North Carolina Press, 1970.

Bodnar, John. "Symbols and Servants: Immigrant America and the Limits of Public History." *The Journal of American History* 73, no. 1 (June 1986): 137–51.

Bodnar, John, Laura Burt, Jennifer Stinson, and Barbara Truesdell. *The Changing Face of the Statue of Liberty.* Center for the Study of History and Memory, Indiana University. A Historical Resource Study for the National Park Service, December 2005.

Boime, Albert. *Hollow Icons: The Politics of Sculpture in Nineteenth-Century France.* Kent, Ohio: Kent State University Press, 1987.

———. "Liberty: Inside Story of a Hollow Symbol." *In These Times,* June 11–24, 1986, 12–13.

———. *The Unveiling of the National Icons: A Plea for Patriotic Iconoclasm in a Nationalist Era.* New York: Cambridge University Press, 1997.

Bolen, Jean Shinoda. *Goddesses in Everywoman: Powerful Archetypes in Women's Lives.* New York: Harper Paperbacks, 2004.

———. *Like a Tree: How Trees, Women, and Tree People Can Save the Planet.* San Francisco: Conari Press, 2011.

———. *The Millionth Circle: How to Change Ourselves and the World—The Essential Guide to Women's Circles.* San Francisco: Conari Press, 1999.

———. *Urgent Message from Mother: Gather the Women, Save the World.* San Francisco: Conari Press, 2008.

———. "Why I Persevere in Advocating a United Nations 5th World Conference on Women." January 30, 2009. www.jeanbolen.com.

Brigham, Clarence S. *Paul Revere's Engravings.* New York: Atheneum, 1969.

Brown, David Jay. Interview with Marija Gimbutas conducted on October 3, 1992. www.mavericksofthemind.com/gim-int.htm. Accessed April 20, 2014.

Brzezinski, Mika. *Grow Your Value: Living and Working to Your Full Potential.* New York: Weinstein Books, 2015.

Bulfinch, Thomas. *The Age of Fable.* New York: Plume, 1995.

Bullock, Steven C. *Revolutionary Brotherhood: Freemasonry and the Transformation of the American Social Order, 1730–1840.* Chapel Hill: University of North Carolina Press, 1998.

Cahn, Naomi, and June Carbone. *Red Families v. Blue Families: Legal Polarization and the Creation of Culture.* New York: Oxford University Press, 2010.

Campbell, Joseph. *Goddesses: Mysteries of the Feminine Divine.* San Francisco: New World Library, 2013.

———. *The Hero with a Thousand Faces.* San Francisco: New World Library, 2008.

———, ed. *The Mystic Vision: Papers from the Eranos Yearbooks,* vol. 6. Princeton, N.J.: Princeton University Press, 1989.

Carter, C. Sue. "The Chemistry of Child Neglect: Do Oxytocin and Vasopressin Mediate the Effects of Early Experience?" *Proceedings of the National Academy of Sciences* 102, no. 51 (2005): 18247–48.

———. "Developmental Consequences of Oxytocin." *Physiology & Behavior* 79 (2003): 383–97.

———. "Motherhood, Monogamy and Health." *Altruism and Health: Perspectives from Empirical Research* (edited by Stephen G. Post). *New York:* Oxford University Press, 2007, pp. 371–88.

———. "Neuroendocrine Perspectives on Social Attachment and Love." *Psychoneuroendocrinology* 23, no. 8 (1998): 779–818.

———. "Oxytocin and Sexual Behavior." *Neuroscience and Biobehavioral Review* 16 (1992): 131–44.

———. "Sex Differences in Oxytocin and Vasopressin: Implications for Autism Spectrum Disorders?" *Behavioural Brain Research* 176 (2007): 170–86.

Carter, C. Sue, Ericka M. Boone, Hossein Pournajafi-Nazarloo, and Karen L. Bales. "Consequences of Early Experiences and Exposure to Oxytocin and Vasopressin Are Sexually Dimorphic." *Developmental Neuroscience* 31 (2009): 332–41.

Carter, C. Sue, and Stephen Porges. "Social Bonding and Attachment." In G. Koob and E. Adkins-Regan, eds. *The Encyclopedia of Behavioral Neuroscience.* New York: Elsevier, 2010.

Chenoweth, Richard. "The Very First Miss Liberty: Latrobe, Franzoni and the First Statue of Liberty, 1807–1814." *Le Libellio d'Aegis* 8, no. 2 (2012): 67–74.

Chireau, Yvonne. *Black Magic: Religion and the African American Conjuring Tradition.* Berkeley: University of California Press, 2006.

Chomsky, Noam. "Humanity Imperiled: The Path to Disaster." www.tomdispatch.com/blog/175707. Accessed June 4, 2013.

Christ, Carol P. "Why Women Need the Goddess." Keynote address at the "Great Goddess Re-emerging" conference at the University of Santa Cruz, Spring 1978. *Goddess Ariadne.* http://goo.gl/UHq2dD. Accessed November 4, 2011.

Cohen, Jonathan. "The Naming of America: Fragments We've Shored against Ourselves." www.uhmc.sunysb.edu/surgery/america.html. Accessed April 21, 2014.

Commager, Henry. *The Empire of Reason: How Europe Imagined and America Realized the Enlightenment.* Garden City, N.Y.: Ancho Press/Doubleday, 1977.

Cunneen, Sally. *In Search of Mary: The Woman and the Symbol.* New York: Ballantine, 1996.

Dashú, Max. "Colonial Hunts in South America," excerpt from *Secret History of the Witches,* 2000. *The Suppressed Histories Archives.* http://suppressedhistories .net/secrethistory/colhuntsouth.html. Accessed August 6, 2011.

———. "Empires Are Doomed to Fall." *Seasonal Salon.* http://rcgi.org/news/ seasonal-salon/37-news/seasonal-salon/fall-equinox-2007/225-empires-are -doomed-to-fall. Accessed August 6, 2011.

———. "Female Divinity in South America." *The Suppressed Histories Archives.* www.suppressedhistories.net/goddess/fdivsa.html. Accessed January 16, 2011.

———. "Icons of the Matrix." *The Suppressed Histories Archives.* http:// suppressedhistories.net/articles/icons.html. Accessed August 6, 2011.

———. "Meanings of Goddess," *Goddess Pages* (Spring 2007). http://goo.gl/ W2hXID. Accessed July 9, 2011.

———. "Racism, History and Lies." *The Suppressed Histories Archives.* www .suppressedhistories.net/articles/racism_history.html. Accessed June 22, 2011.

———. *Women's Power.* DVD. Oakland, Calif.: The Suppressed Histories Archives, 2011.

Davis, Kenneth C. *America's Hidden History: Untold Tales of the First Pilgrims, Fighting Women, and Forgotten Founders Who Shaped a Nation.* New York: Harper Perennial, 2009.

Day, Sara. "'With Peace and Freedom Blest!' Woman as Symbol in America, 1590– 1800." Online version of *American Women: A Library of Congress Guide for the Study of Women's History and Culture in the United States* (Library of Congress, 2001). http://memory.loc.gov/ammem/awhhtml/aw05e/aw05e .html#ack. Accessed March 10, 2014.

Dice, Mark. "What Brad Meltzer's Decoded Missed." *Alex Jones's Infowars,* http:// goo.gl/YcvZjH. Accessed January 17, 2012.

Dillon, Wilton S., and Neil G. Kotler, eds. *The Statue of Liberty Revisited: Making a Universal Symbol.* Washington, D.C.: Smithsonian Institution Press, 1994.

"Divide and Conquer: The 'Indian Experiment' at Hampton Institute." The

American Studies Group at the University of Virginia. http://xroads.virginia
.edu/~CAP/POCA/POC_hamp.html. Accessed June 1, 2013.

Dolan, Eric W. "Belief in Biblical End-Times Stifling Climate Change Action in
U.S.: Study." *RawStory.* http://goo.gl/ZykSdm. Accessed May 11, 2013.

Douglass, Frederick. *Narrative of the Life of Frederick Douglass, an American
Slave, Written By Himself.* New Haven, Conn.: Yale University Press, 2001.
Originally published in 1845.

Dray, Philip. *Stealing God's Thunder: Benjamin Franklin's Lightning Rod and the
Invention of America.* New York: Random House, 2005.

Dubose, Lou. "What Producers of BPA Plastic Learned from Big Tobacco." *The
Washington Spectator.* http://goo.gl/WHVt3T. Accessed December 1, 2013.

Eamon, William. *The Professor of Secrets: Mystery, Medicine, and Alchemy in
Renaissance Italy.* Washington, D.C.: National Geographic Society, 2010.

"Early Suffrage Protests. Miss Blake Tells of Meeting at Statue of Liberty 29 Years
Ago." *New York Times,* July 11, 1915.

Ehle, John. *Trail of Tears: The Rise and Fall of the Cherokee Nation.* New York:
Anchor Books Doubleday, 1997.

Eisler, Riane. *The Chalice and the Blade: Our History, Our Future.* New York:
Harper & Row, 1988.

———. *The Real Wealth of Nations: Creating a Caring Economics.* Oakland,
Calif.: Berrett-Koehler Publishers, 2008.

———. *Sacred Pleasure: Sex, Myth, and the Politics of the Body.* New York: Harper
Collins, 1996.

———. "What's Good for Women Is Good for the World: Foundations for a
Caring Economy." Address at the U.S. Department of State, March 21, 2013.

Elias-Button, Karen. "Athene and Medusa: A Women's Myth." *Anima* 5, no. 2
(1979): 118–24.

Ellis, Joseph. *American Creation: Triumphs and Tragedies in the Founding of the
Republic.* New York: Vintage, 2008.

Fine, Cordelia. "Will Working Mothers' Brains Explode? The Popular New Genre
of Neurosexism." *Neuroethics* 1 (2008): 69–72.

Fischer, David Hackett. *Liberty and Freedom: A Visual History of America's
Founding Ideas.* New York: Oxford University Press, 2004.

———. *Washington's Crossing.* New York: Oxford University Press, 2006.

Fischer, Roger A. "Oddity, Icon, Challenge: The Statue of Liberty in American
Cartoon Art, 1879–1986." *Journal of American Culture* 9, no. 4 (Winter
1986): 63–81.

Fleming, E. McClung. "The American Image as Indian Princess 1765–1783." *Winterthur Portfolio* 2 (1965): 65–81.

———. "From Indian Princess to Greek Goddess the American Image, 1783–1815." *Winterthur Portfolio* 3 (1967): 37–66.

Foner, Philip S., ed. *The Complete Writings of Thomas Paine*. New York: Carol Publishing Group, Citadel Press, 1945.

Forrest, Tuomi. "Maid to Order: Columbus' 'Cannibal Girl' and the Captivity Narrative." *Pocahontas: Icon at the Crossroads of Race and Sex*. http://xroads.virginia.edu/~CAP/POCA/POC-col.html. Accessed June 1, 2013.

Fox, Nancy Jo. *Liberties with Liberty: The Fascinating History of America's Proudest Symbol*. New York: E. P. Dutton, 1986.

Fox, Selena. *Goddess Communion: Rituals and Meditations*. Barneveld, Wisc.: Circle Sanctuary, 1989/2006.

———. "The Goddess of Freedom: From Libertas to Lady Liberty." http://goo.gl/4SQCkv. Accessed November 4, 2013.

Freeman, Jo. "Say It with Buttons." *Ms.* magazine, August 1974, 48–53. www.jofreeman.com/buttons/saybuttons.htm. Accessed June 12, 2012.

Freke, Timothy, and Peter Gandy. *Jesus and the Lost Goddess: The Secret Teachings of the Original Christians*. New York: Harmony, 2002.

Fryd, Vivien Green. *Art and Empire: The Politics of Ethnicity in the U.S. Capitol, 1815–1860*. New Haven, Conn.: Yale University Press, 1992.

———. "Hiram Powers's America: 'Triumphant as Liberty and in Unity.'" *The American Art Journal* 18, no. 2 (1986).

———. "Lifting the Veil of Race at the U.S. Capitol: Thomas Crawford's Statue of Freedom." *Common-Place* 10, no. 4 (July 2010).

———. "The Statue of Liberty: A Chameleon-Like Hollow Icon." Keynote address, "American Icons and Monuments," international conference in cooperation with the John F. Kennedy Institut für Nordamerikastudien and the Terra Foundation for American Art at the Freie Universität Berlin, January 25, 2013.

Gage, Matilda Joslyn. *Woman, Church and State*. Amherst, N.Y.: Humanity Books, 2002. Originally published: Chicago: C. H. Kerr, 1893.

Gaines, James. *For Liberty and Glory: Washington, Lafayette, and Their Revolutions*. New York: W. W. Norton & Company, 2008.

Gallagher, Edward J. "America by Johannes Stradanus (1523–1605)." Lehigh University, December 1997. www.lehigh.edu/~ejg1/ed/strad1.html. Accessed June 1, 2013.

Gates, Henry Louis. *Life upon These Shores: Looking at African American History, 1513–2008.* New York: Knopf, 2013.

George-Kanentiio, Douglas. *Iroquois Culture and Commentary.* Santa Fe, N.Mex.: Clear Light Books, 2000.

———. *Iroquois on Fire: A Voice from the Mohawk Nation.* Lincoln: University of Nebraska Press, 2008.

———. "A rebirth for a sacred place on the Mohawk." *Albany Times Union.* October 16, 2011. http://goo.gl/rnNaAE. Accessed October 16, 2012.

George-Kanentiio, Douglas, and Joanne Shenandoah. *Skywoman: Legends of the Iroquois.* Santa Fe, N.Mex.: Clear Light Books, 1995.

Gill, Sam. *Mother Earth: An American Story.* Chicago: University of Chicago Press, 1991.

Gimbutas, Marija. *The Civilization of the Goddess: The World of Old Europe.* New York: HarperCollins, 1991.

———. *The Language of the Goddess: Unearthing the Hidden Symbols of Western Civilization.* New York: Thames & Hudson, 1989.

———. "The World of the Goddess," public lecture delivered at the California Institute of Integral Studies, San Francisco, 1990. VHS, Green Earth Foundation, El Varano, Calif., 1993. Producer, Richard Sydel; director, Alan Babbitt; project director, Ralph Metzner. http://goo.gl/c5jcje. Accessed September 16, 2014.

Glassberg, David. "Rethinking the Statue of Liberty: Old Meanings, New Contexts." Organization of American Historians, National Park Service, 2003.

Goldwag, Arthur. *The New Hate: A History of Fear and Loathing on the Populist Right.* New York: Vintage, 2012.

Gore, Al. "False Spontaneity of the Tea Party." *Huffington Post.* http://goo.gl/T2CQFk. Accessed July 31, 2015.

Gordon, David, George Smith, and Wendy McElroy. *On Liberty* (by John Stuart Mill) & *Vindication of the Rights of Women* (by Mary Wollstonecraft). Audiobook edition prepared by Ashland, Oreg.: Blackstone Audio, Inc., 2006.

Gough, Hugh. *The Terror in the French Revolution.* New York: Palgrave Macmillan, 2010.

Green, Rayna. "The Pocahontas Perplex: The Image of Indian Women in American Culture." *Native American Voices: A Reader.* Susan Lobo and Steve Talbot, eds. Upper Saddle River, N.J.: Prentice Hall Professional Technical Reference, 1997.

Green, Steven K. "Understanding the 'Christian Nation' Myth." *Cardozo Law Review de novo* 245 (2010): 245–70.

Grinde, Donald A., and Bruce E. Johansen. *Exemplar of Liberty: Native America and the Evolution of Democracy.* Los Angeles: American Indian Studies Center, UCLA, 1991.

Gschaedler, André. *True Light on the Statue of Liberty and Its Creator.* Narberth, Pa.: Livingston Publishing Company, 1966.

Gurevich, Andrew. "50 Shades of Gaia." *The Ecologist.* www.theecologist .org/blogs_and_comments/1564362/50_shades_of_gaia.html. Accessed October 23, 2013.

———. "In Goddess We Trust: America's Spiritual Crossroads." *Reality Sandwich.* http://realitysandwich.com/146191/goddess_we_trust_americas_spiritual_

———. "The Sacred Marriage of Visible Logos & Epigenetic Consciousness: A Paradigm for a New Humanity." *Reality Sandwich.* http://realitysandwich .com/node/162810. Accessed October 19, 2013.

Gutiérrez, Luis T. "Gender Balance in the Post-Patriarchal Age." *Mother Pelican: A Journal of Solidarity and Sustainability* 9, no. 11, November 2013. http:// goo.gl/lSLVLw. Accessed December 16, 2013.

Hamilton, Kendra. "Pocahontas: The Malleability of Race—or the Monster Miscegenation?" http://xroads.virginia.edu/~cap/poca/POC_mix.html. Accessed June 1, 2013.

Hansen, Elaine Tuttle. "The Pocahontas Perplex." *Mother without Child: Contemporary Fiction and the Crisis of Motherhood.* Berkeley: University of California Press, 1997.

Hazelton Jr., George C. *The National Capitol: Its Architecture, Art and History.* New York: J.F. Taylor & Co., 1897.

Heiler, Freidrich. "The Madonna as Religious Symbol" (1934). In *The Mystic Vision: Papers from the Eranos Yearbooks,* vol. 6, edited by Joseph Campbell. Princeton, N.J.: Princeton University Press, 1989.

Hieronimus, J. Zohara Meyerhoff. *Kabbalistic Teachings of the Female Prophets: The Seven Holy Women of Ancient Israel.* Rochester, Vt.: Inner Traditions, 2012.

———. *Sanctuary of the Divine Presence: Hebraic Teachings on Initiation and Illumination.* Rochester, Vt.: Inner Traditions, 2012.

Hieronimus, Robert R., and Laura E. Cortner. *Founding Fathers, Secret Societies: Freemasons, Illuminati, Rosicrucians, and the Decoding of the Great Seal.* Rochester, Vt.: Inner Traditions, 2005.

———. *United Symbolism of America: Deciphering Hidden Meanings in America's*

Most Familiar Art, Architecture, and Logos. Wayne, N.J.: New Page Books, 2008.

Higham, John. "Indian Princess and Roman Goddess: The First Female Symbols of America." *Proceedings of the American Antiquarian Society* 100, pt. 1 (1990): 45–79.

Hill, Rick. "Coming to One Mind: Haudenosaunee Style of Decision-Making." *Turtle Island News,* August 26, 2009, 6–7.

Hislop, Alexander. *The Two Babylons, or, The Papal Worship Proved to be the Worship of Nimrod and his Wife.* Neptune, N.J.: Loizeaux Bros., 1959.

Hobsbawm, Eric. "Man and Woman in Socialist Iconography." *History Workshop Journal* 6 (1978): 121–38.

Hoddinott, John, Harold Alderman, Jere R. Behrman, Lawrence Haddad, and Susan Horton. "The Economic Rationale for Investing in Stunting Reduction." *University of Pennsylvania Scholarly Commons, GCC Working Paper Series, GCC* 13–08.

Hodges, Glenn. "Cahokia: America's Forgotten City." *National Geographic.* January 2011.

Hofstadter, Richard. "The Paranoid Style in American Politics." *Harper's Magazine.* November 1964. http://harpers.org/archive/1964/11/the-paranoid-style-in-american-politics. Accessed August 4, 2014.

Holland, F. Ross. *Idealists, Scoundrels, and the Lady: An Insider's View of the Statue of Liberty–Ellis Island Project.* Chicago: University of Illinois Press, 1993.

Holmes, David L. *The Faiths of the Founding Fathers.* New York: Oxford University Press, 2006.

Honour, Hugh. *The New Golden Land: European Images of America from the Discoveries to the Present Time.* New York: Pantheon Books, 1975.

Horowitz, Mitch. "Interview with Mitch Horowitz." By Dr. Bob Hieronimus. *21st Century Radio,* October 18, 2009.

———. *Occult America: The Secret History of How Mysticism Shaped Our Nation.* New York: Bantam, 2009.

Hurlbut, George C. "The Origin of the Name 'America.'" *Journal of the American Geographical Society of New York* 20 (1888): 183–96.

Inter-Parliamentary Union. "Women in National Parliaments Situation as of June 2015." www.ipu.org/wmn-e/classif.htm. Accessed July 31, 2015.

Irvin, Benjamin. "Benjamin Franklin's 'Enriching Virtues.'" *Common-place* 6, no. 3, (April 2006). www.common-place.org/vol-06/no-03/irvin. Accessed July 31, 2015.

Israel, Jonathan. *A Revolution of the Mind: Radical Enlightenment and the*

Intellectual Origins of Modern Democracy. Princeton, N.J.: Princeton University Press, 2011.

Johansen, Bruce E. *Debating Democracy: The Iroquois Legacy of Freedom.* Santa Fe, N.Mex.: Clear Light Publishing, 1997.

———. *Forgotten Founders: How the American Indian Helped Shape Democracy.* Boston: Harvard Common Press, 1982.

———. *The Global Warming Combat Manual: Solutions for a Sustainable World.* Santa Barbara, Calif.: Praeger, 2008.

———. *Indigenous Peoples and Environmental Issues: An Encyclopedia.* Westport, Conn.: Greenwood, 2003.

———. *The Native Peoples of North America: A History.* New Brunswick, N.J.: Rutgers University Press, 2006.

Johansen, Bruce E., and Barry M. Pritzker, eds. *Encyclopedia of American Indian History.* Santa Barbara, Calif.: ABC-CLIO, 2007.

Jonnes, Jill. *Eiffel's Tower: And the World's Fair Where Buffalo Bill Beguiled Paris, the Artists Quarreled, and Thomas Edison Became a Count.* New York: Viking Adult, 2009.

Joseph, Rebecca M., Brooke Rosenblatt, and Carolyn Kinebrew. "The Black Statue of Liberty Rumor: An Inquiry into the History and Meaning of Bartholdi's *Liberté Éclairant le Monde.*" Northeast Ethnography Program, Boston Support Office, National Park Service, September 2000. www.nps.gov/stli/historyculture/black-statue-of-liberty.htm. Accessed June 7, 2012.

Kaminski, John. *Lafayette: The Boy General.* Madison: University of Wisconsin Press, 2007.

Kammen, Michael. "From Liberty to Prosperity: Reflections upon the Role of Revolutionary Iconography in National Tradition." *Proceedings of the American Antiquarian Society* 86, pt. 2 (October 1976): 237–72.

———. *Spheres of Liberty: Changing Perceptions of Liberty in American Culture.* Jackson: University Press of Mississippi, 2001. First Published by the University of Wisconsin Press, 1986.

Kaufman, Michael, and Michael Kimmel. *The Guy's Guide to Feminism.* Berkeley, Calif.: Seal Press, 2011.

———. "Make Men Your Allies." *New York Times,* February 18, 2013.

Keller, Catherine. *Apocalypse Now and Then: A Feminist Guide to the End of the World.* Boston: Beacon Press, 1996.

Kerber, Linda. *Women of the Republic: Intellect and Ideology in Revolutionary America.* Chapel Hill: The University of North Carolina Press, 1997.

Kimura, Doreen. "Men and Women Display Patterns of Behavioral and Cognitive Differences That Reflect Varying Hormonal Influences on Brain Development." *Scientific American,* May 13, 2002.

Kingsolver, Barbara. "The Weight of a Falling Sky." *Ms.,* Winter, 2015.

Kluge, Kathy Tilghman. "A Vision of Freedom: African Americans and the United States Capitol." Washington, D.C.: U.S. Capitol Historical Society, 2006.

Kolodny, Annette. *The Lay of the Land: Metaphor as Experience and History in American Life and Letters.* Chapel Hill: University of North Carolina Press, 1984.

Koltko-Rivera, Mark. *Freemasonry: An Introduction.* New York: Tarcher, 2001.

Krugman, Paul. "E Pluribus Unum." *New York Times,* July 5, 2013, sec. 1, p. 19.

Laboulaye, Édouard de. *Histoire du Droit de Propriété Fonciére en Occident,* Paris: A. Durand, 1839.

Lacey, Barbara E. *From Sacred to Secular: Visual Images in Early American Publications.* Newark: University of Delaware Press, 2007.

LaDuke, Winona. "The Indigenous Women's Network: Our Future, Our Responsibility." Statement to the United Nations Fourth World Conference on Women, Beijing, China, August 31, 1995. www.ratical.org/co-globalize/WinonaLaDuke/Beijing95.html. Accessed April 22, 2013.

———. *Recovering the Sacred: The Power of Naming and Claiming.* Cambridge, Mass.: South End Press, 2005.

———. *The Winona LaDuke Reader: A Collection of Essential Writings.* Minneapolis, Minn.: Voyageur Press, 2002.

LaDuke, Winona, and Sean Aaron Cruz. *The Militarization of Indian Country.* East Lansing: Michigan State University Press, 2013.

Lambert, Frank. *Religion in American Politics: A Short History.* Princeton, N.J.: Princeton University Press, 2008.

Landes, Joan. *Visualizing the Nation: Gender, Representation, and Revolution in Eighteenth-Century France.* Ithaca, N.Y.: Cornell University Press, 2001.

Le Corbellier, Clare. "Miss America and Her Sisters: Personifications of the Four Parts of the World." *Metropolitan Museum of Art Bulletin* 19.8 (April 1961): 209–23.

Lewis, Claude. "'Liberty' gala perplexes black patriots." Knight-Ridder Newspapers, *Evening Independent,* St. Petersburg, Fla., June 25, 1986.

Liberty! The American Revolution. DVD. Directed by Ellen Hovde and Muffie Meyer. St. Paul, Minn.: Twin Cities Public Television and Public Broadcasting Service, 1997.

Lyons, Oren, and John Mohawk, eds. *Exiled in the Land of the Free: Democracy, Indian Nations and the U.S. Constitution.* Santa Fe, N.Mex.: Clear Light Publishers, 1992.

MacArthur, John D. "How the Great Seal Symbolizes Liberty and Freedom." http://greatseal.com/liberty/index.html. Accessed December 16, 2013.

MacDonald, Kai, and Tina Marie MacDonald. "The Peptide That Binds: A Systematic Review of Oxytocin and Its Prosocial Effects in Humans." *Harvard Review of Psychiatry* (January/February 2010).

Maclean, John. "Selling of Miss Liberty Ignites Outrage." *Chicago Tribune,* April 28, 1986.

Mann, Barbara Alice. *Iroquoian Women: The Gantowisas.* New York: Peter Lang Publishing, 2006.

Mann, Charles. *1491: New Revelations of the Americas before Columbus.* New York: Vintage, 2006.

Marcou, Jules. "Amerriques, Amerigho Vespucci, and America." Smithsonian Institution. Annual Report of the Board of Regents Showing the Operations, Expenditures, and Condition of the Institution to July, 1888, Washington, D.C.: Government Printing Office, 1890, 647–73.

———. "Origin of the Name America." *Atlantic Monthly* 35 (March 1875): 291–96.

Marilley, Suzanne M. *Woman Suffrage and the Origins of Liberal Feminism in the United States, 1820–1920.* Boston: Harvard University Press, 1997.

Markale, Jean. *Women of the Celts.* Rochester, Vt.: Inner Traditions, 1986.

Mayo, Edith. "Be a Party Girl: Campaign Appeals to Women." In *Hail to the Candidate: Presidential Campaigns from Banners to Broadcasts,* edited by Keith Melder, 149–60. Washington, D.C.: Smithsonian Institution Press, 1992.

———. "Ladies and Liberation: Icon and Iconoclast in the Women's Movement." In *Icons of America,* edited by Ray B. Browne and Marshall Fishwick, 209–27. Bowling Green, Ohio: Popular Press, Bowling Green State University, 1978.

———. "Motherhood, Social Service, and Political Reform: Political Culture and Imagery of American Woman Suffrage." http://nwhm.org/online-exhibits/votesforwomen/gallery_1.html. Accessed August 1, 2012.

McCullough, David. *John Adams.* New York: Simon and Schuster, 2002.

McMillen, Sally. *Seneca Falls and the Origins of the Women's Rights Movement.* New York: Oxford University Press, 2009.

Miller, Alice Duer. *Women Are People!* New York: George H. Doran Company, 1917.

Miller, Katya. "An Appreciation of Thomas Crawford's Statue of Freedom." *The*

Capitol Dome Newsletter of the United States Capitol Historical Society 44, no. 4 (Fall 2007): 18–30.

———. "Behold the Statue of Freedom: Sculptor Thomas Crawford and Senator Charles Sumner." *The Capitol Dome Newsletter of the United States Capitol Historical Society* 50, no. 3 (Summer 2013): 16–23.

———. "Freedom Speaks Through Us." www.ladyfreedom.net. Accessed July 17, 2011.

Mitchell, Elizabeth. *Liberty's Torch: The Great Adventure to Build the Statue of Liberty.* New York: Atlantic Monthly Press, 2014.

Monaghan, Patricia. *Encyclopedia of Goddesses and Heroines.* Santa Barbara, Calif.: ABC-CLIO, 2010.

———, ed. *Goddesses in World Culture.* Santa Barbara, Calif.: Praeger, 2010.

Moore, Lisa L., Joanna Brooks, and Caroline Wigginton, eds. *Transatlantic Feminisms in the Age of Revolutions.* New York: Oxford University Press, 2012.

Moreno, Barry. *Ellis Island's Famous Immigrants.* Mt. Pleasant, S.C.: Arcadia Publishing, 2008.

———. *The Statue of Liberty Encyclopedia.* New York: Simon & Schuster, 2000.

———. *The Statue of Liberty* (Images of America). Mt. Pleasant, S.C.: Arcadia Publishing, 2004.

Nelson, Craig. *Thomas Paine: Enlightenment, Revolution, and the Birth of Modern Nations.* New York: Penguin, 2007.

Newton-Small, Jay. "11 Things You Don't Know About the Senate Sisterhood: And Other Stuff I Learned Reporting the Senate Women's Story." Time.com. http://swampland.time.com/2013/10/16/11-things-you-dont-know-about-the-senate-sisterhood. Accessed October 31, 2013.

———. "Women Are the Only Adults Left in Washington." Time.com. http://swampland.time.com/2013/10/16/women-are-the-only-adults-left-in-washington. Accessed October 31, 2013.

"Nineteenth-Century Studies: Icons of Liberty." Lincoln: University of Nebraska. http://ncsmodules.unl.edu/liberty/index.php. Accessed June 7, 2012.

Olmert, Meg Daley. *Made for Each Other: The Biology of the Human-Animal Bond.* Boston: Da Capo Press, 2010.

Olomo, Aina. *The Core of Fire: A Path to Yoruba Spiritual Activism.* Brooklyn: Athelia Henrietta Press, 2003.

———. "Iyami Osoronga: Primordial Mothers of Yoruba Spirituality." In *Goddesses in World Culture,* edited by Patricia Monaghan. Santa Barbara, Calif.: Praeger, 2010.

Ortner, Sherry B. "Is Female to Male as Nature Is to Culture?" In *Woman, Culture, and Society,* edited by M. Z. Rosaldo and L. Lamphere, 68–87. Stanford, Calif.: Stanford University Press, 1974.

———. "The Virgin and the State." *Feminist Studies* 4, no. 3 (Oct., 1978): 19–35.

Our Spirits Don't Speak English: Indian Boarding School. DVD. Directed by Chip Richie. Dallas: Rich-Heape Films, Inc., 2008.

Ovason, David. *The Secret Architecture of Our Nation's Capital: The Masons and the Building of Washington, D.C.* New York: Harper Perennial, 2002.

———. *The Secret Symbols of the Dollar Bill: A Closer Look at the Hidden Magic and Meaning of the Money You Use Every Day.* New York: Harper Perennial, 2004.

Owens, Michael R. H., and Lisa Guernsey. "Lady Liberty: The Changing Face of Freedom." The Capitol Project, Department of American Studies, University of Virginia. http://xroads.virginia.edu/~CAP/LIBERTY/lady_frm.html. Accessed October 5, 2011.

Pagels, Elaine. *Adam, Eve and the Serpent: Sex and Politics in Early Christianity.* New York: Vintage, 1989.

———. *The Gnostic Gospels.* New York: Vintage, 1979/1989.

———. *The Origin of Satan: How Christians Demonized Jews, Pagans, and Heretics.* New York: Vintage, 1996.

———. *Revelations: Visions, Prophecy and Politics in the Book of Revelation.* New York: Penguin Books, 2013.

Paine, Thomas. *The Age of Reason.* Seaside, Ore.: Watchmaker Publishing, 2010. Originally published in 1794.

———. "Liberty Tree." Online at http://greatseal.com/liberty/libertytree.html. Accessed November 4, 2013.

———. *Life and Writings of Thomas Paine.* History of Economic Thought Books, edited by Daniel Edwin Wheeler, 2. Ontario: McMaster University, 1908.

———. *Peter Linebaugh presents Thomas Paine: The Rights of Man and Common Sense.* Brooklyn: Verso, 2009.

Paper, Jordan. *The Deities Are Many: A Polytheistic Theology.* Albany: State University of New York Press, 2005.

———. *The Mystic Experience: A Descriptive and Comparative Analysis.* Albany: State University of New York Press, 2004.

———. *Native North American Religious Traditions: Dancing for Life.* Santa Barbara, Calif.: Praeger, 2006.

————. *Through the Earth Darkly: Female Spirituality in Comparative Perspective.* New York: Continuum, 1997.

Pett, Joel. "Interview with Joel Pett." By Dr. Bob Hieronimus. *21st Century Radio,* June 15, 2014.

Patai, Raphael. *The Hebrew Goddess.* New York: Avon Books, 1967/1978.

Pauli, Hertha, and E. B. Ashton. *I Lift My Lamp: The Way of a Symbol.* New York: Appleton-Century-Crofts, Inc., 1948.

Pellegrino, Greg, Sally D'Amato, and Anne Weisberg. "The Gender Dividend: Making the Business Case for Investing in Women." Deloitte Global Public Sector Report. Published January 13, 2011. http://goo.gl/tslH5y. Accessed April 2, 2013.

Pew Center on the States. "One in 100: Behind Bars in America." February 2008. http://goo.gl/zC11Bf. Accessed July 31, 2015.

Porter, Joy. *Land and Spirit in Native America.* Santa Barbara, Calif.: Praeger, 2012.

————. *Native American Freemasonry: Associationalism and Performance in America.* Lincoln: University of Nebraska Press, 2011.

Powell, Devin. "Columbus' Arrival Linked to Carbon Dioxide Drop." *Science News* 180, nos. 10, 12 (November 5, 2011).

Pray the Devil Back to Hell. DVD. Directed by Abigail E. Disney and Gini Reticker. Sausalito, Calif: Distributed by Roco Films Educational, 2008.

Prison Policy Initiative. "States of Incarceration: The Global Context." www.prisonpolicy.org/global. Accessed July 31, 2015.

Provoyeur, Pierre, and June Hargrove, eds. *Liberty: The French-American Statue in Art and History.* New York: Harper & Row, 1986.

Raboteau, Albert J. *Canaan Land: A Religious History of African Americans.* New York: Oxford University Press, 2001.

————. *Slave Religion: The "Invisible Institution" in the Antebellum South.* New York: Oxford University Press, 2004.

Rachel's Network. "When Women Lead: A Decade of Women's Environmental Voting Records in Congress." http://rachelsnetwork.org/wp/wp-content/uploads/2014/09/WhenWomenLead.pdf. Accessed July 31, 2015.

Richards, Carl. *Greeks and Romans Bearing Gifts: How the Ancients Inspired the Founding Fathers.* Lanham, Md.: Rowman & Littlefield Publishers, 2009.

Roberts, Cokie. *Founding Mothers: The Women Who Raised Our Nation.* New York: Harper Perennial, 2005.

————. *Ladies of Liberty: The Women Who Shaped Our Nation.* New York: Harper Perennial, 2009.

Roger, Philippe. "The Edifying Edifice," Richard Miller, trans. In *Liberty: The French-American Statue in Art and History*, edited by Pierre Provoyeur and June Hargrove. New York: Harper & Row, 1986.

Rozett, Ella. "Black Madonnas and Other Mysteries of Mary." www .interfaithmary.net/pages/blackmadonna.html. Accessed June 1, 2012.

———. "A Constant Stream of Grace: Index/List and Photo Gallery of Black Madonnas Worldwide." http://interfaithmary.net/pages/indexblackmadonnas .htm. Accessed June 1, 2012.

———. "Women of Spirit and Power in the Bible." www.interfaithmary.net/ pages/mary_goddess.html. Accessed June 1, 2012.

Sandberg, Sheryl. *Lean In: Women, Work, and the Will to Lead*. New York: Knopf, 2013.

Schiebinger, Londa. *Nature's Body: Gender in the Making of Modern Science*. Boston: Beacon Press, 1993.

Schwartz, Stephan A. "Social Values, Social Wellness: Can We Know What Works?" *Explore* 8, no. 2 (March/April 2012): 89–91.

———. "The Vagina Battles and National Wellness." *Explore: The Journal of Science and Healing* 8, no. 3 (May 2012): 154–57.

Scott, Pamela. *Temple of Liberty: Building the Capitol for a New Nation*. New York: Oxford University Press, 1995.

Sharlet, Jeff. *The Family: The Secret Fundamentalism at the Heart of American Power*. New York: Harper Perennial, 2009.

Shlain, Leonard. *The Alphabet versus the Goddess: The Conflict between Word and Image*. New York: Penguin Books, 1999.

Shorto, Russell. *The Island at the Center of the World: The Epic Story of Dutch Manhattan and the Forgotten Colony That Shaped America*. New York: Vintage, 2005.

Silverman, Kaja. "Liberty, Maternity, Commodification." *New Formations* 5 (Summer 1988): 69–89.

Singer, Robert C. "Masonry and the Statue of Liberty by the Deputy Grand Master Grand Lodge, F. & A.M., New York." http://washingtons headquar- ters.org/statue-liberty/masonry-statue-liberty. Accessed May 17, 2014.

Slaughter, Anne-Marie. "Why Women Still Can't Have It All." *The Atlantic,* December 30, 2012.

Smith, Andy. "For All Those Who Were Indian in a Former Life." *Women of Power* (Winter 1991). www.thepeoplespaths.net/articles/formlife.htm. Accessed November 17, 2011.

Spar, Debora. "American Women Have It Wrong." *Newsweek,* October 1 & 8, 2012, volume CLX, nos. 14, 15, pp. 40–48.

———. *Wonder Women: Sex, Power, and the Quest for Perfection.* New York: Sarah Crichton Books/Farrar, Straus and Giroux, 2013.

Spiering, Frank. *Bearer of a Million Dreams: The Biography of the Statue of Liberty.* Ottowa, Ill.: Jameson Books, 1986.

Spretnak, Charlene. *Lost Goddesses of Early Greece: A Collection of Pre-Hellenic Myths.* Berkeley, Calif.: Moon Books, 1978.

Statue of Liberty. DVD. Directed by Ken Burns. New York: Florentine Films, WNET, 1985; Arlington, Va.: PBS, 2004.

"The Statue Unveiled." *New York Times,* October 29, 1886.

Stewart, David O. *The Summer of 1787: The Men Who Invented the Constitution.* New York: Simon & Schuster, 2007.

Taibbi, Matt. "Everything Is Rigged: The Biggest Price-Fixing Scandal Ever." *Rolling Stone,* April 25, 2013. http://goo.gl/DTszBv. Accessed April 27, 2013.

Tate, Karen. *Goddess Calling: Inspirational Messages & Meditations of Sacred Feminine Liberation Thealogy.* Alresford Hampshire, England: Changemakers Books, 2014.

Taylor, Joshua. *America as Art.* New York: Harper & Row, 1976.

Taylor, Shelley E. "Tend and Befriend: Biobehavioral Bases of Affiliation under Stress." *Current Directions in Psychological Science* 15, no. 6 (2006): 273–77.

"They Enter a Protest: Woman Suffragists Think the Ceremonies an Empty Farce." *New York Times,* October 29, 1886.

Trachtenberg, Marvin. *The Statue of Liberty.* New York: Viking Press, 1976.

Tuchman, Barbara W. *The First Salute: A View of the American Revolution.* New York: Random House, 1988.

Uvnäs-Moberg, Kerstin. *The Oxytocin Factor: Tapping the Hormone of Calm, Love, and Healing.* Boston: Da Capo Press, 2003.

Vermeule, Cornelius. *Numismatic Art in America: Aesthetics of the United States Coinage,* Boston: Harvard University Press, 1971.

Veverka, James. "The Bible and Gender Equality." http://stopthereligiousright .org/suffrage.htm. Accessed September 24, 2011.

———. "The Classical Temple Architecture and Pagan Statuary of Washington, DC." www.stopthereligiousright.org/washingtondc.htm. Accessed September 3, 2011.

———. "A History of Religious Tests: 323–1961." http://community-2.webtv

.net/tales-of-the-western_world/TESTOATHS. Accessed September 24, 2011.

Wagner, Sally Roesch. *Matilda Joslyn Gage: She Who Holds the Sky.* Aberdeen, S.Dak.: Sky Carrier Press, 1998.

———. *Sisters in Spirit: Iroquois Influence on Early Feminists.* Summertown, Tenn.: Native Voices Book Publishing Company, 2001.

———. *A Time of Protest: Suffragists Challenge the Republic: 1870–1887.* Aberdeen, S.Dak.: Sky Carrier Press, 1992.

The War That Made America. DVD. Directed by Ben Loeterman and Eric Strange. Pittsburgh, Pa.: WQED and Public Broadcasting Service, 2006.

Warner, Marina. *Alone of All Her Sex: The Myth and the Cult of the Virgin Mary.* New York, Knopf, 1976.

———. *Monuments and Maidens: The Allegory of the Female Form.* New York: Atheneum, 1985.

Warren, Mercy Otis. *History of the Rise, Progress, and Termination of the American Revolution interspersed with Biographical, Political and Moral Observations, in Two Volumes.* Indianapolis: Liberty Fund, 1994. Originally published in 1805.

Wasserman, James. *The Secrets of Masonic Washington: A Guidebook to Signs, Symbols, and Ceremonies at the Origin of America's Capital.* Rochester, Vt.: Destiny Books, 2008.

Weatherford, Jack. "Examining the Reputation of Christopher Columbus." *Baltimore Evening Sun,* October 6, 1989.

———. *Indian Givers: How Indians of the Americas Transformed the World.* New York: Crown, 1988.

———. *Native Roots: How the Indians Enriched America.* New York: Ballantine Books, 1991.

———. *The Secret History of the Mongol Queens: How the Daughters of Genghis Khan Rescued His Empire.* New York: Broadway Books, 2011.

Winterer, Caroline. "From Royal to Republican: The Classical Image in Early America." *Journal of American History,* vol. 91, no. 4 (2005): 1264–90.

Wollstonecraft, Mary. *A Vindication of the Rights of Woman.* Mineola, N.Y.: Dover Publications, 1996 (originally published in 1792).

"Women Ask Votes at Liberty's Feet. Read an Appeal at the Base of Bartholdi Statue of Bedloe's Island." *New York Times,* July 6, 1915.

Women in World History Curriculum. "Debating Conflicting Rights, United States 1867–69." www.womeninworldhistory.com/TWR-16.html. Accessed July 19, 2015.

Wood, Gordon S. *The American Revolution: A History.* New York: Modern Library/Random House, 2003.

———. *Empire of Liberty: A History of the Early Republic, 1789–1815.* New York: Oxford University Press, 2010.

———. *The Radicalism of the American Revolution.* New York: Alfred A. Knopf, 1992.

Yellow Bird, Michael. "What We Want to Be Called: Indigenous Peoples' Perspectives on Racial and Ethnic Identity Labels." *The American Indian Quarterly* 23, no. 2 (Spring 1999): 1–21.

Zinn, Howard. *A People's History of the United States: 1492 to Present.* New York: Harper Perennial Modern Classics, 1980/2005.

Index

About the Authors

This photograph of coauthors Laura E. Cortner and Robert R. Hieronimus, Ph.D., was taken inside the head of the Statue of Liberty after the long climb to the top.

Robert R. Hieronimus, Ph.D., is an internationally known historian, visual artist, and radio host. His research has been used by the White House and State Department and published in the congressional record. He has made numerous appearances on documentaries airing on the History, Discovery, BBC, and National Geographic channels as well as many other national and international outlets. His giant murals and painted artcars include the 2,700-square-foot *Apocalypse* and the 1,750-square-foot *We the People,* the Woodstock Bus, and the We the People Artcar. His weekly program, *21st Century Radio,* is the longest running radio show on the new paradigm in the country. He lives in Maryland.

Laura E. Cortner graduated with honors from Goucher College in Towson, Maryland, with a degree in English and a concentration in writing. She has coauthored previous titles with Robert R. Hieronimus, including *Founding Fathers, Secret Societies* and *The United Symbolism of America.* Her work has also appeared regularly in numerous periodicals such as *Lilipoh, UFO Magazine, Fate* magazine, and several Beatles fan publications. She is the director of the Ruscombe Mansion Community Health Center and lives in Maryland.